# Theodicy in Islamic Thought

## *THE DISPUTE OVER AL-GHAZĀLĪ'S "BEST OF ALL POSSIBLE WORLDS"*

*Eric L. Ormsby*

PRINCETON UNIVERSITY PRESS
PRINCETON, NEW JERSEY

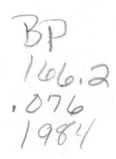

Published by Princeton University Press, 41 William Street,
Princeton, New Jersey 08540
In the United Kingdom: Princeton University Press,
Guildford, Surrey



Library of Congress Cataloging in Publication Data will
be found on the last printed page of this book

ISBN 0-691-07278-7

Publication of this book has been aided by the Paul Mellon
Fund of Princeton University Press

This book has been composed in Linotron Caledonia type

Clothbound editions of Princeton University Press books
are printed on acid-free paper, and binding materials are
chosen for strength and durability. Paperbacks, although
satisfactory for personal collections, are not usually suitable
for library rebinding

Printed in the United States of America by Princeton
University Press, Princeton, New Jersey

*In Memoriam*

*RUDOLF MACH*

# *Preface*

In this work, I describe and analyze the major themes and arguments in a long-lived but little-known debate among Muslim theologians. My first concern has been to present these themes and arguments as clearly and as accurately as I could, and to do so, as often as possible, in the words of the disputants themselves. This seemed especially important to me, since much of the material which I have used exists only in manuscript and so is not always easily accessible.

I have arranged the study topically and have grouped the principal arguments around three central problems: divine power and possibility; divine will and necessity; and divine justice and obligation. In adopting this course, I have followed a procedure often used by the disputants themselves in their treatises. I had at first considered analyzing the debate from a historical viewpoint, but it quickly became clear to me that such an approach would be impracticable. The arguments in the debate were cumulative; each disputant built upon, and recapitulated, the arguments of his predecessors. A chronological approach would have involved either continual repetition and restatement or a narrow concentration on one or two stages of the debate. In my opinion, either course would have misrepresented the significance and potential interest of the debate.

In discussing the arguments in the debate, I have occasionally included references to parallel arguments and themes in Western discussions of theodicy. I did this because the subject may be of interest to students of theology and philosophy beyond the specialized area of Near Eastern studies. However, I would not want to obscure the fact that such references are often problematic.

They are especially so in the instances where reference is made to possible ancient sources—and specifically, Stoic sources—for later Islamic notions and concepts. While it seems undeniable that Muslim authors, from an early date, had access to Stoic thought (or certain portions thereof), it is still unclear by what means, or in what form, Stoic ideas came to them. The transmission of certain Stoic notions to Muslim philosophers and theologians is still a vexed question. Nevertheless, I felt that to omit such references to possible sources would have been, in its own way, equally misleading. In any case, these references, as well as others to medieval Scholastic and modern Western philosophers, are offered here more in the interest of comparison, and as instances of parallel formulations, than out of any desire to suggest, or offer as proved, any direct transmission of ideas or complex of influences.

The three central problems of the dispute, which I treat in Chapters Three through Five below, represent quite complex and significant constellations of problems within the context of Islamic theology. Each might warrant a separate and detailed treatment in its own right. My interest has been to clarify the (often tacit) issues in a rather intricate and protracted dispute, and so I make no claim to offer here definitive discussions of these three problems; rather, I have tried to approach them only as they had bearing on the dispute itself.

I would like to thank several individuals who have helped me during the long time it has taken me to complete this study. My teacher, mentor, and friend, the late Professor Rudolf Mach, first suggested this topic to me and made available the relevant Arabic manuscripts from the Princeton University Library's Garrett and Yahuda Collections. He was always unfailingly generous with his time and with suggestions for the improvement of the work. In addition, he allowed me to use, and cite from, his extensive lexical files of Arabic technical terminology; without these, certain sections of the work, and especially Chapter Three, would have been difficult indeed to write. Furthermore, as my footnotes attest, he was most generous in suggesting further sources that have enriched the work. I have also profited from his precise and nuanced sense of language, which has improved the style of the work in many places. My indebtedness to Rudolf Mach can now never be repaid, but I offer this work, imperfect as it is, to the memory of an incomparable scholar and teacher and a magnanimous friend.

I should also like to thank Professors Manfred Ullmann and Josef van Ess of the University of Tübingen, with whom I was privileged to study and who were helpful to me in the early stages of this work. I thank the Deutscher Akademischer Austauschdienst (DAAD) for making this year of study possible. I am also grateful to Dr. Kennerly L. Woody, my friend and former colleague at the Princeton University Library, and to Professor Calvin Normore, formerly of Princeton's Philosophy Department, for several helpful references to Scholastic sources. Dr. Rafael Danziger kindly suggested references pertaining to 19th-century Algeria. I am also grateful to Mr. Larry Miller for several suggestions and for his encouragement.

I am indebted to Dr. Orest L. Pelech, my friend and former colleague at the Princeton University Library, for generously volunteering to read the entire manuscript in an earlier form. His meticulous attention to detail and his sense of style have improved the work greatly, and I have incorporated many of his suggestions.

I thank Dr. Dieter George of the Staatsbibliothek, West Berlin, for furnishing me with microfilm copies of al-Ghazālī's *al-Imlā'* and al-Samhūdī's *Iḍāḥ al-bayān*. I am also grateful to the Princeton University Library for allowing me to use the Arabic manuscripts in its incomparable collections.

This work is a revision of my doctoral dissertation which I submitted in May 1981 to the Department of Near Eastern Studies of Princeton University. I have revised and corrected the work throughout and have rewritten several sections completely. I should like to thank the faculty of that department for their patience and encouragement. I am especially grateful to Professors Jerome Clinton, John Marks, and Roy P. Mottahedeh for their advice and support.

I also wish to thank Professors George F. Hourani and Michael E. Marmura for making available to me their readers' reports for Princeton University Press. Their comments have saved me from several errors and guided me to further sources which have improved the work; I have incorporated their suggestions throughout. I am grateful, too, to Mr. Sanford G. Thatcher, Assistant Director of Princeton University Press, who has been a most patient and helpful editor.

My wife, Dorothy L. Ormsby, first encouraged me to begin the study of Arabic and she has helped and advised me throughout the preparation of this work. Without her suggestions, criticisms, and support I could have not have completed this work. I am deeply grateful to her.

# *Principal Abbreviations*

| | |
|---|---|
| a. | abū, abī |
| A. | Aḥmad |
| ʿA. | ʿAlī |
| AB | Abū Bakr |
| Ahlwardt | Wilhelm Ahlwardt, *Verzeichnis der arabischen Handschriften* (Berlin) (10 vols.; Berlin, 1887-1899) |
| *AI* | *Annales islamologiques* |
| ʿAl. | ʿAbd Allāh |
| b. | ibn |
| Bouyges | Maurice Bouyges, *Essai de chronologie des oeuvres de al-Ghazālī* (Beirut, 1959) |
| *BSOAS* | *Bulletin of the School of Oriental and African Studies* |
| cmt. | commentary |
| *Dhahab* | Aḥmad ibn Mubārak al-Sijilmāsī al-Lamaṭī, *al-Dhahab al-ibrīz min kalām Sīdī ʿAbd al-ʿAzīz* (Cairo, 1961) |
| *EI*[1] | *The Encyclopaedia of Islam* (4 vols.; Leiden, 1913-1934) |
| *EI*[2] | *The Encyclopaedia of Islam* (new ed.; 4 vols. to date; Leiden, 1960-) |
| *GAL* | Carl Brockelmann, *Geschichte der arabischen Litteratur* (2d ed.; 2 vols.; Leiden, 1943-1949); *Supplement* (= S) (3 vols.; Leiden, 1937-1942) |
| *GAS* | Fuat Sezgin, *Geschichte des arabischen Schrifttums* (8 vols. to date; Leiden, 1967-) |
| *Ḥikmat* | Hamdān b. ʿUthmān al-Jazāʾirī, *Ḥikmat al-ʿārif bi-wajh yanfaʿ li-masʾalah "Laysa fiʾl-imkān abdaʿ mimmā kān"* (Arabic ms., Yahuda #3036) |
| *Iḍāḥ* | Nūr al-Dīn al-Samhūdī, *Iḍāḥ al-bayān li-man arāda al-ḥujjah min "Laysa fiʾl-imkān abdaʿ mimmā kān"* (Arabic ms., Berlin; Pm. 226, Ahlwardt #5102) |

| | |
|---|---|
| *Iḥyā'* | Abū Ḥāmid al-Ghazālī, *Iḥyā' 'ulūm al-dīn* (4 vols. Cairo, 1334/1916) |
| *Itḥāf* | Murtaḍā al-Zabīdī, *Itḥāf al-sādat al-muttaqīn* (10 vols. Cairo, 1311/1894) |
| *JA* | *Journal asiatique* |
| *JAOS* | *Journal of the American Oriental Society* |
| *K.* | *kitāb* |
| Kaḥḥālah | 'Umar Riḍā Kaḥḥālah, *Mu'jam al-mu'allifīn* (15 vols. Damascus, 1957-1961) |
| Lane | Edward William Lane, *An Arabic-English Lexicon* (8 vols. London, 1863-1885) |
| M. | Muḥammad |
| Mach | Rudolf Mach, *Catalogue of Arabic Manuscripts (Yahuda Section) in the Garrett Collection, Princeton University Library* (Princeton, 1977) |
| *Mughnī* | 'Abd al-Jabbār al-Asadābādī, *al-Mughnī fī abwāb al-tawḥīd wa'l-'adl* (Cairo, 1962-). |
| *Qur.* | *Qur'ān (Koran)* |
| *R.* | *risālah* |
| *RAAD* | *Revue de l'Académie Arabe de Damas* |
| *REI* | *Revue des études islamiques* |
| *SI* | *Studia Islamica* |
| *SVF* | J. von Arnim, *Stoicorum veterum fragmenta* (4 vols. Leipzig, 1903-1924) |
| *Tahdīm* | Ibrāhīm b. 'Umar al-Biqā'ī, *Tahdīm al-arkān min "Laysa fi'l-imkān abda' mimmā kān"* (Arabic ms., Garrett #464H) |
| *Tashyīd* | Jalāl al-Dīn al-Suyūṭī, *Tashyīd al-arkān min "Laysa fi'l-imkān abda' mimmā kān"* (Arabic ms., Yahuda #3030) |
| *ZDMG* | *Zeitschrift der Deutschen Morgenländischen Gesellschaft* |
| Ziriklī | Khayr al-dīn al-Ziriklī, *al-A'lām. Qāmūs tarājim* (new ed. 8 vols.; Beirut, 1979) |

# *Contents*

*THEODICY IN ISLAMIC THOUGHT*

"This question . . . is celebrated among the *ʿulamāʾ*. When one begins to speculate upon it, it seems easy, but upon reflection it is a puzzle, in the solution of which many *shaykhs* have grown weary. Their views diverge, their disagreements multiply, they scatter into factions. . . ."—Murtaḍā al-Zabīdī, *Itḥāf al-sādat al-muttaqīn*, vol. 9, p. 440.

# Introduction

## I
## THE PROBLEM OF THEODICY

This study deals with a debate among Muslim thinkers which centered on a single disputed sentence and which persisted, with remarkable tenacity, from the early 12th century until well into the 19th. The debate is of signal interest, not only for its longevity and the level of intensity sustained throughout, but for the light it casts on the way in which Muslim theologians approached one of the perennial problems of human thought: the problem, or rather complex of problems, subsumed under the heading of theodicy.

The term "theodicy," originally coined by Gottfried Wilhelm Leibniz (1646-1716), in his *Essais de Theodicée* (1710), from the Greek words for "God" (θεός) and "justice" (δίκη), is commonly used in two senses. In its first, original, and proper sense, theodicy denotes the attempt to demonstrate that the divine justice remains uncompromised by the manifold evils of existence; it is the attempt, in Milton's words, "to justify the ways of God to men."[1]

More precisely, according to Immanuel Kant (1724-1804), ". . . by theodicy is understood the defense of the creator's supreme wisdom against the charge which reason brings on the basis of what is contrary to purpose (*das Zweckwidrige*) in the world."[2]

The term "theodicy" has developed a second, broader sense as well. It has come to signify God's concern and solicitude for creation in general, and so often appears as synonymous with providence itself. This secondary usage of the term will not concern us greatly in what follows, even though the attitude it rep-

[1] *Paradise Lost* (Book I, line 26), in N. Frye (ed.), *Paradise Lost and Selected Poetry and Prose* (NY, 1962), p. 6.

[2] "Ueber das Misslingen aller philosophischen Versuche in der Theodicee," in *Werke* (Akademie-Textausgabe), VIII, 255.

resents is well attested in Islamic literature.[3] We are concerned here primarily with theodicy in its original sense. The question of God's justice and goodness occupied Muslim thinkers as seriously as it did their Western counterparts, even if, for a variety of reasons, the allied problem of evil does not appear to assume the dominant position in Islamic theology which it often occupies in Western tradition.

Even more narrowly, we will be concerned with what we term the special question of theodicy, the problem of optimism. Is this world the best, the optimal, world possible, or could God create a superior world at will? This special question entails a certain shift of emphasis. Divine justice is still at stake: if God could make a better world than this world and yet refuses to do so, can He properly be characterized as just? But the divine power is also at issue, and perhaps even more acutely so: is God capable of creating another world, or does this world represent the full expression of His creative power?

Justice and power form the twin horns of the classic dilemma of theodicy; the fact of evil calls these attributes into question. In solving the dilemma, one must account for evil in a plausible way, and without sacrificing either God's justice or His power. If the solution places too great an emphasis on omnipotence, justice will suffer; however, if it emphasizes justice unduly, omnipotence will be curtailed.

David Hume offered this terse and elegant version of the dilemma: "Is he (God) willing to prevent evil, but not able? then is he impotent. Is he able, but not willing? then is he malevolent. Is he both able and willing? whence then is evil?"[4]

Optimism is an extreme response to this dilemma. The optimist asserts not merely that there is no evil, or that evil is not what it seems, but that in fact this world is the best of all possible worlds. When the skeptic calls into question the goodness and power of divinity, as in the above dilemma, the optimist, in response, takes these attributes as given and incontrovertible

[3] So, among many possible examples, *Qur*. 2:164; see, too, the description of spring by the Persian poet Saʿdī (d. 691/1292), in which the earth is portrayed as a child whom God nourishes and adorns, *Gulistān* (ed. Platts), p. 2.

[4] *Dialogues concerning Natural Religion* (ed. Pike), p. 88. This is, of course, Hume's version of the classic formulation by Epicurus, for which see below, p. 63.

and then proceeds boldly to call into question the very reality of evil.

Optimism is unfashionable today. The very word has come to denote a maudlin and distorted view of reality. Optimism, as a legitimate philosophic position, is often decried and dismissed as hopelessly myopic. Critics censure it as too abstract or as too rationalistic; it is seen as callous to lived human experience.[5] Many no doubt would agree with William James, who noted, in regard to Leibniz and his theodicy, ". . . truly there is something a little ghastly in the satisfaction with which a pure but unreal system will fill a rationalist mind."[6]

We shall consider some of these criticisms of optimism, and of theodicy in general, in the section immediately following. We shall also attempt to assess its distinctive merits. The object in this is not to take sides, but to trace the predominant themes in a perennial debate. Certain of these themes reappear in the Islamic debate; it may be helpful to view them from a wider and, at the same time, more familiar perspective.

The question at issue in both traditions is the same: is this world the best that can possibly be, or are there other, superior worlds which God could create at will? The answers to this question, and the reasons for those answers, will differ markedly in each tradition at many points; and yet, as we might expect, there is common ground as well.

## II
## OPTIMISM AND ITS CRITICS

"The best of all possible worlds is horribly ridiculous," writes Voltaire in a letter dated September 17, 1756, and he

[5] For a view of theodicies as ultra-rationalistic, see the work of the Russian existentialist theologian Lev Shestov, *In Job's Balances* (London, 1932), pp. 36-37; for a more judicious view of rationalist optimism in general, see M. Merleau-Ponty, *Signs* (Evanston, 1964), p. 147ff. Theodicies may be unfashionable, but they still have their advocates; see, for example, the posthumously published works of the influential Austrian philosopher Franz Brentano (1838-1917), especially his *Vom Dasein Gottes* (Leipzig, 1929) and *Religion und Philosophie* (Bern, 1954). More recently, the Jesuit thinker Pierre Teilhard de Chardin (1881-1955) has espoused a rather exuberant optimism; see his *The Phenomenon of Man* (NY, 1961), especially pp. 309-311.

[6] *Pragmatism* (Cambridge, Mass., 1978), p. 18.

adds, "One must see everything with stoic eyes. But how, when one suffers and witnesses suffering?"[7]

The question had occupied Voltaire increasingly during the previous year. His perplexity and bitter dissatisfaction with the fashionable optimism of his time were consequences of a single momentous event. On November 1, 1755, at 9:40 a.m., a tremendous earthquake had destroyed the city of Lisbon. This earthquake, the worst in recorded history, claimed tens of thousands of victims in Lisbon alone, while its total force extended over an area of one million square miles.[8] The day and the hour of the disaster are significant: it was All Saints Day, and by mid-morning the churches of Lisbon were packed. There seemed a monstrous irony in this timing.

Earthquakes and other natural disasters had often been interpreted as visitations of providence, or were considered terrible but necessary components of some "universal system" of divine wisdom. Thus, William King (1650-1729), the learned archbishop of Dublin, in an essay written some fifty years earlier, had suggested that:

> Earth-quakes, Storms, Thunder, Deluges and Inundations . . . are sometimes sent by a just and gracious God for the punishment of mankind; but often depend on other natural causes, which are necessary, and could not be removed without greater damage to the whole. These Concussions of the Elements are indeed prejudicial, but more Prejudice would arise to the Universal System by the Absence of them. . . . The Earth then must either not be created at all, or these things be permitted.[9]

[7] Voltaire, *Correspondance* (ed. Besterman; Paris, 1978), IV, 851.

[8] The Lisbon earthquake has been estimated at 8.9, or even 9, on the Richter Scale; for details, see H. Tazieff, *When the Earth Trembles* (NY, 1964), pp. 83-85. For the repercussions of the disaster on European thought, see H. Weinrich, "Literaturgeschichte eines Weltereignisses: Das Erdbeden von Lissabon," in *Literatur für Leser* (Stuttgart, 1971), pp. 64-76. As Weinrich shows, the earthquake had a decisive effect on several generations of intellectuals and helped to hasten the decline of philosophic optimism. For a vivid account, see also Otto Friedrich, *The End of the World* (NY, 1982), pp. 179-212.

[9] *An Essay on the Origin of Evil* (London, 1731), pp. 121-122; King's work, written originally in Latin, first appeared in 1702 under the title *De origine mali*. The explanation King advances is of Stoic origin; see A. A. Long, *Hellenistic*

In Lisbon, however, providence surpassed itself. The very earth, in the words of one witness, had moved "like a horse shaking itself."[10] Those who were not crushed in the churches were killed as they fled the successive aftershocks, or in the great fire that burned everywhere out of control. Those who sought refuge in the harbor, away from the toppling buildings, were engulfed by tidal waves.

Within two months of the earthquake, Voltaire had written and published his celebrated *Poème sur le désastre de Lisbonne*. The immediate target of Voltaire's indignation was the English poet Alexander Pope (1688-1744), but the poem was actually an indictment of optimism in general. Formulated by Leibniz, systematized by Christian Wolff (1679-1754), and popularized in verse by Pope, optimism found expression in the dictum "Tout est bien," or, as Pope put it, "Whatever is, is right."[11]

For Voltaire, this saying had become "nothing but an insult to the sufferings of our life."[12] In the *Poème*, Voltaire writes out of disillusionment as much as of outrage: he, too, had once been an unthinking—if uneasy—adherent of optimism. Nevertheless, the tone of the poem is still far from the savage ridicule of *Candide*, which was to appear in 1758.[13]

Voltaire was not alone in his critique of optimism. David Hume, in his *Dialogues concerning Natural Religion*, written during the 1750's, sharply questioned its claims; he noted, for example, that "the only method of supporting Divine benevolence . . . is to deny absolutely the misery and wickedness of man."[14] Samuel

---

*Philosophy* (London, 1974), p. 169, citing the view of Chrysippus that "the evil which occurs in terrible disasters has a rationale peculiar to itself . . . and is not without usefulness in relation to the whole."

[10] Cited in Voltaire, *Correspondance*, IV, 1397.

[11] In his *An Essay on Man* (I.x): "All Nature is but Art, unknown to thee; / All Chance, Direction, which thou canst not see; / All Discord, Harmony not understood; / All partial Evil, universal Good: / And, spite of Pride, in erring Reason's spite, / One truth is clear, Whatever Is, Is Right." A classic study of optimism is A. O. Lovejoy, *The Great Chain of Being* (Cambridge, Mass., 1976); for Pope, see p. 183ff.

[12] Preface to the "Poème sur le désastre de Lisbonne," in *Mélanges* (Paris, 1965), p. 302.

[13] For Voltaire's initial attack on Leibniz, see *Mélanges*, p. 308.

[14] *Dialogues concerning Natural Religion*, p. 90

Johnson, in 1757, published his masterful review of Soame Jenyns's *A Free Enquiry into the Origin of Evil.* The *Enquiry* represented optimism at its most fatuous, and Johnson lost no opportunity to savage it.[15]

The most penetrating critique of optimism, and of theodicy in general, was not to come, however, for another forty years. In 1791, Immanuel Kant, who in his youth had defended the optimist position,[16] published his "Ueber das Misslingen aller philosophischen Versuche in der Theodicee." In this essay Kant reviewed the various attempts to reconcile divine wisdom with the undeniable fact of evil in the world, and found all such attempts doomed to failure. Human reason, he argued, is by its nature incapable of fathoming the problem. Man must content himself with a purely "negative wisdom" (*eine negative Weisheit*); i.e., he must recognize the necessary limitation of his reason, which is incapable of grasping "what is too high for us."[17]

Kant concludes his article with a fervent disquisition on the *Book of Job*, and for good reason. Kant's position is one of pious skepticism here. He regards the question of theodicy not merely as insoluble in itself, but as in some measure presumptuous. This is a problem that dumbfounds reason and stills speculation:

[15] Johnson's review appeared in *The Literary Magazine* (London), vol. 2 (1757) and has been reproduced in facsimile in Richard B. Schwartz, *Samuel Johnson and the Problem of Evil* (Madison, 1975), pp. 98-112.

[16] In his 1759 essay "Versuch einiger Betrachtungen über den Optimismus," in *Werke*, II, 27-36. It should be noted, too, that in 1756, Kant had written three scientific essays on the Lisbon earthquake, and on earthquakes in general, in one of which he declared that "even the frightful instruments of affliction to the human race—the convulsive upheavals of countries, the rage of the sea stirred to its depth, the fire-spewing mountain peaks—summon mankind to reflection, and are not set by God as a rightful consequence of constant laws in nature any less than other, more usual causes of disturbance, which are deemed more natural, only because we are more accustomed to them." Kant could argue, further, that such disasters as the Lisbon earthquake were "instructive," for by study of them man could correct his presumption that the laws of nature were arranged purely for his comfort and convenience. See "Geschichte und Naturbeschreibung der merkwürdigsten Vorfälle des Erdbebens . . ." in *Werke*, I, 431.

[17] "Ueber das Misslingen aller philosophischen Versuche in der Theodicee," p. 263

Then Job answered the Lord and said,
Behold, I am vile; what shall I answer thee?
I will lay mine hand upon my mouth.
Once I have spoken; but I will not answer.[18]

We shall encounter this attitude of pious skepticism more than once in the following pages. The view that the problem is too high for human reason, and that the very discussion of it transgresses human limits and affronts God, played an important part in the Islamic debate.

A far more radical reaction against optimism occurred in the 19th century. For Arthur Schopenhauer (1788-1860), for example, it is no longer a question of skepticism, pious or otherwise, but of outright pessimism. Schopenhauer, perhaps following Johann Gottlieb Fichte (1762-1814) here,[19] argued that this world, far from being the best, is in fact the worst of all possible worlds:

> Now this world is arranged as it had to be if it were to be capable of continuing with great difficulty to exist; if it were a little worse, it would no longer be capable of continuing to exist. Consequently, since a worse world could not continue to exist, it is absolutely impossible; and so this world itself is the worst of all possible worlds.[20]

For Schopenhauer, optimism is "a bitter mockery of the unspeakable sufferings of mankind."[21] In challenging it, he follows the traditional strategy of opponents of optimism and confronts its sweeping pretension with quite specific instances of misery, evil, and imperfection:

[18] *Job* 40:3-5. Because of the vast literature surrounding it, it is impossible to do more than allude to this most famous of all theodicies; for a discussion of *Job* in its ancient Near Eastern context, see Marvin H. Pope (tr.), *Job* (NY, 1965), pp. l-lxviii.

[19] According to the arch-pessimist Eduard von Hartmann (1842-1906): "Fichte declares the natural world to be 'the worst of all worlds that can be' and consoles himself for this only with a belief in the possibility of rising into the bliss of a transcendent world by means of pure thought." *Philosophie des Unbewussten* (Leipzig, 1889), II, 286.

[20] *Die Welt als Wille und Vorstellung* (Zürcher Ausgabe), vol. II/2, p. 683; tr. E.F.J. Payne, II, 583

[21] *Die Welt als Wille und Vorstellung*, vol. I/2, p. 408; tr. Payne, I, 326.

> If we were to conduct the most hardened and callous optimist through hospitals, infirmaries, operating theatres, through prisons, torture-chambers, and slave-hovels, over battlefields and to places of execution; if we were to open to him all the dark abodes of misery, where it shuns the gaze of cold curiosity, and finally were to allow him to glance into the dungeon of Ugolino where prisoners starved to death, he too would certainly see in the end what kind of a world is this *meilleur des mondes possibles*. For whence did Dante get the material for his hell, if not from this actual world of ours?[22]

This, too, is a position we shall meet again in the Islamic debate, though not, to be sure, as the result of any pessimism, such as Schopenhauer's. When the optimist points to the grand structure and noble design of the universe, his skeptical adversary points, with unerring precision, to the cracks in the ceiling, the mice in the wainscoting, and the refuse in the corners. Such was the procedure in antiquity: Carneades (d. 129? B.C.), the leader of the New Academy, had developed it to perfection in combatting the confident optimism of the Stoic Chrysippus (d.c. 206 B.C.).[23]

So far we have dwelt on the undeniable shortcomings of optimism, and have viewed it through the eyes of critics. What may be said of its distinctive merits?

In the first place, the optimist is not quite so blind to "reality" as his opponent maintains. It is obviously in the interest of optimism to confront evil and imperfection directly, if only in order to present a stronger argument against it. For example, the Cartesian optimist philosopher Nicolas Malebranche (1638-1715),

[22] *Die Welt als Wille und Vorstellung*, vol. I/2, p. 406; tr. Payne, I, 325. Schopenhauer's pessimism seems pale indeed in comparison to the bleak views of his younger contemporary, the great Italian poet Giacomo Leopardi (1798-1837), who wrote in his *Zibaldone* for April 22, 1826: "Everything is evil. That is, all that is, is evil; that each thing exists, is an evil; each thing exists for an evil end; existence is an evil and directed toward evil. . . . There is no good other than non-being. . . . Existence, by its nature and proper and general essence, is an imperfection, an irregularity, a monstrosity." In *Tutte le Opere*, IV, 1004.

[23] See, for example, E. Norden, "Beiträge zur Geschichte der griechischen Philosophie," *Fleckeisens Jahrbücher* (*Jahrbücher für classische Philologie*), 19. Supplementband (Leipzig, 1893), pp. 431-439.

in seeking to demonstrate the ultimate perfection of things as they are, had his hypothetical adversary exclaim: "The universe is, then, the most perfect that God can make? How, indeed! So many monsters, so many turmoils, this great number of the impious—all this contributes to the perfection of the universe?"[24]

More importantly, however, theodicies strive for a consistent and coherent view of the world. Theodicies are not only attempts to "justify the ways of God to men"; they are also attempts to render an intelligible account of existence. This is no mean undertaking and, while often misguided, is not to be despised. An optimist philosopher might with justice reply to William James that there is something a little ghastly as well in the satisfaction with which the anti-rationalist contemplates impure reality. The optimist errs in glossing over "reality," but his opponent too often offers nothing but this reality in all its mute and irreducible particularity.

The optimist assumes a universal vantage-point whence he sees the world as a harmonious and unified whole in which nothing is without its reason or role. In such a world, all things are entwined and interconnected; they are all in some sense necessary:

> For it must be known that all things are connected in each one of the possible worlds: the universe, whatever it may be, is all of one piece, like an ocean: the least movement extends its effect there to any distance whatsoever, even though this effect becomes less perceptible in proportion to the distance.
>
> Therein God has ordered all things beforehand once for all, . . . and each thing as an idea has contributed, before its existence, to the resolution that has been made upon the existence of all things; so that nothing can be changed in the universe.[25]

[24] *Entretiens sur la métaphysique et sur la religion*, in *Oeuvres complètes* (Paris, 1965), XII, 211; cited in F. Billicsich, *Das Problem des Übels in der Philosophie des Abendlandes* (Vienna, 1952), II, 95-96.

[25] Leibniz, *Essais de Theodicée* (ed. Gerhardt), pp. 107-108; tr. E. M. Huggard, p. 128. Moreover, each substance mirrors the whole universe and the divine glory, for each is "like a whole world and like a mirror of God or, indeed, of the entire universe, which each expresses in its own way." Leibniz, *Discours de métaphysique* (ed. Lestienne), p. 37.

In a best of all possible worlds, nothing is insignificant, nothing is dispensable; if one part, however minute, be removed, the whole structure suffers. In such a universe, nothing can truly be lost. We find this expressed in a strange and rather moving passage in which Leibniz, in a mood of religious exaltation, wrote:

> For finally, nothing is neglected in nature; nothing is lost with God; all our hairs are numbered, and not a glass of water will be forgotten; *qui ad justitiam erudiunt multos fulgebunt quasi stellae*; no good action without reward, no evil one without some punishment; no perfection without a series of others unto infinity.[26]

In this view, nothing is commonplace. Leibniz's unforgotten glass of water will have its counterpart, too, in the Islamic debate, where it is said that not even the least thing—a gnat's wing or a speck of dust—can be removed from the universe without detriment.

The notion that the universe is a harmonious union of disparate but necessary components is common in defenses of divine power and wisdom. If nothing can be removed without harm, by the same token nothing can be improved; everything is interdependent: "For one part to be improved out of recognition would spoil the proportions of the whole design; overstretch one lute-string and the melody is lost."[27]

For the optimist, the world is unalterably good because divine wisdom has fashioned it. The saving notion of divine wisdom is important in most theodicies, and held an especially strong position in the Islamic version, as we shall see. Leibniz, for example, declared that God's "supreme wisdom, united to a goodness that is no less infinite, cannot but have chosen the best"; there is, to be sure, "an infinitude of possible worlds," but God

[26] Leibniz, *Philosophical Papers and Letters*, ed./tr. Loemker (Dordrecht, 1976), pp. 219-220.

[27] St. Thomas Aquinas, *Summa theologiae*, Ia.25,6, ad 3; tr. T. Gilby *et al.*, V, 177. The conception of the universe in musical terms, hearkening back to Pythagorean notions, is common in such discussions; cf. St. Bonaventura: ". . . The universe is like a most beautiful song which flows according to the best harmonies, each of its parts following after the others. . . ." *Liber I. Sententiarum* (Dist. XLIV, art. I, quaest. iii), in *Opera theologica selecta* (Quaracchi, 1934), I, 625.

"must needs have chosen the best, since he does nothing without acting in accordance with supreme reason."[28]

The world reflects this supreme wisdom, but it is often well concealed. The optimist proposes to seek it out and trace its effects in all facets of creation. The divine wisdom is nowhere more cunningly concealed, however, than in the many afflictions, miseries, vexations, and imperfections that beset existence.

It is in the effort to explain these evils, which should have no place in a "best of all possible worlds," that the advocate of theodicy most often comes to grief. There is, for example, disease to be explained, as in Milton's sonorous catalogue of woes:

> Convulsions, epilepsies, fierce catarrhs,
> Intestine stone and ulcer, colic pangs,
> Demoniac frenzy, moping melancholy,
> And moon-struck madness, pining atrophy,
> Marasmus, and wide-wasting pestilence. . . .[29]

Furthermore, the optimist must account for moral evil and, specifically, human sin and wickedness. Finally, he must explain what Leibniz termed "metaphysical evil," i.e., the "original imperfection in the creature."[30]

There is a variety of more or less ingenious explanations for the problem of evil—the problem *par excellence* of theodicy—to which we can only allude here.[31] These explanations range

[28] Leibniz, *Essais de Theodicée*, p. 107; tr. Huggard, p. 128.

[29] *Paradise Lost* (Book XI, lines 480ff.), p. 274. The passage is cited by Hume, *Dialogues*, p. 85.

[30] Leibniz, *Essais de Theodicée*, p. 115.

[31] A bibliography on the problem of evil would be a considerable undertaking in its own right. Some works which I have found useful are the following: (1) *overviews*: John Hick, "The Problem of Evil," *The Encyclopedia of Philosophy* (NY, 1972), III, 136-141; P. Lobstein, "Vorsehung," in A. Hauck (ed.), *Realencyklopädie für protestantische Theologie und Kirche* (3d rev. ed.; Leipzig, 1908), XX, 740-762; "Theodizee," in K. Galling (ed.), *Die Religion in Geschichte und Gegenwart* (3d ed.; Tübingen, 1972), VI, 739-747. (2) *separate monographs*: the most thorough treatment is Friedrich Billicsich, *Das Problem des Übels in der Philosophie des Abendlandes* (3 vols.; Vienna, 1952-59); for a useful anthology of texts, see Nelson Pike (ed.), *God and Evil: Readings on the Theological Problem of Evil* (Englewood Cliffs, NJ, 1964). See also John Bowker, *Problems of Suffering in Religions of the World* (Cambridge, 1970); Paul Ricoeur, *The Symbolism of Evil* (Boston, 1969). An interesting discussion, with reference to Karl Barth's

from the familiar belief, common to many religions, that suffering is the result of sin, or that evil is an unavoidable consequence of human free will, to the rather more complex and rarefied concepts of evil as a "privation of good" (*privatio boni*) or as, in the Stoic view, a "necessary concomitant" of the good.[32]

The notion of evil as the privation of good provides an instructive example of both the strengths and the weaknesses of such explanations. The notion, which goes back to Plotinus,[33] is widespread; it is the preferred explanation for evil in Western Scholasticism, for example, and particularly Thomism,[34] as well as in the writings of Islamic philosophers, such as Ibn Sīnā (Avicenna, d. 428/1037).[35] Briefly put, the privative theory of evil states that evil is actually a lack, or privation, of the good. Evil as such has no essence; it is a deficiency, in varying degrees, of the good appropriate for a creature or thing. Just as being and the good are convertible, so, too, are non-being and evil. Thus, St. Augustine could claim that "there is no such entity in nature as 'evil'; 'evil' is merely a name for the privation of good."[36]

---

views is; William M. Frierson, *The Problem of Evil: a Metaphysical and Theological Inquiry* (Ph.D. dissertation, Emory University, 1977). A brilliant recent treatment may be found in Leszek Kolakowski, *Religion* (Oxford, 1982), pp. 19-58.

Two exceptional studies of the problem in Indian thought deserve mention: Arthur L. Herman, *The Problem of Evil and Indian Thought* (Delhi, 1976), and Wendy D. O'Flaherty, *The Origins of Evil in Hindu Mythology* (Berkeley, 1980). Little has been written on the problem in Islamic thought, but mention may be made here of Herman Stieglecker's useful article "Die islamische Lehre vom Guten und Bösen," *Orientalia*, NS 4 (1935), pp. 239-245.

[32] *SVF* II, 1170 (evil occurs κατὰ παρακολούθησιν), cited in M. Pohlenz, *Die Stoa* (Göttingen, 1970), II, 57.

[33] *Enneads*, I.8.3; III.2.5. As J. Hirschberger notes, the privative theory of evil has its ultimate origin in Plato, though the latter did not develop it as such; *Geschichte der Philosophie* (12th ed.; Freiburg, 1976), I, 83.

[34] See, for example, St. Thomas Aquinas, *Summa contra Gentiles*, III: 6-15. As we might expect, Leibniz also employs this explanation; see his *Essais de Theodicée*, p. 201.

[35] Ibn Sīnā, *al-Shifā'*, *Ilāhīyāt*, II, 415; *al-Najāh*, p. 284ff. Cf. also, p. 229, line 3ff.; *Dānish-nāmah-i 'alā'i*, pp. 164-165. There is a summary in al-Ghazālī, *Maqāṣid al-falāsifah*, p. 297ff. The notion gains special prominence with the philosophers of the Isfahan school; see, e.g., Mīr Dāmād (d. 1041/1631), *K. al-qabasāt* (Tehran, 1977), p. 428ff. A useful general discussion is in the recent work, in Persian, of Ḥusayn Khalīqī, *Āfirīnish va naẓar-i faylasūfān-i islāmī dar bārah-i ān* (Tabriz, 1975), pp. 370-375

[36] *The City of God*, XI.22; tr. H. Bettenson, p. 454; cf. also, XI.9 (tr. p. 440): ". . . evil is not a positive substance: the loss of good has been given the name

If we apply this explanation to specific evils, we find that illness, for example, is not truly an evil, but the lack, in greater or lesser degree, of the good that is health; furthermore, sin or crime is a falling-away in the moral sphere from the good or perfection of virtue; and, finally, the evil in the limitation of our natures, as created, contingent beings, is no true evil, but merely a lesser degree of good or being. What we call evil in all these circumstances is not some positive, active factor but, rather, the absence of a greater good. Evil arises in the diminishment of being.

The explanation is ingenious, and it is plausible. Unfortunately, like most such explanations, it cannot withstand the touch of experience. As the contemporary Austrian philosopher Ernst Topitsch notes:

> The wobbly chair, the boot full of holes, the dull knife are just as real as their counterparts that are fit for use; if one designates them "unreal," this is merely another way of saying that they lack a full capacity for function and use. It is, therefore, a purely verbal operation, viz., the definition of "being" through value, on the strength of which one terms what is contrary to value as "non-being." The empirical fact is totally unaffected by this procedure.
>
> For example, the clinical diagnosis and prognosis of cancer remain wholly unchanged, whether one affirms or denies of it the predication of being. Indeed, the attitude of the sick person, in gauging his suffering, can hardly be influenced in any essential way; it relieves him little if one assures him that his disease is, in reality, something non-existent.[37]

This is a common criticism, but it is hardly the last word on the subject; indeed, the privative theory of evil still has its advocates.[38] It may be argued, for example, against Topitsch's

---

of 'evil,' " and XII.3 (p. 474); also, *Confessions* VII.12 (Loeb ed.; p. 374ff.). On the Augustinian theodicy, see John Hick, *Evil and the God of Love* (London, 1966); and J. Kopperschmidt, "Rhetorik und Theodizee. Studie zur hermeneutischen Funktionalität der Rhetorik bei Augustin," *Kerygma und Dogma* 17 (1971), pp. 273-291.

[37] *Vom Ursprung und Ende der Metaphysik* (Munich, 1972), pp. 266-267.

[38] See, for example, J. Gredt, *Elementa philosophiae aristotelico-thomisticae* (13th ed.; Barcelona, 1961), II, 33-34; and J. Hirschberger, "Omne ens est bonum," *Philosophisches Jahrbuch der Görres-Gesellschaft* 53 (1940), pp. 292-305, es-

comments, that the evil in a cancer is, nevertheless, "something non-existent," whether or not the sufferer recognizes it as such, or derives any consolation from this recognition. Furthermore, it is not entirely correct to say that, according to the privative theory, a "wobbly chair" is "unreal." Rather, it exists, and as an existing thing it is good; however, it lacks that full measure of good, and so of being, that a sturdy chair possesses.

In this brief survey, we have concentrated on one phase of Western optimism, and on the reactions against it that arose in the wake of an unusually decisive event, the Lisbon earthquake of 1755.[39] Many of the themes and arguments we have noted here will reappear in the Islamic debate. Before broaching that debate, however, we must ask how the question of theodicy took shape within the Islamic milieu.

## III
## ISLAMIC FORMULATIONS OF THEODICY

Theodicy in Islam was first formulated in reaction to conceptions of God that stressed his unqualified omnipotence. These early formulations, associated especially with the Muʿtazilite school of theology, sought to temper a quite literal conception of omnipotence with a rationalistic notion of divine justice. In the eyes of many early theologians, this attempt went to excess,

---

pecially p. 294. See also the clear discussion in Jeffrey Burton Russell, *The Devil* (NY, 1979), p. 146.

[39] The effects of the earthquake extended not only throughout Europe, but to the south as well, and especially in Morocco. There it was known as "the Meknes earthquake," for it devastated that royal city, as well as nearby Fez; see Magali Morsy, "Le tremblement de terre de 1755 d'après des témoignages d'époque," *Hespéris Tamuda* 16 (1975), pp. 89-98. Fearful destruction prevailed throughout Morocco, from Tetuan in the north at least as far south as Casablanca, which had to be abandoned. According to a contemporary account, in the Portuguese port of Mazagan (today known as al-Jadīdah), the first of November, 1755, dawned "so serenely . . . as to seem to wish to take all sadness from human hearts," but soon, "all was confusion . . . all was misery"; *Relaçaõ do grande terremoto, que houve na Praça de Mazagam em o primeiro de Novembro de 1755* (Lisbon, 1756), p. 4. For other accounts, see Muḥammad al-Qādirī, *Nashr al-mathānī: The Chronicles* (ed. Cigar; London, 1981), pp. 106-108 [Arabic text]; pp. 230-232 [translation]; and G. Vajda, *Un recueil de textes historiques judéo-marocains* (Paris, 1951), p. 41. For an Islamic viewpoint on earthquakes, see the discussion in our Conclusion below.

and so a further reaction set in. The Ashʿarite school of theology, which broke away from Muʿtazilism in the 4/10th century and was to become the dominant "orthodox" school of Islamic theology, returned decisively to the earlier emphasis on omnipotence, but it did so in a way that allowed for the incorporation within its system of certain carefully qualified rationalistic elements taken over from Muʿtazilism. The Ashʿarite insistence on divine omnipotence led to a rejection of belief in free will and causality; it further entailed a radical revision of the very basis of the Muʿtazilite theodicy: the notion of an objective, intellectually discernible good and evil.

The Ashʿarite emphasis on divine omnipotence, far from resolving the problem of theodicy, gave rise to further difficulties. These difficulties arose from the very definition of omnipotence, and they came to light only at a somewhat later period, especially in the writings of the theologian and mystic Abū Ḥāmid al-Ghazālī (d. 505/1111). These difficulties are, in large measure, the subject of this study. They were the focus of vigorous debate during a long period in the history of Islamic dialectical theology (*kalām*) that is often characterized as one of stagnation and of progressive petrification of dogma. The debate, and the optimistic theodicy that emerged from it, drew heavily on the past. Nevertheless, it was not entirely a resumption of earlier arguments, but often involved a redefinition and further elaboration of established points of doctrine.

The notion of God's illimitable omnipotence was of great importance in early Islam. The Qur'ān stresses repeatedly, for example, that "He is powerful over everything" (2:20 and *passim*). Ignaz Goldziher summarized the impact of this notion, as follows:

> The idea of absolute dependence had generated the crudest conceptions of God. Allah is a potentate with unbounded power: "He cannot be questioned about His acts" (21:23). Human beings are playthings in His hands, utterly without will. One must hold the conviction that God's will cannot be measured by the yardstick of human will, which is encompassed with limitations of all kinds, that human capacity shrivels to nothing next to the limitless will and absolute might of Allah. Allah's might also

> includes the determination of human will. A human being can perform an act of will only as God directs his will. Such is the case also in man's moral conduct: the volition in making a moral choice is determined by God's omnipotence and eternal decree.[40]

In this conception, God is the only true agent; He alone creates actions (*af'āl*). This notion, which obviated all secondary causality, could be applied quite literally, e.g., in the case of infectious disease:

> The Prophet of God said: "There is neither contagion nor augury nor jaundice (?) nor bird of evil omen." A bedouin asked: "O Prophet of God, how is it then that my camels were in the sand (as healthy as) gazelles, and then a mangy camel mingled with them and made them mangy?" The Prophet replied; "Who infected the first (camel)?"[41]

Acute difficulties arose from this conception, especially in relation to the problem of belief and free will. If God is the sole agent, He determines belief and disbelief. Consequently, God not only creates disbelief but then punishes the unbeliever for a disbelief which He Himself has implanted in him. This, too, had a Qur'ānic basis, e.g., 2:7: "God has set a seal on their hearts and on their hearing, and on their eyes is a covering, and there awaits them a mighty chastisement."[42]

Reactions arose early. They, too, could be justified on the basis of opposing Qur'ānic verses in which God plainly delegated responsibility for misdeeds to human agency.[43] And, in

[40] *Vorlesungen über den Islam* (Heidelberg, 1925), p. 82; tr. Hamori, *Introduction to Islamic Theology and Law* (Princeton, 1981), p. 77. For the appearance of this theme in the later debate, and the use of *Qur.* 21:23, cited by Goldziher, see Chapter Three below.

[41] For this tradition, see Aḥmad ibn Ḥanbal, *Musnad*, II, 267; al-Bukhārī, *Ṣaḥīḥ*, IV, 55. For a discussion, and opposing traditions, see M. Ullmann, *Die Medizin im Islam* (Leiden, 1970), p. 243; the meaning of the word *ṣafar*, here translated "jaundice," is obscure, as Ullmann notes.

[42] Translations from the Qur'ān are from A. J. Arberry, *The Koran Interpreted* (NY, 1967); for this verse, see p. 30.

[43] See, for example, 3:165 and 4:79: "Whatever good visits thee, it is of God; whatever evil visits thee is of thyself" (Arberry, p. 112). See also Goldziher, *Vorlesungen*, p. 83 ff.; tr., pp. 78 ff.

any case, does the Qur'ān not state that "God shall not wrong (*lā yaẓlim*) so much as the weight of an ant" (4:40)?[44]

Thus, in response to the question of whether God damns eternally those whom He Himself has not guided to Islam, the influential early ascetic al-Ḥasan al-Baṣrī (d. 110/728) declared: "Our God is too merciful (*arḥam*), too just (*aʿdal*), and too generous (*akram*) to do that to His servants."[45] Again (probably with reference to *Qur.* 2:18),[46] al-Ḥasan stated: "Our God is too just and too fair to blind a man and then say to him, 'See! or else I shall punish you,' or to deafen him and then say, 'Hear! or I shall punish you,' or to strike him dumb and then say, 'Speak! or else I shall punish you.' "[47]

In this epistle, written in reply to a request from the Umayyad caliph ʿAbd al-Malik (reigned 65-86/685-705), al-Ḥasan al-Baṣrī argued in favor of human free will, but he did so in order to exculpate God from any imputation of caprice or injustice. al-Ḥasan belonged to no specific school or sect; nevertheless, his influence was enormous, and nowhere more so than on the early school of theology known as the Muʿtazilah.[48]

The Muʿtazilah are often credited with the establishment of dialectical theology in Islam.[49] The school originated in Basra, in the 2/8th century; its founders Wāṣil ibn ʿAṭā' (d.131/748) and ʿAmr ibn ʿUbayd (d. 144/761) had been members of the circle of al-Ḥasan al-Baṣrī. A rival school was established somewhat later in Baghdad by Bishr ibn al-Muʿtamir (d. 210/825). Partly in reaction to the exaggerated emphasis on divine omnipotence

[44] Arberry, p. 106; cf. R. Paret, *Der Koran* (Stuttgart, 1979), p. 64.

[45] Arabic text in H. Ritter, "Studien zur Geschichte der islamischen Frömmigkeit, I," *Der Islam* 21 (1933), p. 79, line 16. For al-Ḥasan al-Baṣrī, see *GAS* I, 591-594.

[46] "Deaf, dumb, blind—so they shall not return" (Arberry, p. 31); see also 2:20.

[47] Ritter, "Studien . . . ," p. 74, line 17.

[48] Later Muʿtazilites would claim al-Ḥasan as an early exemplar and progenitor; see Ibn al-Murtaḍā, *Ṭabaqāt al-Muʿtazilah* (ed. Diwald-Wilzer; Wiesbaden, 1961), p. 18 ff. al-Ḥasan was thus claimed as well by Ashʿarites and Ḥanbalites. On his famous epistle, see M. Schwarz, "The Letter of al-Ḥasan al-Baṣrī," *Oriens* 20 (1967), pp. 15-30.

[49] H. S. Nyberg, "al-Muʿtazilah," *EI*[1], III, 421-427 (still the best brief account of the Muʿtazilites).

which characterized such purely predestinarian sects as the Mujbirah (Jabrīyah), the Muʿtazilites early espoused the doctrine of free will; in this, as in certain other respects, they originally formed part of the wider and more diffuse movement of the Qadarīyah, the advocates of free will.[50]

The Qadarīyah and the Muʿtazilah were also known as "the party of justice" (*ʿadlīyah*), and their defense of free will was inseparably linked with their insistence on divine justice.[51] The principle of divine justice (*ʿadl*) was of cardinal importance for the Muʿtazilah. Justice formed one of the five fundamental tenets of the school; indeed, originally it was listed first in order of the five and only at a later date relegated to second place, following "divine unity" (*tawḥīd*).[52]

A concern with divine justice characterized the Muʿtazilah from its inception. Wāṣil ibn ʿAṭāʾ is said to have composed, while in prison, a *rajaz* poem of 40,000 verses on the subjects of "divine justice, unity and the threat" (*al-waʿīd*); this poem, "the like of which people had not heard" before, prompted a public outcry for his release.[53] Wāṣil firmly maintained the position that no relation may exist between God and evil:

> The creator being wise and just, it is forbidden to establish a relation between Him and evil (*sharr*) or wrong (*ẓulm*). . . . So man is the author of good, evil, faith, unbelief, obedience, and transgression, and is rewarded or punished for his acts.[54]

To be sure, this would lead to other questions; the categorical denial of any relation between God and evil would seem to restrict His power. For our purpose, however, what is important

[50] For the Mujbirah, see, among others, al-Shahrastānī, *K. al-milal wa'l-niḥal* (Cairo, 1951), p. 133; "The doctrine of 'compulsion' (*jabr*) entails a denial of the capacity for action in any true sense from man and its ascription to God." See also, Goldziher, *Vorlesungen*, p. 89; tr., p. 82. For the Qadarīyah, see *EI*², IV, 368-372 (s.v. "Ḳadariyya").

[51] For the designation *ʿadlīyah*, see Ibn al-Murtaḍā, *Ṭabaqāt*, p. 2; J. van Ess, *Frühe muʿtazilitische Häresiographie* (Beirut, 1971), p. 93.

[52] W. Madelung, *Der Imam al-Qāsim ibn Ibrāhīm* (Berlin, 1965), p. 18.

[53] al-Malaṭī, *K. al-tanbīh* (ed. Dedering; Istanbul, 1936), p. 30. For Wāṣil, see *GAS* I, 596.

[54] A. J. Wensinck, *The Muslim Creed* (Cambridge, 1932), p. 81, citing Shahrastānī, *K. al-milal*, p. 66.

is that this affirmation laid the basis for the first characteristic form of Islamic theodicy.

To declare God just, meant, in Muʿtazilite terms, to hold that He "does no wrong nor does He choose it, nor does He fail to fulfill what is obligatory upon Him, and all His acts are good."[55] Furthermore, divine justice meant not only that God performed the good and, indeed, even the obligatory, but that He was in some way obliged to provide "the optimum" (*al-aṣlaḥ*: "the most salutary") for his creatures.[56]

The doctrine of the optimum took hold in Muʿtazilite thought in the early 3/9th century and was particularly associated with the brilliant and versatile theologian Ibrāhīm ibn Sayyār al-Naẓẓām (d. between 220-230/835-845).[57] The doctrine was not unanimously accepted, even among the Muʿtazilites. This is hardly surprising. The Muʿtazilites were notorious for their contentiousness. According to one early heresiography, there were more than a thousand questions on which the two main schools of Baghdad and Basra differed, and members of one school frequently accused members of the other of "disbelief" (*kufr*).[58]

On the doctrine of the optimum, the two schools generally concurred in proclaiming God "obliged" to provide the best, but they differed over the extent of that obligation. The Baghdad school usually held that God must perform the optimal for man in both religious and worldly matters (*fi'l-dīn wa'l-dunyā*), and they understood "the optimal" as "the most appropriate" (*awfaq*) in terms of the divine wisdom and providence. The Basra school, on the other hand, held that God's obligation extended to matters of religion only, and they interpreted the "optimal" as denoting "benefit" (*nafʿ*).[59]

The lines of division between the two schools were not hard

[55] *Sharḥ al-uṣūl al-khamsah*, p. 301. For the author of this commentary, a pupil of the *qāḍī* ʿAbd al-Jabbār known as Mānkdīm Shishdīv or (less oddly!) A.b.a. Hāshim al-Ḥusaynī (d. 425/1034), see D. Gimaret, "Les Uṣūl al-ḫamsa du Qāḍī ʿAbd al-Jabbār," *AI* 15 (1979), p. 58.

[56] For the doctrine of *al-aṣlaḥ*, see Chapter Five below.

[57] van Ess, *Frühe muʿtaz. Häresiographie*, p. 130. For al-Naẓẓām, see *EI*¹, III, 892-893, and *GAS* I, 618-619.

[58] al-Malaṭī, *K. al-tanbīh*, p. 32.

[59] al-Bāqillānī, *K. al-tamhīd* (ed. McCarthy; Beirut, 1957), p. 255.

and fast. al-Naẓẓām, nominally a Basra Muʿtazilite, agreed with the more extreme Baghdad faction.[60] (al-Naẓẓām was, in any case, declared heretical by his fellow Basrans for his extreme position.)[61] By contrast, Bishr ibn al-Muʿtamir, the founder of the Baghdad school, originally rejected the notion of any obligation upon God in matters other than religion. Thus, he declared: "It is not obligatory for God to do the best of things for man; indeed, this is absurd because there is no end and no term to the beneficence which God can perform. He is obliged to do for men only what is best for them in their religion."[62]

The doctrine of the optimum rested on a notion that was to prove wholly unacceptable to later theologians of the Ashʿarite school. The Muʿtazilites held that the human intellect, unaided by divine revelation (as expressed in the law), could discern good and evil in acts. This was a necessary consequence of their belief in divine justice: if the intellect could not recognize the good, how could it come to know God as just?

The Muʿtazilite theodicy represented an early instance of rationalist optimism. Following their principles, the Muʿtazilites sought to discover the "rational aspect" beneath every circumstance and event. This would lead, in some cases, to spectacular theological contortions. Since God did nothing without some wise purpose, and since everything He did had as its ultimate object the specific well-being of individual creatures, it was necessary to discover and defend this wise action in the most unseemly events. How, it might be asked, was punishment in hell "optimal" for the damned? The answer might be, for example, that it was indeed optimal, since if God released the damned, they would only commit worse sins and so eventually be relegated to an even lower level of hell.[63]

The extreme emphasis on divine justice, exemplified in the doctrine of the optimum, provoked a sharp reaction. Against the

[60] *Ibid*.

[61] al-Baghdādī, *al-Farq bayn al-firaq* (Cairo, 1910), p. 117.

[62] al-Ashʿarī, *Maqālāt al-islāmīyīn* (ed. Ritter; Istanbul, 1929-33), I, 246. Bishr is said to have recanted before his death and espoused the more extreme position; see al-Khayyāṭ, *K. al-intiṣār* (ed. Nader; Beirut, 1957), p. 53.

[63] al-Juwaynī, *Irshād* (ed. Luciani; Paris, 1938), p. 169; tr., pp. 259-260.

position of al-Naẓẓām, who held, for example, that "evil is an intrinsic feature of the evil act. . . . The doer of justice (i.e., God) may not be described as having power to commit injustice,"[64] both the more moderate members of the Basra Muʿtazilah as well as members of stricter, more literalist groups, such as the Karrāmīyah and the Ḥanbalites, recoiled in alarm and cried "Heresy!"

Ashʿarism, too, represented a reaction against Muʿtazilism. Abū al-Ḥasan al-Ashʿarī (260-324/874-935), the eponymous founder of the school, had himself been a member of the Basra Muʿtazilah under the leadership of Abū ʿAlī al-Jubbāʾī (d. 303/915).[65] In the year 300/912, al-Ashʿarī broke decisively with the school. His doubts and disagreements over the doctrine of the optimum are often said to have precipitated the break.

According to an oft-cited story, al-Ashʿarī questioned his master al-Jubbāʾī as to whether God had done "the optimum" in the case of three individuals: a believer, an unbeliever, and a child, all of whom died and were, respectively, rewarded, punished, and "neither rewarded nor punished."[66] What, asked al-Ashʿarī, if the child who had died should say, "O Lord, if only you had let me live, it would have been better (*aṣlaḥ*), for then I would have entered paradise?" God, replied al-Jubbāʾī, would say to the child, "I knew that if you had lived, you would have become a sinner and then entered hell." But then, countered al-Ashʿarī, the unbeliever in hell would exclaim, "O Lord! Why did you not kill me as a child, too, so that I would not sin and then enter hell?" At this, according to the accounts, al-Jubbāʾī was left speechless.

Against the Muʿtazilite theodicy, al-Ashʿarī and his followers

[64] al-Shahrastānī, *K. al-milal*, p. 77.

[65] For al-Ashʿarī, see *EI*², I, 694-695; *GAS* I, 602-604; al-Subkī, *Ṭabaqāt al-Shāfiʿīyah al-kubrā* (Cairo, 1964-76), IV, 347-444. For an excellent discussion, which seeks to correct oversimplified views of the Ashʿarite school and its relation to al-Ashʿarī, see G. Makdisi, "Ashʿarī and the Ashʿarites in Islamic Religious History," *SI* 17 (1962), pp. 37-80; 18 (1963), pp. 19-39.

For al-Jubbāʾī, see *GAS* I, 621-622; Ibn al-Murtaḍā, *Ṭabaqāt*, pp. 80-85. On the writings of al-Jubbāʾī and his more famous son Abū Hāshim (d. 321/933), see D. Gimaret, "Matériaux pour une bibliographie des Ǧubbāʾī," *JA* 264 (1976), pp. 277-332.

[66] al-Ījī, *Mawāqif* (Cairo, 1905-07), VIII, 197.

embraced the earlier tendency of Islam that declared God, in His unlimited omnipotence, the author of good as well as evil. They rejected belief in free will; God alone can "create acts," according to an early Ashʿarite creed.[67] Their position was exemplified in the oft-invoked pious formula: "What He wills, is; what He does not will, is not."[68] All things, from human acts to natural events in the world, were the direct result of divine decree; and this decree was to be accepted without question: "Good and evil (occur) through the decree and power of God. We believe in God's decree and power—the good as well as the evil, the sweet as well as the bitter."[69]

Nevertheless, the Ashʿarites, despite these austere articles of faith, represented a middle course. If they reacted against an excessive Muʿtazilite stress on divine justice and God's "obligations," they at the same time eschewed the severe predestinarianism of the Mujbirah. God alone created acts; man, however, "acquired" these acts and so could be deemed legally responsible for his deeds.

Furthermore, in rejecting its parent school of Muʿtazilism, Ashʿarism did not by any means reject its distinctive methods: the reliance on dialectic, the use of a precise theological terminology, and, more generally, a rationalist and speculative approach to dogmatic issues. For this reason, stricter schools, such as the Ḥanbalite, looked with disapproval on Ashʿarism as riddled with reprehensible "innovations" (*bidaʿ*).[70]

In reverting to a more literal conception of divine omnipotence, the Ashʿarites ran the risk of raising questions about divine justice in even more exacerbated form. They resolved such incipient questions in a radical manner. Ashʿarism denied outright that good and evil had any objective basis. Rather, good and evil were determined by divine fiat. This characteristic Ashʿarite principle, which we shall encounter frequently in the following pages, was given admirable expression by the great

[67] al-Ashʿarī, *al-Ibānah ʿan uṣūl al-diyānah* (Cairo, 1977), p. 23.
[68] al-Ashʿarī, *al-Ibānah*, p. 15.
[69] al-Ashʿarī, *al-Ibānah*, p. 25; see also, al-Ashʿarī, *Maqālāt*, I, 291.
[70] Goldziher, *Vorlesungen*, p. 266; tr., p. 240.

early codifier of Ashʿarite theology, the *qāḍī* Abū Bakr Muḥammad al-Bāqillānī (d. 403/1013):

> We emphatically deny that there is in the intellect, acting on its own, any way to know the evil of an act or its goodness, its legal prohibition or legal neutrality, or its obligatory nature. These judgments, in their totality, may not be posited for acts except through the divine law, and not through any determination of the intellect.[71]

The Ashʿarite school (together with the equally "orthodox" school of al-Māturīdī, d. 333/944)[72] was to become dominant in Islamic theology.[73] It might be thought that this fact would spell an end to any further developments of theodicy within Islamic theology. It seems improbable that an optimistic theodicy of the sort propounded by the Muʿtazilites could emerge within Ashʿarism. In a system that frankly acknowledges God to be the author of evil as well as of good, what need could there be for theodicy or, indeed, optimism of any kind? Is not Ashʿarite theology the very embodiment of the "*Fatum Mahometanum*" against which Leibniz inveighed, comparing it to the "lazy sophism" of antiquity and stating that it is this belief that "causes the Turks not to shun places ravaged by plague?"[74]

The frank ascription to God of evil as well as of good, the strict reliance on the sovereign efficacy of the divine will, the belief that everything that occurs is the direct and inevitable result of the divine decree—these elements, which do represent a severe form of fatalism, are also, however, the very elements upon which a distinctive Islamic version of theodicy would be

[71] al-Bāqillānī, *K. al-tamhīd*, p. 105. For al-Bāqillānī, see *GAS* I, 608-610. On the early Ashʿarite conception of evil, see P. Antes, "The First Ašʿarites' Conception of Evil and the Devil," *Mélanges offerts à Henry Corbin* (Tehran, 1977), pp. 177-189.

[72] For al-Māturīdī, whose school was especially widespread in Central Asia, see *EI*[1], III, 414-415; *GAS* I, 604-606.

[73] Muʿtazilism continued as a force well into the 5/11th century, especially under the Būyids in Iran; its influence seems to have waned after the death of the *qāḍī* ʿAbd al-Jabbār in 415/1025. The last prominent representative was the Qur'ān commentator and grammarian al-Zamakhsharī (d. 538/1144).

[74] Leibniz, *Essais de Theodicée*, p. 132; tr., p. 153.

erected. "Fatalism," after all, may itself be a response to the dilemma of theodicy.

Whatever the merits of the Muʿtazilite theodicy or the Ashʿarite response to it, fundamental questions persisted. In the 5/11th century, for example, the Syrian poet and skeptic Abū al-ʿAlāʾ al-Maʿarrī (d. 449/1057) could write:

> Someone may ask whether God wills nothing but the good. Regarding evil, one of two things may be: either God knows it, or He does not. If He knows it, one of two things may be: either He wills it, or He does not.
>
> If He does will it, it is as though He were the agent, just as it is said, "The prince cut off the thief's hand," even though he did not perform the act himself. If God does not will (evil), then what is not permitted against an earthly prince, is permitted against Him; for whenever something is done in his realm that displeases him, the prince repudiates it and commands its cessation.
>
> This is a difficulty which the theologians have exerted their powers of reasoning to solve, but to no avail.[75]

Furthermore, in the Qurʾān God is repeatedly described as merciful and compassionate. If He is truly compassionate, His compassion should extend to all creatures, and not merely to man; but this, as al-Maʿarrī further noted, is manifestly not the case:

> Since it is stated that the creator is merciful and compassionate, why does the lion spring to attack gentle creatures that are neither harmful nor robust? And how many have perished through snakebite, including many famous people! (Why) do hawk and falcon swoop upon the grain-gleaning bird? The grouse leaves her thirsting chicks and sets out early to reach water which she would carry to them in her craw, but a hawk finds her far from them and devours her. So her chicks perish of thirst.[76]

[75] Yāqūt, *Irshād al-arīb* (ed. Margoliouth; Leiden, 1913), I, 199; cited in H. Ritter, "Risālat Ibn Sīnā fī'l-arzāq," *RAAD* 25 (1950), p. 200.

[76] Yāqūt, *Irshād*, I, 200. al-Maʿarrī raises the question of the unmerited suffering of animals in the context of a defense of his vegetarianism. The question

Such questions were hardly new in Islam. The Muʿtazilites, for example, had devoted much ingenuity to the problem of unmerited suffering, particularly that of infants and animals.[77] In a certain sense, however, al-Maʿarrī's way of asking the question was new. It did not proceed from preconceived dogmatic axioms involving "justice" and "omnipotence." It raised the question of evil without obvious preconceptions and in terms of the world as given by experience. It was a skeptical and philosophical way of posing the question of theodicy.

Islamic philosophers, and especially Ibn Sīnā, a contemporary of al-Maʿarrī, raised such questions and provided their own distinctive answers.[78] In so doing, they introduced into Islamic thought several classical solutions for the problem of evil, e.g., the privative theory of evil, or the notion of evil as a necessary concomitant of a greater good. These answers occurred, moreover, within the framework of elaborate and complex philosophical systems, heavily indebted to Greek thought; such systems, like that of Ibn Sīnā, with its conception of a providence (*ʿināyah*) in which all existing things emanated necessarily from the divine nature, possessed an autonomy that posed a threat to dogmatic theology.[79] Such a system offered a coherent and plausible account of the world, and it did so without relying on revelation.

During the period roughly from the 3/9th to the 5/11th centuries, the various attempts to resolve the problem of theodicy which we have here briefly reviewed, stood as rival, competing solutions, each of which could claim its group of adherents. Each, moreover, represented a distinctive point of view that seemed incompatible with its rivals.

---

was raised by others as well; cf. the discussion by the great philosopher Abū Bakr M. b. Zakarīyā' al-Rāzī (d. ca. 320/923) in his *K. al-sīrah al-falsafīyah* in *Rasā'il falsafīyah* (ed. Kraus; Cairo, 1939), p. 104.

[77] See Chapter Five below.

[78] Such questions are paraphrased by al-Ghazālī, *Maqāṣid al-falāsifah* (ed. Dunyā; Cairo, 1961), pp. 296-297: "We see the world teeming with evils, disasters and abominations, such as thunderbolts, earthquakes, floods and beasts of prey. So, too, in human souls: lust, wrath and the like. How does evil issue from God? Is it by decree, or not? If not, then something is beyond God's power and will. . . . If so, then how can He who is sheer goodness ordain evil?"

[79] See Chapter Four below for a discussion.

In the 11th and 12th centuries, however, the Ashʿarite school struggled to gain the ascendancy, and succeeded in winning a large measure of prominence and influence. This occurred for a variety of reasons; for our purposes, what is of moment is that this prominence was very much the result of the work of a single thinker, the theologian and mystic Abū Ḥāmid al-Ghazālī.

al-Ghazālī[80] was born in 450/1058 in Ṭūs, in the Iranian province of Khurāsān. He came from a family of scholars—his father had been an expert in jurisprudence (*fiqh*)—and he received a thorough traditional education. For a time, he studied under the celebrated *Imām al-Ḥaramayn* al-Juwaynī (d. 478/1085). In 485/1091, the Seljuq vizier Niẓām al-Mulk appointed him to a teaching position at the newly founded Niẓāmīyah *madrasah* in Baghdad.[81]

In 488/1095, al-Ghazālī underwent a severe spiritual crisis. In his "spiritual autobiography," written some fifteen years later, al-Ghazālī described this crisis.[82] Quite early in his career, he had undergone a period of radical skepticism; the very bases of knowledge seemed shaken.[83] In a quest for the science that might provide certain knowledge, al-Ghazālī investigated, in turn, dialectical theology (*kalām*), Ismāʿīlī authoritarian teaching (*taʿlīm*), philosophy (*falsafah*), and Ṣūfī mysticism.[84] In each of these areas, al-Ghazālī wrote treatises in which he attempted to survey the

[80] On the spelling Ghazālī—as opposed to Ghazzālī—, see W. M. Watt, *EI*², II, 1038, but also *GAL* SI, 744, note 1.

[81] For a useful, if somewhat dated, biographical account, to which I am indebted, see D. B. Macdonald, "The Life of al-Ghazzālī, with especial reference to his religious experiences and opinions," *JAOS* 20 (1899), pp. 71-132; the disputed question which forms the subject of the following pages is briefly discussed on p. 121. Further biographical details may now be found in the introduction to R. J. McCarthy, *Freedom and Fulfillment* (Boston, 1980), esp. pp. ix-xxiv. See also *GAL* I, 535-546; SI, 744-756; al-Subkī, *Ṭabaqāt*, VI, 191-389; al-Ṣafadī, *al-Wāfī biʾl-wafayāt*, I, 274; Kaḥḥālah, II, 266ff; Ziriklī, VII, 22f. On the Niẓāmīyah, see G. Makdisi, "Muslim Institutions of Learning in 11th Century Baghdad," *BSOAS* 24 (1961), pp. 1-56.

[82] His *al-Munqidh min al-ḍalāl*, probably written in 502 or 3/1108 or 9, a few years before his death.

[83] *al-Munqidh min al-ḍalāl* (ed. Jabre; Beirut, 1959), pp. 12-17; French tr., pp. 63-66. On skepticism in Islam, see J. van Ess, "Skepticism in Islamic Religious Thought," *al-Abḥāth* 21 (1968), pp. 1-18.

[84] *al-Munqidh*, p. 15ff.; tr., p. 67ff.

distinctive features and arguments of its adherents. His method of mastering a branch of learning consisted ultimately in assimilating it to the extent that he could compose a thorough account of it.

Thus, in the case of *kalām*, he produced the compendium of dogmatic theology entitled *al-Iqtiṣād fi'l-iʿtiqād*. In philosophy, he summarized the views of the philosophers, and especially those of Ibn Sīnā, in his *Maqāṣid al-falāsifah*, and he then subjected those views to a harsh critique in his *Tahāfut al-falāsifah*. His polemical treatment of Ismāʿīlism is contained principally in the works known as *al-Quṣṭās al-mustaqīm* and *al-Mustaẓhirī*.[85]

al-Ghazālī's quest for a basis of certain knowledge ended with his conviction that Ṣūfism offered the only satisfactory approach. However, he found himself incapable of renouncing his prestigious position and embracing the Ṣūfī way of poverty and asceticism. His indecision precipitated the actual crisis. For six months, he struggled with himself to no avail. Finally, as he recounts it:

> I wavered incessantly between the strong pull of worldly desires and the promptings of the next world for almost six months from the month of Rajab, 488 (July 1095). Then, in that month, I crossed the boundary from free will into constraint (*iḍṭirār*). God locked my tongue so that I was unable to teach. I used to exert all my effort so that I might be able to teach for one day . . . but my tongue could not master a single word.[86]

[85] For these works, see the standard bibliography by M. Bouyges, *Essai de chronologie des oeuvres de al-Ghazālī* (Beirut, 1959); ʿAbd al-Raḥmān Badawī, *Muʾallafāt al-Ghazzālī* (Cairo, 1961), is also useful. The *Mustaẓhirī*, so named in honor of the ʿAbbāsid caliph al-Mustaẓhir (*reg.* 487-512/1094-1118), was edited, in an incomplete form, by I. Goldziher as *Streitschrift des Ġazālī gegen die Bāṭinijja-Sekte* (Leiden, 1916); for an Ismāʿīlī reply to al-Ghazālī's work, see now Henry Corbin, "The Ismāʿīlī Response to the Polemic of Ghazālī," in S. H. Nasr (ed.), *Ismāʿīlī Contributions to Islamic Culture* (Tehran, 1398/1977), pp. 69-98.

For recent literature on al-Ghazālī, see J. van Ess, "Neuere Literatur zu Ġazzālī," *Oriens* 20 (1967), pp. 299-308; and Kōjirō Nakamura, "A Bibliography on Imām al-Ghazālī," *Orient* (Tokyo), 13 (1977), pp. 119-134. There is a useful annotated bibliography in McCarthy, *Freedom and Fulfillment*, pp. 383-392.

[86] *al-Munqidh*, p. 37.

This strange aphasia was accompanied by other symptoms. He could scarcely eat; he lapsed into a state of extreme enervation. The doctors were powerless to cure him. Finally, under pretext of performing the pilgrimage, he left Baghdad, resigning his teaching post in favor of his brother Aḥmad.[87] He spent two years in Damascus, where he devoted himself to prayer and solitude. In 490/1097, he made the pilgrimage. al-Ghazālī spent the next nine years in seclusion; and it was during this period of reflection that he began to write his huge work entitled the *Iḥyāʾ ʿulūm al-dīn.*

In the *Iḥyāʾ*, al-Ghazālī attempted to order the religious sciences under the aegis of Ṣūfī mysticism. The work is in effect a synthesis, but it is no impartial *summa*; it is a highly tendentious and programmatic work. Its object is to lead the uninitiated to an understanding and acceptance of the Ṣūfī way, and then to guide and instruct him in its application. To this end, it draws on a wide range of sources; in the eyes of more traditional readers, these sources often betrayed suspect, and even heretical, tendencies.

There can be no question of describing this work in further detail here.[88] Its originality has perhaps been exaggerated, as one author has recently suggested.[89] The fact is indisputable, however, that to succeeding generations the *Iḥyāʾ* stood as a unique and even indispensable guide to religious study and practice. The work established al-Ghazālī's position as the "renewer of religion" for his age and earned him the honorific title "Proof of Islam" (*ḥujjat al-Islām*). As we shall see, his prestige and spiritual authority after his death became, at times, virtually unassailable.

al-Ghazālī was persuaded to return briefly to teaching and

[87] Shihāb al-dīn Aḥmad al-Ghazālī (d. 520/1126), an influential mystic and author in his own right; see *GAL* I, 546.

[88] For an outline and précis of the contents of the *Iḥyāʾ*, see G. H. Bousquet, *Ih'ya ou Vivification des sciences de la foi* (Paris, 1955).

[89] So P. Nwyia, *Ibn ʿAṭāʾ Allāh et la naissance de la confrérie šāḏilīte* (Beirut, 1971), pp. 8-9; "The exceptional character of this work has been too often emphasized, as though it were one of its kind . . . [al-Ghazālī's] work appears much less original when it is placed in the line of attempts made before his time to render Sufism intelligible."

then became the leader of a small group of Ṣūfīs. He wrote several summaries of the *Iḥyā'*, in which he explained or reaffirmed his positions there, and, in some cases, even developed them further; and he wrote his celebrated autobiography. In his last works, he returned to the subjects of *kalām* and the principles of jurisprudence (*uṣūl al-fiqh*), e.g., his *Kitāb al-mustaṣfā* (written in 503/1109)—subjects which had occupied him in his early career, before his "conversion."[90] He died, in Ṭūs, in 505/1111, at the age of 55.

al-Ghazālī is in many respects the central figure in the following study and so we have dwelt here in some detail on his life. In several passages of his later Ṣūfī works, al-Ghazālī raised the question of theodicy in a rather novel form. He offered a solution to the problem that combined many aspects of earlier approaches—the Muʿtazilite, the Ashʿarite, and the philosophical—and he did so by casting all of these approaches into a single distinctive formulation.

[90] His last work, completed a few days before his death, was an anti-*kalām* tract entitled *K. iljām al-ʿawāmm ʿan ʿilm al-kalām*, on which see Bouyges, pp. 80-82 (no. 63).

# ONE

# *The Perfect Rightness of the Actual*

## I
## THE PROBLEM

"There is not in possibility anything more wonderful than what is" (*laysa fi'l-imkān abdaʿ mimmā kān*). This statement, ascribed to Abū Ḥāmid al-Ghazālī (d. 505/1111), engendered a controversy that lasted from his own lifetime until well into the 19th century. Opposition to the statement and all that it implied was fierce and bitter. Thus, Ibrāhīm ibn ʿUmar al-Biqāʿī (d. 885/1480), one of al-Ghazālī's most implacable critics, would not shrink from accusing him of outright heresy.[1] In turn, al-Ghazālī's defenders mounted a vigorous counterattack leading, on at least one occasion, to violence: in Damascus an angry mob attacked and almost killed al-Biqāʿī after the contents of his treatise against the "Proof of Islam" became known.[2] Nor were the disputants above spiteful gibes at opponents: one of al-Ghazālī's lesser-known defenders would remark sneeringly that al-Biqāʿī should have entitled his treatise, not "The Triumph," as he had intended, but rather "Onion Peels" (*qushūr al-baṣal*), because of its "stink."[3]

What in this statement provoked such controversy? The fact that it was attributed to none other than al-Ghazālī, the renowned renewer of religion, is of course significant. For a possibly suspect doctrine to be affirmed by so celebrated a figure could not but elicit passionate interest, and this is a factor that must be kept in mind. Nevertheless, the debate itself, stubborn and protracted as it was and ranging from puerile taunts to ex-

[1] *Tahdīm*, fol. 44a (For al-Biqāʿī and the other disputants discussed here, see Chapter Two.)

[2] al-Suyūṭī, *K. al-taḥadduth bi-niʿmat Allāh* (ed. Sartain; Cambridge, 1975), p. 187.

[3] M. b. Ḥāmid al-Shāfiʿī, *al-Dalīl*, fol. 133b.

ceedingly subtle and intricate argumentation, arose out of certain central issues in Islamic theology.

Thus, the statement is said to lead to "a restriction of the divine omnipotence" (*ḥaṣr al-qudrah*) in the critics' view and so must be rejected.[4] This is in fact the crux of the problem; for if nothing in possibility is "more wonderful," or more perfect, than what actually exists here and now, then God's omnipotence seems severely compromised. This world with all its undeniable defects and afflictions will be taken as the full and final manifestation of God's power.

This objection is well summarized by one of al-Ghazali's last champions, the 19th-century writer Hamdān ibn ʿUthmān al-Jazāʾirī, as follows:

> (The statement's) incompatibility with the principles of the *ahl al-sunnah* is for three reasons. First, the creed of the orthodox, which must be believed, is that the things of which God is capable (*maqdūrāt Allāh*) stop at no limit and end; and that the order of this world, even if it is in perfect wisdom and excellent design—even so, God is capable of creating one more excellent than it, and one still more excellent than that most excellent *ad infinitum*.
>
> But the meaning of al-Ghazālī's statement is that the creation of what is more perfect and more wonderful than this world is outside the sphere of possibility. . . . So the divine power is not connected with the creation of a world better and more excellent than this world. Rather, the divine power terminates at this limit of greatest excellence and highest perfection.[5]

This is the first and gravest difficulty with al-Ghazālī's statement, and it represents a "great audacity" (*jurʾah ʿaẓīmah*) on his part; indeed, it may even be termed a "breach of orthodox consensus" (*ijmāʿ*).[6] And, as if to complicate matters further, al-Ghazālī has himself affirmed, in several other works, the orthodox doctrine that God's power is limitless, a fact which al-Jazāʾirī and others are quick to point out.[7]

[4] al-Yāfiʿī, *Marham al-ʿilal* (ed. Ross; Calcutta, 1910), p. 17.

[5] *Ḥikmat*, p. 12.

[6] *Ibid.*

[7] So in al-Ghazālī's *K. al-arbaʿīn* (Cairo, 1344), p. 5: "The objects of God's

The apparent constraint on God's omnipotence leads to two further difficulties noted by al-Jazā'irī. One of these is that the statement seems compatible with the condemned doctrine of the philosophers according to which God creates, not out of free choice (*ikhtiyār*), but out of a necessity intrinsic to His nature (*ījāb dhātī*). And, lastly, critics will note a perilously close kinship, both in form and meaning, between al-Ghazālī's assertion and the formulations of the Muʿtazilite doctrine of "the optimum" (*al-aṣlaḥ*). This doctrine was repudiated by the orthodox, who found especially abhorrent its insistence upon an obligation on God's part to provide what is most beneficial and most salutary for His creation.[8]

This is but the barest summary of problems to which it will be necessary to return in later chapters. It is given here only to set al-Ghazālī's statement within the context of the debate. The bone of contention is the possible infringement of the divine prerogatives of omnipotence and free choice. The suspicion that al-Ghazālī's position reflects the influence of philosophers and the Muʿtazilites "who cling to their shirt-tails"[9] will serve only to sharpen the acrimony of the debate.

Before considering the development of the debate itself, with its many disputants and their works, and before embarking on an analysis of the theological difficulties adumbrated above, we must examine the controversial statement in its context in the various works of al-Ghazālī in which it appears. This will enable us to form a clearer conception of al-Ghazālī's "theodicy," if it may indeed be so termed.[10]

We shall need further to ascertain whether this theodicy is consistent with his viewpoint as expressed elsewhere in his work, or whether it is indeed an aberration, or lapse (*zallah*) on his

---

power are innumerable" (*lā tuḥsā maqdūrātuhu*), as also in his *al-Iqtiṣād fi'l-iʿtiqād* (ed. Çubukçu; Ankara, 1962), p. 82 [For these works, see Bouyges, nos. 38 and 24, respectively.]

[8] *Ḥikmat*, pp. 14-15.

[9] *Ibid.*

[10] According to Wensinck, al-Ghazālī's emphasis on strict predestination is so rarely reconciled in the *Iḥyā'* with the "human and tender" traits of God that "one can scarcely speak of theodicy in Ghazzālī," *La pensée de Ghazzālī* (Paris, 1940), p. 17.

part, as at least one of his opponents will charge.[11] We shall have to keep in mind that consistency is perhaps a tenuous criterion in relation to al-Ghazālī, as has often been pointed out.[12]

Finally, we should be in a position to determine whether the disputed sentence is in fact correctly attributed to al-Ghazālī or whether, as certain commentators will claim, it is after all an alien notion interpolated (*madsūs*) into his work by later meddling or malicious hands.

# II
# THE TEXTS

The commentators single out four works by al-Ghazālī in which the offending statement occurs.

It appears first in the discussion of "trust in God" (*tawakkul*) in the fourth part of the *Iḥyā' 'ulūm al-dīn*, where, in speaking of the "necessarily right order" of the world, al-Ghazālī declares: "There is not in possibility anything whatever more excellent, more complete, or more perfect than it is."[13] This sentence, together with the entire passage in which it appears, will provide the *locus classicus* for the debate in all later discussions.

al-Ghazālī reaffirmed his position in a later treatise entitled *al-Imlā' fī mushkilāt al-Iḥyā'*. This work was in fact composed in response to critics who had attacked certain debatable points in the *Iḥyā'*. Here al-Ghazālī writes: "There is not in possibility anything more wonderful (*abda'*) than the form of this world or more excellent in arrangement or more complete in construction."[14]

In a third work, written after the *Iḥyā'* and paraphrasing its major doctrines, al-Ghazālī will omit the controversial sentence

[11] *Tahdīm*, fol. 37b.

[12] See W. M. Watt, "The Study of al-Ghazālī," *Oriens* 13/14 (1961), p. 128; and Wensinck, *La pensée de Ghazzālī*, pp. 83-85 and 98ff.

[13] *Iḥyā'*, IV, 223, lines 6-7: *laysa fi'l-imkān aṣlan aḥsan minhu wa-lā atamm wa-lā akmal.*

[14] *al-Imlā'* (Berlin ms., Pm. 545 [Ahlwardt II, 316, no. 1714]), fol. 16a. Also printed on the margin of *Itḥāf* I, 193ff. For this work (variously known as *al-Ajwibah al-muskitah 'an al-as'ilah al-mubhitah* and *al-Intiṣār li-mā fi'l-Iḥyā' min al-asrār*), see Bouyges, nos. 61 and 116; and *GAL* I, 422; S I, 748, no. 25.

in the corresponding passage (which is otherwise almost verbatim) but will introduce it elsewhere. This work is the *Kitāb al-arbaʿīn*, intended as a sequel to his *Jawāhir al-Qurʾān*. (The commentators, confusingly enough, often cite the *Kitāb al-arbaʿīn* merely as "*Jawāhir*.") There, in discussing the notion of "contentment with the divine decree" (*riḍāʾ biʾl-qaḍāʾ*), a Ṣūfī principle closely connected with *tawakkul*, he writes that these decrees "are ordered in the most perfect and most excellent of ways" (*ʿalā akmal al-wujūh wa-aḥsanihā*), such that "nothing in possibility is more excellent than they, nor more perfect" (*wa-laysa fiʾl-imkān aḥsan minhā*).[15]

The fourth work mentioned by the disputants is the *Maqāṣid al-falāsifah*, an exposition of the doctrines of the philosophers, and particularly those of Ibn Sīnā. As is well known, al-Ghazālī intended this work as an introduction to his stringent critique of philosophy, the *Tahāfut al-falāsifah*. In the Latin West, however, the *Maqāṣid* came to be mistakenly identified as a favorable presentation of the philosophers' doctrines, and "Algazel" joined the ranks of Avicenna, Averroes, and Avempace in the scholastic tradition.[16] At times it will seem as though certain of his opponents in the present debate make the same mistake and confuse al-Ghazālī's position with that of the philosophers whom he elsewhere attacks.

It must be admitted that this is not wholly without foundation. Certain philosophical doctrines, such as that of the world's eternity (*qidam al-ʿālam*), were indisputably repugnant to al-Ghazālī, and he criticized them vehemently. In the case of others, however, such as the doctrine of providence (*ʿināyah*), it is not entirely clear that he rejected them *in toto*. There is evidence to suggest that he accepted certain aspects of such doctrines, with significant modifications, and then incorporated them in thinly disguised form in later works such as the *Iḥyāʾ*.

This, too, is a subject to which we shall be obliged to return in a later chapter. Here let us merely note that the passage in

[15] *K. al-arbaʿīn*, p. 270.

[16] See E. Gilson, *History of Christian Philosophy in the Middle Ages* (NY, 1955), p. 216. For the *Maqāṣid*, see Bouyges, p. 23 (no. 17), who dates it at 487; G. Hourani, "The Chronology of Ghazālī's Writings," *JAOS* 79 (1959), p. 227, dates the work at 486/1094, i.e., four years before the *Iḥyāʾ* was begun.

question appears in al-Ghazālī's discussion of providence, where he says: "All existing things, from the number of the stars and their measure, the earth's shape and that of animals and everything that exists, exist as they do only because it is the most perfect way to be (*akmal wujūh al-wujūd*). Any other possibilities are defective in regard to it (sc. the actual order)."[17]

All of these variations, but especially those in the *Iḥyā'* and the *Imlā'*, came to be compressed into a single rhyming formula under which the entire problem and its discussion were subsumed, i.e.: "There is not in possibility anything more wonderful than what is" (*laysa fi'l-imkān abdaʿ mimmā kān*).[18]

# III
# THE STATEMENT IN CONTEXT

The following passage from the *Iḥyā'* represents al-Ghazālī's most sustained formulation of theodicy. It is, moreover, the passage to which all later discussions refer; an understanding of it will be necessary in following the course of the dispute. This does not mean, however, that we shall attempt at this point to decide "what al-Ghazālī really meant." Such an attempt would be premature before the comments of his critics and supporters have been considered. Hence, we shall try to present here as fully as possible what he in fact wrote, keeping in mind the differing interpretations to which his words gave rise.

Our object at this state is exposition rather than analysis. We shall concentrate on the text of the *Iḥyā'*, bringing in citations from other of his works where they may serve to illumine his intention; we shall have particular recourse to his own comments in the *Imlā'* as well. The difficulty here will be to refrain from deciding the issue (if indeed it can be decided); no exposition, however well intentioned, can remain completely neutral. But our ultimate interest should be not only to determine al-Ghazālī's original meaning but to learn what his commenta-

[17] *Maqāṣid al-falāsifah*, p. 238; cf. also p. 237: "The essence of the One is an essence from which necessarily every existing thing emanates in the most complete and perfect manner" (*ʿalā al-wajh al-atamm wa'l-akmal ʿalā tartībihi*).

[18] Most later treatises employ this formula: thus al-Suyūṭī will entitle his work *Tashyīd al-arkān min "Laysa fi'l-imkān abdaʿ mimmā kān."*

tors made of his remarks. What we here term a Muslim version of theodicy is the product of many minds arguing pro and con over a span of centuries in an attempt to understand what is contained *in nuce* in the original text.

## A. *THE IḤYĀ' TEXT*

It should be made clear at the outset that we are dealing, not with a systematic or even a closely reasoned proof of theodicy, but with an exhortation to a specific stage (*maqām*) on the Ṣūfī path. al-Ghazālī's defenders take his critics to task for ignoring this, and rightly so.

Thus, according to Murtaḍā al-Zabīdī (d. 1205/1791), ". . . his purpose in this is to incite man to the utmost in reliance on God (*tawakkul*)—that is what this question is all about—and to contentment with every decree of God . . . so that man may not despair over an evil which befalls him or a good which eludes him."[19]

This hortatory intent is obvious when the entire passage is seen and so it will be given here in full, despite its length, as is almost invariably done in the commentaries themselves.

In his discussion of the realization of the divine unity (*tawḥīd*), which is the basis (*aṣl*) of trust in God, al-Ghazālī states that to reach the stage of trust, it is necessary that:

> . . . one believe with utter certainty in which there is neither weakness nor doubt that if God had created all creatures with the intelligence of the most intelligent among them and the knowledge of the most learned among them; and if He had created for them all the knowledge their souls could sustain and had poured out upon them wisdom of indescribable extent; then, had He given each one of them the knowledge, wisdom, and intelligence of them all, and revealed to them the consequences of things and taught them the mysteries of the transcendent world and acquainted them with the subtleties

[19] *Itḥāf*, IX, 450, line -3ff.

of divine favor and the mysteries of final punishments, until they were made well aware of good and evil, benefit and harm; then, if He had ordered them to arrange this world and the transcendent world in terms of the knowledge and wisdom they had received, (even then) that act of arrangement on the part of all of them, helping each other and working in concert, would not make it necessary to add to the way in which God has arranged creation in this world and the next by (so much as) a gnat's wing, nor to subtract from it (by so much as) a gnat's wing; nor would it raise a speck of dust or lower a speck of dust; (their arrangement) would not ward off sickness or fault or defect or poverty or injury from one so afflicted, and it would not remove health or perfection or wealth or advantage from one so favored.

But if people directed their gaze and considered steadfastly everything that God has created in heaven and earth, they would see neither discrepancy nor rift.

Everything which God apportions to man, such as sustenance, life-span, pleasure and pain, capacity and incapacity, belief and disbelief, obedience and sin, is all of it sheer justice, with no injustice in it; and pure right, with no wrong in it.

Indeed, it is according to the necessarily right order, in accord with what must be and as it must be and in the measure in which it must be; and there is not in possibility anything whatever more excellent, more perfect, and more complete than it.

For if there were and He had withheld it, having power to create it but not deigning to do so, this would be miserliness contrary to the divine generosity and injustice contrary to the divine justice. But if He were not able, it would be incapability contrary to divinity.

Indeed, all poverty and loss in this world is a diminution in this world but an increase in the next. Every lack in the next world in relation to one individual is a boon in relation to someone else. For were it not for night, the value of day would be unknown. Were it not for illness, the healthy would not enjoy health. Were it not for hell, the blessed in paradise would not know the extent of their blessedness. In the same way, the lives of animals serve as ransom for human souls; and the power to kill them which is given to humans is no injustice.

Indeed, giving precedence to the perfect over the imperfect is justice itself. So too is heaping favors on the inhabitants of paradise by increasing the punishment of the inhabitants of hell. The ransom of the faithful by means of the unfaithful is justice itself.

As long as the imperfect is not created, the perfect will remain unknown. If beasts had not been created, the dignity of man would not be manifest. The perfect and the imperfect are correlated. Divine generosity and wisdom require the simultaneous creation of the perfect and the imperfect.

Just as the amputation of a gangrenous hand in order to preserve life is justice, since it involves ransoming the perfect through the imperfect, so too the matter of the discrepancy which exists among people in their portion in this world and the next. That is all justice, without any wrong; and right in which there is no caprice.

Now this is a vast and deep sea with wide shores and tossed by billows. In extent it is comparable to the sea of God's unity. Whole groups of the inept drown in it without realizing that it is an arcane matter which only the knowing comprehend. Behind this sea is the mystery of predestination where the many wander in perplexity and which those who have been illuminated are forbidden to divulge.

The gist is that good and evil are foreordained. What is foreordained comes necessarily to be after a prior act of divine volition. No one can rebel against God's judgement; no one can appeal His decree and command. Rather, everything small and large is written and comes to be in a known and expected measure. "What strikes you was not there to miss you; what misses you was not there to strike you."[20]

*1. The Perfect Rightness of the Actual* (lines 1-40)

The world as it is and not otherwise, the actual state-of-affairs, is superior to any merely hypothetical alternative order. This is true of the least detail: the gnat's wing or the speck of dust. Not one iota of the actual may be changed for the better.

The striking opening lines of the passage, with its extended hypothetical sentence, are based very closely on a passage in the *Qūt al-qulūb* of Abū Ṭālib al-Makkī (d. 386/996).[21] As is well known, the *Qūt al-qulūb*, together with works by ʿAbd al-Karīm al-Qushayrī (d. 465/1072) and al-Ḥārith ibn Asad al-Muḥāsibī (d. 243/857), were favorite Ṣūfī sources for al-Ghazālī in composing the *Iḥyā'*. Indeed, al-Jazā'irī for one will see the entire passage above as little more than a commentary on al-Makkī's text.[22]

The original passage in the *Qūt al-qulūb*, corresponding roughly to lines 1-26 of the above translation, begins with the same premise as al-Ghazālī's. For both authors, this world is not only right and just as it is, it is insuperably so. Even if God were to increase human knowledge and wisdom to the fullest extent

[20] *Iḥyā'*, IV, 222-223; cf. also the translation by H. Wehr, *al-Ġazzālī's Buch vom Gottvertrauen* (Halle, 1940), p. 37. The final quotation in the passage is from *ḥadīth*; see Aḥmad ibn Ḥanbal, *Musnad* V, 183, 185, 189, and Ibn Mājah, *Sunan*, I, 30 (no. 77).

[21] *Qūt al-qulūb* (Cairo, 1351/1932), III, 52. al-Ghazālī's indebtedness to al-Makkī was well known; it is noted, for example, in *Itḥāf*, IX, 450. See also Wehr, *al-Ġazzālī's Buch vom Gottvertrauen*, p. 111, note 164. For al-Ghazālī's dependence on his predecessors, see P. Nwyia, *Ibn ʿAṭā' Allāh*, pp. 8-9: "Ibn ʿAbbād noted it already in the 14th century: Ghazālī borrowed the best part of his *Iḥyā'* from Muḥāsibī and from the *Qūt al-qulūb* of Makkī."

[22] *Ḥikmat*, p. 39.

imaginable and grant man unlimited freedom to rearrange the cosmos, even then it could not be improved. al-Makkī intensifies this assertion with a sentence omitted in al-Ghazālī's reworking: "Even if God were to assist and strengthen" man, his attempt to redesign the world order would be unavailing.[23]

As noted earlier, the passage is part of an exhortation to trust in God, and the same is true of al-Makkī's text as well. In a sense we may regard the entire long opening sentence as the reply to an unexpressed but ever-present question: Why is the world as it is? It would plainly be improved if. . . . (and indeed, such questioning, though for different motives, will appear in al-Biqāʿī's attack.) This dissatisfaction with things as they are forms an obstacle to the trust in God which both authors are eager to inculcate. Elsewhere al-Makkī points out that the very particles of the hypothetical conditional and of the future may become instruments of impiety:

> If a person says, "Were it not for so-and-so, I would have perished," "Were it not thus, it would be so,"—this is polytheism (*shirk*) . . .
>
> *sawfa* is one of the armies of Iblīs.[24]

Such statements reflect an assumption that agents other than God exist; they suggest that things might have been otherwise, and so they undermine trust in God. Furthermore, the human self is by nature presumptuous and arrogantly eschews its proper subservience. In his discussion of fortitude (*ṣabr*), al-Ghazālī notes that "there is no self which does not have hidden within it what Pharaoh openly proclaimed, i.e., 'I am your lord the most high!' " for "the self by its very nature shuns servanthood (*ʿubūdīyah*) and craves lordship (*rubūbīyah*)."[25]

This apotheosis of the self, to which human beings naturally

[23] *Qūt al-qulūb*, III, 52.

[24] *Ibid.*, III, 6. Cf. Ibn Mājah, *Sunan*, I, 31: *law taftaḥu ʿamal al-shayṭān.* According to Abū Sulaymān al-Sijistānī, as reported by al-Tawḥīdī, when one submits without question to divine law, " 'why?' falls away, 'how?' is invalidated, 'why not?' vanishes and 'if only' and 'would that' disappear in the wind!" *al-Imtāʿ wa'l-muʾānasah* (ed. Amīn; Beirut, 1953), II, 6-7. [*sawfa* is the future particle in Arabic.]

[25] *Iḥyāʾ*, IV, 61.

tend, along with a false reliance on worldly means, make a genuine trust in God impossible. The aspirant to *tawakkul* must crave not lordship, however, but to be "like an infant who knows no refuge other than his mother's breast."[26] Or, as another famous saying has it, he must be "in God's hands like a corpse in the corpse-washer's hands who turns him however he wishes, for there is no motion or self-direction in him."[27] But it is not enough to be *Kadavergehorsam*; the aspirant must achieve a changed perception of the world, and this entails more than mere "resignation to the course of fate's decrees," even if this is a prerequisite.[28] What is ultimately required is "good opinion of God,"[29] leading to complete faith in the divine mercy and wisdom. Whereas "the recognition of God's oneness produces contemplation of the Causer of causes, . . . faith in the divine mercy and capability . . . produces trust in the Causer of causes. *Tawakkul* is imperfect without trust in the agent (*wakīl*) . . . and peace of mind in the contemplation of the Protector."[30]

The aspirant to trust in God must therefore learn to see the world as it really is—not as the product of blind chance or of any series of causes and effects, nor as the arena of his own endeavors, but as the direct expression of the divine will and wisdom, down to the least particular. Trust in God presupposes the recognition of the perfect rightness of the actual. The world is to be viewed, not from the personal perspective of hope and fear, but "from above:" "Abū Sulaymān al-Dārānī said, 'When you see things from above, you discover another flavor (*ṭaʿm*) in them.' "[31]

From this vantage point the aspirant sees world and self without reference to self; whatever befalls him is perceived not in terms of his own natural desires but in terms of the divine wis-

[26] al-Qushayrī, *al-Risālah al-Qushayrīyah* (Cairo, 1966), I, 375.

[27] al-Qushayrī, I, 368.

[28] al-Qushayrī, I, 372. Cf. al-Kalabādhī, tr. Arberry, *The Doctrine of the Sufis* (Cambridge, 1935), p. 92.

[29] *ḥusn al-ẓann*. "ʿAbd Allāh ibn Dāwūd said: 'I consider *tawakkul* as good opinion of God,' " cited in B. Reinert, *Die Lehre vom tawakkul in der klassischen Sufik* (Berlin, 1968), p. 44. See also P. Nwyia, *Ibn ʿAṭāʾ Allāh*, p. 105.

[30] *Iḥyāʾ*, IV, 222.

[31] Cited in *Qūt al-qulūb*, III, 53.

dom which dictates it. This permits him to realize that this world is indeed the best possible world, for the existence of everything in it is the result of the divine will. Not even the least thing—a gnat's wing—can be added or subtracted without detriment.[32]

a. *The Divine Wisdom: The Natural Order*. The example of the gnat's wing is introduced for a purpose. To be sure, this is in one sense no more than saying "the least trifle" (as Wehr brings out in his translation: "die geringste Kleinigkeit").[33] But something more is involved as well.

A signal characteristic of most attempts at theodicy is the belief that no aspect of the world, however insignificant it may seem, is without some redeeming reason. This is a result of the so-called "principle of sufficient reason" which often goes hand-in-hand with theodicy. The classic formula for this principle was stated by Christian Wolff (1679-1754): "*nihil est sine ratione sufficiente, cur potius sit, quam non sit*;"[34] i.e., nothing is without a sufficient reason why it is rather than is not; or, in Schopenhauer's terse translation: "Nichts ist ohne Grund warum es sei."[35] (It is this principle, of course, which occasions some of the most telling satire at the expense of Leibniz in Voltaire's *Candide*.)

In following this principle, the proponent of theodicy will be compelled to discover the sufficient reason for the existence of such manifestly destructive, noxious, or at best nugatory creatures as bedbugs, flies, lice, etc., as well as of such catastrophes as earthquakes, floods, hurricanes, and the like. Debates over the role of such creatures or events in the divine scheme were common from antiquity on. The Stoic Chrysippus (c. 280-206 B.C.), for example, is often credited with the defense of a wise providence. Max Pohlenz, a leading historian of Stoicism, has paraphrased some of the justifications imputed to him: "The wild

[32] On the connection between *tawakkul* and the view of this world as the best possible, see also Reinert, *Die Lehre*, p. 45 (with reference to the early Ṣūfī Sahl al-Tustarī).

[33] Wehr, *al-Ġazzālī's Buch vom Gottvertrauen*, p. 37.

[34] *Philosophia prima sive Ontologia* (2d ed.; Frankfurt, 1736; rpt. Hildesheim, 1962), p. 47, cited in Schopenhauer, *Über die vierfache Wurzel des Satzes vom zureichenden Grunde*, in *Werke*, V, 17.

[35] Schopenhauer, *Werke*, V, 17.

beasts are there to test the power of humans, the poison fangs of the serpents furnish medicine, the mice teach alertness, and the bedbugs take care that we not sleep too long."[36] Of course, the defender of this view may select just such examples at the outset; for if the divine wisdom can be made plain in gnats and flies, then how much the more so in admittedly noble and worthwhile beings?[37]

The unalterable rightness of the actual is evinced in the least things. al-Makkī, in commenting of his own choice of the gnat as an example, states: "The gnat and the mustard seed are the smallest of animate and inanimate things which God created, but in each of them are 360 instances of wisdom (*hikam*)."[38] The gnat is, of course, commonly used as an example of something small or trivial (cf. *Qur*. 2:26), but it is in just such despicable objects that the wonders of divine wisdom are revealed. Thus, for al-Jāḥiẓ, the gnat's wing is an object lesson for the thoughtful who can perceive in its "long scrolls" an "abundance of wonders."[39]

In various passages of his later works, but especially in the *Iḥyā'*, al-Ghazālī delights in demonstrating the marvels concealed in the tiny, the commonplace, and the familiar. If the divine wisdom may be made apparent in such banal objects, how much the more will it shine forth in the undeniably grand and majestic aspects of creation? It is al-Ghazālī's guiding principle that "the lowest is explicatory of the highest."[40] In this, he follows a well–established tradition, common from antiquity and perhaps best exemplified in Galen's *De usu partium*, which was

[36] Pohlenz, *Die Stoa*, I, 100 (citing *SVF* II, 1173, 1163); cf. also W. Capelle, "Zur antiken Theodicee," *Archiv für Geschichte der Philosophie* 20 (1907), esp. pp. 178-179 and 188. For Talmudic parallels, see H. Goitein, *Das Problem der Theodicee in der älteren jüdischen Religionsphilosophie* (Königsberg, 1890), p. 34. For comparable Islamic discussions, see al-Māturīdī, *K. al-tawḥīd*, p. 108, and al-Damīrī, *Ḥayāt al-ḥayawān*, I, 266.

[37] See, for example, al-Jāḥiẓ, *K. al-ḥayawān*, II, 109.

[38] *Qūt al-qulūb*, III, 52.

[39] al-Jāḥiẓ, *K. al-ḥayawān*, I, 208-209.

[40] *Jawāhir al-Qur'ān*, p. 41: *al-adnā bayyinah 'alā 'l-a'lā*. The procedure is comparable to the Rabbinic *ḳal wa-ḥomer*, or conclusion *a minori ad majus*; see M. Jastrow, *A Dictionary of the Targumim, The Talmud Babli and Yerushalmi, and the Midrashic Literature* (NY, 1971), p. 436.

translated early into Arabic and from which, indeed, many of his examples of wisdom ultimately derive.[41]

At the same time, such lowly creatures as the gnat are themselves inexhaustible mines of wonder, before which the human intellect must confess itself checked and baffled. "Indeed," says al-Ghazālī, "even if we wished to mention the marvels in a bedbug, an ant, a bee or a spider—for these are the tiniest animals—in the way they construct their dwellings, gather their food, consort with their mates and store provisions, . . . we would be unable to do so."[42] In resorting to such examples, al-Ghazālī wishes to rekindle the sense of amazement which is dulled by familiarity; for when "we see an unfamiliar creature, even if it is a worm, the mind's amazement is renewed."[43] It will be one of his favored strategies, therefore, to present familiar creatures as though they were to be seen afresh for the first time. When man's sense of amazement is stimulated, he is driven to reflection; through reflection, he comes to recognize the unalterable wisdom of things as they are.

A meticulous wisdom is revealed in the actual placement of things within creation, and the order of the world discloses a

[41] Galen's influential work was translated into Arabic in the 3d/9th century by Hubaysh ibn al-Ḥasan and then revised by Ḥunayn ibn Isḥāq (d. 260/873), under the title *K. fī manāfiʿ al-aʿḍāʾ*. See M. Steinschneider, *Die arabischen Übersetzungen aus dem Griechischen*, pp. 286-287; G. Bergsträsser, "Hunain ibn Ishaq über die syrischen und arabischen Galen-Übersetzungen," *Abhandlungen für die Kunde des Morgenlandes* 17:2 (1925), p. 27; and M. Ullmann, *Die Medizin im Islam*, p. 41.

In regard to al-Ghazālī's purpose in the example of the gnat, compare Galen's remark à propos of the flea: "If the Creator's skill is such when displayed incidentally . . . in insignificant animals, how great must we consider his wisdom and power when displayed in animals of some importance!" *De usu partium* (ed. Helmreich), II, 449; tr. May, *On the Usefulness of the Parts of the Body*, II, 732.

[42] *Iḥyāʾ*, IV, 375. Cf. Galen, I, 5; tr. May, I, 71. See also, *De usu partium*, II, 448 [tr. May, II, 731]: ". . . any other animal you may care to dissect will show you as well both the wisdom and skill of the Creator, and the smaller the animal the greater the wonder it will excite, just as when craftsmen carve something on small objects."

[43] *Iḥyāʾ*, IV, 376. Elsewhere, al-Ghazālī seeks to stimulate wonder by noting a microcosmic correspondence between creatures; thus, the gnat is no less wonderful than the majestic elephant, for the Creator endowed both with trunks! See *Iḥyāʾ*, IV, 273; and for an earlier source for this comparison between gnat and elephant, see Jāḥiẓ, *K. al-ḥayawān*, VII, 169.

fundamental justice in its very structure. In this, al-Ghazālī adheres to a traditional Islamic notion of justice (*ʿadl*), by which is meant the proper placement of things, each in its own most fitting place. In propounding the alliance of justice with wisdom in the very design of the world, al-Ghazālī follows earlier, "orthodox" theologians: al-Māturīdī (d. 333/944) had already countered the Muʿtazilite doctrine of the optimum (*al-aṣlaḥ*) with a concept of wisdom which he defined as "appositeness" (*iṣābah*), or the proper placement of things.[44]

The notion of divine wisdom is central to an understanding of the Ghazālian theodicy; at the same time, it should be noted that this concept, which plays so large a part in his thought, was repugnant to many of his fellow Ashʿarites, for whom any attempt to rationalize God's actions was suspect. In the dispute, objections will be raised to al-Ghazālī's reliance on the notion of wisdom. Moreover, to members of other theological schools, Ashʿarism was to appear dangerously lacking in any appreciation of the importance of divine wisdom in the scheme of things; the criticism was to be levelled not only by Muʿtazilite and Shīʿite theologians, but even by more strictly traditionalist schools, such as the Ḥanbalite. Two centuries after al-Ghazālī's death, for example, the great Ḥanbalite theologian Ibn Taymīyah (d. 728/1328) will fault the Ashʿarites for their neglect of the principle of divine wisdom; the Ashʿarites, he states, "affirm will without wisdom, and volition without mercy, love, and approval."[45] In this light, al-Ghazālī's pronounced emphasis on the role of wisdom may have represented an attempt—not entirely successful, in any case—to modify the strict Ashʿarite doctrine of God's sovereign unaccountability, or, at least, to rationalize and render palatable this doctrine.

For al-Ghazālī, the divine wisdom pervades each creature. The gnat may seem an eccentric example, but it is one to which

[44] *K. al-tawḥīd*, p. 97. This notion of justice will be further discussed in Chapter Five below.

[45] *Majmūʿat al-rasāʾil al-kubrā* (Cairo, 1323), I, 333. For Ibn Taymīyah's own understanding and use of the concept of wisdom, see Joseph N. Bell, *Love Theory in Later Ḥanbalite Islam* (Albany, 1979), p. 69ff.

he frequently has recourse.[46] God's wisdom is such that human intelligence, even acting in concert with all the creatures of heaven and earth, is incapable of fathoming its wonders in the structure of a noxious insect. For within these minuscule creatures "are such marvels that if the first and the last were to join together [to attempt] to comprehend their natures, they would be unable to grasp the truth."[47] The gnat confutes human presumption. How much the more futile will a concerted action prove, on the part of all humanity, to envisage, let alone realize, another order of things?

For al-Ghazālī, nothing in creation is more indicative of the divine wisdom than the human body itself. Each of our limbs and organs displays the perfect rightness of the actual. The human body is a particularly apt and persuasive example. It is most immediate and most familiar to us; it is also most revelatory of the Creator's grandeur. Man, however, persists in remaining brutishly unaware of this. "Man," states al-Ghazālī, "is the most amazing of animals, and yet he is not amazed at himself."[48]

In his zeal to awaken a sense of amazement, al-Ghazālī dwells in detail on specific features of the human body, and he does so dramatically. At times it is as though he were peeling back be-

[46] *Jawāhir al-Qur'ān*, p. 39; *Iḥyā'*, IV, 273. There is a strikingly similar passage in the work traditionally ascribed to al-Ghazālī and entitled, fittingly, *al-Ḥikmah fī makhlūqāt Allāh* (Cairo, 1352/1934), p. 54; however, I now think this work incorrectly ascribed to al-Ghazālī. There are not only pronounced stylistic differences between *al-Ḥikmah* and al-Ghazālī's indisputably genuine works, but the former work displays throughout a decisively Muʿtazilite cast of thought and expression; see, for example, pp. 7, 9, 12, 13 and 17. Furthermore, the work espouses a highly anthropocentric doctrine of providence, which al-Ghazālī expressly rejects. It may be noted, too, that none of al-Ghazālī's commentators alludes to, or cites from, *al-Ḥikmah fī makhlūqāt Allāh*; nor does he himself refer to it. The ascription of authorship to al-Ghazālī was probably due to the important role he reserves for wisdom in his later work, which made him seem a likely author, as well as to the fact that many passages in *al-Ḥikmah* parallel passages in the *Iḥyā'*. These parallels, however, are due to a common reliance on Galen and other scientific authors and are, in any case, hardly unique to al-Ghazālī. (I am grateful to Professor George F. Hourani for his comments, which have prompted me to this conclusion.)

[47] *Iḥyā'*, IV, 274.

[48] *Iḥyā'*, IV, 376: *al-insān aʿjab al-ḥayawānāt wa-laysa yataʿajjab min nafsihi.* In commenting on this passage, Murtaḍā al-Zabīdī cites the following verse: "Do you think that you are [merely] a little mass (*jirm ṣaghīr*), when the greater world is enfolded within you?" *Itḥāf*, X, 204.

fore the eyes of startled onlookers the various intricate layers and components of their own bodily forms. His examples derive from the medical texts, but he infuses them with a sense of the marvelous. Beneath such demonstrable marvels as the number and structure of the bones, the intricacy and elegance of the nerves and muscles, the manifold actions of tendons and ligaments, or even the complex orchestration of the tiny muscles that move our eyelids, lie unsearchable depths of divine wisdom. This awareness of hidden dimensions of meaning in the very sinews and tissues of our bodies enables al-Ghazālī to turn the brute facts of the physician and the anatomist to telling effect. As he himself notes: "The physician considers these [sc. the bones] so that he may know a way of healing by setting them, but those with insight consider them so that through them they may draw conclusions about the majesty of Him who created and shaped (the bones). What a difference between the two who consider!"[49]

Thus, there is a rigorous justice and rightness in the least aspect of our bodies. Nothing could have been different, nothing could have been better; no limb or organ could have been arranged or appointed in other than its actual form and position. For example, God "composed the eye of seven layers, each of which has a specified characteristic and a specified shape, and if one of these layers were missing or removed, the eye would be deprived of sight."[50] The human eye could function properly in no other position than that in which it actually is:

> He placed the eye in the place in the body most fitting for it. Had He created it on the back of the head or on the leg or on the hand or on top of the head, it would be obvious what shortcoming would befall it, and what exposure to injuries.[51]

Even the design and positioning of the nose display wisdom, for

> . . . you must know that nothing has been created in a place without being specifically intended for it. If (the nose) were to the right or to the left, or lower or higher, it would be defective

[49] *Iḥyā'*, IV, 372.
[50] *Ibid.*; see also *al-Maqṣad al-asnā*, p. 82.
[51] *al-Maqṣad al-asnā*, p. 106.

> or useless or ugly or disproportionate, displeasing to the sight. Therefore, He created the nose in the center of the face. Had He created it on the forehead or on the cheek, defect would attend its uses.[52]

al-Ghazālī discusses the human skin, the various muscles of the body, the nerves, veins, and arteries; he dwells on the twenty-four muscles necessary to move the pupil and the eyelid.[53] He enumerates and describes the 248 bones of the human body; he discusses their various sizes, shapes, and functions. Not a single bone could be added or subtracted from the body without detriment.[54] His descriptions are precise, for he wishes to emphasize the meticulous rightness of things as they are.

Certain bodily features, such as the human hand, compel special admiration. Our opposable thumb reveals great ingenuity of design:

> He placed the fingers on one side and the thumb on the other side, so that the thumb could curve around them all. Now if the first and the last cooperated to devise by subtle thought another way of placing the fingers except as they have been placed—with a distance from the thumb to the fingers and a difference in the fingers' length and their order in a single row—they could not do this. For by this arrangement the hand is best suited (*ṣalaḥat*) for grasping and letting go.[55]

Man's very fingernails are of crucial importance, for if they "were lacking in man, and an itch befell him, he would be the most impotent and the weakest of creatures. Nothing could take the (nail's) place in scratching his body."[56]

After he has laid bare the integuments of that most obvious and immediate source of amazement, the human body itself, al-

[52] *al-Maqṣad al-asnā*, p. 107; *Iḥyā'*, IV, 373. Cf. Galen, *De usu partium*, II, 153; tr. May, II, 530. There is a parallel passage in *al-Ḥikmah fī makhlūqāt Allāh*, p. 21.

[53] *Iḥyā'*, IV, 372.

[54] *Ibid.*

[55] *Iḥyā'*, IV, 373, line -4. Cf. Galen, I, 7; tr. May, I, 72. See also, *al-Ḥikmah fī makhlūqāt Allāh*, p. 22. A similar line of reasoning may be found also in Job of Edessa, *Book of Treasures* (ed. Budge), p. 321 [Syriac text]; p. 45 [translation].

[56] *Iḥyā'*, IV, 374. Cf. *al-Ḥikmah*, p. 22.

Ghazālī reminds his reader that all of this grew from a turbid drop of semen within the secret darkness of the womb.[57] And he exhorts his reader:

> Turn now to the drop of semen and consider its state at first and what it then becomes. Reflect that if *jinn* and men had joined together to create for the drop of semen, hearing or sight or intellect or power or knowledge or spirit, or to create in it bones, veins, nerves, skin, or hair—would they have been able to do that? Assuredly not! Even if they wished to know its real nature, and how it took shape after God created it, they would be incapable of that.[58]

The human body is marvelous and perfectly right in every particular. Nevertheless, it is not the highest example of the wonders of divine wisdom. al-Ghazālī rejects anthropocentrism; even the least speck of dust (*dharrah*) in the realm of the heavens is not only "most wise in its creation and most perfect in its construction," but also includes "more marvels than the human body."[59] Indeed, "on earth there is no relation to all the wonders of the heavens."[60] The gnat, small and lowly as it is, prompts astonishment and reveals the marvels of higher creatures; so, too, does man, in all the manifest wonder and beauty of his form, serve to lead reflection to still higher and more amazing realms of divine wisdom:

> Consider now man's outward and inward aspect, and his body and its features; for in these you see wonders and craft that compel amazement. All this God made in a drop of dirty water. From this you see His craft in a drop of water and what He made in the realm of the heavens and the stars, and His wisdom in their positionings, forms and magnitudes.[61]

b. *The Divine Wisdom: The Social Order.* The perfect rightness of the actual extends not only to the natural world, it obtains with equal force in the world of human affairs (lines 36-40, 80-

[57] *Iḥyā'*, IV, 374.
[58] *Iḥyā'*, IV, 373.
[59] *Ibid.* See also *al-Maqṣad al-asnā*, p. 107.
[60] *Ibid.*
[61] *Iḥyā'*, IV, 372, line 3.

83). There is complete justice and right in every condition of life. At times, little distinction seems to be made between the natural and the social orders; for, indeed, both are the result of the divine will. This encompasses the most mundane objects: one of God's greatest blessings toward man, says al-Ghazālī, lies in the creation of the *dirham* and the *dīnār*, since the world is supported by them. They are mere metals without any intrinsic benefit and yet all are compelled to use them.[62]

The doctrine that God directly wills whatever occurs—indeed, He is the only real agent—makes this unavoidable; every action of man is the result of God's will.[63] Moreover, nothing simply "happens" to man; there is neither caprice nor carelessness in the administration of the world. Whatever happens is intentional and not random; and it is God who intends it. The navigator believes that the wind drives his ship through the sea; the scribe thinks that his hand guides the pen to form letters on the page; the king issues edicts in the belief that it is he who incites to action. All three are deluded.[64] Whatever occurs in this world, from "the creeping of a black ant on a hard stone in a pitchdark night" to the "atom's motion in the open air," God knows,[65] and it is the direct expression of His will. It is He, and only He, who causes actions.

This is not to say that for al-Ghazālī man has no sphere of action or of choice. Indeed, he praises the Ashʿarite school of theology, to which he adhered, just for steering a middle course between more extreme schools on this subject, and for teaching that actions are from God in one sense and from man in another.[66] He rejects as absurd the teaching of the Jabrīyah, who in the effort to avoid any constraint on God's power hold that human beings are on the level of inorganic matter as regards free choice. One who questions them, he says, "should strike them and rend their garments and turbans, claw their faces,

[62] *Iḥyā'*, IV, 79.
[63] See al-Ashʿarī, *al-Ibānah ʿan uṣūl al-diyānah* (Cairo, 1977), p. 23.
[64] I have here paraphrased *Iḥyā'*, IV, 213-214.
[65] *K. al-arbaʿīn*, p. 5; cf. *Iḥyā'*, I, 96, *paen.*
[66] *K. al-arbaʿīn*, pp. 10, 13.

pluck out their hair, their mustaches, and their beards, and then excuse himself as these fools do" (i.e., by claiming that all acts are from God alone).[67] At the other extreme, however, both the Qadarīyah and the Muʿtazilah are also to be rejected, for in their insistence on man's free will they tend to render God powerless.[68]

This is a complex question and requires fuller discussion than is possible here.[69] It should be noted that in the *Iḥyāʾ* passage (and indeed in treatments of *tawakkul* generally), greater stress is placed on the sole agency of God than usual; the *mutawakkil* must recognize no agent other than God (though this will not absolve him from responsibility, in the legal sense, for the consequences of his actions).

The divine agency extends to all facets of human existence, such as sustenance, span of life, pleasure and pain, etc. It is God who allots to man all that he has; and it would be false to assume, for example, that a man could increase or decrease his allotted share of nourishment (*rizq*) in this life. The sustenance of each creature is foreordained and is as inevitable as death: "If a man were to flee from his allotted nourishment, it would overtake him just as death, if he were to flee from it, would overtake him."[70]

al-Ghazālī describes the role of the divine will in human life, in a passage which reinforces his position in the *Iḥyāʾ*, as follows:

> God wills existing things and sets things created in time in order, for there occur in this world and in the transcendent world neither few nor many, small nor great, good nor evil, benefit nor harm, belief nor unbelief, recognition nor denial, gain nor loss, increase nor diminishment, obedience nor disobedience, except as a result of God's decree and predestination and wisdom and will. What He wishes, is; what He does not wish, is not.

[67] *K. al-arbaʿīn*, pp. 9-10, 12.
[68] *Ibid.*
[69] On the question of free will, probably the most vexed topic of early Islamic theology, W. Montgomery Watt's *Free Will and Predestination in Early Islam* (London, 1948) is still the standard introduction.
[70] al-Makkī, *Qūt al-qulūb*, III, 27.

> Not even the casual glance of a spectator nor the stray thought in the mind come to be outside the sphere of His will. He is the originator; He causes recurrence (*al-muʿīd*); He is the effecter (*faʿʿāl*) of what He wills.[71]

And, once again, al-Ghazālī has recourse to the kind of hypothetical statement employed in the *Iḥyāʾ* text as he tries to clinch this point: "Were men, *jinn*, angels, and devils to join together in order to set in motion a single atom in this world, or to bring it to rest, without God's will and volition, they would be incapable of that."[72]

In his summary of human conditions, al-Ghazālī makes no effort to present pain, incapacity, illness, or poverty as anything other than the evils they are. Nor are such misfortunes the result of social inequity or accident or human wickedness. God intends poverty or pain or disbelief for certain individuals, just as He intends wealth, well-being, and belief for others. No attempt is undertaken here to absolve God from responsibility for these circumstances. This does not mean that al-Ghazālī will not offer a variety of explanations for evil, and particularly the evil of suffering, but that the question of the ultimate authorship of evil does not arise, or at least does not occupy the central position, in his version of theodicy, that it occupies in Western versions.

A bizarre form of optimism, this, that can look on disease, destitution, social inequity, and the like, and unflinchingly pronounce it right and just! The later discussions will be quite specific and consistent in pursuing this theme. To note but one example: it is right, indeed God desires, that certain people be relegated to the so-called "base professions" (*al-ḥiraf al-khasīsah*, such as tanning, for this contributes to the perfect orderliness of the world as it is. The perfect rightness of the actual encompasses the status quo.[73]

[71] *K. al-arbaʿīn*, p. 6.

[72] *Ibid.* See also al-Ghazālī's *Naṣīḥat al-mulūk* (ed. Humāʾī; Tehran, 1315-17), p. 5, for a parallel passage in Persian; tr. F.R.C. Bagley, *Ghazālī's Book of Counsel for Kings* (London, 1964), pp. 8-9.

[73] So al-Samhūdī, *Iḍāḥ al-bayān*, p. 134, and al-Suyūṭī, *Tashyīd al-arkān*, fol. 3b. Indeed, even cupidity and the "profit motive" serve; according to al-Ghazālī, God utilizes merchants who are driven by love of money and the lust for profit

It would be a mistake to conclude from this that al-Ghazālī is blind to the realities of existence or that a kind of Panglossian obtuseness dictates his remarks. The point would seem to be rather the Ashʿarite insistence that there is no intrinsic good or evil in any of these conditions.[74] So, for example, in disputing the contention of certain Muʿtazilites that the religious obligations (*taklīf*) enjoined on man by God are good in themselves (on the ground that an earned reward in the hereafter is more satisfying than a gratuitous one), al-Ghazālī denies that there is any intrinsic merit in *taklīf*:

> How can any intelligent man say that there is benefit in a creation where *taklīf* exists? Benefit has meaning only if *taklīf* is absent. For *taklīf* is in its essence the imposition of constraint (*ilzām kulfah*), and that is pain.[75]

True benefit would in fact presuppose the complete avoidance of this earthly life:

> There would be benefit for man had he been created in paradise without pain or grief; but as for the existing state-of-affairs, all intelligent men desire non-being. One says, "Would that I were oblivious and forgotten!" Another says, "Would that I were nothing!" And still another, "Would that I were this piece of straw that is swept from the earth!" And yet another says while pointing to a bird, "Would that I were that bird!"
>
> These are the words of prophets and saints who are intelligent men. Some of them desire the cessation of existence while others desire the cessation of responsibility in order to be inanimate matter or a bird.[76]

---

to bring together and make available, even at peril of their lives, the foodstuffs widely scattered over the earth. See *Iḥyāʾ*, IV, 102. For a general treatment of the theme, see J. Viner, *The Role of Providence in the Social Order* (Princeton, 1972).

[74] In his Persian correspondence, al-Ghazālī notes that all things at all times enjoy only a figurative (*majāzī*) existence, whereas God's existence alone is real (*ḥaqīqī*); thus, each thing's "non-existence and existence are not from itself, but rather from the divine nature." *Makātīb-i fārsi-yi Ghazzālī* (ed. Iqbāl; Tehran, 1333), p. 20.

[75] *al-Iqtiṣād fi'l-iʿtiqād*, p. 176. For a Muʿtazilite discussion of the question, see ʿAbd al-Jabbār, *Mughnī*, XIV, 137ff. The matter is also treated, as Professor Michael Marmura kindly informed me, in Ashʿarī, *Maqālāt*, I, 248.

[76] *al-Iqtiṣād*, p. 176.

This passage will be cited by his critics as evidence that al-Ghazālī does believe in the possibility of a superior world; and they will claim that on this point, as on others, he contradicts himself.

Leaving this question in abeyance for the moment, let us note that al-Ghazālī here wishes to refute the notion, dear to certain Muʿtazilites, that God enjoined the religious obligation upon man because it was good in and of itself; and, further, that He enjoined it for the ultimate benefit of each individual. The notion rests on the Muʿtazilite belief in the autonomy of the human intellect to discern good and evil, unaided by the directives of the divine law. And it is this which al-Ghazālī, in good Ashʿarite fashion, here strives to refute. For him, as for Ashʿarism generally, good and evil have no objective validity. God did not impose *taklīf* because it was good in itself; it is good only because God established it. Indeed, God could abrogate the current obligations and command other obligations contrary to those now in force; and these newly ordained obligations would be immediately normative.

Furthermore, while the actual order of things is insuperably right and just, as the *Iḥyā'* text proclaims, it is so "from above," i.e., from the divine perspective, and not from the limited (and interested) viewpoint of each individual. All that exists in the natural world as well as in the sphere of human affairs is "most excellent" and "most perfect," but this supreme excellence is disclosed only to the gaze schooled in "trust in God." It is perhaps for this reason, too, that examples such as that of the gnat recur so frequently in such works, not only because it is a small and contemptible creature but exactly because it is obnoxious to man. The perfect rightness of the actual must be demonstrable in what plagues and pesters man, as well as in what benefits him.[77]

[77] Such pestiferous creatures swarm through the wisdom literature, especially in the early hexaemeron works. St. Basil the Great, for example, deals with scorpions and other poisonous creatures, as well as with carnivores and such oddities as the elephant's trunk and the camel's neck; see S. Giet (ed.); *Homélies sur l'Hexaémeron* (Paris, 1968), 200b. St. Basil states his guiding principle thus: "Nothing is without cause. Nothing is by chance. Everything possesses some ineffable wisdom" (*ibid.*, 113a). See also St. Augustine, *De Genesi ad litteram*

c. *The Intrinsic Superiority of Existence.* The doctrine that any actual existent is intrinsically superior to any non-existent or possible is seen by at least one of al-Ghazālī's supporters as explaining his affirmation of the perfect rightness of the actual. This doctrine al-Ghazālī expresses in the dictum: "Existence is *per se* better than non-existence."[78]

The application of this dictum leads to obvious difficulties. Hostile commentators will charge that in this view the *kāfir*'s disbelief is superior to his possible future belief.[79] In reply it is pointed out that whatever exists, exists only because God has determined that there will be a preponderating good (*maṣlaḥah rājiḥah*) in its existence. The fact that certain things, such as the *kāfir*'s belief, do not exist simply indicates that the preponderating good lay in their not coming to be.[80]

The *shaykh al-Islām* Zakarīyā' al-Anṣārī (d. 926/1520) will interpret al-Ghazālī's statement in accord with this dictum.[81] al-Jazā'irī, who transmits his interpretation, comments:

> I say that the meaning of al-Ghazālī's expression is that those possible worlds which have not sniffed the scent of existence are numerous but the world which is honored with the light of existence is more perfect, more wonderful, and more excellent than they, since existence is superior to non-existence.[82]

Nevertheless, al-Jazā'irī immediately qualifies this interpretation by stating that it does not really fit the context of al-Gha-

---

(Paris, 1972), III.xv.24—xviii.28; and the 9th-century Syriac author Moses Bar Kepha, in L. Schlimme, *Der Hexaemeronkommentar des Moses Bar Kepha* (Wiesbaden, 1977), II, 496ff. An extreme, later example: in 1738, F. C. Lesser published his *Insecto-Theologia* in which the ravages of insects are seen as "so many marks of the power, the justice, the wisdom, and even of the goodness of God," cited in Viner, *The Role of Providence*, p. 23.

[78] *Maqāṣid al-falāsifah*, p. 237: *al-wujūd khayr min al-'adam fī dhātihi.* Cf. the Scholastic precept that *ens et bonum convertuntur* in, e.g., Aquinas, *Summa theologiae*, 1A.5,3. See also, St. Bonaventura, *Itinerarium mentis in Deum*, VI. 2: "Omnino melius est esse quam non esse." For a discussion, see J. Hirschberger, "Omne ens est bonum," *Philosophisches Jahrbuch der Görres-Gesellschaft* 53 (1940), pp. 292-305.

[79] *Itḥāf*, IX, 449.

[80] *Itḥāf*, IX, 450.

[81] Cited in *Ḥikmat*, p. 31.

[82] *Ibid.*

zālī's remarks; and also, presumably, because of the dictum's origin in the doctrines of the philosophers.

*d. The Hiddenness of the World's Perfection.* The perfect rightness of the actual is emphasized, on at least one level, as a check to human presumption and as an incitement to trust in God. But it may also suggest some overriding necessity in the nature of things to which even God is subject. Does not al-Makkī state that even "with God's assistance" man would be unable to devise a better world? To be sure, the intention may be only, as one commentator will rather lamely suggest, "to glorify the creator's work."[83] This would, indeed, be consistent with al-Ghazālī's emphasis, in the *Iḥyā'* and other works, on "the perception of God's wisdom in each existing thing which He created, since He created nothing in the world without wisdom in it."[84]

Nevertheless, this suggestion would be more plausible had al-Ghazālī continued to follow his source-text for the remainder of the *Iḥyā'* passage. Abū Ṭālib al-Makkī avoids any imputation of constraint on God by declaring that the excellence of the world is simply imperceptible to most people. Thus, for him, it is more a question of the limited nature of the human intellect; the presumption that a better world is possible is only a result of that limitation. Any reflection on the divine power remains unexpressed:

> God lets (the world order) take its course in conformity with the intellect's own order and the meanings of the customary and usual course of events, through well-known means and accepted instrumentalities, to the measure of that with which intellects are imprinted by nature and for which they have an innate propensity.
>
> So God conceals the ends and veils mysteries . . . hence, the excellence of the world-order and the beauty of the divine decree are by their very nature hidden. Most people are ignorant

[83] Badr al-dīn al-Zarkashī (d. 794/1392) offers this reading; cited in *Ḥikmat*, p. 19.

[84] *Iḥyā'*, IV, 78

> of the underlying principles (*ḥikam*) except for those who trust in God.[85]

The world is aligned with the human mind in such a way that the mind cannot see it except in terms of its habitual perspective.[86] Moreover, God has the world follow this course intentionally, and He conceals its true excellence. Man is not apt to perceive this excellence in the normal pattern of events because the world and the mind are attuned in such a way that he cannot. But if man, through attainment of trust in God, were to see the world as it is, he would recognize its supreme excellence and beauty; and he would know that neither "illumined intellects" nor mystic knowledge can "necessitate anything other than this world-order.[87] He would know the true perfection of things as they are, which is a hidden perfection.

Now what is merely latent in al-Makkī's text—what indeed is not at issue there at all, the question of God's power—is cast into rather bold relief in al-Ghazālī's reworking. In the face of this, certain commentators would be tempted to return to al-Ghazālī's source and to propose that perhaps nothing more was meant than what al-Makkī had originally put forth, i.e., that the human mind is simply incapable of conceiving a better order of things because of its own limitations. al-Jazā'irī considers, but quickly rejects, this interpretation:

> If it were said that (the possibility of a better world) stands in relation to those things knowable to people and to their capacities, and that they are not able to imagine anything better and more wonderful than this world, then it would be valid and conceded (*ṣaḥḥa wa-sullima*). But not in relation to God's omnipotence.[88]

[85] *Qūt al-qulūb*, III, 52. The same idea, more clearly expressed, occurs in the *K. al-yanābīʿ* of the early Ismāʿīlī author Abū Yaʿqūb al-Sijzī, in H. Corbin (ed.), *Trilogie ismaélienne* (Tehran, 1961), p. 41.

[86] A similar thought (though in a wholly different context!) in Johann Peter Hebel, *Schatzkästlein des rheinischen Hausfreundes* (Zürich, n.d.), p. 16: "The greatest wisdom is revealed in the simple and natural arrangement of things, and one does not recognize it, just because everything is so simple and natural."

[87] *Qūt al-qulūb*, III, 52.

[88] *Ḥikmat*, p. 12.

Whether or not al-Makkī foresaw the implications of his position and drew back to avoid a looming dilemma or whether these remained nascent and unrecognized cannot, of course, be determined. The fact is that al-Ghazālī has reworked the text in such a way as to lay bare all its hidden consequences. For both al-Makkī and al-Ghazālī the world is perfect as it is. But whereas al-Makkī concentrates on the inability of the human mind to perceive this, al-Ghazālī forces the issue. He affirms the impossibility of a more excellent state-of-affairs, and he does so in terms that could not but be controversial.

*2. The Disputed Statement (lines 41-51)*

As we have seen, it was these lines which particularly aroused the ire of critics. Even some of al-Ghazālī's admirers were scandalized. His former pupil, the Andalusian *qāḍī* Abū Bakr ibn al-ʿArabī (d. 543/1148), is said to have exclaimed:

> Our *shaykh* Abū Ḥāmid al-Ghazālī has said something stupendous for which the Iraqis have criticized him. And, as God is my witness, this is indeed occasion for criticism! For he said, "There is nothing in the divine omnipotence (*qudrah*) more wonderful than this world in its perfection and wisdom."[89]

Now in al-Ghazālī's texts the word *imkān* (possibility), and not *qudrah* (power), is invariably used. This will be a crucial point in the debate. Whether Ibn al-ʿArabī's version represents a legitimate variant or a simple misreading, or whether indeed the two terms can have been taken as co-extensive, are matters that will be treated in Chapter Three below.

If read in context, and if one keeps in mind the unalterable rightness of the actual so forcefully affirmed in the opening lines, the statement seems to follow inexorably: if nothing can be added to, or subtracted from, creation without detriment, if all the circumstances of life are insuperably right and just, then indeed nothing in possibility is more excellent than what is.

And yet, the statement remains outrageous. It flies in the face of common experience. Who could not list dozens, indeed hun-

[89] Cited in almost all the discussions; see, for example, *Dhahab*, p. 473, and *Itḥāf*, IX, 442, line 13ff.

dreds, of examples from his own or others' experience which are indisputably not "right and just"? Furthermore, the lines seem to lead inescapably to the conclusion that God could not change, let alone improve, the actual order of things; that, as Spinoza put it, "things could have been produced by God in no other manner and in no other order than that in which they have been produced."[90]

These are the immediate difficulties; still others spring to mind. For does the statement mean merely that God has, as it were, exhausted all possibilities in the creation of this world; that in effect nothing remains unactualized in the order of existence (as Massignon, for one, understood the phrase)?[91] Or does it rather mean that out of all possible things God selected the most excellent, perfect, and complete, but that there are other possible things which He did not, but could, create? Could God select other *possibilia*? Could He, for example, select *possibilia* that are less excellent, less perfect, less complete? And, if not, does this entail some constraint as well on His power or freedom of choice?

Furthermore, does the statement mean that there is some necessary order of things which alone is most excellent, perfect, and complete, an order which God Himself must respect? And, lastly, to state that something is "most excellent" or "most wonderful"—that there obtains what later commentators will term a condition of "most-wonderfulness" (*abdaʿīyah*)—is to imply that God's power reaches to a specific limit but no further; but on the other hand, to state that God's power stops at no limit is to

[90] *Ethics*, I, proposition 33: "Res nullo alio modo, neque alio ordine à Deo produci potuerunt, quàm productae sunt," in *Werke* (ed. Blumenstock), II, 136; tr. Gutmann, p. 68. It was partly in reaction to this proposition that Leibniz fashioned his own theodicy; for an excellent discussion, see G. Friedmann, *Leibniz et Spinoza* (Paris, 1962), esp. p. 136.

[91] *La passion de Ḥusayn Ibn Manṣûr Ḥallâj* (new ed.; Paris, 1975), III, 83, note 5. In this note, which is a capsule account of the dispute, Massignon claimed that al-Ghazālī abandoned his controversial position, and he offered the works *al-Iqtiṣād fi'l-iʿtiqād* and *al-Mustaṣfā min ʿilm al-uṣūl* in evidence (albeit without specific references). We now know, however, that *al-Iqtiṣād* was written before the *Iḥyāʾ* (see Bouyges, pp. 33-34); furthermore, I find no support for Massignon's claim in the *Mustaṣfā* itself, a work on *uṣūl al-fiqh* completed in 503/1109 (Bouyges, no. 59).

imply that His power remains unconnected with any supreme or utmost perfection.

Dilemmas abound here. al-Ghazālī compounds them by introducing in lines 46-51 what is in many respects the classic dilemma of theodicy:

> But if there were (a more excellent world possible) and God had withheld it, having power (*qudrah*) to do it but not deigning to do so, this would be miserliness (*bukhl*) contrary to the divine generosity (*jūd*) and injustice (*ẓulm*) contrary to the divine justice (*ʿadl*).
> But if He were not able, it would be incapability (*ʿajz*), contrary to divinity.[92]

This is the familiar dilemma: if God has withheld (literally, "hoarded": *iddakhara*) a better world which He could have created, He is miserly, but this is in contradiction to His generosity and justice; and if He could not have created a better world, He is somehow deficient in power, but this is in contradiction to the nature of divinity. Therefore, this world is the best and most excellent possible.

It is true that the question of a better possible world arises only because of our awareness of the evils of existence. If this world did not present so many obvious imperfections and disparities, alternative and superior states-of-affairs would not spring so readily to mind. al-Ghazālī's formulation of the dilemma presupposes this fact. Nevertheless, there is a difference of emphasis. The classic formulations of the dilemma are designed to cast doubt on the goodness and/or power of the deity, or at least to raise questions about these, because of the fact of evil. al-Ghazālī's formulation is intended to buttress his conviction that this is the most excellent world possible; the problem of the authorship of evil is sidestepped.

This is apparent if we compare al-Ghazālī's statement with what is perhaps the earliest and most celebrated formulation of the dilemma, that attributed to Epicurus:

[92] *Iḥyāʾ*, IV, 223, lines 7-8.

> God either wishes to take away evils and cannot, or he can and does not wish to, or he neither wishes to nor is able, or he both wishes to and is able. If he wishes to and is not able, he is weak, which does not fall in with the notion of God. If he is able to and does not wish to, he is envious, which is equally foreign to God. If he neither wishes to nor is able, he is both envious and weak, and therefore not God. If he both wishes to and is able, which alone is fitting to God, whence, therefore, are there evils, and why does he not remove them?[93]

The terms of both formulations are close, but it is the disturbing question "whence . . . are there evils?" (*unde . . . sunt mala*?) which is stressed in Epicurus' version for the purpose of casting doubt on the providence or the very existence of deity, whereas al-Ghazālī emphasizes the inconceivability of predicating miserliness, injustice, or impotence of God. If you deny that this is the most excellent world possible, you impugn these attributes of God. Part of the furor which the statement provoked raged about these very lines, for they seem to make God's perfection in His attributes hinge on the world's perfection; and while most would accept the former perfection, few would view the idea of the perfection of the world—a created thing, after all—as obvious or even demonstrable.

In the debate, this very emphasis of al-Ghazālī's will occupy the foreground. The problem of the nature and origin of evil will play a lesser role. What will be very much at issue is the question of whether God is capable of creating another and better world.[94]

It should be noted that not only al-Ghazālī's conclusion but his very choice of words will provoke censure as well. Even if he is not actually seen as imputing "miserliness" to God, to some of his critics the very usage of such a term, even in a hypothet-

[93] Lactantius, *De ira Dei*, XIII.20:21; tr. McDonald *The Wrath of God*, pp. 92-93 (I have modified this translation slightly).

[94] On the related point of suffering, see the interesting generalization of J. Bowker, *Problems of Suffering in Religions of the World* (Cambridge, 1970), p. 102: "Whereas in Christianity suffering occurs as a problem because it conflicts with the assertion that God is love, in Islam it occurs principally because it conflicts with the belief that God is omnipotent."

ical way, will smack of impiety. Certainly the terms had been used often enough before, and in similar discussions.[95] Then, too, the stress which he places on justice (*ʿadl*), with its Muʿtazilite connotations, would arouse suspicion.

No doubt the suggestion that God's generosity and justice might in some way depend on the perfect excellence of the world order was particularly objectionable; but we should also keep in mind that any discussion of the topic at all could seem problematic to some. This is perhaps in accordance with the saying of the mystic al-Junayd (d. 297/910): "The denial of a fault where (the existence of) a fault is impossible is (in itself) a fault.[96]

### 3. *The Correlation of Perfect and Imperfect (lines 52-84)*

In attempting to justify the perfect rightness of the actual, al-Ghazālī will offer several closely related explanations derived from the notion that there is a correlation of perfection and imperfection (lines 73-74 above: *al-kamāl wa'l-naqṣ yuẓhar bi'l-iḍāfah*).

At the outset (lines 52-56), this seems to involve no more than the familiar idea of compensation common to most religions: losses suffered in this life are made good in the hereafter.[97] So, too, in the *Qūt al-qulūb* we read: "Loss in this world is increase in the hereafter; increase in this world is loss in the hereafter. Whoever is given something of this world has it subtracted from his portion in the hereafter."[98]

[95] Cf. the discussion in al-Ashʿarī, *K. al-lumaʿ* (ed. McCarthy), p. 20ff., where God's generosity (*tafaḍḍul*) or miserliness (*bukhl*) is debated. Later, al-Bayḍāwī (d. ca. 685/1286), commenting on *Qur.* 2:245, will claim that God is stingy (*yaqtur ʿalā*) to some, but generous to others: *Anwār al-tanzīl* (ed. Fleischer), I, 127, line 11. In some accounts, e.g., *Itḥāf*, IX, 451, line 21, a line of the poet al-Mutanabbī is misquoted to this effect: "He did not lavish when He bestowed the world, but was stingy." See *Sharḥ dīwān al-Mutanabbī* (ed. Yāzijī), p. 14, line 9, for the accepted version of this line.

[96] Cited in Ibn Khaldūn, *Muqaddimah* (tr. Rosenthal; 2d ed.; Princeton, 1967), III, 54.

[97] Cf. the New Testament parable of Dives and Lazarus in *Luke* 16:19-31; for some parallels in Judaism, see R. Mach, *Der Zaddik in Talmud und Midrasch* (Leiden, 1957), pp. 35-36.

[98] *Qūt al-qulūb*, III, 40. The Ḥanbalite theologian Ibn Qayyim al-Jawzīyah (d. 751/1350) gives vivid expression to this belief: "Whoever drinks wine in this life

As the passage continues, however, it becomes clear that more is involved than simple reward or punishment. There is a kind of equilibrium whereby loss and gain are balanced both in this world and the next, such that gain here is counterbalanced by loss in the afterlife, and loss by gain.[99] Moreover, the loss or gain of one requires the corresponding loss or gain of another. The saying "One man's loss is another man's gain" applies here on a cosmic scale: "Every lack in the next world in relation to one individual is a boon in relation to someone else" (lines 54-56).

This is further explained by examples purporting to show that it is through opposites that we acquire knowledge; that we come to appreciate a good thing, for example, by comparison with a bad, or less good, thing: day by night, health by sickness, heaven by hell, etc. This is of course a familiar notion, and one of great antiquity: "Sickness makes health pleasant, evil good, hunger excess, toil repose.[100] But beyond this al-Ghazālī seems to hold that the existence of the imperfect is requisite for the existence of the perfect, and that the one without the other would not exist.

The Ṣūfī ʿAyn al-Quḍāh al-Hamadhānī (d. 525/1131), who was himself influenced by al-Ghazālī, remarks in this regard:

---

does not drink it in the hereafter; whoever wears silk in this life does not wear it in the hereafter; whoever eats from plates of gold and silver in this life does not eat from them in the hereafter. . . . As the Prophet said, 'In this world, it belongs to them [i.e., the affluent], but in the next world, it belongs to you." See his *Ḥādī al-arwāḥ ilā bilād al-afrāḥ* (Cairo, 1962), p. 191.

[99] This world and the next exist in a continuum; see al-Ghazālī, *al-Qusṭās al-mustaqīm* (Beirut, 1959), p. 69, *paen*. According to Fakhr al-dīn al-Rāzī (d. 606/1209), *Mafātīḥ al-ghayb*, I, 205-206: "The hereafter stands in a relation to this world like the root in relation to the branch and like the body in relation to its shadow; for everything that is in this world must have its root in the hereafter, or else it is like a mirage or an idle fancy. And everything in the hereafter must have a simulacrum in this world, or else it is like a tree without fruit. . . . There must be between these two juncture, connection and affinity." Later in the same work, al-Rāzī affirms that "the life of this world is wisdom and right," and he supports this affirmation by resorting to the (Muʿtazilite) notion that "the essential natures of things do not differ by being in this world or in the hereafter," *Mafātīḥ al-ghayb*, VIII, 135.

[100] Heraclitus, fr. 111 (Diels-Kranz, I, 175). Cf. Aristotle, *De anima* 430b.22-23 (Loeb ed.; p. 174), and Aquinas, *Summa theologiae*, IA. 48, 1.

> Wisdom is that whatever is, was, or will be is not and cannot be except that its contrary also exist. Whiteness can never be without blackness; heaven is not fitting without earth; substance without accident is inconceivable. Muḥammad cannot be without Iblīs. Virtue without vice, disbelief without belief. So with all the contraries: "Things are explicable through their contraries" (*wa-bi-ḍiddihā tatabayyan al-ashyā'*).
>
> Muḥammad's faith cannot exist without the disbelief of Iblīs (*īmān-i Muḥammad bī kufr-i Iblīs na-tavānast būdan*).[101]

It is once again the Stoic Chrysippus with whom this idea is most usually associated; thus, in his lost work *On Providence* he stated:

> There is absolutely nothing more foolish than those men who think that good could exist, if there were at the same time no evil. For since good is the opposite of evil, it necessarily follows that both must exist in opposition to each other, supported as it were by mutual adverse forces; since as a matter of fact no opposite is conceivable without something to oppose it.
>
> For how could there be an idea of justice if there were no acts of injustice? or what else is justice than the absence of injustice? How too can courage be understood except by contrast with cowardice? . . . For it is in the same way that good and evil exist, happiness and unhappiness, pain and pleasure. For, as Plato says, if you take away one, you will have removed both.[102]

[101] *Tamhīdāt*, in *Muṣannafāt* (ed. ʿUṣayrān; Tehran, 1962), pp. 186-187. See also the statement of the later Iranian philosopher Mullā Ismāʿīl Khwājūʾī [Mullā Ismāʿīl al-Māzandarānī] (d. 1173/1759) that heaven and hell exist correlatively and that neither can exist or continue without the other; his *Thamarat al-fuʾād fī nubadh min masāʾil al-maʿād*, in Ashtiyānī (ed.), *Anthologie des philosophes iraniens* (Mashhad, 1358), IV, 161.

[102] Cited in Aulus Gellius, *Noctes atticae*, VII, 1; see also, *SVF*, II, 1169 (reference in de Vogel, *Greek Philosophy*, III, 80). For a Scholastic critique of the notion, see Albertus Magnus, *Summa theologiae*, in *Opera omnia*, XXXIV/1 (Aschendorff, 1978), p. 199ff.

The idea originates in the famous passage of Plato's *Theaetetus*, 176a, where it is said that "evils . . . can never be done away with, for the good must always have its opposite" (tr. Cornford, *Collected Dialogues*, p. 881). In his commentary on *Timaeus* 30a (ed. Diehl, I, 373), Proclus states: "If the inferior did not exist, the superior would have no place" (τοῦ δὲ χείρονος οὐκ ὄντος οὐκ ἔχει χώραν τὸ κρεῖττον). Aristotle, in *Cat.* 14a.8-13 (Loeb ed., pp. 96-97), rejects the notion.

Although in al-Ghazālī's use of this notion there appears no suggestion that this correlation of opposites is the result of anything other than the divine wisdom and generosity, which require the simultaneous creation of both perfect and imperfect, his introduction of it into his theodicy will draw rebuke. Why, it is asked, could not God have created only a single imperfect individual? One disfigured, diseased, or simply ugly individual would have sufficed to apprise us of the benefits and superiority of health and beauty; hosts of such afflicted individuals are superfluous.

A more troublesome objection centers on the charge that a fallacy is involved in this line of reasoning. The fallacy lies in confusing contraries (such as black/white, rich/poor, good/evil) with correlative terms (such as right/left, north/south, etc.).[103] Correlative terms are understood by reference to each other; they are mutually implicative. Contraries, on the other hand, are extreme opposites and not mutually implicative; and "perfect/imperfect" would seem to belong to this category of opposition.

If we say, "All things created by God are perfect," then its subaltern, "Some things created by God are perfect" is implied; but not its contradictory, "Some things created by God are not perfect." Between two sub-contraries, such as "Some things created by God are perfect" and "Some things created by God are not perfect," there is compatibility (both may be true), but there is no mutual implication.

The objection would thus seem to be that there is really no reason why recognition of the perfect requires the existence of the imperfect; these are not true correlatives. (And indeed, even if they were, there would be no causal connection between them.)[104] And, in any case, the objection will continue, why could not God simply have given us knowledge through some other means, not requiring the misery and unhappiness of so many?

al-Ghazālī nevertheless uses this concept as a means of justi-

[103] See Aristotle, *Cat.* 11b.15ff (Loeb ed., p. 80ff); also, al-Ghazali, *Miʿyār al-ʿilm* (Beirut, 1978), pp. 92, 233.

[104] J. van Ess, *Die Erkenntnislehre des ʿAḍudaddīn al-Īcī* (Wiesbaden, 1966), pp. 381, 386.

fying virtually every facet of existence. For not only are perfect and imperfect correlated; the imperfect serves as a "ransom" for the perfect.[105] In this way the disturbing problem of the unmerited suffering of animals, which had preoccupied the Muʿtazilites earlier, will find its "solution": animals reveal the superiority of man by the very fact of their "lower" level of existence (lines 71-73), and they also serve as sacrifices whereby human souls are ransomed. The same applies to other forms of imperfection: the diseased, the destitute, the damned themselves. All exist solely as sacrifices for the perfect.

Obviously, such a notion may be used to justify any monstrosity. The further explanation that such a state-of-affairs is required by the "divine generosity and wisdom" will hardly serve to blunt its effect. Even such an admirer and defender of al-Ghazālī as al-Jazāʾirī will find this justification of the actual hard to stomach. We may detect a pained note, and even a certain empathy, in his summary of the objections to this idea. It is, he admits, good form (*adab*) not to bring objections against God, and yet, if what al-Ghazālī asserts is true, an afflicted person could complain:

> Why am I a spectacle of distress in this world or the next, just so that the healthy may enjoy health and the happy their happiness and just so that they may know the value of those blessings which they have been given?
>
> Why am *I* not among those blessed in this world or the next, so that I might enjoy health or happiness? . . . And why is their knowledge of the degree of their favor provided for by means

[105] According to *ḥadīth*, Muslims may be ransomed from hell by Christians and Jews whom God then sets in their places; see Muslim, *Ṣaḥīḥ*, IV, 2119. The *amīr* ʿAbd al-Qādir, the final commentator on the disputed statement, recounts an amusing anecdote regarding the "ransom" of the perfect by the less perfect. Thus, he writes: "Intellects differ from one another in accord with the way in which God created people; thus, the intellects of the prophets are not like those of other people. The intellect of Abū ʿAlī Ibn Sīnā surpasses other intellects by far. It is told that al-Rāzī said one day to al-Āmidī, 'Why is the destruction and sacrifice of animals for man's sake considered proper?' al-Āmidī replied, 'The destruction of the inferior for the benefit of the superior is justice itself.' And so al-Rāzī rejoined, 'In that case, it would be just to sacrifice you for the sake of Abū ʿAlī Ibn Sīnā!' " See his *Dhikrā al-ʿāqil wa-tanbīh al-ghāfil* (Beirut, 1966), p. 52; tr. G. Dugat, *Le livre d'Abd-El-Kader* (Paris, 1858), pp. 37-38.

of my misery? Why isn't *my* knowledge of the value of divine favor provided for through *their* misery?[106]

This would, indeed, seem to be an unanswerable objection, like the famous story with which al-Ashʿarī silenced his former master al-Jubbāʾī in their debate over *al-aṣlaḥ*.[107] The only answer offered—it is perhaps the only answer possible—is that things are so ordered by the inscrutable predestination of God. It is to this answer, which occupies the closing lines of the *Iḥyāʾ* passage, that we now turn.

*4. The Secret of Predestination (lines 84-100)*

The world as it is, in its unalterable perfection, comes to be necessarily (*wājib al-ḥuṣūl*) but only after—indeed, only because of—a prior act of divine volition (*baʿd sabq al-mashīʾah*). al-Ghazālī's critics will lay emphasis on the "necessary" coming-to-be of the world, his supporters on the preceding act of divine will. Predestination is not at issue here; that is accepted by both sides. At issue is the implication, conveyed by the term "necessary," that God must act in a certain way, that anything in this world may be described as necessarily coming to be.

Although elsewhere al-Ghazālī offers other arguments for the perfect rightness of things as they are, his final position is that all is just and right solely because God has willed it. The guaranty of his theodicy is the unassailable fact of the divine predestination. It is only this that permits the seeker after trust in God any certainty. Something similar was expressed by Martin Luther in his own defense of predestination: "For if you doubt, or disdain to know that God foreknows and wills all things, not contingently but necessarily and immutably, how can you believe confidently, trust to and depend upon his promises?"[108]

Predestination is usually discussed under two aspects in Islamic theology, for which the terms are *qaḍāʾ* and *qadar*. *Qaḍā*

[106] *Ḥikmat*, p. 51.

[107] For this oft-cited story, see, e.g., al-Ghazālī, *al-Qusṭās al-mustaqīm*, pp. 95-96; al-Baghdādī, *Uṣūl al-dīn*, pp. 151-152; al-Ijī, *Mawāqif*, VIII, 197. The version given by al-Subkī, *Ṭabaqāt*, III, 356, is translated in Tritton, *Muslim Theology*, p. 166. See also our Introduction above.

[108] *The Bondage of the Will* (tr. Cole), p. 44.

denotes "the eternal will and divine providence which fulfills the order of existing things according to a particular arrangement."[109] It is in this sense that al-Ghazālī states in the *Iḥyā'* text that "good and evil are foreordained" (*maqḍīy*, line 93).

*Qadar*, on the other hand, "connects that will with things at particular moments.[110] It is God's "production of things in a particular measure and specific decree expressed through their very natures and states."[111] Although the term *qadar* serves to denote the whole subject of predestination generally, we may think of *qaḍā'* as applying to the divine foreordainment in the broadest sense, and *qadar* as applying to individual destinies. *Qadar* in this sense is well illustrated in a famous *ḥadīth*:

> The Prophet said: "When one of you is created, he is held in his mother's womb for 40 days, then he is a clot of blood for that long again, then he is a lump of flesh for that long again. Then God sends the angel who is commanded to write down four words for him: "Write down his action, his term of life, his allotted nourishment, and "damned" or "saved."[112]

Another version adds "and nothing will be added to or subtracted from the decree."[113] It is thus that nothing can be added to or subtracted from the actual, for it has been foreordained by the divine will. As such, it cannot but be more excellent than anything in possibility.

In the *Kitāb al-arbaʿīn*, al-Ghazālī quotes another *ḥadīth* to illustrate his belief that good and evil are foreordained:

> God says: "I create good and I create a people for it. I create evil and I create a people for it. Happiness is for him whom I created for good, and I multiply it for him. But evil is for him whom I create for evil; I multiply evil for him.[114]

[109] *K. al-arbaʿīn*, p. 11.

[110] *Ibid.*

[111] al-Tahānawī, *Kashshāf iṣṭilāḥāt al-funūn* (ed. Sprenger; Calcutta, 1862), II, 1234.

[112] Ibn Mājah, *Sunan*, I, 29; see also, Wensinck, *Muslim Creed*, p. 54, and J. van Ess, *Zwischen Ḥadīṯ und Theologie* (Berlin, 1975), p. 1ff., for a discussion of this *ḥadīth*.

[113] Wensinck, *Muslim Creed*, p. 54.

[114] *K. al-arbaʿīn*, p. 265.

As for those who question this order of things: "Woe upon woe for whomever asks 'why?' and 'how?' "[115]

Here, however, we must pull back somewhat and note that while al-Ghazālī does offer this as the ultimate justification for the rightness of things as they are, it is simplistic to assume that nothing further in extenuation of this view is offered. In the same book of the *Iḥyā'* in which our vexed question occurs al-Ghazālī presents rather extended arguments in an attempt to reconcile this strict predestination with some highly qualified notion of free will. It must be remembered, too, that predestination was one of the most controversial questions in Islamic theology from the earliest period.[116] The tensions inherent in the question are apparent from a saying attributed to Muslim ibn Yasār (d. 100 or 101/718 or 720): "(Free will and predestination) are two deep valleys where people stray without ever reaching bottom. Act therefore like someone who knows that only his own acts can still save him; and trust in God like someone who knows that only that will strike him which was meant for him."[117]

In lines 84-86, al-Ghazālī uses the metaphor of a vast storm-tossed sea to convey the incomprehensibility of predestination.[118] This is a matter "which only the knowing comprehend" but which they "are forbidden to divulge."

This is the final point in the passage that will provoke censure. al-Ghazālī will be accused of disclosing secrets to ordinary people which it is impermissible to discuss. And does he not himself say, "Disclosure of the secret of God's lordship is *kufr*?"[119] Such secrets are not part of the "practical aspects" (*muʿāmalāt*) of Ṣūfism which the *Iḥyā'* purports to detail, addressed as it is to

[115] *Ibid.*

[116] See Tritton, *Muslim Theology*, p. 54ff.; Wensinck, *Muslim Creed*, p. 36ff.; van Ess, *Zwischen Ḥadīṯ und Theologie, passim.*

[117] Cited by van Ess, *ibid.*, pp. 152-153, who sees it as an attempt at compromise between strict predestinarians and advocates of free will.

[118] A common metaphor in such discussions. ʿAlī, for example, was credited with the remark, "Predestination (*qadar*) is a deep sea; do not set out upon it!" See G. F. Hourani, "Ibn Sīnā's 'Essay on the Secret of Destiny,' " *BSOAS* 29 (1966), p. 28.

[119] *Iḥyā'*, IV, 213, line 1.

the average Muslim, and not to the initiate.[120] And yet, it is sometimes necessary to discuss the more esoteric, or "illuminative aspects" (*mukāshafāt*) of such mysteries as trust in God or the realization of the divine unity, in order to enable people to put them into practice in their lives. "Knowledge of the practical aspect is incomplete without (knowledge of) the illuminative."[121]

Later in the *K. al-tawakkul*, al-Ghazālī addresses himself to such practical concerns as, for example, how the father of a family (*mu'īl*) may strive for the kind of utter trust in God that *tawakkul* demands; or what the proper attitude is when one's property is stolen; or the course to observe in resorting to the use of medicaments, or refraining therefrom (*tark al-tadāwī*), etc.[122] Here, however, it is his concern to establish a suitable foundation so that the aspirant will act neither blindly nor in a purely perfunctory manner in striving for trust in God.

His critics will seize on this as an example of irresponsibility at best and outright heresy at worst. This charge may seem strange in connection with the final lines of the *Iḥyā'* text: nothing is affirmed there which is in any way unorthodox, let alone controversial. In fact, al-Ghazālī seems rather to pull back from entering into any discussion of the "secret of predestination" (*sirr al-qadar*).

Of course, it is true that according to certain early traditions the subject of *qadar* is best not discussed at all. "He who discusses predestination in any way will be held accountable for it on the Day of Judgement; he who does not discuss it will not be held accountable."[123] This may account for his critics' charges to some extent; but their chief objection is that he broaches

[120] See Wehr's remarks in the introduction to his translation, *al-Ġazzālī's Buch*, p. xxii.

[121] *Iḥyā'*, IV, 212, line 1.

[122] For *tawakkul al-mu'īl*, see *Iḥyā'*, IV, 234ff. (Wehr, p. 66ff.); theft of property, *Iḥyā'*, IV, 242ff. (Wehr, p. 86ff.); *tark al-tadāwī, Iḥyā'*, IV, 246ff. (Wehr, p. 91ff.)

[123] Ibn Mājah, *Sunan*, I, 33; cf. the apocryphal remark in Abū Nu'aym, *Ḥilyat al-awliyā'*, IV, 182 (cited in van Ess, *Zwischen Ḥadīṯ und Theologie*, 153): "Do not speak about *qadar*. It is God's secret; do not give away His secret."

forbidden subjects in a work intended for the common folk (*ʿawāmm*). For these critics any discussion, let alone any questioning, of such doctrines as *qadar* in such a context will appear reprehensible.

In his later paraphrase of this passage in the *K. al-arbaʿīn*, al-Ghazālī states that only initiates perceive the hidden explication (*taʾwīl*) of the world, while the common folk hold simply that "what strikes you was not there to miss you, what misses you was not there to strike you."[124] This "predestinarian axiom,"[125] of questionable origin, found its way into at least one early form of the creed, the *Fiqh Akbar* I.[126] In the *Iḥyāʾ* passage, al-Ghazālī cites it as a seemingly straightforward conclusion to his whole discussion, but his remarks in the *K. al-arbaʿīn* reveal that this was intended only for the common folk. Those with mystic knowledge, the *ʿārifūn*, understand that in everything there is a hidden meaning which is the direct effect of God's wisdom and will; they understand that what is "must be" (*wājib al-ḥuṣūl*) by the decree of the eternal will (*al-mashīʾah al-azalīyah*).[127]

It must be admitted that throughout his discussion of *tawḥīd* and *tawakkul* in the *Iḥyāʾ*, al-Ghazālī will seem to waver between silence on a particular issue and disclosure. Thus, in speaking of the fourth, and highest, stage of *tawḥīd*, he briefly characterizes it but refrains from further discussion because "an explanatory treatment of this is not allowed."[128] Nevertheless, on the same page, after remarking that "disclosure of the mystery of God's lordship is *kufr*," he will engage in a rather guarded treatment of a difficult point, i.e., how something can represent a unity and a multiplicity at one and the same time.[129] And in

124 *K. al-arbaʿīn*, p. 243.

125 van Ess, *Zwischen Ḥadīṯ und Theologie*, p. 79ff.

126 The axiom is seen as originating in protest to the doctrines of the Qadarīyah, advocates of human free will; see Wensinck, *Muslim Creed*, pp. 103 and 107ff.

127 *K. al-arbaʿīn*, p. 245. Elsewhere al-Ghazālī states that "everything that enters into existence enters only through necessity (*wujūb*), for it is necessary that it exist, even though it is not necessary on account of its own intrinsic nature, but necessary because of the divine decree." *al-Maqṣad al-asnā*, p. 103.

128 *Iḥyāʾ*, IV, 213, line 17.

129 *Ibid.* (line 2ff).

describing the third stage of *tawḥīd*, he presents an extensive explanation of the two chief obstacles which Satan presents to man in order to weaken belief in the divine unity: the belief in causality in nature and in the capacity for free choice in animals (*ikhtiyār al-ḥayawānāt*.[130]

Such "disclosures" will strengthen his critics' hands but his defenders will find in them the confirmation of al-Ghazālī's status as "one of the great among the *ahl al-bāṭin*"[131] (i.e., those possessing esoteric knowledge, in contradistinction to the *ahl al-ẓāhir*, exponents of exoteric, literal knowledge). The latter are not entitled to find fault with such authorities as al-Ghazālī "because the *ahl al-bāṭin* are most aloof from passion and closest to God-given success; and they are even more successful because of their accurate grasp of the supreme truth (*iṣābat al-ḥaqīqah*)."[132] According to this defense, al-Ghazālī is one of those privileged to perceive the "unity of existence" (*waḥdat al-wujūd*); and the following saying will be applied to him: "When you see all things as one thing from a single source and with a single substance, you see what you did not see before, you hear what you have not heard and you understand what creatures do not understand."[133] Does not al-Ghazālī state in his discussion of gratitude in the *Iḥyā'* itself that "the whole is like a single thing in which one thing is connected to the other the way the limbs of the body are connected to each other"?[134]

And yet, by his own testimony, such subjects as *qadar* and *tawḥīd* may not be treated in detail in a work written for the ordinary person, for these subjects belong properly to the *'ilm al-mukāshafāt*. Such subjects dazzle the weak, the ignorant, and the unprepared: "Do not lift the curtains which hide the sun from the gaze of the bats lest they perish!"[135]

It will be finally for lifting these curtains, or at least appearing to, that al-Ghazālī will be severely rebuked.

[130] *Ibid.* (line -10ff).
[131] *Itḥāf*, IX, 459.
[132] *Ibid.*
[133] *Itḥāf*, IX, 460; cf. also *Qūt al-qulūb*, III, 53.
[134] *Iḥyā'*, IV, 95.
[135] *Iḥyā'*, IV, 84.

## *B. AL-GHAZĀLĪ'S OWN COMMENTARY*

In *al-Imlā' fī mushkilāt al-Iḥyā'*, al-Ghazālī presents a brief defense of the controversial passage in the *Iḥyā'*.[136] Unfortunately, the text as we have it is corrupt; in parts it is intelligible only when the Berlin manuscript, the printed version, and the citations in later treatises are collated. Rather than present it translated *in extenso* here, we shall offer a synopsis of the main arguments.

al-Ghazālī begins by repeating his original statement with some important modifications: "There is not in possibility (anything) more wonderful (*abdaʿ*)[137] than the form (*ṣūrah*)[138] of this world."[139]

[136] See note 14 above. See also, *Iḍāḥ*, pp. 72-73; *Dhahab*, p. 474 (partial text); *Ḥikmat*, pp. 19-20.

[137] The word *abdaʿ* seems peculiar, though none of the disputants calls attention to it. *Badīʿ*, of course, denotes what is novel and surprising, "unknown before" (Lane, 166). Ahlwardt renders it accordingly as "überraschenderes" (*Verzeichnis*, II, 316). Asín Palacios takes it as equivalent to *aḥsan* or *afḍal*: "más excelente" (*La espiritualidad*, IV, 11), as does Humā'ī: "bihtar" (*Ghazzālī-nāmah*, p. 428).

The word is commonly used in regard to poetry: *atā bi'l-badīʿ*, "he produced a new saying" (Lane, 166) and also signifies a branch of rhetoric (*ʿilm al-badīʿ*). In this sense, it may be conjectured that al-Ghazālī wanted to emphasize the startling and admirable artistry of the world order, and to do so with a term not associated with the Muʿtazilites and their doctrine of *al-aṣlaḥ*. (For an interesting hypothesis that the whole notion of *badīʿ* in poetry developed out of Muʿtazilite *kalām*, see Suzanne P. Stetkevych, "Toward a Redefinition of '*Badīʿ*' Poetry," *Journal of Arabic Literature* 12 (1981), pp. 1-29.)

The word and its derivatives have other technical meanings. In *Qur.* 2:117 and 6:101, God is called *al-badīʿ* ("creator"), and the 4th and 8th forms of the verb came to mean "to create *ex nihilo*." See, e.g., al-Kindī, *Rasā'il*, I, 183; al-Rāghib al-Iṣfahānī, *Tafṣīl al-nash'atayn*, pp. 15-16; al-Jurjānī, *Taʿrīfāt*, p. 3; Aḥmadnagarī, *Dustūr al-ʿulamā'*, I, 17. The term *ibdāʿ* is, of course, a technical term in Ismāʿīlī theology as well; see, among others, Ḥamīd al-dīn al-Kirmānī, *Rāḥat al-ʿaql* (ed. Ḥusayn & Ḥilmī; Cairo, 1953), p. 59.

Massignon seems to have had this latter sense in mind when he translated the sentence as "Rien de plus ne se trouve dans le possible que dans l'existentialisé" (*Passion*, III, 83, note 5), as though it meant: "Nothing more creatable *ex nihilo* remains in possibility," in accord with his interpretation of the passage.

[138] Cf. *al-Maqṣad al-asnā*, p. 81: "The name *muṣawwir* (he who forms) is apt for God since He orders the forms of things in the most excellent order (*aḥsan tartīb*) and provides them with the most excellent form (*ṣawwarahā aḥsan taṣwīr*)." See also p. 79 of the same work.

[139] *al-Imlā'*, fol. 16a. In the Berlin ms., there is a lacuna where the word *abdaʿ* appears in other texts.

It is probable that his contemporaries, the Iraqis whom Abū Bakr ibn al-ʿArabī mentions, took particular objection to the seeming denial of God's free choice (*ikhtiyār*), for he here introduces a defense of his position in those terms.

God is a free agent (*fāʿil mukhtār*); as such, He may choose to create or not to create. But when He does choose to create, His creation must be the utmost of "what wisdom demands" (*mā taqtaḍīhi al-ḥikmah*).[140] To say that God is somehow incapable for freely choosing not to create is like accusing him of miserliness for His "delay" in bringing the world from non-existence into existence.

The question of God's deferral of creation (*ta'khīruhu bi' l-ʿālam qabla khalqihi*) is rather complicated.[141] To claim that He did not defer creation is to make the world coeval with Him; it is thus to maintain the doctrine of the world's eternity. To assert, however, that God did defer creation is to raise the troubling question of whether He was previously unable or unwilling to create the world. Did He "hoard" a good He might have given? It also leads to the question of whether some preponderating factor (*murajjiḥ*) influenced His will to create the world at one time rather than at another; and yet, the presence of such a factor would seem to impugn the sovereignty of the divine will.[142]

al-Ghazālī's introduction of the question of God's deferral of creation is strategically astute. He wishes to equate this question with that raised by his own disputed sentence. He asks in effect: What is the difference between saying that miserliness (or in-

[140] For this phrase, see also al-Rāghib al-Iṣfahānī, *Tafṣīl*, pp. 17 and 39, and al-Bayḍāwī, *Anwār al-tanzīl*, I, 127.

[141] This question and the related question of what God did prior to creation elicited impatient and perplexed responses from Western theologians. Typical is the comment of Albertus Magnus: "This seems to me a foolish question" (*Videtur mihi esse stulta quaestio*), *In I Sententiarum* [Dist. XLIV, B, art. 1], in *Opera omnia* (Paris, 1893), XXVI, 391. And, according to John Milton: "Anyone who asks what God did before the creation of the world is a fool; and anyone who answers him is not much wiser," *Christian Doctrine*, in *Complete Prose Works* (New Haven, 1973), VI, 299. For an Islamic discussion, see the work of the great Ismāʿīlī poet and thinker Nāṣir-i Khosraw, *Zād al-musāfirīn* (Berlin, 1341?), p. 275ff.

[142] See the discussion in al-Ījī, *Mawāqif*, VIII, 85-86.

capacity or injustice) follows from God's creation of a less than perfect world and saying that such defects follow from His deferral of the world's creation? In other words, we know that God deferred creation, that He created the world at one time rather than another, and yet this does not lead us to accuse Him of miserliness. Why, then, should the disputed statement lead ineluctably to this conclusion? God's creation of the world at a particular moment, and not sooner, results from His free choice and sovereign will, and so, too, His creation of the world in the most perfect and excellent way.

From the beginning, it would seem, critics charged al-Ghazālī with holding, or at least supporting, the doctrine of necessary creation; and this charge would recur. A consequence of this doctrine is the world's eternity, a notion inadmissible to orthodox theologians; for it not only sets up a "rival" to God but severely circumscribes His power and freedom of choice. al-Ghazālī's introduction of the question of deferral of creation is thus in part an effort to dissociate himself from such suspect doctrines. And so he replies: to hold that miserliness or impotence may be imputed to God on this basis is tantamount to holding that they also follow God's deferral of creation; i.e., it is to accept the very premises of the philosophers who do so argue.

This response will not escape censure. Aḥmad ibn Mubārak al-Sijilmāsī al-Lamaṭī (d. 1156/1742), for one, will argue that it allows God free choice before creation but strips it from Him afterward. He can choose to create or not to create, but when He does, He must create the best.[143] It is probably in anticipation of some such objection that al-Ghazālī so vigorously stresses the role of divine wisdom: it is divine wisdom which dictates that things be as good as possible, and not some necessity to which God is subject.

Other initial objections to the *Iḥyā'* passage may have dwelt on the manifest imperfections of this world, for al-Ghazālī now attempts, in the *Imlā'*, to turn these very imperfections to ad-

[143] *Dhahab*, p. 475.

vantage. This is a further elaboration of his belief in the correlation of perfect and imperfect.

To say that the world is perfectly right and just does not mean that every individual in it is equal to every other in perfection. On the contrary, it is the best possible world because it contains imperfection as well as perfection. It is the best possible world because it is in accord with what wisdom demands; and wisdom, as we know, demands the simultaneous creation of perfect and imperfect.

Furthermore, this world of perfect and imperfect beings is itself decisive proof (*dalīl qāṭiʿ*) of God's perfection. Imperfection is as necessary here as perfection:

> If everything that God created were deficient (*nāqiṣ*) in comparison with something else that He could create (but did not, the lack that is brought in evidence against this existence that He did create would be obvious), just as it is obvious in those particular individuals whom He did create deficient, in order to show thereby the perfection of what He created otherwise, and all of this would be a kind of proof for the deficiency of what He did make, and decisively so; while the predication to Him of power to make the more perfect would be mere opinion (*ẓann*).[144]

We cannot say that this world is inferior to some other possible state-of-affairs unless everything within it is deficient by comparison with that hypothetical world. If that were so, and everything that God created were deficient, we could say decisively that the present creation is less than the best possible. Furthermore, we could not know whether God is capable of creating anything better. As it is, however, we see grades of perfection. The more perfect shows what God is capable of, and we recognize the more perfect by means of what is less so. God gave human beings intellects and powers of understanding so that they would perceive this: ". . . inasmuch as He taught them a perfection that shows them defect, He also informed them of His power by means of incapacity."[145]

[144] *Imlā'*, fol. 16b, lines 6-9. The sentence in parentheses is lacking in al-Samhūdī's citation, *Iḍāḥ*, pp. 72-73.
[145] *Imlā'*, fol. 16b.

It is the sign of wisdom that the perfect and the imperfect coexist; their coexistence indicates that the world is the product of wisdom, and not of any intrinsic necessity or obligation. The world would not be as good as possible if the imperfect were lacking. al-Ḥāmid al-Shāfiʿī illustrates this with an analogy:

> If there were a king who had many storehouses—a storehouse of jewels, a storehouse of gold, a storehouse of silver, and a storehouse of coins—and he then gave alms from all his storehouses, he would be absolutely generous. But if he gives from one storehouse and not from the others he can be deemed miserly in relation to what he has not given.
>
> But there is no doubt that God, in this world that He produced, gives from all His storehouses.[146]

The king of course represents God, the jewels are His prophets, the gold His saints, the silver His believers, and the coins represent unbelievers and hypocrites. It would have been less than generous of God to have withheld the latter. Furthermore, without the coins, we would not be able to recognize the value and distinction of the gold, the silver, and the jewels.

The wisdom in God's creation is unimpeachable. Only he can find fault with it who is unaware of the "measure of the world" (*miqdār al-ʿālam*) and the way in which it is arranged in accordance with the next world. There is a continuum of perfect and imperfect, gain and loss, extending between this life and the next. Such a doubting person has not yet "glimpsed the transcendent world with the vision of the heart" (*bi-baṣar qalbihi*) nor crossed the limits to what is lowest in his own nature; i.e., he has not realized that these extremes coexist within his own nature as well.

By contrast, one who is aware that all that ultimately matters is the divine pleasure or wrath sees that

> He brought forth the world in its totality from non-existence, which is sheer negation (*nafy maḥḍ*), into existence, which is sound affirmation (*ithbāt ṣaḥīḥ*) and He measured it into levels

[146] *al-Dalīl*, fol. 135a, line 22ff. This is based on a similar passage in al-Ghazālī's *al-Maqṣad al-asnā*, pp. 230-231.

> and set an appointed term for it. Hence there exist living and dead, moving and unmoving, wise and ignorant, wretched and happy, near and far, small and large, majestic and mean, rich and poor, commanded and commanding, believer and unbeliever, ingrate and grateful, male and female, earth and sky, this world and the next, and other things too numerous to count.[147]

And all of this, he continues, "subsists in God, exists through His power, continues through His knowledge . . . and indicates His far-reaching wisdom. There is nothing more perfect than its temporal creation except His eternity, nor (more perfect) than its administration except for His absolute rule. . . ."[148]

This inventory of correlated opposites reinforces what was declared in the *Iḥyāʾ*. Conditions such as happiness and sadness, belief and disbelief, are placed on equal terms with male and female, earth and sky, and the like. No distinction is made between what we would regard as transitory or permanent qualities. This is, of course, because none of these subsists in itself but only in God; what reality they have is apparent and fictive.

If the objection is brought that things do change—a happy person may grow sad, a rich become poor, etc.—and so, another state obtains that must be judged either the same (then what of change?), or worse (then it is no longer the best possible), or better (then the former state was not the best possible), the reply once again will be that it is divine wisdom which dictates things as they are. Things have no intrinsic excellence; the excellence they possess proceeds from the fact that divine wisdom selected them to be. This objection, base on the undeniable fact of change, will impel al-Suyūṭī and al-Samhūdī to develop their theories of "relative perfection" in response.

The assertion that things as they are, are optimal because of the dictates of divine wisdom will provide al-Ghazālī's defenders one of their strongest and most useful arguments. Through it they will struggle to refute the charge that he merely parrots philosophers and Muʿtazilites. But the appeal to wisdom, far

[147] *Imlāʾ*, fol. 16b. See also, *Iḍāḥ*, p. 73; and al-Yāfiʿī, *Marham al-ʿilal*, p. 18.
[148] *Imlāʾ*, fol. 16b.

from mitigating the disapprobation of the critics, will serve instead only to complicate and intensify the debate.

## IV
## SUSPECT SOURCES

al-Ghazālī's immediate source for the controversial passage was, as we know, the *Qūt al-qulūb* of Abū Ṭālib al-Makkī; but the critics claim that other, more insidious sources and influences shaped his viewpoint. This charge is certainly not without foundation. However al-Ghazālī's defenders will ultimately elaborate and refine his position in order to prove its conformity to orthodox (i.e., Ashʿarite) doctrine, the statement reveals a certain striking affinity with various Muʿtazilite and philosophical formulations.

Thus, the early Muʿtazilite ʿAbbād ibn Sulaymān (d. c. 250/864), in rejecting the notion that God could provide better for man than He has already done, remarked: "It is not possible (*lā yajūz*) that God forgo anything which He can do by way of benefit in order to do some other benefit. . . . If He had something more salutary (*aṣlaḥ*) and more excellent (*afḍal*) than what He has done for people, and He were to prevent them from having it, He would be miserly (*bakhīl*) and unjust (*ẓālim*) to them."[149]

And Abū al-Hudhayl al-ʿAllāf (d.c. 227/840) held the view that "there is no goodness better than what He has already done" (*lā ṣalāḥ aṣlaḥ mimmā faʿala*).[150]

The Muʿtazilite doctrine of *al-aṣlaḥ* was, of course, more nuanced than these isolated citations reveal and was by no means unanimously accepted even among the Muʿtazilites themselves, the degree of God's "obligation" to His creatures forming a point of special disagreement.

Still more troubling to al-Ghazālī's critics will be the suspicion that the doctrines of the philosophers lie at the heart of the statement. This suspicion is all the more disturbing in that al-Ghazālī was credited with the most telling critique of these doc-

[149] Ibn Ḥazm, *al-Fiṣal*, III, 120, cited in Massignon, *Passion*, III, 83, note 5, who considers it the prime source of al-Ghazālī's statement. Cf. also, al-Bazdawī, *K. uṣūl al:dīn*, pp. 126-127.

[150] al-Ashʿarī, *Maqālāt*, I, 239, cited in Wensinck, *Muslim Creed*, p. 74.

trines in his *Tahāfut al-falāsifah*. For his friends, of course, this very fact will provide proof positive that he cannot have meant the statement as it was taken by hostile readers.

Tāj al-dīn al-Subkī (d. 771/1370), for example, will declare that philosophers like Ibn Sīnā are "among the damned and so how could al-Ghazālī have relied on him? Philosophy has no place in the *Iḥyā'* which he wrote only after he had belittled it as a science."[151]

Nevertheless, the charge is not so lightly to be dismissed. In his section on providence in the *Shifā'*, Ibn Sīnā (d. 428/1037) states:

> God knows by His nature what exists in the order of good; and is by His very nature a cause of goodness and perfection insofar as possible (*bi-ḥasab al-imkān*) and He wills it. . . . He knows the order of the good in the widest possible way (*'alā wajh al-ablagh fi'l-imkān*) so that there emanate from Him the order and good that He knows in the widest way in an emanation most perfectly conducive to order in accord with possibility (. . . *fayaḍān 'alā atamm ta'dīyah ilā al-niẓām bi-ḥasab al-imkān*).[152]

Still another suspect source mentioned is the *Rasā'il* of the Ikhwān al-Ṣafā', and, indeed, in the section on fortitude (*ṣabr*) in that work, we learn that prophets are able to withstand calamities because they hold the conviction that "the world has a maker who is one, living, powerful, and wise and that He has arranged the world's affairs in the most excellent order, and its order in the perfection of wisdom, such that nothing small or great occurs unless there be in it varieties of wisdom and types of benefits no one but He knows."[153]

The underlying principle in these passages (as, it would seem in al-Ghazālī's) is that the world as a product of a perfect creator must be as excellent as possible; otherwise, defects or deficien-

[151] Cited in *Itḥāf*, IX, 442.

[152] *K. al-shifā'*, *Ilāhīyāt*, II, 415. Cf. the paraphrase by Ibn Sīnā's pupil, Bahmanyār ibn al-Marzubān (d. 430/1038) in his *al-Taḥṣīl* (ed. Muṭahharī; Tehran, 1349), p. 663: *hādha al-niẓām huwa al-niẓām al-ḥaqīqī lā niẓāma afḍal minhu wa-lā atamm.*

[153] *Rasā'il* (Beirut, 1957), IV, 72-73.

cies would reflect on its maker: "from the perfect only the perfect may issue."[154]

These formulations seem to have as their common source the famous passage of Plato's *Timaeus* (29A-30B) in which it is stated that "the work of the supremely good" cannot "be anything but that which is best" (τὸ κάλλιστον). When the demiurge shaped the universe he "fashioned reason within soul and soul within reason, to the end that the work he accomplished might be by nature as excellent and perfect as possible."[155] The demiurge, the "best of causes" (ἄριστος τῶν αἰτίων) fashions the cosmos "the best of things that have become" (κάλλιστος τῶν γεγονότων).[156] And it is because the demiurge is good and without any jealousy (φθόνος) that he desires to make a cosmos as excellent as possible.[157]

In Galen's compendium of the *Timaeus*, translated into Arabic by Ḥunayn ibn Isḥāq (the Greek original is lost), the corresponding passage bears a striking similarity to al-Ghazālī's formulation:

> It is not possible that (the world) be in any condition more excellent than that in which it is (*lā yumkin an yakūna ʿalā ḥāl afḍal min ḥālihi allatī huwa ʿalayhā*).[158]

And the compendium continues:

> The reason for the creation of the world is God's generosity (*jūd*) . . . for there is neither envy nor miserliness (*bukhl*) with the generous one (*al-jawād*) toward anything at any time. Hence when he wanted to set in order the corporeal substance moving at random and without order in the best possible way (*fī ghāyat mā yumkin*) it could be ordered, he created the world.[159]

There are certain obvious affinities here with the Ghazālian text: the surpassing excellence of creation is predicated on the

[154] *Ḥikmat*, p. 15.
[155] *Timaeus* 30B; tr. Cornford, *Plato's Cosmology*, pp. 33-34.
[156] *Timaeus* 29A; tr. Cornford, p. 23.
[157] *Timaeus* 29E; tr. Cornford, p. 33. For the early Greek notion of the grudging nature of the gods, see A. J. Festugière, "Réflexions sur le problème du mal chez Eschyle et Platon," in *Etudes de philosophie grecque* (Paris, 1971), p. 8ff.
[158] *Galeni Compendium Timaei Platonis*, p. 5 [Latin translation, p. 39].
[159] *Ibid.*

perfect generosity of its creator; to deny this excellence is to impugn the creator. His generosity is such that He acts to the very limit of the possible (*fī ghāyat mā yumkin*). In the *Maqāṣid al-falāsifah*, his exposition of the philosophers' views, al-Ghazālī explains what this means: "The One poured forth (*afāḍa*) existence upon all existing things just as it must be, and in accord with what must be without hoarding (*iddikhār*) any possible thing."[160] There is, therefore, good reason to assume that the *Timaeus* passage, or some variation thereof, stood as al-Ghazālī's ultimate source, and to understand the phrase "there is not in possibility" (*laysa fī' l-imkān*) as meaning that God has not hoarded or withheld any possibility.

The implications of the *Timaeus* passage were drawn out far more explicitly in another long-lived debate in the Latin West. Under the influence of the *Timaeus*, as mediated by the 4th-century commentator and translator Calcidius, Peter Abelard (1079-1142), al-Ghazālī's younger contemporary, posed the question "whether God can make better or more things than He does make, or whether He can in any way cease from making those things which He does make?"[161] Abelard acknowledges the difficulties to which either affirmation or denial of this question leads, but he argues that "God indeed does all the things of which He is capable, and does them as well as He can."[162] If we expect from ourselves the good acts of which we are capable, how much the more so shall we expect them of God, who is supremely good and for whom no action is onerous? For Abelard, therefore, this world is the best possible, for "God cannot do more than He already does, or better; nor can He refrain from doing those things He does do."[163] To say that the world could be better is to say that God is less good or just or generous than He might have been.

Abelard's question and response engendered a debate within

[160] *Maqāṣid*, p. 242

[161] *Theologia Christiana*, in *Opera* (ed. Cousin; Paris, 1859), II, 560. See also Lovejoy, *Great Chain of Being*, pp. 70-73.

[162] *Ibid.*, II, 561: *Facit itaque omnia quae potest Deus, et tantum bene quantum possit.*

[163] *Ibid.*: *plura Deus nullatenus facere possit quam facit; aut melius facere, aut ab his cessare.*

Latin Scholasticism; his position was sharply disputed at first by such theologians as Hugh of St. Victor (1096-1141) and Peter Lombard (ca. 1095-1160) and later by virtually every Scholastic thinker of note. Continuing comment on the issue was assured because Peter Lombard incorporated the question in the first book of his massively influential compilation known as the *Sentences*. The *Sentences* formed an integral part of the medieval curriculum, and commentary upon them was prerequisite to academic advancement.[164]

As in the Islamic debate, objections to Abelard's position centered on the implicit curtailment of divine omnipotence; in the words of Hugh of St. Victor, such a view as Abelard's threatened "to subject divine omnipotence to a measure" (*sub mensura coarctare*).[165] Or, as Alexander of Hales (ca. 1170-1245), the teacher of Bonaventura, put it: "If God cannot act in a better way than He does act, then His power is limited, which is false."[166]

The history of this Scholastic debate, which elicited extensive discussion from Abelard's time well into the 14th century and the works of William of Ockham (ca. 1290-1349) and his followers, deserves a study in its own right.[167] In general, Scholastic

[164] For the text, see *Magistri Petri Lombardi Parisiensis episcopi Sententiae in IV libris distinctae*. 3d ed. (Grottaferrata, 1971), I/2, 298-306. For the vast commentary literature, see Friedrich Stegmüller, *Repertorium Commentariorum in Sententias Petri Lombardi*. 2 vols. (Würzburg, 1947).

[165] *De sacramentis*, I.ii.22, in Migne, *Patrologia Latina*, vol. 176, p. 214. Hugh's comments are taken up by the Lombard and cited in all the later discussions. In passing, it is perhaps worth mention that Origen (ca. 185-253) did in fact hold that God's power was limited, and that through His will, God called into existence only that number of beings which He could administer; see his *De principiis*, II 9, 1 (ed. Görgemanns & Karpp, Darmstadt, 1976), p. 401.

[166] *Summa theologica* (ed. Klumper; Quaracchi, 1924), I, 224; the work is traditionally ascribed to Alexander, but is in fact the work of several hands.

[167] In addition to those cited above, see, e.g., Albertus Magnus, *Opera omnia* (Paris, 1893), XXVI, 387ff.; Duns Scotus, *Opera omnia* (Paris, 1893), X, 742ff; Thomas Aquinas, *In quatuor libros Sententiarum Magistri Petri Lombardi*, in *Opera* (Parma, 1852-1873), VI, 346ff; and *Summa theologiae*, I.25, 6; Bonaventura's discussion is one of the most extensive and impressive Scholastic treatments, in his *Opera theologica selecta* (Quaracchi 1934), I, 604-632; see also, William of Ockham, *Scriptum in librum primum Sententiarum*, in *Opera theologica* (St. Bonaventure, NY, 1979), IV, 650-660. As my friend Professor Calvin Normore kindly informs me, there is also a brief discussion by Robert Grosseteste (1175-1253) in his *De libero arbitrio*, ed. L. Baur, *Die philosophischen Werke des Robert Grosseteste* (*Beiträge zur Geschichte der Philosophie des Mit-*

theologians affirmed that God could indeed create a better world, or worlds, than this, but they could not satisfactorily resolve the underlying dilemma—indeed, who could? They struggled to do so by seizing on distinctions. What is actually meant, they asked, by "better" or by "world"? If by "better" one refers to God's actions, then it must be said that He cannot act in any better way, i.e., with "better" wisdom or goodness or power; however, if by "better" one refers to the objects of God's power, then it is true to say that things may be made better than they are.[168]

Again, in discussion of the question a favorite strategy was to distinguish between the essential and the accidental being or goodness of things or of the world itself. The substantial being or goodness of the world or its parts could not be improved, but accidental goodness or being could become better or worse.[169] A man, for example, might be made stronger or more intelligent or more eloquent than he is, for these are accidental to what he is *qua* man, but he could not be made more a "rational animal" than he is, for this is his very nature. The substantial nature of a thing cannot be changed without altering its identity, and this reflects, not limitation of power on God's part, but the very natures of things as they are.

Hence, for the consensus of Scholastics, this world in its essential nature cannot be better, for then it would not be this world, but another; on the other hand, its accidental goodness might be immeasurably improved. There could be, as Aquinas noted, the creation of further species, or the addition of further parts to the world, or the improvement of its individual constituents.[170]

Such a solution has a certain elegance. It affirms the essential nature of the creation to be unalterably good, and so it preserves the creator's justice and goodness; at the same time, it meets

---

*telalters*, 9), p. 180. There are very few scholarly discussions of the question, but see A. Maurer, "Ockham on the Possibility of a Better World," *Mediaeval Studies*, 38 (1976), pp. 291-312; and F. Copleston, *A History of Philosophy*, II/1, 299-300 (Bonaventura), and II/2, 89-90 (Aquinas).

[168] Alexander of Hales, *Summa*, I, 224.

[169] Albertus Magnus, *In I Sentent. Dist. XLIV*, in *Opera*, XXVI, 391; cf. also, Th. Aquinas, *Summa theologiae*, I.25,6.

[170] Aquinas, *In quatuor libros Sententiarum*, in *Opera*, VI, 354.

squarely our common sense of dissatisfaction by acknowledging that numerous individual aspects of the world might indeed be better, if only "accidentally." To be sure, this left the question as to why the creator did not remedy such individual defects; to such a question, as, for example, why God does not increase the capacities of finite things, Albertus Magnus (1206-1280) could only declare: "I say that in His wisdom, He was not inclined to give more, and He was unwilling to give more; but why He was unwilling, I do not know. He, however, knows."[171]

The Scholastic debate appears clear-cut and predictable, even from this cursory glance, in comparison with the Islamic dispute. None of al-Ghazālī's critics cites such sources as the *Timaeus* to support the contention that philosophical doctrine shaped his views. For such critics, a suspicious turn of phrase, a technical term, the foreign cast of the whole passage, would have been sufficient to alert them, had not the content already alarmed and outraged their sensibilities. And they proceed to attack by innuendo and by frankly *ad hominem* arguments.

In turn, al-Ghazālī's defenders will claim that his sources are unimpeachably orthodox. They will adduce Qur'ānic precedents, e.g., "the All-mighty, the All-compassionate, who has created all things well (*alladhī aḥsana kull shay' khalaqahu*);[172] and especially, "We . . . created man in the fairest stature" (*laqad khalaqnā al-insān fī aḥsan taqwīm*).[173]

What seems to a modern reader obvious—that al-Ghazālī in some way submitted to the influence of those philosophers whom he, nevertheless, largely repudiated—is ignored or disavowed by his defenders. To admit the influence of ancient or Islamic philosophers upon al-Ghazālī was tantamount to surrender for his supporters; and this held true, even with such later defenders as Murtaḍā al-Zabīdī and al-Jazā'irī, in the 18th and 19th centuries respectively.

Thus, the notion of the correlation of perfect and imperfect will be supported by appeal to those Qur'ānic passages in which

[171] *Opera*, XXVI, 392.
[172] *Qur*. 32:7 (tr. Arberry, p. 117), cited in al-Suyūṭī, *Tashyid*, fol. 3a.
[173] *Qur*. 95:4 (Arberry, p. 343), cited in *ibid.*

the creation of things in pairs is mentioned, e.g., "and of everything created We two kinds."[174]

Furthermore, the principle that "from the perfect only the perfect may issue" will be grounded in the verses: "And heaven—We built it with might, and We extend it wide. And the earth—We spread it forth; O excellent Smoothers!"[175]

These are but scattered examples; and, to be sure, the critics will easily find opposing verses with which to refute the defenders. Much of the dispute will turn on such exchanges of Qur'ānic passages.

## V
## THE AUTHENTICITY OF THE ASCRIPTION

The difficulties involved with al-Ghazālī's position and, in particular, the suspicion that it represented heretical doctrines, induced some commentators to conclude that the passage in question could not be accurately ascribed to him, but had been interpolated into the *Iḥyā'* by other hands. This suspicion was strengthened by the apparent inconsistencies (and even contradictions) between certain of his other works and the *Iḥyā'* passage. We have already called attention to two of these alleged inconsistencies: in *al-Iqtiṣād fi'l-i'tiqād*, his doctrinal *kalām* work, al-Ghazālī postulates a superior state-of-affairs in the absence of the religious obligation imposed upon man; and in more than one passage he explicitly upholds the accepted doctrine that the objects of God's power are endless. The thought that a figure of such authority and eminence could have subscribed to repudiated doctrines, and doctrines which he had himself refuted, gave additional support to this argument.

It was, of course, conceivable that the statement was a simple lapse (as al-Biqā'ī, not without malice, would suggest); but it was preferable to believe that the statement had been smuggled into the *Iḥyā'* in an attempt to buttress unpopular opinions with the prestige of a universally venerated authority.

[174] *Qur.* 51:49 (Arberry, p. 239), cited in *ibid.* al-Suyūṭī understands this to refer to the opposition of day and night, black and white, belief and unbelief, etc.

[175] *Qur.* 51:47 (Arberry, p. 239), cited in *Itḥāf*, IX, 454.

Tempting as this theory may seem, it remains highly implausible. There can be little serious doubt that the statement is correctly ascribed to al-Ghazālī. First, we have the evidence that objections to the statement sprang up with al-Ghazālī's own lifetime, and that he himself addressed those objections in the *Imlā'*. It is hardly credible that an entire treatise, dealing with other disputed points as well, would be fabricated, and that within the supposed author's lifetime, nor that such a fabricator would then proceed to sprinkle parallel passages throughout other of al-Ghazālī's works.

Furthermore, there is the disapproving testimony of Abū Bakr ibn al-ʿArabī, al-Ghazālī's own pupil, that he did indeed hold this position. The matter would seem to have been a subject of open discussion and debate, as ibn al-ʿArabī's reference to the "Iraqis" suggests. Then, too, al-Ghazālī did not disown the statement, as he might easily have done, but rather vigorously reaffirmed it in the *Imlā'* and included it, in paraphrase, in the *Kitāb al-arbaʿīn.*

The passage would seem to be more or less in accord with al-Ghazālī's later Ṣūfī position, as expressed in other works composed after the *Iḥyā'*. Again and again, in such treatises as *Jawāhir al-Qur'ān, Kitāb al-arbaʿīn,* and *al-Maqṣad al-asnā* (as well as in many sections of the *Iḥyā'*), we find a recurrent affirmation of the perfect rightness of the actual. These affirmations occur, moreover, in such a way as to suggest that they form an important part of his own particular mystical viewpoint.

There was a further, perhaps more urgent, consideration for al-Ghazālī's supporters in accepting the authenticity of the ascription, whatever difficulties it caused for them. If one such passage in the *Iḥyā'* were deemed spurious, others might be rejected as well. No assurance would remain that any text was free of such fabrications. According to al-Jazā'irī:

> The idea that the *Iḥyā'*, after its perfect renown in the author's lifetime, should offer an opening to the Muʿtazilites to record their machinations and mix in their invalid teachings is impossible. The possibility of this is an infringement on a matter of religion.

> Were we to assume the possibility of this, no confidence in books on law and theology would remain for us, and the arguments of the *mujtahids* . . . would not remain sound for us. For it might be said in an effort to weaken them, "Perhaps this is an interpolated and forged doctrine," and as soon as the possibility entered, the argument would collapse.[176]

For al-Jazā'irī, as for others, it was a matter of integrity as well as of evidence to accept the ascription to al-Ghazālī. To permit the suggestion of interpolation was to invite the destruction of rational discussion as well as tradition. No issue would then be faced on its merits. And, more dangerously, it might be asked, if we cannot rely on the authenticity of al-Ghazālī's works, how may we be sure of any other respected authority's works?

This is, of course, no proof of the genuineness of the ascription, but it does give some sense of the tenor of the dispute. Even those who claim to accept the theory of interpolation, such as al-Biqāʿī and al-Lamaṭī, do not content themselves with a mere dismissal of the issue on the grounds that it is spurious; rather, they pursue the question tenaciously to all its final consequences.

The issue, to be sure, had a vitality of its own. The underlying problems had never been resolved to satisfaction despite the ascendancy of "orthodox" doctrine; but, then, neither were they to be resolved in the West. It is perhaps in the nature of the case that the problem of theodicy, at least as traditionally posed, cannot be convincingly resolved.[177]

Often it seems that the arguments for interpolation are intro-

[176] *Ḥikmat*, p. 40.

[177] Recently, Benson Mates has argued that "the principal traditional problems of philosophy are genuine intellectual knots; they are intelligible enough, but at the same time they are absolutely insoluble." *Skeptical Essays* (Chicago, 1981), p. 3. Mates does not deal with the problem of theodicy in his discussion, but his formulation and analysis of such "intelligible but insoluble" problems seem to me to apply with special aptness to theodicy; see pp. 3-13 of the above work for his discussion.

For other philosophers, the problem is fatally skewed; for example, the contemporary German philosopher Hermann Schmitz considers the traditional discussion of the "best of all possible worlds" to be based on a historic misapprehension and misapplication of the very notion of possibility. See his *System der Philosophie*, Bd. I: *Die Gegenwart* (Bonn, 1964), esp. pp. 364ff.

duced as face-saving gestures. It was risky to attack such an authority as al-Ghazālī whose prestige, by the 15th and 16th centuries, for example, when most of the debate took place, was well-nigh unassailable. It was more discreet to attack the position while at the same time declaring that the "Proof of Islam" had never really held it.

TWO

# *The Disputants and Their Works*

## I

## THE FORM OF THE DEBATE

Theology in Islam is a science based on dialectic. Indeed, as has often been pointed out, the Arabic term for theology, *ʿilm al-kalām*, means "the science of discourse."[1] A position is taken and established in the face of opposing positions; correct doctrine is determined by examination, and demolition, of rival and opposing doctrines. "Theology in Islam, more perhaps than in other religions, is a contentious science. . . ."[2]

This contentious science early developed characteristic modes of argumentation. Scholastic disputation (*munāẓarah*) followed well-defined procedures. The various types of argument were codified; a specialized body of technical terminology emerged; rules governing the conduct of disputants, from procedural formulae to the observance of certain proprieties, were elaborated. All facets of disputation were the province of the art of dialectic (*ādāb al-baḥth*), itself the subject of a considerable body of literature.

The controversy engendered by al-Ghazālī's statement, while not a formal disputation, draws heavily on the rules, procedures, and terminology of the *ādāb al-baḥth*. Thus, an author may assume the position of the opponent (*sāʾil*) in addressing an adversary, who is then assigned the role of respondent (*mujīb*). The respondent may be expected to act as the *muʿallil*; i.e., he must demonstrate the basis, or rationale (*ʿillah*), of his position. A thesis (*daʿwā*) may be advanced, or an objection (*muʿāraḍah*) mounted; thus, those who oppose al-Ghazālī are said "to object"

[1] J. van Ess, "Disputationspraxis in der islamischen Theologie. Eine vorläufige Skizze, *REI* 44 (1976), p. 23.

[2] *Ibid.*

to his statement (*ʿāraḍūhu*), i.e., they raise objections based on contrary arguments.[3]

Despite the codification of Islamic theology in *summae*, such as the *Mawāqif* of al-Ijī (d. 756/1355), in which an attempt was made to systematize all aspects of belief, certain seemingly minor questions persisted unresolved. These irksome questions provided the subject of recurrent debate which flourished on the fringes of the ever-continuing refinement and perfection of the formal systems of theology. The questions provoked by al-Ghazālī's statement are one such example; in this case, explication of a few brief passages—indeed, of a single sentence—would lead to confrontation with central issues in Islamic theology.

Another comparable debate, though not so long-lived as that surrounding al-Ghazālī's words, sprang from the assertion by Muḥyī al-dīn Ibn al-ʿArabī (#5, below) that Pharaoh had been granted faith by God and had died a believer.[4] At stake here was the immediate issue of whether such a notorious malefactor as Pharaoh could truly have believed, but other broader questions relating to the problem of free will and determinism were also drawn into play. And, as in the present debate, the "ortho-

[3] With the notable exception of the article cited in the preceding note, no study has been devoted to the important subject of *ādāb al-baḥth*. Here we can only allude to certain of the key terms and forms of argumentation. A thorough study would require, and deserves, an extensive investigation in its own right.

A useful modern manual on the subject is Muḥammad Muḥyī al-Dīn ʿAbd al-Ḥamīd, *R. al-ādāb* (Cairo, 1361/1942). There is a discussion in G. Makdisi, *The Rise of Colleges* (Edinburgh, 1981), p. 128ff. (Makdisi is concerned, however, with the place of disputation in the traditional curriculum, and not with the terminology or forms of argumentation as such). For a brief, interesting account of *disputatio* in the Latin Scholastic tradition and curriculum, see Anthony Kenny and Jan Pinborg, "Medieval Philosophical Literature," in *The Cambridge History of Later Medieval Philosophy* (Cambridge, 1982), pp. 21-29.

[4] The controversial passage, based on Ibn al-ʿArabī's interpretation of Qur'ān 10:90, occurs in his *Fuṣūs al-ḥikam* (ed. ʿAfīfī), p. 201. Ibn al-ʿArabī's position was defended by Jalāl al-Dīn al-Dawwānī (d. 907/1501) in his *R. fī imān Firʿawn* (Yahuda ms. 2180; see *GAL* II, 282, no. 7; S II, 307); for other treatises, see Mach, #2179-2185. See also the *Mīzān al-ḥaqq fī ikhtiyār al-aḥaqq* of the great Turkish scholar Ḥājjī Khalīfah (d. 1657), (Istanbul, 1286) pp. 60-64; tr. G. Lewis, *The Balance of Truth*, pp. 75-79. I intend to deal with this dispute in a forthcoming article entitled "The Faith of Pharaoh: the History of a Disputed Question in Late Mamluk and Early Ottoman Egypt."

doxy" of the originator of the opinion was also involved; although it should be noted that Ibn al-ʿArabī remained (and remains) a far more controversial figure than al-Ghazālī.[5]

The present debate is distinguished by its longevity as well as by the number of eminent participants it attracted. Leaving aside the authors who merely mention the issue in passing or who refer to it in the course of discussion of other points, we may count some twenty-six active contributors to the dispute. In some cases, to be sure, the contribution amounts to no more than a terse statement of position vis-à-vis the disputed question, but there are also seventeen independent treatises by various authors and several extended discussions in works devoted to other topics.

These contributions fall into two broad divisions. The first represents what we term the major course of the dispute, involving consideration of the question from the viewpoint of traditional scholastic theology. Paramount here is the question of the divine omnipotence, together with the allied questions of divine wisdom and free choice. Authors in this tradition—e.g., Ibn al-Munayyir (#8), al-Biqāʿī (#18), al-Suyūṭī (#26), and al-Samhūdī (#28)—follow a fairly consistent pattern in their discussions: the author ordinarily cites the texts by al-Ghazālī in which the statement occurs; he produces the opinions of various commentators pro and con and affirms or denies them, often having recourse to proof texts from the Qur'ān and *ḥadīth*, or to the pronouncements of oustanding authorities of earlier generations, as well as to logical arguments; in his conclusion, he may invoke al-Ghazālī's eminence as a mystic or, if he is opposed, he may draw attention to al-Ghazālī's reputed unreliability in some discipline such as *ḥadīth*.

This is, of course, a composite description; the order of discussion is anything but invariable. Certain general features are worthy of note. Commentators are careful to furnish a scrupulous account of opposing arguments and objections. This is not

[5] Mr. Michael Albin, Field Director of the Library of Congress, Cairo, informed me in May, 1979, that publication of the critical edition of Ibn al-ʿArabī's *al-Futūḥāt al-makkīyah* had been temporarily halted by the authorities on "religious grounds." I understand that publication has since been resumed.

so much in the interest of objectivity but in order the better to refute such arguments. If anything, we may even suspect that an opposing opinion has often been presented in its strongest form, so that the refutation will appear all the more convincing.

The debate possesses a striking continuity for this reason. The comments of, e.g., Abū Bakr ibn al-ʿArabī, a younger contemporary of al-Ghazālī, are transmitted with unwavering fidelity century after century until the final treatment in the 19th century. This enables us to determine the position of several participants whose comments have not survived in their original form.

The continuity of the debate is due to the fact that each disputant built on the work of his predecessors. In the course of time, more and more opinions had to be assembled and examined, and so the later treatises, especially those of al-Lamaṭī (#36), Murtaḍā al-Zabīdī (#37), and al-Jazā'irī (#38), are in effect histories of the debate as well as active contributions to it. It should not be thought, however, that the course of the debate brought with it a mere accumulation of transmitted opinions; a progressive refinement of certain arguments is at work as well.

Thus, a point that is thrown out seemingly without development by an earlier commentator may be picked up and elaborated with great precision by a later author. We note this, for example, in a point made by al-Yāfiʿī (#12) in the 14th century which al-Samhūdī, in the 16th, will make a bulwark of his defense. Even in the penultimate treatise of the debate, that of al-Jazā'irī, we discover several new developments of old arguments.

The second broad division of the debate is what, for want of a better term, we shall call the "esoteric" tradition of interpretation. This tradition takes its impetus from the espousal of al-Ghazālī's statement by the Ṣūfī mystic Muḥyī al-dīn Ibn al-ʿArabī (although most of the elements on which Ibn al-ʿArabī bases his comments are present in al-Ghazālī's own works). The themes of the *coincidentia oppositorum*, for example, and the covert wisdom discernible in each facet of creation will be important in this tradition.

On occasion we suspect that certain commentators, such as

al-Shaʿrānī (#32), took up the disputed statement merely as part of a more general exposition of the teachings of Ibn al-ʿArabī. It should be noted too that support from such suspect quarters did not make the task of defending al-Ghazālī's orthodoxy any easier for his supporters; in the view of hostile commentators, endorsement of a position by Ibn al-ʿArabī or his followers constituted proof positive of the doctrine's heterodoxy. In turn, it is quite likely that Ibn al-ʿArabī's supporters, in an effort to legitimate their master's views, seize on the passage in order to link him with the prestigious figure of al-Ghazālī.

The esoteric interpretations of the disputed statement arise more from an attempt to gloss al-Ghazālī's or Ibn al-ʿArabī's texts than from the desire to contest rival opinions, and so are not usually offered as theses in a disputation. Nevertheless, these interpretations fueled the larger debate and became incorporated in all later accounts. al-Lamaṭī for one will dismiss all such interpretations as irrelevant; but others, like al-Jazāʾirī, will combine both approaches in their treatises, invoking the mystical theosophy of Ibn al-ʿArabī and the cogent rational arguments of al-Samhūdī in turn in an attempt to defend al-Ghazālī. The convergence of these two traditions occurs in other disputants as well, if to a lesser degree.

Naturally, these two rather broad divisions do not neatly encompass all the participants, nor does every author fit precisely in one or the other group. Furthermore, there are individuals whose participation in the debate cannot be verified directly but who are listed in later accounts. This is the case, for example, with Ibn al-Jawzī (#4), Ibn Qayyim al-Jawzīyah (#10), and Ibn al-Ṣalāḥ al-Shahrazūrī (#6), among others. They are included here for the sake of completeness and also because the very fact of their inclusion by the disputants is itself significant: the name of a famous authority, invoked at a critical juncture, may itself be a weapon of debate. Thus, al-Biqāʿī, in seeking to strengthen his case against al-Ghazālī, will invoke the name of Ibn al-Jawzī, who had earlier criticized al-Ghazālī's untrustworthy use of *ḥadīth*. Other early opponents of al-Ghazālī will also be drawn into the later debate, even if their objections were not to the question at issue but rested on more general grounds. These figures play a posthumous role, as it were, in the development of the debate. al-Ṭurṭūshī (#1) and al-Māzarī (#2) are good examples of this.

## II
## CHRONOLOGICAL LIST OF DISPUTANTS

In the list that follows, an attempt has been made to include all known participants in the debate. Individuals are grouped by century and listed chronologically by death date within each century. The form of the name first listed is that to which reference is made in the texts themselves; fuller names are provided for lesser known figures. Dates of birth and death appear according to the Muslim and Christian calendars after each name. The position taken pro or con the disputed statement is indicated for each participant in the right-hand margin; in some cases, of course, this was not ascertainable.

Our purpose here is to identify each participant as fully but as succinctly as possible, and to indicate the source(s) of their comments, either in their own works or in the citations of later commentators.

In some cases, it seemed desirable to present the opinions of certain participants at greater length, either because they are of paramount importance for the course of the debate, or, conversely, because these opinions are anomalous and not taken up elsewhere. An asterisk is used to identify those authors whose views are discussed in the narrative portion following each section of the list.

The footnotes contain (1) references to the works in which an individual's opinions are cited and to the original source of these opinions, where ascertainable; (2) a summary of the disputant's position, if not treated more fully elsewhere; (3) references to pertinent bio-bibliographical sources where further information may be found, with reference first given to C. Brockelmann's *Geschichte der arabischen Litteratur* (*GAL*). In some cases, brief characterizations of authors, indicating doctrinal affiliations, etc., are also included.

## A. THE 6/12TH CENTURY

| | | |
|---|---|---|
| *1. | Abū al-Walīd al-Ṭurṭūshī (*or*: al-Ṭarṭūshī), i.e. Abū Bakr M.b. al-Walīd b. Khalaf al-Ṭurṭūshī al-Fihrī b.a. Randaqa (451-520 or 525/1059-1126 or 1131).[6] | *contra* |
| *2. | Abū ʿAbd Allāh al-Māzarī, i.e., Abū A. M. b. A. al-Tamīmī al-Imām al-Māzarī (d.536/1141).[7] | *contra* |
| *3. | Abū Bakr Ibn al-ʿArabī, i.e., Abū Bakr M.b. ʿAl. b. A. b. al-ʿArabī al-Andalusī al-Ishbīlī (468-543/1073-1148).[8] | *contra* |
| 4. | Abū al-Faraj Ibn al-Jawzī (508 or 510-597/1116-1200).[9] | *contra* |

### *al-Ṭurṭūshī and al-Māzarī: the Roots of the Opposition*

Both of these authors, younger contemporaries of al-Ghazālī, voice a common objection to his teaching which will resound throughout the debate: al-Ghazālī bases his views on the heretical doctrines of the philosophers—Ibn Sīnā, Abū Ḥayyān al-Tawḥīdī, and the Ikhwān al-ṣafā' are singled out[10]—and on the

[6] al-Ṭurṭūshī (i.e., from Tortosa in Spain) is mentioned as an opponent in *Itḥāf* I, 28-29 and IX, 442. (For the vocalization al-Ṭarṭūshī, see Maqqarī, *Nafḥ al-ṭīb* II, 87; Yāqūt, *Muʿjam al-buldān* III, 529; and Subkī, *Ṭabaqāt* VI, 242, note 1). Cf. also Maqqarī, *Nafḥ*, II, 27; Ibn al-Khaṭīb, *Iḥāṭah*, III, 267; I. Goldziher, *Le livre de Mohammed Ibn Toumert*, p. 37. A recent discussion is: ʿAlī Sāmī al-Nashshār, "Abū Ḥāmid al-Ghazālī wa-muʿāriḍūhu min ahl al-sunnah," *Majallat Kullīyat al-Ādāb* (Baghdad), I (1959), pp. 195-211; for al-Ṭurṭūshī, see p. 199. [*GAL* I, 600; S I, 829; Maqqarī, *Nafḥ*, II, 85-90; Ibn Khallikān, III, 393.]

[7] al-Māzarī (i.e., from Mazara in Sicily) is cited in Subkī, *Ṭabaqāt*, VI, 242ff. and *Itḥāf*, I, 28-29 (following Subkī) and IX, 442; see also al-Nashshār, "Abu Ḥāmid al-Ghazālī . . . ," p. 197ff. [*GAL* S I, 663; Ibn Khallikān, III, 413.]

[8] His comments on the statement were transmitted by ʿAbd Allāh al-Qurṭubī in his *Sharḥ asmā' Allāh al-ḥusnā*, and are cited in *Iḍāḥ*, p. 66; *Dhahab*, p. 473; *Itḥāf*, I, 33 and IX, 442, line 11. See also ʿAmmār Ṭālibī, *Arā' Abī Bakr Ibn al-ʿArabī al-kalāmīyah*; (2 vols.; Algiers, 1974), vol. 2 of which contains an edition of Ibn al-ʿArabi's *al-ʿAwāṣim min al-qawāṣim*. [*GAL* I, 525; S I, 663, 732; Ibn Khallikan, III, 423.]

[9] Cited in opposition in *Tahdīm*, fol. 41a and *Itḥāf*, I, 33 and IX, 442. A work cited as "*Iʿlām*" is said to contain his views, but this is in fact the *Iʿlām ahl ʿālim bi-taḥqīq nāsikh al-ḥadīth wa-mansūkhihi* of his teacher M. b. al-Nāṣir (d. 556/1160); see Bankipore, V, 2, 312 and *GAL* S I, 917 (but cf. al-Ṣafadī, *al-Wāfī*, I, 275). For Ibn al-Jawzī's criticism of al-Ghazālī as a careless transmitter of *ḥadīth*—a common Ḥanbalite accusation—see Goldziher, *Muslim Studies*, II, 146. [*GAL* I, 659; S I, 914; Ibn Khallikān, II, 321.]

[10] *Itḥāf*, IX, 442, line 17ff.

"cryptic utterances" (*rumūz*) of such Ṣūfis as al-Ḥallāj (executed 309/922).[11] al-Māzarī admits that he has not read any of the works by al-Ghazālī that he denounces but has judged them on the basis of students' accounts.[12] al-Ṭurṭūshī, more reasonably, acknowledges al-Ghazālī's preeminence in the various sciences of religion but claims that his conversion ruined him.[13]

Both opponents see in the works written after al-Ghazālī's conversion to Ṣūfism a dangerous and corrupting mixture of mysticism and philososphy. Moreover, al-Ghazālī is seen as a mere dabbler in both disciplines. The charge is, thus, not only that al-Ghazālī attempts to introduce the suspect teachings of Ṣūfis and philosophers into orthodoxy, but that he does so in an inconsistent, irresponsible, and ultimately incompetent manner. Nor was this disapproval voiced only by Mālikī authors, such as al-Ṭurṭūshī and al-Māzarī, who after all had a bone to pick with al-Ghazālī for his attack on the eminence accorded the study of applied jurisprudence (*ʿilm al-furūʿ*);[14] it was voiced as well by the philosophers themselves, and most notably by Ibn Rushd.

al-Ṭurṭūshī, a pupil of Ibn Ḥazm and author of a well-known *Fürstenspiegel* entitled *Sirāj al-mulūk* (written to rival al-Ghazālī's own *Naṣīḥat al-mulūk*),[15] seems to have been the first to hurl this charge.[16] In a (lost) work entitled *Marāqī al-ʿārifīn*, he writes:

> Those who pursue the mystic path incur great injury from the books of this fellow from Ṭūs (*hādha al-rajul al-ṭūsī*). He copies the Ṣūfis but does not adhere to their doctrines; he mixes the doctrines of the philosophers in with their doctrines until people fall into error.

[11] Subkī, *Ṭabaqāt*, VI, 243.

[12] *Itḥāf*, I, 28; Subkī, *Ṭabaqāt*, VI, 240.

[13] *Itḥāf*, I, 29.

[14] On the bitter opposition of the Mālikis to al-Ghazālī's disparagement of the importance accorded the *furūʿ* and the profession of *faqīh*, see Goldziher, *Le livre de Mohammed Ibn Toumert*, p. 27ff.

[15] For this work, written originally in Persian, see Bouyges, no. 47 (pp. 61-63).

[16] He is said to have written a treatise refuting the *Iḥyāʾ*, but the work has not survived; see Goldziher, *Le livre de Mohammed Ibn Toumert*, p. 37.

> But I say that his reach in philosophy was limited and that he copied the *shaykh* Abū ʿAlī Ibn Sīnā in his philosophy, which he transmitted in the *Maqāṣid*; and in his logic, which he transmitted in the *Miʿyār al-ʿilm*; but he [sc. al-Ghazālī] fell short of him.[17]

This charge seems somewhat disingenuous; no mention is made of the *Tahāfut al-falāsifah*, al-Ghazālī's attack on the philosophers. Indeed, the *Maqāṣid* is seen as an attempt to disseminate Ibn Sīnā's thought; such would also be the case in the Latin West, as we have noted. This may be attributable to a popular conception of al-Ghazālī, prevalent at the time, which emphasized a certain inconsistency, if not outright insincerity, on his part. One apocryphal anecdote has him writing the *Maqāṣid* (perceived as a work in favor of philosophy) in the mornings, and the *Tahāfut*, his attack on philosophy, in the evenings.[18]

Lest it be thought that these accusations are merely the indiscriminate outbursts of obscurantists, it should be mentioned that the same suspicion of inconsistency was echoed by members of an opposing camp. No less a figure than the philosopher Ibn Ṭufayl (c. 501-581/1105-1185), in his *Ḥayy ibn Yaqẓān*, declared al-Ghazālī's works "confused" (*muḍṭarib*), and he stated: "In one place he binds and in another looses; he declares some things heretical and then declares them permissible."[19] In the same passage, Ibn Ṭufayl also mentions the rumor that al-Ghazālī authored various esoteric works embodying a secret teaching.[20] This perhaps lent support to the later defense of al-Ghazālī as the master of an esoteric doctrine which placed him above reproof.

Ibn Rushd (520-595/1126-1198), al-Ghazālī's opponent in another, more celebrated debate, presses Ibn Ṭufayl's point with far greater acerbity. In his *Faṣl al-maqāl* he writes: "He does

[17] Cited in Ibn al-Khaṭīb, *Iḥāṭah*, III, 267.

[18] M. Schreiner, "Beiträge zur Geschichte der theologischen Bewegungen im Islam," *ZDMG* 52 (1898), p. 503, citing the Jewish writer Abraham Gavison (d. 1578) of Tlemcen, who recounts the anecdote in his *ʿOmer ha-Shikhḥah*.

[19] *Ḥayy ibn Yaqẓān* (ed. Gauthier), p. 15; cf. also *Iḥāṭah*, III, 265.

[20] *Ibid.*

not adhere to any one way in his books; with the Ashʿarites we see him as an Ashʿarite, with the Muʿtazilites as a Muʿtazilite, with the philosophers as a philosopher, and with the Ṣūfīs as a Ṣūfī."[21] Moreover, even though "he meant nothing but good," al-Ghazālī in fact corrupts the unsophisticated; and, given Ibn Rushd's program to reconcile philosophy and the *sharīʿah*, this is the most serious charge: al-Ghazālī impairs the causes of both religion and philosophy. Thus, he "wanted to increase the number of learned men but in fact he increased the number of the corrupted!"[22] And for this reason, if for no other, says Ibn Rushd, ". . . the *imāms* of the Muslims ought to forbid those of his books which contain learned matter to all save the learned."[23]

In these earliest of al-Ghazālī's opponents we find accusations that will be brought repeatedly: he dabbles in philosophy and mysticism, mingling half-understood precepts from these fields in with acceptable teachings; he is inconsistent in theory and in practice; he blurs the lines of distinctive disciplines, creating dangerous amalgams; he leads the unwary astray.

His Mālikite opponents, like al-Ṭurṭūshī and al-Māzarī, fault his espousal of philosophy and, in particular, his acceptance of Aristotelian logic. Indeed, it will be al-Ghazālī whom the formidable Ḥanbalite master Ibn Taymīyah (d. 728/1327), basing himself on these early critics, will hold responsible for introducing Aristotelian logic into *kalām*.[24] On the other hand, his opponents among the philosophers accuse him of divulging abstruse doctrines to the vulgar and of misinterpreting them to boot.

### *Abū Bakr Ibn al-ʿArabī: "Possibility" vs. "Omnipotence"*

Ibn al-ʿArabī's position is rather more complex. He seems to have believed that al-Ghazālī's motives were sound in attack-

[21] *Faṣl al-maqāl* (ed. Hourani; Leiden, 1959), pp. 27-28; tr. G. Hourani, *Averroes on the Harmony of Religion and Philosophy* (London, 1961), p. 61. See also, *Iḥāṭah*, III, 266.

[22] *Faṣl al-maqāl*, p. 27; tr., p. 61.

[23] *Ibid.* See also, *Iḥāṭah*, III, 266.

[24] Ibn Taymīyah, *Radd ʿalā al-manṭiqīyīn* (Bombay, 1949), p. 15.

ing philosophy but that he then became entangled in the very doctrines he had set out to discredit: "Our *shaykh* Abū Ḥāmid entered deeply into philosophy (*dakhala fī baṭn al-falsafah*); then he wanted to extricate himself but could not."[25]

al-Ghazālī's preferred method of immersing himself in the techniques and terminology of his adversaries the better to refute them may lie at the heart of this charge; certainly his adoption of Aristotelian logic aroused deep suspicion. In the work entitled *al-ʿAwāṣim min al-qawāṣim*, his own attempt at a *destructio philosophorum*, Abū Bakr Ibn al-ʿArabī sought to follow his teacher al-Ghazālī's method without, however, availing himself of any of the philosophers' techniques, such as logic.

Abū Bakr Ibn al-ʿArabī was associated with al-Ṭurṭūshī, referring to him as "my master in asceticism" (*shaykhī fī al-zuhd*);[26] and al-Ṭurṭūshī's disapproval of al-Ghazālī may have influenced the younger man. Nevertheless, he is circumspect and carefully qualifies his rejection of the disputed statement; the deference he felt for his former teacher is apparent here, as it is in fact throughout *al-ʿAwāṣim min al-qawāṣim*.

Thus, in a second comment on the disputed statement he exclaims, "Even though we are a drop in his (al-Ghazālī's) ocean, indeed we oppose him in nothing but this," and he goes on to say, "Praise be to Him who perfected for this our *shaykh* the virtues of created things but then turned him from these clear paths!"[27]

As noted above, however, it is Abū Bakr Ibn al-ʿArabī who introduces the term "omnipotence" (*qudrah*) into the disputed statement, instead of "possibility" (*imkān*), and by so doing sets one of the major themes of the dispute. The belief that al-Ghazālī posed a limit to divine power will underlie the attacks of both Ibn al-Munayyir (#8) and al-Biqāʿī (#18), and will not be clearly corrected until the response of Zakarīyā' al-Anṣārī (#30).

[25] Cited by Ibn Taymīyah, *Bayān muwāfaqat ṣarīḥ al-maʿqūl li-ṣarīḥ al-manqūl*, printed on the margin of *Minhāj al-sunnah al-nabawīyah* (Būlāq, 1321), I, 3.

[26] Abu Bakr ibn al-ʿArabī, *Sirāj al-murīdīn*, fol. 57, cited in Ṭālibī, *Arā' Abī Bakr*, I, 209.

[27] Cited in *Iḍāḥ*, p. 66; *Ḥikmat*, p. 18.

*B. THE 7/13TH CENTURY*

*5. Muḥyī al-dīn Ibn al-ʿArabī (560-638/1165-1240).[28] *pro*
6. Ibn al-Ṣalāḥ al-Shahrazūrī (577-643/1181-1243).[29] *contra*
7. Sharaf al-dīn Ibn al-Tilimsānī (567-644/1172-1246).[30]
*8. Aḥmad ibn al-Munayyir, i.e., A.b.M.b. Manṣūr b. Abī al-Qāsim b. Mukhtār b. AB al-Judhāmī al-Iskandarī (620-683/1223-1284).[31] *contra*

Discussion of the statement in the 13th century takes two opposing directions: the influential Ṣūfī theologian Muḥyī al-dīn Ibn al-ʿArabī enthusiastically endorses it, going so far as to incorporate it (usually without ascription) into his own works; and the Mālikite *qāḍī* Aḥmad Ibn al-Munayyir composes the first thorough and systematic critique of al-Ghazālī's remarks, a critique, moreover, which will provide a foil for the later elaborate justification of theodicy by al-Samhūdī. Ibn al-ʿArabī's espousal of the statement in the light of his own complex mystical system led to the introduction of new and rather idiosyncratic interpretations, most of which will be dismissed as wholly irrelevant by later commentators. Ibn al-Munayyir's attack may be seen, at least in part, as the articulation of earlier objections which often remained inchoate and vague.

*Ibn al-ʿArabī*

Muḥyī al-dīn Ibn al-ʿArabī seems to have been the first to accept the disputed statement without reservation, though he

[28] Cited in al-Shaʿrānī, *Ajwibah*, fol. 126b, line 11, and *al-Yawāqīt wa'l-jawāhir*, I, 34; see also *Itḥāf*, IX, 451ff. and *Ḥikmat*, p. 2. [*GAL* I, 571; S I, 790.]

[29] Cited in *Itḥāf*, IX, 442; probably his rejection of philosophy, and of logic in particular, underlies this ascription. See his *Fatāwā* (Cairo, 1348), esp. p. 35: "*Falsafah* is the basis of stupidity and weakness. . . . Whoever philosophizes has his insight blinded into the manifest merits of the *sharīʿah*"; and his interdict on studying the works of Ibn Sīnā whom he calls (p. 34) "a Satan." See, too, al-Nashshār, "Abū Ḥāmid al-Ghazālī . . .," p. 204ff.; Ṭālibī, *Arā' Abī Bakr*, I, 16. [*GAL* I, 440; S I, 610.]

[30] His position is unknown; cited in *Dhahab*, p. 482; *Itḥāf*, IX, 457; *Ḥikmat*, p. 33. [Kaḥḥālah, VI, 133.]

[31] Cited in *Iḍāh*, *passim*; *Dhahab*, p. 474; *Itḥāf*, I, 33 and IX, 442. [*GAL* I, 529; S I, 738; Kutubī, *Fawāt*, I, 149-150; Suyūṭī, *Bughyat al-wuʿāh*, p. 168; Kaḥḥālah, II, 161-162.]

does so very much for his own purposes. The statement appears in at least five passages of his works; three of these may be found in his vast *al-Futūḥāt al-makkīyah.*

The statement first appears in his work to illustrate the idea, elaborated earlier by Abū Bakr Ibn al-ʿArabī, among others, that the divine attributes are mirrored in the world. That wrath (*ghaḍab*), for example, is attributable to God entails that there exist an object of this wrath; the fact that God is forgiving entails that man commit acts for which forgiveness is requisite (although, to be sure, no responsibility for man's acts redounds to God). Ibn al-ʿArabī cites the *ḥadīth*, "If you did not sin, God would bring forth a people who sin and then seek forgiveness, so that He might forgive them," and he comments.

> He (Muḥammad) points out that everything that occurs in the world is for no other reason than to display the application of a divine name. Since this is so, there does not remain in possibility anything more wonderful than this world, nor more perfect. There remain in possibility only simulacra (*amthāl*), *ad infinitum.*[32]

In a second passage, commenting on the *ḥadīth* "God is beautiful and loves beauty,"[33] Ibn al-ʿArabī introduces the idea of the world as the "mirror of God" (*mir'āt al-ḥaqq*). Every aspect of creation reflects its creator; and since He is supremely beautiful, so, too, are all His "reflections." This interpretation, together with the passage cited earlier, may be understood in the light of Ibn al-ʿArabī's doctrine of creation. Creation for him is a continuous theophany (*tajallin*), in contradistinction to the traditional doctrine of creation *ex nihilo*. There is no "beginning" to creation; it is, rather, an incessant manifestation of divinity.[34] In such a theophany, in which the world itself is God "in some way," though most emphatically not God in another, neither ugliness nor imperfection can be said truly to exist:

> God is the world's creator and the producer of its form, so the world is utterly beautiful; there is nothing ugly in it (*mā fīhi*

[32] *al-Futūḥāt al-makkīyah* (Būlāq, 1293/1876), II, 126, line 19ff.

[33] See, among others, Aḥmad ibn Ḥanbal, *Musnad*, IV, 151.

[34] For a discussion, see H. Corbin, *Creative Imagination in the Ṣūfism of Ibn ʿArabī* (Princeton, 1969), p. 184ff.

> *shay' min al-qubḥ*). God combined in it all excellence and beauty so there is not in possibility more beautiful, more wonderful, and more excellent than the world.[35]

Ibn al-ʿArabī goes on to reiterate the notion that there exist in possibility no possibilities that have not been already realized: "Were He to create what He created to infinity, it would be like what He has (already) created, because the divine beauty and excellence are encompassed and manifested in it. . . . Were anything lacking from it, it would fall from the level of perfection He created and be ugly."[36] The act of creation entails a ceaseless self-manifestation within creation; and this is why we may say that God has produced an unsurpassably beautiful world: it reflects the consummate realization of all His attributes.

This is made more explicit in the relevant passage from the *Fuṣūṣ al-ḥikam* where creation is envisaged as God's "outward form":

> There is nothing in possibility more wonderful than this world because it is in the form of the Merciful. God produced it, i.e., He manifested His existence in manifesting the world, just as man is manifested through the existence of his natural form. For we are His outward form, and His essential nature (*huwīyah*) is the spirit of this form which it directs.[37]

Just as man's spirit animates the body that manifests his existence, so, too, does God's spirit animate and direct the visible creation which is, as it were, His body.

This leads us to Ibn al-ʿArabī's third usage of the disputed statement in the *Futūḥāt*, where it will be applied to the "perfect

[35] *al-Futūḥāt al-makkīyah*, III, 586, line 11ff.

[36] *Ibid.* The strange statement that there is no ugliness in creation is explained as follows by Ibn al-ʿArabī's later commentator ʿAbd al-Karīm al-Jīlī (#16 below): "Ugliness exists in the world only relatively. The judgment of absolute ugliness in existence is to be denied; there remains only absolute beauty. Don't you see that the ugliness of sins is manifest only in relation to their prohibition, and the ugliness of a stinking smell is so only relative to one whose nature is not attuned to it? . . . Don't you see that being burnt by fire is ugly only in relation to him who perishes or is injured by it, whereas for the salamander, it is extremely beautiful?" *al-Insān al-Kāmil* (Cairo, 1328), I, 53.

[37] *Fuṣūṣ al-ḥikam*, p. 172; cf. the recent translation by R.W.J. Austin, *The Bezels of Wisdom* (Ramsey, NJ, 1980), p. 215, which misinterprets the passage, in my opinion. See also the comment by Muṣṭafā Bālī-zādeh (d. 1658), where "outward form" is interpreted as the *sharīʿah*, *K. sharḥ Fuṣūṣ al-ḥikam* (s.1., 1309/1891), p. 330.

man" (*al-ʿabd al-kāmil*). The perfect man is "the most perfect manifestation, than which nothing is more perfect. Concerning him, Abū Ḥāmid (al-Ghazālī) states, 'There is not in possibility more wonderful than this world,' because of the perfected existence of all realities within it."[38]

The "perfect man" is first and foremost the prophet Muḥammad himself, who, as ʿAbd al-Karīm al-Jīlī remarks, stands in relation to the saints and other prophets as "the most perfect" in relation to the merely perfect.[39] But it may also be understood as applying to man himself, as a kind of mystical prototype. In an early work entitled *Kitāb al-tadbīrāt al-ilāhīyah fī iṣlāḥ al-mamlakah al-insānīyah*, Ibn al-ʿArabī again introduces the disputed statement in a way that may help us to understand his seemingly capricious application of it.

Thus, man, because of his "elevated rank" over all other animals, is an epitome (*mukhtaṣar*) of the cosmos, and "nothing remains in possibility that has not been lodged in him . . . so that he appears in the utmost perfection."[40] Man is perfect because "there is in existence no miserliness" nor is there defect in the divine power; and it is for this reason that "one of the *imāms*" says, "There is nothing more wonderful than this world in possibility."[41]

"This world," then, is taken to apply to the "little world" (*al-ʿālam al-ṣaghīr*), or microcosm, known as man.[42] The world is a

[38] *al-Futūḥāt al-makkīyah*, II, 136.

[39] *al-Insān al-kāmil*, II, 44. al-Jīlī is the most famous proponent of the "perfect man," an important notion in Ṣūfī theosophy; cf. also the work of the 13th-century Persian mystic ʿAzīz al-Dīn Nasafī, *K. al-insān al-kāmil* (ed. Molé; Tehran, 1962). For discussions, see R. A. Nicholson, *Studies in Islamic Mysticism*, pp. 77-162, and the same author's brief discussion in "A Moslem Philosophy of Religion," *Le Muséon* 1 (3d series; 1915), pp. 83-87; the most comprehensive treatment is H. H. Schaeder, "Die islamische Lehre vom Vollkommenen Menschen," *ZDMG* 79 (1925), pp. 192-268.

[40] *K. al-tadbīrāt*, ed. H. Nyberg in *Kleinere Schriften des Ibn al-ʿArabī* (Leiden, 1919), p. 106.

[41] *Ibid.*

[42] The idea of the microcosm is commonplace in Islamic thought and derives from classical antiquity. See, e.g., the Arabic translation of pseudo-Galen, ed. and tr. by G. Bergsträsser as *Pseudo-Galeni in Hippocratis de Septimanis commentarium* (Corpus medicorum graecorum, XI, 2, 1; Leipzig, 1914), p. 4: "Galen says that Hippocrates compared man to the world and called him a little world," and *passim*. A. Götze argued for an Iranian origin of this notion; see his "Per-

"divine copy" (*nuskhah ilāhīyah*) and is "correct": it is lacking in neither "letter nor meaning," and man, the microcosm, a perfected mirror of that world which is itself the "mirror of God," is by extension equally perfect.[43]

*Aḥmad Ibn al-Munayyir*

With the work of Aḥmad Ibn al-Munayyir we come to the earliest systematic critique of the disputed statement. An expert in many disciplines, including grammar, rhetoric, Qur'ān commentary, and jurisprudence, Ibn al-Munayyir served as Mālikite *qāḍī* in Alexandria. From one biographical account we learn that he intended to write a refutation of the entire *Iḥyā'*, but was dissuaded by the opposition of his mother, who exclaimed, "You finish contending with the living and you begin to contend with the dead!"[44]

The treatise which Ibn al-Munayyir did write, but which has apparently not survived, addressed itself wholly to our disputed statement and was entitled *al-Ḍiyā' al-mutala'li' fī ta'aqqub al-Iḥyā' lil-Ghazālī*.[45] Luckily, it is possible to reconstruct the contents of this work from the formidable response written by al-Samhūdī in the 16th century. What follows here is an outline of Ibn al-Munayyir's main points, as cited or paraphrased in al-Samhūdī's *Iḍāḥ al-bayān*:

*Khuṭbat al-risālah* (*Iḍāḥ*, p. 137, lines 16-20): In several pas-

---

sische Weisheit in griechischem Gewande. Ein Beitrag zur Geschichte de Mikrokosmos-Idee," *Zeitschrift für Indologie und Iranistik* 2 (1923), pp. 60-98.

For Islamic discussions, see, among others, Jāḥiẓ, *K. al-ḥayawān*, I, 212ff.; al-Baghdādī, *Uṣūl al-dīn*, pp. 34-35; al-Bayḍāwī, *Anwār al-tanzīl*, I, 6; Nasafī, *K. al-insān al-kāmil*, p. 142ff.; and Afẓal al-Dīn M. Maraqī Kāshānī, *Jāvidān-nāmah*, in *Muṣannafāt* (ed. Mīnūvī; Tehran, 1331), I, 274ff. For a general treatment, see S.H. Nasr, *An Introduction to Islamic Cosmological Doctrines* (rev. ed.; London, 1978), pp. 96-104.

For a witty *reductio ad absurdum* of the whole idea, see the early work of Ludwig Feuerbach (1804-1872), entitled *Gedanken über Tod und Unsterblichkeit* (1830) in his *Werke* (Frankfurt, 1975), I, 140-143. Finally, there is an interesting discussion of the subject in K.A.H. Hidding, "Der Hochgott und der mikrokosmische Mensch," *Numen* 18 (1971), pp. 94-102.

[43] *K. al-tadbīrāt*, p. 109.

[44] al-Suyūṭī, *Bughyat al-wu'āh* (Cairo, 1326), p. 168; the story turns on the verbal play between *Iḥyā'* and *aḥyā'* ("living"), and is meant to illustrate Ibn al-Munayyir's contentious temperament.

[45] So, e.g., in *Itḥāf*, I, 33, among others.

sages of the *Iḥyā'*, al-Ghazālī states that disclosure of the secret of predestination is *kufr*, but he then proceeds to disclose it. Thus, he not only contradicts himself; he is guilty of *kufr* as well.

(1) *First Precept* (*qā'idah*) (*Iḍāḥ*, p. 79, lines 10-13): Against the implication that God could be termed miserly if He had created less than the most perfect. Non-generosity (*'adam al-jūd*) is mere negation; it does not occur because there is in generosity some attribute subsisting in God's nature. Generosity is rather an attribute of action (not, that is, an "essential" attribute). How, then, may its absence entail the attribute of "stinginess?"

(2) *Second Precept* (*Iḍāḥ*, p. 79, lines 10-13): There is no opposition (*taḍādd*) between generosity and miserliness, nor between justice and injustice. Logical opposition occurs only when qualities within a genus are concerned, e.g., blackness and whiteness. Miserliness and injustice, however, are merely legal judgments, and so too are justice and generosity. The law can declare miserliness good and generosity bad.

(3) *Third Precept (Iḍāḥ*, p. 80, line 3): al-Ghazālī's declaration that the creation of other than the perfect is impossible is based on the fact that otherwise it would be necessary to designate God miserly; i.e., al-Ghazālī claims that creation is perfect not because it truly is so but because if he did not he would feel compelled to term God miserly. In other words, his claim is little more than a *pia fraus*.

(4) *Fourth Precept* (*Iḍāḥ*, p. 125, *paen.*—p. 126, line 5): The conventional notion that incapacity (*'ajz*) is lack of power (*'adam al-qudrah*) is erroneous: a stone has no power, but it is not termed "incapable." The eternal power stands in no nexus to the impossible, but this is not incapacity. (This point is raised in opposition to the phrase in the *Iḥyā'* passage, "If there were (a more wonderful world possible) and He did not produce it . . .").

(5) *Fifth Precept* (*Iḍāḥ*, p. 97, *ult.*—p. 98, line 3): al-Ghazālī's statement is consistent with the doctrines of the philosophers who claim that God creates *per necessitatem naturae* (*bi-ījāb dhātī*), i.e., that He cannot by His very nature create anything

but the best. (Ibn al-Munayyir repeats this charge in the *khātimah* of his treatise as well.)

(6) *Sixth Precept* (*Iḍāḥ*, p. 106, line 14; p. 124, line 17): Other than what is known (*khilāf al-maʿlūm*) is possible, contrary to the implications of the disputed statement.

(7) *Seventh Precept* (*Iḍāḥ*, p. 85, line 10): al-Ghazālī reveals himself in this statement as an adherent of the Muʿtazilite doctrine of "the optimum" (*al-aṣlaḥ*).

(8) *Eighth Precept* (*Iḍāḥ*, p. 112, line 11; p. 124, line 10): al-Ghazālī limits divine omnipotence. But how can we accept a divine power restricted to, e.g., a number that cannot be exceeded or a limit that cannot be surpassed?

Such is the bare outline of Ibn al-Munayyir's treatise. We shall consider some of his major arguments more fully in later chapters. With his treatise the debate proper begins. All later disputants will have to confront one or another of his eight points.

## *C. THE 8/14TH CENTURY*

9. al-Ḥāfiẓ al-Dhahabī, i.e., Abū ʿAlī b. Qāymāz Shams al-dīn al-Dhahabī (673-748/1274-1348).[46]
10. Ibn Qayyim al-Jawzīyah (691-751/1292-1350).[47]
11. Taqī al-dīn al-Subkī (683-756/1284-1355).[48] *pro*

*12. Abū M. ʿAl. b. Asʿad al-Yāfiʿī (698-768/1298-1367).[49] *pro*

13. ʿAbd al-Wahhāb b. ʿA. Tāj al-dīn al-Subkī al-Shāfiʿī (727-771/1327-1370).[50] *pro*

[46] Cited in *Itḥāf*, I, 33 and IX, 442, as providing a summary of the dispute in his monumental *Taʾrīkh al-Islām*. [*GAL* II, 57; S II, 45.]

[47] Cited in *Itḥāf*, IX, 442. This famous disciple of Ibn Taymīyah is probably cited for his more general opposition to al-Ghazālī's use of logic [*GAL* II, 127; S II, 126.]

[48] Cited in *Itḥāf*, IX, 442 and 447. He apparently defended al-Ghazālī on the ground that the remark was interpolated. [*GAL* II, 106; S I, 680.]

[49] His comments appear in his *Marham al-ʿilal al-muʿḍilah* (ed. Ross), pp. 17-20. [*GAL* II, 226; S II, 227; Subkī, *Ṭabaqāt*, X, 33; Taşköprüzāde, *Miftāḥ al-saʿādah*, I, 217; *EI*[1], IV, 1144-1145.]

[50] al-Subkī does not discuss the disputed question as such, but provides an account of the general objections of al-Ṭurṭūshī and al-Māzarī in his *Ṭabaqāt al-Shāfiʿīyah al-kubrā* (Cairo, 1964-76), VI, 240ff.

14. Yūsuf al-Dimashqī, i.e., ʿAbd al-Wahhāb b. Yūsuf b. Ibrāhīm al-Dimashqī (698-782/1299-1380).[51]

*15. Badr al-dīn M. b. Bahādur al-Zarkashī (745-794/1344-1392).[52] *pro*

During the 14th century, discussion of the statement is limited to passing references or to rather brief and sometimes fragmentary paraphrases of earlier interpretations. However, certain of the arguments advanced will play an important role in later stages of the debate, and so deserve mention.

*al-Yāfiʿī*

The Yemenite author al-Yāfiʿī offers a succinct defense of al-Ghazālī in his anti-Muʿtazilite treatise *Marham al-ʿilal al-muʿḍilah*. Although he is cited by name in none of the later accounts—even the well-nigh exhaustive account of Murtaḍā al-Zabīdī fails to include him—his arguments illustrate lines of defense that were to be taken increasingly in following centuries.

His first argument is the familiar one that the creation is a sign of its creator; and a defective creation betokens a deficient creator. Those who oppose al-Ghazālī are forced to the conclusion that this creation is inferior to a more perfect possible creation; and they thereby impute deficiency to the creator.[53]

On the contrary, argues al-Yāfiʿī, this creation is indeed most wonderful. The existence of something more wonderful than the most wonderful is impossible (*wujūd abdaʿ min al-abdaʿ muḥāl*). Therefore, the existence of a world more wonderful than this is impossible.[54]

Secondly, to the objection that this view entails a restriction on omnipotence, al-Yāfiʿī replies that there is no nexus (*taʿalluq*) between omnipotence and the impossible.[55] This is a point that

[51] Cited in *Itḥāf*, IX, 442; his position is unknown. [Kaḥḥālah, VI, 231.]

[52] Cited in *Dhahab*, pp. 474 and 478; Suyūṭī, *Tashyīd*, fol. 6b; *Itḥāf*, IX, 447 and 452; *Ḥikmat*, pp. 19 and 25-26. [*GAL* II, 112; S II, 108; Ibn Ḥajar al-ʿAsqalānī, *al-Durar al-kāminah*, III, 397; Ibn al-ʿImād, *Shadharāt al-dhahab*, VI, 335.

[53] *Marham al-ʿilal*, p. 17: *kamāl al-ṣanʿah yadullu ʿalā kamāl al-ṣāniʿ waʾl-naqṣ ʿalā al-naqṣ*.

[54] *Ibid.*

[55] *Ibid.* This point will be discussed more fully in Chapter Three below; for a

will play an important part in the later debate, especially in al-Samhūdī's work.

Finally, al-Yāfiʿī offers a lengthy inventory of creation in terms of the *coincidentia oppositorum*. In this world, there exist "instances of wisdom" (*ḥikam*), the hidden splendors of which are superior to the outwardly manifest splendors. Human intellects perceive merely the least of these hidden splendors (*al-maḥāsin al-bāṭinah*). Ordinary vision (*baṣar*) is inadequate; insight (*baṣīrah*) is required. But whoever, like al-Ghazālī, attains this insight realizes that all opposing aspects of existence necessarily coexist and conceal hidden beauty. Here al-Yāfiʿī inserts a long list of such opposites, ranging from predictable pairs such as good/evil, rich/poor, beautiful/ugly, etc., to clarity/turbidity, roughness/smoothness, the fragrant/the stinking, and, in fact, all the various orders of existence: inanimate matter, animals, men, *jinns*, angels, and devils. Each thing contains its own mystic wisdom; thus, certain plants are toxic or contain medicinal properties; jewels possess magical effects, etc.[56] The occult and the commonplace exist side-by-side. Nothing may be disregarded or dismissed.

These are themes that we have already encountered, and they will recur. The conviction that such authorities as al-Ghazālī are endowed with a spiritual perspicacity enabling them to discern hidden properties in all aspects of creation pervades the defenses of al-Samhūdī, Murtaḍā al-Zabīdī, and al-Jazāʾirī.

### *Badr al-dīn al-Zarkashī*

Testimony concerning the position of this disputant is somewhat confusing. He is said to have considered the statement interpolated into al-Ghazālī's works,[57] and yet he offers several arguments in defense of it.[58]

al-Zarkashī is often cited as having held that the disputed

---

brief treatment in another context, see T. Izutsu, "Creation and the Timeless Order of Things," *The Philosophical Forum*, 4 (1972), p. 129ff.

[56] *Marham al-ʿilal*, pp. 18-19.

[57] In *Itḥāf*, IX, 447, he is listed among proponents of interpolation.

[58] al-Zarkashī's comments are said to appear in his "*Tadhkirah*," a work I have been unable to identify.

statement is one of those "barren sayings" (*al-kalimat al-ʿuqum*) which ought not be applied to the creator; and, furthermore, as having suggested that al-Ghazālī intended by it nothing more than a glorification of the creator's handiwork.[59]

Elsewhere, it is reported, al-Zarkashī follows Ibn al-ʿArabī in applying the statement to man "because he contains the principles of all the species in existence" and is himself "the farthest possibility" (*ghāyat al-mumkin*).[60] Man, however, represents the utmost possibility only in this world; in the hidden realm of God the principles of existence are boundless and marvels are inexhaustible.

The disputed statement then applies only to this world and is true only because human perception is limited:

> The mystic's judgment is to the measure of his perception (*idrāk*), not to the measure of God's judgments. God comprehends everything; but no one can comprehend a single one of his species in every way.[61]

This goes back, of course, to the line of reasoning in Abū Ṭālib al-Makkī's *Qūt al-qulūb*. As a possible interpretation of al-Ghazālī's position it will not gain credence with later commentators; and al-Lamaṭī, in particular, will single it out for attack.[62]

### *D. THE 9/15TH CENTURY*

*16. ʿAbd al-Karīm al-Jīlī (765-832/1365-1428).[63] *pro*

*17. Abū al-Mawāhib al-Tūnisī (d.850/1446).[64] *pro*

[59] *Tashyīd*, fol. 6a; *Dhahab*, p. 474; *Itḥāf*, IX, 452.

[60] *Tashyīd*, fol. 6a; in *Itḥāf*, IX, 452, al-Zarkashī is said to have based this on *Qur*. 16:8 ("He creates what you do not know"), since "man is the most wonderful thing we know God to have created."

[61] *Tashyīd*, fol. 6a; *Ḥikmat*, p. 25.

[62] *Dhahab*, p. 478.

[63] Cited in al-Shaʿrānī, *al-Ajwibah*, fol. 126b; *Dhahab*, p. 476; *Itḥāf*, IX, 453, lines 13-28; *Ḥikmat*, p. 22. [*GAL* II, 264; S II, 283; *EI*², I, 71; and see above, notes 36 and 39.]

[64] Cited in *Dhahab*, p. 480; *Itḥāf*, IX, 457; *Ḥikmat*, p. 30. [Kaḥḥālah, IX, 142.]

*18. Ibrāhīm b. ʿUmar Burhān al-dīn al-Biqāʿī (809-885/1404-1480).[65] *contra*
19. M. b. Ḥāmid al-Shāfiʿī (fl. 885/1480).[66] *pro*
*20. Muḥammad b. ʿAbd al-Raḥmān Jalāl al-dīn al-Bakrī (807-891/1404-1486).[67] *pro*
21. Burhān al-dīn al-Anṣārī al-Khalīlī.[68]
22. ʿAbd al-Raḥmān b. M. b. Ḥājjī b. Faḍl al-Zayn al-Santawī (827-896/1421-1490).[69] *pro*
23. A. b. Zarrūq al-Burnusī al-Fāsī (846-899/1442-1493).[70] *pro*
24. Badr al-dīn al-Saʿdī al-Ḥanbalī (d. 900/1495).[71] *contra*

[65] *Tashyīd*, fol. 1b; Ibn Ḥajar al-Haythamī, *Fatāwā* (Cairo, 1937), p. 47; *Itḥāf*, I, 33 and IX, 442-444, 447, 449. [*GAL* II, 179; S II, 177; Sakhāwī, *Ḍaw'*, I, 101-111; al-Suyūṭī, *al-Taḥadduth*, p. 187; Ismāʿīl Pasha al-Baghdādī, *Hadīyat al-ʿārifīn* (Istanbul, 1951), pp. 21-22; F. Rosenthal, *History of Muslim Historiography*, p. 107.]

[66] Author of the treatise *al-Dalīl wa'l-burhān ʿalā annahu laysa fi'l-imkān abdaʿ mimmā kān*, Yahuda ms. 598 (Mach 3027).

[67] Cited in *Dhahab*, p. 477; *Itḥāf*, I, 33 and IX, 458; *Ḥikmat*, p. 25. Jalāl al-Bakrī was al-Suyūṭī's predecessor as *shaykh* of the Baybarsīyah, the Ṣūfī *khānqāh*, and held this post until his death; see Sartain, *Jalāl al-Dīn al-Suyūṭī*, I, 45. [Sakhāwī, *Ḍaw'*, VII, 284; Kaḥḥālah, X, 134; Ziriklī, VI, 194.]

[68] Author of a brief treatise entitled *R. fī "Laysa fi'l-imkān abdaʿ mimmā kān"* which is in the Raza Library, Rampur; according to the *Catalogue* (IV, 38), the treatise was in response to a question by Zayn al-dīn ʿAbd al-Raḥīm b. Ibrāhīm al-Abnāsī (d. 891/1486), hence its placement here in the 9/15th century. I am grateful to Prof. R. Mach for this reference.

[69] Author of the treatise *al-Sayf al-ḥusām fī al-dhabb ʿan kalām Ḥujjat al-Islām*, Yahuda ms. 2249 (Mach 3028), fol. 1b-20b. On fol. 11b, al-Santawī explains that a friend requested him to write on this subject, but he left the matter to God; then, in a dream, he beheld someone reciting *ḥadīth* incorrectly and when he awoke, the interpretation of the disputed statement was clear. He knew that "those who attack al-Ghazālī distort his meaning. And at this, God opened my heart . . . and so, I drew the sword" (*salattu al-ḥusām*). [Sakhāwī, *Ḍaw'*, IV, 127-128.]

[70] His comments are in his *Sharḥ ʿAqīdat al-Ghazālī*, printed on the margin of ʿAbd al-Qādir al-Fākihī's *al-Kifāyah fī sharḥ Bidāyat al-hidāyah* (Cairo, 1296). Cited in *Dhahab*, p. 478; *Itḥāf*, IX, 458; *Ḥikmat*, p. 27. [*GAL* II, 328; S II, 360; Sakhāwī, *Ḍaw'*, I, 222; Ibn Maryam, *al-Bustān fī dhikr al-awliyā' wa'l-ʿulamā' bi-Tilimsān* (Algiers, 1326/1908), pp. 45-50; Kaḥḥālah, I, 155; Ziriklī, I, 91; see also ʿAl. Gannūn, *Aḥmad Zarrūq* (Tetuan, 1954) and A. Khushaim, *Zarrūq the Ṣūfī* (Tripoli, 1976).]

[71] Author of the (untitled) treatise, Yahuda ms. 3166 (Mach 3029), "*Jawāb su'āl ʿan qawl al-Ghazālī. . . .*" He sides with al-Biqāʿī (#18) on the disputed question.

During the 15th and 16th centuries, the dispute reaches its high point and becomes a public issue. Many leading figures are drawn into the controversy; numerous treatises are composed; the statement joins the roster of disputed questions which occupied the attention of the *ʿulamāʾ* in late Mamluk and early Ottoman Egypt, where the debate now chiefly flourishes.

Experts were commonly requested to formulate opinions on such troublesome points and their opinions were then subject to attack by rival experts. These attacks in turn engendered further opinions pro or con. In the present instance, the opinion of al-Biqāʿī spawned several dissenting opinions, almost unanimously opposed to his; indeed, the intensity of the dispute in this period was largely the result of his powerful, if unbalanced, attack on al-Ghazālī.

*ʿAbd al-Karīm al-Jīlī*

al-Jīlī accepts the disputed statement on the following grounds:

> God's eternal knowledge precedes every actually existing thing (*kull wāqiʿ fi'l-wujūd*); hence, it is not possible that it rise above its level in the divine knowledge, or descend below it. So the *imām*'s remark is valid: "There is not in possibility more wonderful than what is."[72]

The idea that God's prior knowledge necessitates the existence of things as they are will be important in the later discussions. Here, al-Jīlī, following Ibn al-ʿArabī, notes that existence occurs on one of two levels: the level of primordial eternity (*qidam*), which is exclusively God's, and the level of things created in time (*ḥudūth*). Of temporally created things, each occupies a level assigned to it in God's prior knowledge and cannot either rise above or sink below this level, for that would imply some defect in omniscience.

*Abū al-Mawāhib al-Tūnisī*

al-Tūnisī, author of a commentary on the *Ḥikam* of the Ṣūfī Ibn ʿAṭāʾ Allāh, advances the viewpoint that al-Ghazālī's

[72] Cited in *Itḥāf*, IX, 453, line 13ff.

statement refers, not to the "possibility of divine omnipotence," but to the "possibility of divine wisdom" (*imkān al-ḥikmah al-ilāhīyah*).[73] In other words, what actually exists is a manifestation of the full extent of God's wisdom, but not of His power, which is unlimited.

Critics will be quick to point out that such a solution saves omnipotence at the expense of wisdom; and limitations on the divine wisdom are equally to be eschewed.

*Ibrāhīm Ibn ʿUmar al-Biqāʿī*

al-Biqāʿī, a Shāfiʿite scholar well known for his writings on *ḥadīth*, Qur'ān commentary, and history, composed two treatises attacking al-Ghazālī's remarks.

The first is entitled *Tahdīm al-arkān min "Laysa fi'l-imkān abdaʿ mimmā kān"* and, to judge from the responses of his opponents, who cite it repeatedly, is the more important of his two works on the subject.[74]

The second work is entitled *Dalālat al-burhān ʿalā anna al-imkān abdaʿ mimmā kān*; it appears to be in the main a recapitulation of the *Tahdīm*.[75]

al-Biqāʿī's method of attack in the *Tahdīm* is two-pronged: he begins by attempting to discredit al-Ghazālī, both for his reputed weakness in *ḥadīth* and for his approval of disputed practices, such as the supererogatory community prayers of the first Friday in the month of Rajab (*ṣalāt al-raghā'ib*).[76] He then launches his attack proper on the statement itself. al-Biqāʿī employs what might be termed a "common sense" approach to the question. The world, as anyone can see, is patently imperfect; numerous examples of this imperfection can be adduced. al-Biqāʿī proceeds to list example after example of such manifest imper-

[73] Cited in *Itḥāf*, IX, 457, *paen.*

[74] I have used the Garrett ms. 464H (Hitti 798); there is also a ms. in the Yale University Library (vol. L156; Nemoy 1401).

[75] There is a copy of this work in the State Central Library, Hyderabad, but I have been unable to obtain a microfilm, despite the kind efforts of Mr. Y. Lakshman Rao, the librarian (see Āṣafīyah, II, 1304, 109).

[76] On this question, see Ḥājjī Khalīfah, *Mīzān al-ḥaqq*, pp. 81-86; tr. pp. 97-100; and also M. J. Kister, " '*Rajab* is the Month of God . . .' A Study in the Persistence of an early Tradition," *Israel Oriental Studies* 1 (1971), pp. 191-223.

fections and deficiencies in order to demonstrate that almost anything in creation could have been otherwise, and indeed would have been markedly improved by being otherwise. His arguments form a curious reversal of the notion of the wisdom hidden in creation so dear to al-Ghazālī and his defenders.

al-Biqāʿī's object in this is not to arraign the divine wisdom; rather, he wishes above all to uphold the illimitable omnipotence of the creator. This world, such as it is, simply cannot be the full manifestation of that infinite power. If the world is a "sign" for al-Biqāʿī, as it so clearly is for al-Ghazālī and his followers, it is a sign of what God could have done, had He so willed; its glaring imperfection proclaims how little the world may be taken as a reflection of the divine power. In his zeal to preserve this power, al-Biqāʿī seems to be hurling a jeremiad at creation, but this is far from his true purpose, which is rather to assail the complacent optimism that discovers "God's purpose" in every aspect of existence.

These arguments will be treated in greater detail in the following chapter. Here let us note that they do not themselves seem to have been the only catalyst for the outrage which engulfed al-Biqāʿī. The public hue and cry, which kept him a prisoner for some time in his own house (and which may account for the opprobrium in which certain of his contemporaries held him)[77] arose more from the object of his attack—the "Proof of Islam," al-Ghazālī, deemed by many the "renewer" (*mujaddid*) of religion in his own time—than from his actual arguments. al-Biqāʿī's disrespectful tone could not have helped matters, in any case.

It is a strange fact that whereas many, if not most, of the contemporary defenses of al-Ghazālī were provoked by al-Biqāʿī's onslaught, the points which he raised would excite little comment in later discussions.[78] al-Samhūdī, for example, although

[77] For an example of this, see the hostile biography by al-Sakhāwī (known, to be sure, for his spiteful treatment of contemporaries), *Ḍaw'*, I, 101ff., and the verses quoted, with evident relish, on p. 105: "Were al-Biqāʿī, loathsome in his indecency and deceit, / His absurdity and his recalcitrance, to say: 'The sun appears in the sky,' / Intelligent men would give him no credence." But cf. the rather laudatory account in al-Suyūṭī's *Naẓm al-ʿiqyān* (ed. Ḥittī), pp. 24-25.

[78] The treatises of al-Santawī, al-Saʿdī al-Ḥanbalī, Ḥāmid al-Shāfiʿī, and al-Suyūṭī, among others, were responses to al-Biqāʿī.

he mentions al-Biqāʿī disparagingly, disdains to address his arguments; and al-Jazāʾirī, in the 19th century, fails even to include al-Biqāʿī in his list of participants.

al-Biqāʿī's attack was not as perverse as it might seem. Disputes had raged among the *ʿulamāʾ* over the degree of orthodoxy of various controversial figures, chief among whom were Muḥyī al-dīn Ibn al-ʿArabī and the mystical poet Ibn al-Fāriḍ (d. 632/1235);[79] and charges of "disbelief" (*kufr*) were rather freely hurled. Moreover, the obstreporous and often insulting tone which al-Biqāʿī adopts was common to such disputes. According to E. M. Sartain:

> Disputes between scholars over such problems caused great animosity, and the participants were often incredibly intolerant of any view which differed from their own. Shams al-dīn al-Bānī was always prescribing punishment . . . for those who opposed him . . . and al-Suyūṭī himself had a tendency to accuse people of unbelief (*kufr*), for which the penalty was death. While these pronouncements infuriated those they were aimed at, there does not seem to have been much danger of such punishments being carried out. Each scholar wrote his little pamphlets to defend his own opinions and refute his opponent's, and factions supporting rival sides would be formed.[80]

No supporting faction would embrace al-Biqāʿī's position. Others would oppose the disputed statement, but none would throw in his lot wholeheartedly with al-Biqāʿī in an unbridled attack. It was clearly one thing to assail suspect figures, such as Ibn al-ʿArabī (as indeed al-Biqāʿī did in one of his other works),[81] and quite another to attack such a venerated and even sacrosanct figure as al-Ghazālī.

### *Jalāl al-dīn al-Bakrī*

al-Bakrī, an Egyptian jurisprudent and later *qāḍī* of Alexandria, advances what may perhaps be termed the "funda-

[79] For a brief account of these disputes, see Sartain, *Jalāl al-Dīn al-Suyūṭī*, I, 54-55.

[80] *Jalāl al-Dīn al-Suyūṭī*, I, 131. For vivid examples of typical acrimonious exchanges and repartee in an earlier period, see G. Makdisi, *The Rise of Colleges*, pp. 134-140.

[81] In his *Maṣraʿ al-taṣawwuf* (ed. ʿAbd al-Raḥmān al-Wakīl; Cairo, 1372/1953).

mentalist" argument: creation of a more wonderful world is impossible because Qur'ān and *sunnah* do not mention such a possibility. "If it were possible, the Qur'ān would mention it. God says, 'We have not neglected anything in the Book' (*Qur*. 6:38). The *sunnah* does not mention it; if it had, the *'ulamā'* would have said so. . . ."[82]

As might be expected, this argument will be easily countered with opposing proof-verses.

## *E. THE 10/16TH CENTURY*

| | | |
|---|---|---|
| 25. | Abū ʿAbd Allāh M. b. ʿUmar al-Maghribī al-Shādhilī (d. 910/1500).[83] | *pro* |
| 26. | Jalāl al-dīn al-Suyūṭī (849-911/1445-1505).[84] | *pro* |
| 27. | Kamāl al-dīn Ibn Abī Sharīf (d. 906/1500 or 1501).[85] | *contra* |
| *28. | al-Sayyid al-Samhūdī, i.e., Nūr al-dīn Abū al-Ḥasan A.b. ʿAl. al-Samhūdī al-Shāfiʿī (844-911/1440-1505 or 1506).[86] | *pro* |
| 29. | Burhān al-dīn Ibrāhīm Ibn Abī Sharīf (d. 921/1516).[87] | *pro* |

[82] Cited in *Dhahab*, p. 477; *Itḥāf*, IX, 458; *Ḥikmat*, p. 25.

[83] al-Suyūṭī's *shaykh* in his Ṣūfī instruction, he follows the interpretation of al-Tūnisī that the statement applies to divine wisdom: in God's realm the more wonderful is possible. Cited in *Itḥāf*, IX, 454, line 5ff.; *Ḥikmat*, p. 23; see also al-Shaʿrānī, *al-Ṭabaqāt al-kubrā* (Cairo, 1954), II, 116, for a further reference to his opinion.

[84] al-Suyūṭī's treatise is entitled *Tashyīd al-arkān min "Laysa fi'l-imkān abdaʿ mimmā kān,"* Yahuda ms. 303 (Mach 3030). Cited in *Dhahab*, p. 482; *Itḥāf*, I, 32 and IX, 444, 456; *Ḥikmat*, p. 32. [*GAL* II, 200, no. 265; S II, 195; Ahlwardt, IV, 435; A. Iqbal, *Maktabat al-Jalāl al-Suyūṭī* (Rabat, 1977), p. 134. For his life and times, see E. M. Sartain, *Jalāl al-Dīn al-Suyūṭī*, vol. 1: *Biography and Background* (Cambridge, 1975).]

[85] In his commentary on the *Musāyarah* of Kamāl al-dīn Ibn al-Humām al-Sīwāsī entitled *al-Musāmarah fī sharḥ al-Musāyarah* (ed. ʿAbd al-Ḥamīd; Cairo, 1940), p. 61, he associates the statement with the philosophers' doctrines. Cited in *Dhahab*, p. 474; *Itḥāf*, IX, 457; *Ḥikmat*, pp. 18-19. [*GAL* II, 122; S II, 117.]

[86] He discusses the question in his *Iḍāḥ al-bayān* (Berlin ms. Pm. 226; Ahlwardt, IV, 435, #5102). Cited in *Dhahab*, p. 473; *Itḥāf*, IX, 453-454; *Ḥikmat*, p. 33ff. [*GAL* II, 223; S II, 223; Sakhāwī, *Ḍaw'*, V, 245ff.; *EI*[1], IV, 134-135.]

[87] The younger brother of Kamāl al-dīn Ibn Abī Sharīf (#27). Cited in *Dhahab*, p. 479; *Itḥāf*, IX, 457; *Ḥikmat*, p. 29. [*GAL* S II, 142.]

*30. Zakarīyā' al-Anṣārī al-Shāfi'ī (826-926/1422-1520).[88] *pro*

31. Ibn Ṭūlūn al-Ṣāliḥī (890-953/1485-1546).[89]

32. 'Abd al-Wahhāb al-Sha'rānī (898-973/1493-1565).[90] *pro*

*33. Aḥmad Ibn Ḥajar al-Haythamī (911-973/1505-1565).[91] *pro*

*al-Samhūdī*

If the 15th century was dominated by the attack of al-Biqā'ī and the various responses it provoked, the 16th century was dominated by the defense of al-Samhūdī; his treatise, entitled *Iḍāḥ al-bayān li-man arāda al-ḥujjah min "Laysa fi'l-imkān abda' mimmā kān,"* is perhaps the most impressive treatment of the whole issue. al-Samhūdī, a native of upper Egypt who lived for long periods in Medina (and whose history of that city remains a standard source),[92] addresses his arguments to the objections raised two centuries earlier by Aḥmad Ibn al-Munayyir (#8 above).

In his brief introduction to the treatise, al-Samhūdī remarks that "questions are numerous concerning what has been ascribed to . . . al-Ghazālī . . . and people have become engrossed

[88] Cited in *Dhahab*, p. 480; *Itḥāf*, IX, 455, line 12ff.; *Ḥikmat*, p. 31. [*GAL* II, 122; S II, 117.]

[89] In his *al-Fulk al-mashḥūn fī aḥwāl M. b. Ṭūlūn*, Ibn Ṭūlūn (who had been a student of al-Suyūṭī in Cairo) mentions a responsum he had written on the question and entitled *Qalā'id al-'iqyān fī ajwibat mas'alah "Laysa fi'l-imkān abda' mimmā kān,"* on which see his *Rasā'il tārīkhīyah* (Damascus, 1348), p. 43. I am indebted to Prof. R. Mach for this reference. [*GAL* II, 481; S II, 494; Ibn al-'Imād, VIII, 298.]

[90] This prolific Ṣūfī author and follower of Ibn al-'Arabī cites the statement in his *al-Ajwibah al-marḍīyah 'an a'immat al-fuqahā' wa'l-ṣūfīyah*, Yahuda ms. 584 (Mach 2821), fol. 126b; and in *al-Yawāqīt wa'l-jawāhir* (Cairo, 1312), I, 34. Cited in *Dhahab*, p. 475; *Itḥāf*, I, 32 and IX, 457; *Ḥikmat*, p. 21. [*GAL* II, 444; SII, 466; A. J. Arberry, *Sufism* (London, 1950), pp. 123-128; *EI*[1], IV, 318; Michael Winter, "Sha'rānī and Egyptian Society in the Sixteenth Century," *Asian and African Studies* (Jerusalem), 9 (1973), pp. 313-338.]

[91] A brief discussion in his *al-Fatāwā al-ḥadīthīyah*, p. 47, cited in Massignon, *Passion*, III, 83, note 5. [*GAL* II, 508; S II, 527.]

[92] His *Wafā' al-wafā' bi-akhbār Dār al-Muṣṭafā* (4 vols.; Cairo, 1954-55); see also A. Morabia, "Surnaturel, prodiges prophétiques et incubation dans la ville de l'Envoyé d'Allah," *SI* 42 (1975), pp. 93-114.

in its complexity in past and present because for many it is difficult to understand what (al-Ghazālī) meant by it."[93]

The *Iḍāḥ al-bayān* is divided into two sections. In the first section, al-Samhūdī cites the texts by al-Ghazālī in which the problematic statement occurs. In the second section (constituting the bulk of the treatise: pp. 73-143), he deals with Ibn al-Munayyir's objections. This entails, for example, a discussion of the various meanings of "necessity" (*wujūb*) (*faṣl* 1, pp. 73-77); a comparison of the Muʿtazilite doctrine of good and evil with al-Ghazālī's (*faṣl* 2, pp. 77-93); an analysis of possibility and impossibility (*faṣl* 3, pp. 93-98); a consideration of the doctrine of the "optimum" (*al-aslaḥ*; *faṣl* 4, pp. 98-105); the problem of whether al-Ghazālī's statement limits the "objects of God's power" (*maqdūrāt Allāh*; *faṣl* 5; pp. 105-113); and an examination of the context of the disputed statement, i.e., the exhortation to trust in God (*faṣl* 7, pp. 126-143).

It is al-Samhūdī's contention that the disputed statement owes nothing to the doctrines of either philosophers or Muʿtazilites. Moreover, al-Ghazālī does not even "clearly state" (*lam yufṣiḥ*) that creation of the more wonderful is beyond the divine omnipotence.[94] Rather, the troublesome statement is to be understood thus: "There is not in the possibility by which every possible is to be described more wonderful than what exists because perfect generosity and wisdom, which precede the divine volition to create in accord with them, require that what exists be specified by the characteristic of 'most-wonderfulness.' "[95]

This is a complex reformulation, and one that it will be necessary to explore more thoroughly in the following pages. Despite its apparent opacity, it represents an attempt to cast al-Ghazālī's elusive and imprecise statement into a rigorous form, and to do so with formulaic compression. The entire *Iḍāḥ al-bayān* may in a sense be regarded as an elaboration of this restatement.

[93] *Iḍāḥ*, p. 65, line 10ff.

[94] *Iḍāḥ*, p. 66, line 18.

[95] *Ibid.*: *laysa fi'l-imkān alladhī yūṣaf bihi kull mumkin abdaʿ mimmā wujida l'iqtiḍā' kamāl al-jūd wa'l-ḥikmah allatī sabaqat al-mashī'ah bi'l-ījād ʿalā wafqihā taʿayyun ittiṣāf al-mawjūd bi'l-abdaʿīyah.*

al-Samhūdī's treatise is the most exhaustive and far-ranging analysis of the problems raised by al-Ghazālī's assertion. It is, furthermore, the most successful synthesis of arguments offered by earlier disputants, and as such it represents a high point in the debate. al-Samhūdī's chief concern is to defend the orthodoxy of al-Ghazālī against the attacks of Ibn al-Munayyir, and he does so in a systematic manner, with scrupulous attention to the issues. His work may justifiably be considered a significant contribution in its own right to the literature of theodicy.

*Zakarīyā' al-Anṣārī*

The *shaykh al-Islām* Zakarīyā' al-Anṣārī was often called in to mediate other disputes because of his reputation for impartiality, and this may have been the case here. He offers a crucial distinction, intended to correct the version of the statement transmitted by Abū Bakr Ibn al-ʿArabī. Thus, "possibility" (*imkān*), he points out, is not to be confused with "divine power" (*qudrah*). Rather, "*imkān* occurs (here) in its familiar meaning opposite to impossibility (*imtināʿ*) and to necessity (*wujūb*). . . . Hence, the meaning of al-Ghazālī's remark is that 'there is not on the side of possibility' (*fī jānib al-imkān*), or 'there is not in the possible' (*fi'l-mumkin*) more wonderful than that with which the divine power is connected."[96]

Moreover, the statement is entirely correct. And it has no connection with Muʿtazilite doctrines. They affirm that God is incapable of producing anything more wonderful than what He has already produced; but al-Ghazālī has himself disproved this doctrine and so he cannot have subscribed to it.[97]

As noted earlier, Zakarīyā' al-Anṣārī also defended the statement on the grounds of the superiority of existence to non-existence.

*Ibn Ḥajar al-Haythamī*

al-Haythamī's interpretation of the statement is as follows: when God created the world, He destined one part of it

[96] Cited in *Ḥikmat*, p. 31.
[97] *Ibid.*

eventually to cease and another to continue "to no fixed term" (*lā ilā ghāyah*).[98] (These parts correspond to heaven and hell.) This means that God cannot wholly annihilate the world; not, to be sure, because annihilation (*iʿdām*) is in itself impossible, but because He had originally ordained the continuance of the world, or at least certain portions of it. Hence, "since its annihilation is impossible, . . . its original creation is the utmost in wisdom and perfection and is the most wonderful which can exist."[99]

This oddly circular argument seems to mean that God cannot annihilate the world because that would represent an abrogation of His prior decree that the world continue; such annihilation would indicate either that His prior decree required modification (in which case it was less than perfect), or that the divine omniscience had somehow suffered alteration (which is contrary to the nature of omniscience). But both consequences are inadmissible. Therefore, this creation is the most wonderful in possibility.

## *F. THE 11/17TH CENTURY*

34. ʿAbd al-Qādir b. Muṣṭafā al-Saffūrī al-Dimashqī al-Shāmī (d. 1081/1670).[100] *pro*

## *G. THE 12/18TH CENTURY*

35. Shaykh M. b. al-Shaykh A. ʿAqīlah al-Makkī (d. 1150/1737).[101]

[98] *al-Fatāwā al-ḥadīthīyah*, p. 47.

[99] *Ibid.* The idea that God could not wholly annihilate the world was advanced by certain Muʿtazilite theologians, as well as by members of an opposing sect, the Karrāmīyah; see al-Baghdādī, *Uṣūl al-dīn*, p. 94. Also, Suhayr Mukhtār, *al-Tajsīm ʿind al-muslimīn, madhhab al-Karrāmīyah* (Alexandria, 1971), p. 217; and R. M. Frank, *The Metaphysics of Created Being* (Istanbul, 1966), pp. 25-26.

[100] The only disputant known for the 17th century; the grounds of his defense of al-Ghazālī are not mentioned. Cited in *Itḥāf*, IX, 458. [*GAL* I, 532; S I, 740; N II, 476.]

[101] Author of a short treatise called *R. fayḍ al-mannān fī maʿnā "Laysa fi'l-imkān . . ."* which remained unknown to later authors. The ms., now in the Majlis Collection, was unavailable to me; see Ḥā'irī, *Fihrist-i kitābkhānah-i Majlis-i Shūrā-yi millī* (Tehran, 1346/1968), IX: 1, 35, #2716 (I am indebted to Prof. R. Mach for this reference). [*GAL* II, 506; S II, 522; Kaḥḥālah, VIII, 264.]

*36. Ahmad ibn Mubārak, i.e., Aḥmad ibn Mubārak al-Sijilmāsī al-Lamaṭī (1090-1156/1679-1742).[102] *contra*

*37. M. b. M. Murtadā al-Zabīdī (1145-1205/1732-1791).[103] *pro*

With the 18th century a somewhat different emphasis appears in the discussions of the disputed question: the main authors strive to furnish a survey of all previous opinions on the issue. To be sure, this represented no new departure; previous authors had cited or summarized the views of their predecessors. Their citations or summaries, however, were introduced more to shore up an argument or to further a given thesis than out of any desire to present the entire range of opinions on the subject.

In the works of al-Lamaṭī, al-Zabīdī, and, in the 19th century, al-Jazā'irī, we become aware of an interest in compiling a history of the dispute; they strive for completeness, including even the names of earlier authors whose position vis-à-vis the statement remained unknown, or only partially attested. These three are, then, the historians of the dispute; and, while they are fully engaged in argument either for or against the controversial statement, they possess a historical perspective on the issue to a far greater degree than their predecessors. As a result, virtually the whole history of the debate may be reconstructed from their works alone.

*al-Sijilmāsī al-Lamatī*

It is fitting, given al-Ghazālī's earliest opponents, that the last dissenting voice in the dispute belong to an adherent of the Mālikite school of law, the Moroccan jurisprudent and mystic Aḥmad ibn Mubārak al-Sijilmāsī al-Lamaṭī. A native of Sijilmasa, al-Lamaṭī moved in his youth to Fez in order to pursue his stud-

[102] His treatment occupies one chapter of his *al-Dhahab al-ibrīz min kalām Sīdī ʿAbd al-ʿAzīz* (Cairo, 1380/1961), pp. 472-507. Cited in *Itḥāf*, I, 33, and IX, 445, line -11ff.; *Ḥikmat*, p. 17 and *passim*. [*GAL* II, 614; S II, 704; al-Kattānī, *Salwat al-anfās*, II, 203; Kaḥḥālah, II, 56. NB: The death date given in *GAL* is incorrect.]

[103] His discussion, in his cmt. on the *Iḥyā'* entitled *Itḥāf al-sādat al-muttaqīn* (Cairo, 1311/1894) occurs twice: a summary in I, 32-33, and again, in great detail, in IX, 429-460. He also wrote a separate treatise entitled *Luqṭat al-ʿajlān fī taḥqīq "Laysa fi'l-imkān,"* for which see *Fihrist al-makhṭūṭāt al-muṣawwarah*, sect. 5, #205 (I thank Prof. R. Mach for this reference). [*GAL* II, 371; S II, 398; al-Kattānī, *Fihris al-fahāris*, I, 398-413; Ziriklī, VII, 70.]

ies; there he passed the remainder of his life, becoming a disciple of the Ṣūfī *shaykh* ʿAlī ibn Masʿūd al-Dabbāgh al-Ḥasanī, whose sayings he collected in his *al-Dhahab al-ibrīz*.

al-Lamaṭī directs his arguments chiefly against al-Samhūdī, but he is unsparing in his attacks on lesser figures, often dismissing an opinion with a few scathing comments. His discussion is of the first importance, both for the information it provides on earlier disputants and for his own careful and subtle arguments. Murtaḍā al-Zabīdī, who calls him one of the "fanatic opponents" of al-Ghazālī, will attempt to refute his attack on al-Samhūdī;[104] and al-Jazā'irī, although he disagrees with him at every turn, will perforce construct most of his own account on that given in al-Lamaṭī's work.

Such is al-Lamaṭī's opposition to the disputed statement that he is willing to entertain the possibility that not only the statement itself, but its defense in the *Imlā'*, are both fabrications interpolated into al-Ghazālī's works.[105] He takes care, however, to assure his readers that his objections are directed to the offensive statement itself, and not to the person or reputation of al-Ghazālī. Thus, his *shaykh*, shortly after his death, appeared to him while al-Lamaṭī was "between sleep and waking," and informed him that he had spoken with al-Ghazālī in the next world. al-Ghazālī, he revealed to him, is one of the "great saints" and worthy of reverence.[106]

al-Lamaṭī acknowledges that he had formerly been suspicious of al-Ghazālī, but this fact does not affect his impartial treatment of the disputed question, for now his whole being is filled with the reverence which his late *shaykh* imparted to him:

> God guarded me through our *shaykh* from Abū Ḥāmid. . . . When I decided to refute this question and invalidate it and explain the evil of its absurdity, the *shaykh* stood before me and filled my mind with reverence for Abū Ḥāmid; he exalted

[104] *Itḥāf*, IX, 445.

[105] *Dhahab*, p. 496. W. M. Watt considers the introduction to the *Imlā'* suspect and probably spurious; see "The Authenticity of the Works Attributed to al-Ghazālī," *JRAS* (1952), p. 42. There seems to be no reason to doubt the authenticity of the bulk of the work, or of the passage in which the disputed statement occurs.

[106] *Dhahab*, p. 498.

> him in my view and magnified him in my sight, so that my whole inner being was filled therewith. Thus, my refutation was directed to the question, and detracted in no way from Abū Ḥāmid himself.[107]

*Murtaḍā al-Zabīdī*

It is to the great lexicographer and commentator Murtaḍā al-Zabīdī that we owe the most thorough and detailed treatment of all aspects of the dispute. A native of India,—he was born in Bilgram—al-Zabīdī emigrated to Cairo, where he spent most of his very active life. He was especially celebrated, among all his other accomplishments (not least of which was his compilation of the huge dictionary *Tāj al-ʿarūs*), for his legendary mastery of the science of *ḥadīth*.

al-Zabīdī's magisterial commentary on the disputed question is the fruit of a promise made some ten years earlier. At the outset of his discussion of the first book of the *Iḥyā'*, he refers to the dispute and offers a fleeting account of various disputants and their views. He expresses the hope that he will be able to treat the topic more fully when he reaches the *Kitāb al-tawakkul*, one of the last books of the *Iḥyā'*.

A decade later, in the 9th massive volume of his commentary, he remarks:

> Earlier I promised, in the preface to the Book of Knowledge, . . . that when God allowed me to arrive at the Book of Trust (where this question is written), I would discuss it, using my understanding, assisted by God, for the entirety of the *imāms'* discussion,—those who concur, those who oppose, those who criticize. And now, behold, God has granted to me . . . that I reach this stage after nearly ten years have elapsed from the date of the promise until today.[108]

Of the question itself, he remarks:

> This question, for which we are now adducing proof-texts (*shawāhid*), is celebrated among the *ʿulamā'*. When one begins to speculate upon it, it seems easy, but upon reflection it is a puzzle, in the solution of which many *shaykhs* have grown weary.

[107] *Dhahab*, p. 497.
[108] *Itḥāf*, IX, 440, line -5ff.

> Their views diverge, their disagreements multiply, they scatter into factions. . . .[109]

His method in dealing with this vexatious and divisive question will be, therefore, as follows:

> It appears to me now that I should assemble the discussions of these factions and discourse upon them in an equitable manner (*bi'l-inṣāf*), shunning the path of aimless wandering (*sabīl al-i'tisāf*). But what is correct is from God; what is incorrect is the result of my poor comprehension and the stupidity of my nature![110]

This exaggerated modesty should not deceive us. al-Zabīdī deals with an astonishing range of arguments, and does so with dispassionate accuracy. At the same time, he is a strongly committed advocate of al-Ghazālī's position; and his ultimate defense will rest on the, by now, familiar view of al-Ghazālī as the master of a spiritual insight beyond the grasp of ordinary mortals.

We human beings are unable, he says, even to comprehend fully the laws governing the apportionment of legacies (*al-mawārīth*); how should we presume to know God's decrees?[111] And he cites approvingly the remark attributed to Ibn 'Abbās: "Those who would understand God's decree are like those who stare at the sun's flames: the more they look, the more they are dazzled!"[112] A very few, however, like al-Ghazālī, are granted a brief but penetrating insight into some higher truth. These are the true spiritual masters; they are not bound by the usual strictures of the human condition, and so they are above cavil and reproof.

### *H. THE 13/19TH CENTURY*

*38. Hamdān b. 'Uthmān al-Jazā'irī (c. 1188-1255 or 1257/1773-1840 or 1845).[113] *pro*

[109] *Ibid.*

[110] *Itḥāf*, IX, 441, lines 1-3.

[111] *Itḥāf*, IX, 438, line 3.

[112] *Itḥāf*, IX, 440, line 19. (Ibn 'Abbās is 'Abd Allāh ibn al-'Abbās (d. 68/686), known as "al-Ḥibr" or "al-Baḥr," and credited with establishing the science of Qur'ān commentary; see *EI*², I, 40-41.)

[113] His treatment of the question is entitled *Ḥikmat al-'ārif bi-wajh yanfa' li-mas'alat "Laysa fi'l-imkān abda'. . . ."* Autograph ms., Yahuda 3036 (Mach 3031);

*39. Abū Muḥyī al-dīn ʿAbd al-Qādir b. Muḥyī al-dīn al-Jazāʾirī al-Dimashqī al-Ḥasanī (d. 1300/1883).[114] *pro*

*The End of the Dispute: Hamdān ibn ʿUthmān al-Jazāʾirī*

The dispute comes to a close in the 19th century with the work of the Algerian scholar and man-of-letters Hamdān ibn ʿUthmān al-Jazāʾirī (or: Hamdān ibn ʿUthmān Khawājah, as he is often called). His is the last summation of the dispute, as well as the last original contribution to it.

al-Jazāʾirī's complicated role in French-Algerian relations at the time of the conquest of Algeria has received attention of late; by some he is viewed as a mere opportunist, by others as a defender of Islam and "Algeria for the Algerians."[115]

These issues need not concern us here. What is less well known is that this self-professed admirer of European civilization, who spoke French and English (as well as Arabic and Turkish), who indeed had lived in France and translated some of the works of Benjamin Constant, one of his favorite authors, into Arabic and who, if he did not welcome French rule in Algeria, at least accepted it, in the beginning, with outward equanimity—it is not well known, in short, that this complex and cultivated man turned his attention, at the end of his life, to a defense of the rightness of things as they are. In 1836, al-Jazāʾirī could write to a friend, in reference to the "horrors" committed by the French against the subject Algerians: "God has contempt for those who endure and suffer contempt";[116] and he could appeal to the Ottoman sultan to intervene on behalf of Algeria.

---

cf. *Idāḥ al-maknūn*, I, 414. [Kaḥḥālah, VIII, 75; Ismāʿīl Pasha al-Baghdādī, *Hadīyat al-ʿārifīn*, I, 335.]

[114] ʿAbd al-Qādir cites approvingly, and comments on, lines 3-43 of the *Iḥyāʾ* passage in his *K. al-mawāqif fīʾl-taṣawwuf waʾl-waʿẓ waʾl-irshād* (Damascus, 1966-67), I, 285. As Prof. R. Mach kindly informed me, ʿAbd al-Qādir also wrote a separate, brief response on the question entitled *Ijābat al-Amīr ʿAbd al-Qādir li-baʿḍ al-ʿulamāʾ*; the ms. is in the Ẓāhirīyah Library, Damascus, but I have been unable to obtain a copy of it. See *Fihris al-makhṭūṭāt . . . , al-taṣawwuf*, I (Damascus, 1978), p. 10 (#11). [*GAL* II, 655; S II, 886; Kaḥḥālah, V, 304; Ziriklī, IV, 45; *EI*², I, 67-68; R. Danziger, *Abd al-Qadir and the Algerians* (NY, 1977).]

[115] See A. Temimi, *Recherches et documents d'histoire maghrébine* (Tunis, 1971), p. 111ff.

[116] Cited in *ibid.*, p. 114; cf. also, G. Yver, "Si Hamdan ben Othman Khodja,"

Nevertheless, a few years later, after he had returned to Istanbul, his birthplace, al-Jaza'irī would state in the opening pages of his work on plague: "Just as the date of one's death is foreordained and can neither be advanced or deferred, so, too, sickness and health, wealth and poverty, movement and rest, disease and healing, . . . and indeed, all the conditions of all created beings are foreordained and set to an appointed time; and none of them can overstep the time foreordained for them in the prior knowledge of God."[117]

More important for our purpose is the treatise that al-Jazā'irī composed, probably in 1257/1845, and which he dedicated to the Ottoman poet and *shaykh al-Islām* ʿĀrif Ḥikmat (1786-1859).[118] In this work, entitled *Ḥikmat al-ʿārif*, as a tribute to its dedicatee, al-Jazā'irī embraced both the mysticism of Ibn al-ʿArabī and the strict scholasticism of al-Samhūdī in order to justify and explain al-Ghazālī's statement. His position is made clear at the outset, in terms with which we have become familiar:

> It is obvious to the perspicacious that the visible world is like a mirror in relation to us, a model of the invisible world; and that the acts of the wise creator are exalted far above any caprice, imperfection and flaw. . . . Nothing which exists is without its principle; and within that are other principles which show you the breadth of God's power in what He ordains and commands. The divine power is equal to every possible thing; He, however, chooses the most marvelous. . . .[119]

The treatise is divided into two parts. In the first part, al-Jazā'irī gives a list of the disputants known to him and discusses their opinions on the disputed question. Often he interjects his own views in the midst of a discussion, or recounts an anecdote,

*Revue africaine* 57 (1913), p. 113; and, in general, Ibn ʿAbd al-Karīm, *Hamdān ibn ʿUthmān Khūjah al-Jazā'iri* . . . (Algiers, 1972).

[117] *Itḥāf al-munsifīn wa'l-udabā' bi-mabāḥith al-iḥtirāz ʿan al-wabā'* (Istanbul, 1254), p. 8. For a discussion of theological questions connected with plague, see M. Dols, *The Black Death in the Middle East* (Princeton, 1977), pp. 109-121.

[118] *Iḍāḥ al-maknūn*, I, 414, gives the date as 1252, but the autograph ms. bears the date 1257 on p. 6, line 5. For ʿĀrif Ḥikmat, see A. Altunsu, *Osmanlı şeyhülislâmları* (Ankara, 1972), p. 188f.

[119] *Ḥikmat*, p. 2.

so that the work has a lively and engaging quality. The second part is a biography of al-Ghazālī, based very closely on that of al-Subkī (#13 above).

Although he relies on al-Samhūdi's arguments in interpreting and defending the disputed statement, al-Jazā'irī never read that author's *Iḍāh al-bayān*; what he knows of this work he has gleaned from al-Lamaṭī's hostile summary in *al-Dhahab al-ibrīz*. al-Jazā'irī is then in the singular position of having to rely on the very opponent whom he wishes to refute for the arguments with which to refute him![120]

al-Jazā'irī also has recourse to the spiritual sovereignty of al-Ghazālī as a defense. There is a consensus, he says, that "special spiritual sovereignty and leadership (*quṭbanīyah*) exist in renowned individuals and in saints . . . and in the illuminated mystics (*mukāshafūn*), whose pronouncements may be relied upon, and their revelations conceded," as long as these pronouncements and revelations are not in conflict with doctrinal principles.[121] Whenever an apparent incompatibility occurs, the statements of such individuals are to be considered like the "ambiguous statements" (*mutashābihāt*) in the Qur'ān and *sunnah*; and their validity is to be granted. This is true, to be sure, only in the case of masters like al-Ghazālī, whose authority has been established by consensus (*ijmā'*). While the statements of such spiritual authorities do not have "the force of the text of Qur'ān and *sunnah*," nevertheless, they are to be conceded; those who utter them possess a teaching "to be relied upon and deemed a support in whatever does not jar with any religious fundamental."[122]

### *'Abd al-Qādir*

al-Jazā'irī's compatriot, the *amīr* 'Abd al-Qādir, the resistance leader whose campaign against the French in Algeria ended in defeat in 1847, commented approvingly on the disputed statement and even composed a brief treatise on it. Like al-Jazā'irī, 'Abd al-Qādir was an ardent follower of Ibn al-'Ara-

120 *Ḥikmat*, p. 37, line 4.
121 *Ḥikmat*, p. 44.
122 *Ibid.*

bī, as his great *Kitāb al-mawāqif* amply attests. He accepts the disputed passage in the *Iḥyā'*, however, not in accord with the idiosyncratic interpretation of his master Ibn al-ʿArabī, but very much as al-Ghazālī himself wrote it: whatever God gives or withholds is sheer justice and right, for God acts solely out of wisdom and knowledge.[123] ʿAbd al-Qādir adduces the following *ḥadīth* in support of the rightness of things as they are:

> Among My servants is he for whom only poverty is suitable; if I were to make him rich, it would corrupt him. Among My servants is he for whom only affluence is suitable; if I were to render him destitute, it would corrupt him.[124]

In the same work, ʿAbd al-Qādir also produced a remarkable and extended mystical disquisition on the wisdom and profound rightness of all aspects of creation; in this, too, he stands squarely at the close of a tradition persuasively articulated by al-Ghazālī, and elaborated with great subtlety by Ibn al-ʿArabī and his followers.[125]

It is fitting that ʿAbd al-Qādir, the final contributor to the debate, should stand in the same line as Ibn al-ʿArabī, the first to endorse the controversial statement. This fact imparts a sense of closure to the whole long debate, and serves to accentuate its striking continuity and coherence. In this regard, it is worth noting that at his death, in 1883, ʿAbd al-Qādir was buried alongside his master in the Mosque of Ibn al-ʿArabī, which stands on the slope of Mt. Qāsiyūn in the Ṣāliḥīyah Quarter of Damascus. There is perhaps a symbolic rightness in this final juxtaposition.[126]

## *I. ANONYMOUS WORKS*

For the sake of completeness, the following anonymous treatises dealing with the disputed question are listed here, beginning with the single title which can be dated.

[123] *K. al-mawāqif*, I, 285.

[124] *Ibid.*

[125] See, for example, the impressive treatment in his *K. al-mawāqif*, II, 633-743.

[126] In 1966, ʿAbd al-Qādir's remains were removed to Algeria where they now rest.

40. *Tathbīt qawāʿid al-arkān bi-an laysa fi'l-imkān* . . . (Yahuda ms. 3233, Mach #3026).[127] *pro*
41. *Risālah fī sharḥ "Laysa fi'l-imkān* . . ." (Awqāf Library, Baghdad, ms. 3339).[128]
42. *Farīdat al-bayān fī qawl al-Ghazālī* . . . (Azhar ms.)[129]
43. Untitled ms., 3 fols. in length, against those who oppose al-Ghazālī's statement that "effects derive from their causes in the most perfect and excellent of ways," and "there is nothing in possibility," etc. (Cairo, Khedival Library)[130] *pro*

## III

## THE PRESTIGE OF AL-GHAZĀLĪ AS A FACTOR IN THE DEBATE

We have drawn attention on several occasions to the extreme veneration which al-Ghazālī's defenders, and even some of his opponents, express in his regard in their discussions of the vexed question. It is difficult to assess the effect of this veneration on the course of the dispute, but its importance should not be ignored.

Sometimes it is possible to detect a certain discomfort, or embarrassment, on the part of al-Ghazālī's defenders. In the case of al-Zarkashī, for example, we note that he first terms the statement "a barren saying which ought not be applied to the creator," and yet he then proceeds to justify it. It is as though he were saying: al-Ghazālī could not have said this, but if he did. . . . This may explain as well the tenacity of the interpolation

[127] The work was written in refutation of al-Biqāʿī and was completed in 884/1479. There is a Cairo ms. of the same work, attributed to Shihāb al-dīn M.b.M.b. ʿAl. al-Balātunusī; see *Fihrist al-makhṭūṭāt* (Cairo, 1961-63), I, 126, cited in Mach, p. 257.

[128] ʿAl. al-Jubūrī, *Fihris al-makhṭūṭāt al-ʿarabīyah fī Maktabat al-Awqāf* (Baghdad, 1973-74), II, 273.

[129] *Fihris al-kutub al-mawjūdah bi'l-Maktabah al-Azharīyah* (Cairo, 1946-52), III, 612.

[130] *Fihrist al-kutub al-ʿarabīyah al-maḥfūẓah bi'l-Kitābkhānah al-Khidīwīyah al-Miṣrīyah* (Cairo, 1308), VII, 259. (I thank Professor R. Mach for these last three references.)

theory. As long as one accepted the attribution to al-Ghazālī as genuine, it was hazardous to attack the statement. Even al-Biqāʿī would argue that the statement had been interpolated, although this did not save him from the abuse of his contemporaries.

We have already mentioned that an angry crowd kept al-Biqāʿī a virtual prisoner in his house in Damascus after his attack on the statement became known. This was not to be the last misfortune which he suffered as a result of his imprudence; according to Ibn Ḥajar al-Haythamī:

> . . . al-Biqāʿī's fanaticism (*taʿaṣṣub*) led him to rebuke al-Ghazālī for his statement, "There is not in possibility more wonderful than what is." al-Biqāʿī calumniated (al-Ghazālī) in a way that inflamed passions. It went to the point that when he came to pay his respects to a certain learned man and found him in a secluded place, that man took his sandal and struck al-Biqāʿī with it until he was nearly dead.
>
> While beating him, he kept scolding him and saying, "*You* are the one who rebukes al-Ghazālī! *You* are the one who says such-and-such concerning al-Ghazālī!" until people gathered and rescued him.
>
> Afterwards (al-Biqāʿī's) contemporaries turned against him and opposed him; they composed many books in defence of al-Ghazālī and in rebuttal of al-Biqāʿī.[131]

Obviously, it is the fact that al-Biqāʿī had attacked al-Ghazālī that is at issue in this anecdote, and not the particular theological position which he sought to uphold. Such resentment toward al-Ghazālī's detractors would smoulder throughout the debate in the pages of his defenders.

Even during his lifetime, al-Ghazālī enjoyed an enormous prestige, and this continued to swell after his death. He not only was credited with authority in traditional religious matters, but he gained an aura of sanctity. Furthermore, he was seen as a wonder-worker, endowed with gifts of divination. The esoteric knowledge which God had granted to ʿAlī and to Jaʿfar al-Ṣādiq had descended next on al-Ghazālī. In the popular mind, al-Gha-

[131] *al-Fatāwā al-ḥadīthīyah*, p. 47.

zālī evolved into a kind of sorcerer; he was deemed capable of telling the future through magic spells derived from Qur'ānic verses, or of devising charms through which enemies might be destroyed and desires realized, etc.[132]

At the same time, al-Ghazālī was seen as the "renewer of religion" for his age. In Spain and in the Maghrib, to be sure, resistance to such works as the *Iḥyā'* was at first considerable. al-Jazā'irī recounts an anecdote which illustrates both this initial resistance and the almost magical power with which al-Ghazālī's works were endowed by his followers:

> The *Iḥyā'* became famous during its author's lifetime and circulated widely. Manuscripts came to the Maghrib and to al-Andalus. It is said that the *'ulamā'* of al-Andalus issued legal opinions (*fatwā*) permitting it to be burned. They did this out of envy; and, reportedly, they did have it burnt. al-Ghazālī heard of this and said, "They rend my book! May God rend their rule!"
>
> By the decree of the hearing and knowing God, their sovereignty vanished after that and the Spaniards seized their realms![133]

The effect of this exaggerated reverence is evident in at least one instance in the present debate. al-Sijilmāsī al-Lamaṭī conducted a kind of opinion-poll on the question, interviewing both simple folk and scholars. The results, which are not without humor, deserve mention:

> I asked one of the common folk about this question. He said, "Isn't the divine power efficacious for every possible thing that may be supposed?" I answered that it was. Then he asked, "Is not restricting it to some possibles, but not others, (to declare the divine power) limited or incapable?" I answered, "Yes." Then he said, "Is not incapability in regard to the creator an impossibility?" I answered, "Yes." Then he replied, "The question is plain: what, then, is abstruse about it?"[134]

al-Lamaṭī next approached a learned man:

[132] See Goldziher, *Le livre de Mohammed Ibn Toumert*, p. 14ff, for the details on which this paragraph is based.
[133] *Ḥikmat*, p. 40.
[134] *Dhahab*, p. 478.

> I said to one of the legal experts, "What is your opinion on Abū Ḥāmid's saying, 'There is not in possibility more wonderful than what is?' " He answered, "The *shaykh* al-Shaʿrānī has already discussed this, and so have others."
>
> I said, "I am asking only for *your* opinion on it!" He answered me, "What opinion should *I* have on it?" I exclaimed, "Curse you! It is an article of faith! Don't you see, if someone should say to you, 'Is our Lord capable of producing more excellent than this creation?' " Then, he replied, "I would say to him that the objects of God's power are infinite; so He is able to produce more excellent than this creation by a thousand degrees, and then more excellent than that excellent, and so *ad infinitum*."
>
> I said, "His statement 'There is not in possibility more wonderful than what is,' is contrary to that." At that point he grasped the import of the statement ascribed to Abū Ḥāmid.[135]

Moreover, this was not an uncommon experience for al-Lamaṭī: "The very same thing happened to me with many of the learned. When I asked them about the statement of Abū Ḥāmid, they became conscious of the lofty stature (*jalālah*) of the *imām*, the "Proof of Islam," and so they vacillated. But when I altered the statement, as in the previous case with the simple folk, they affirmed the all-encompassing nature of the divine power (*ʿumūm al-qudrah*) and the infinitude of its objects."[136]

[135] *Dhahab*, p. 471.
[136] *Ibid.*

THREE

# *Divine Power and Possibility*

## I
## THE ATTACK OF AL-BIQĀʿĪ

al-Biqāʿī reverses the disputed statement and proclaims: "There is in possibility more wonderful than what is."[1] Had God, for example, made all men as wise as Adam, this world would have been more wonderful, for Adam knew everything without study and when the spirit blew upon him, he gave all things their names.[2] God could have made all men as comely as Joseph, or endowed them with memories as retentive as al-Bukhārī's.[3] He could have enabled man to see the *jinn* who watch man, unbeknowst to him (*Qur.* 7:27); or taught him the language of birds and beasts so that, like David and Solomon, he might bend them more easily to his will; or, better still, He could have endowed all people from birth with a knowledge of Arabic, "the best of tonques," so that they might receive the Qur'ānic revelation without devoting a lifetime to the study of grammar and syntax.[4]

God chose to do none of these things, even though He knew that He might thereby improve the world immeasurably. And yet, God cannot be accused of either stinginess or injustice. God acts, not "as wisdom requires," but as He will: "He is not to be held accountable for what He does" (*Qur.* 21:23).[5]

That this world would be more wonderful if God had made all people wise and beautiful "no reasonable person can doubt,"

[1] *Tahdīm*, fol. 48a: *kāna fi'l-imkān abdaʿ mimmā kān.*

[2] *Tahdīm*, fol. 47b; for Adam, see *Qur.* 2:31, and al-Kisā'ī, *Qiṣaṣ al-anbiyā'* (tr. Thackston), p. 28.

[3] *Tahdīm*, fol. 47b. Joseph is the paragon of male beauty; see *Qur.* 12:31, and al-Kisā'ī, *Qiṣaṣ*, p. 167. al-Bukhārī, the renowned compiler of traditions, was noted for his prodigious memory.

[4] *Tahdīm*, fol. 48a.

[5] Cited in *Tahdīm*, fol. 45b.

for man is subject not only to outer defects such as lameness, blindness, leprosy, and the like, but to such inner defects as "guile, iniquity, hatred, and impotence, resulting from the pursuit of outward abominations"; and these vices are such that, "had they an odor, existence would stink with them and everything should flee them."[6]

al-Biqāʿī's arguments are straightforward and appeal to common sense, somewhat like Samuel Johnson's celebrated "refutation" of Berkeley's idealism. al-Biqāʿī says in effect: Can you look at this world and call it "the most wonderful in possibility"? Who, after all, cannot think of scores of possible improvements in the way things are? This is not, be it noted, out of any pessimism on al-Biqāʿī's part; it proceeds, rather, from his indignation at the presumption of those who, like al-Ghazālī, venture to pronounce this world a fitting manifestation of the divine power.

al-Biqāʿī seeks to show what God could have done; he relies on two basic arguments to this end. First, he appeals to our common recognition of the world's manifold imperfections; and, second, he points out that changes occur in the world, and even changes for the better. How may we allow for the fact of change in a "best of all possible worlds"? In his argumentation, al-Biqāʿī relies on numerous examples illustrative of possible improvements in the present world—these examples are often fanciful, and perhaps deliberately so—and on proof-texts from Qur'ān and *sunnah*.[7]

al-Biqāʿī's arguments follow a rather predictable pattern: he introduces his examples with the phrase "God is capable of . . ." (*kāna qādiran ʿalā an* . . .) and follows them with the assertion that, had God so acted, our lot would have been more wonderful than that which we presently have (*hādha abdaʿ mimmā naḥnu fīhi*). His thesis is that God, who created the heavens and earth

[6] *Tahdīm*, fol. 47b.

[7] This was a time-honored method of argumentation; cf. al-Ashʿarī, *al-Ibānah*, pp. 7-33, where it is employed against the Muʿtazilites. In his gloss entitled *al-Nukat wa'l-fawā'id* (on al-Taftāzānī's cmt. on al-Nasafī's *ʿAqā'id*), al-Biqāʿī impatiently dismisses intellectual proofs in favor of those based on scripture; thus, speaking of God's oneness, he comments: "As for *tawḥīd*, the truth is that proof based on tradition suffices to establish it, contrary to what the *shaykh* says," *al-Nukat wa'l-fawā'id* (Yahuda ms. 2245), fol. 7a, *ult.*

in six days, is undoubtedly capable of making the world more wonderful in an instant (*fī laḥẓah*).[8] That He does not do so, however, scarcely entitles us to conclude that this world represents the utmost of what He is capable of doing.

## A. WHAT GOD COULD HAVE DONE

We have already seen some examples of what, in al-Biqāʿī's opinion, God could have done to improve the world; it will suffice to mention a few further such examples here, in order to convey some sense of the tone and style of his treatise.

Thus, in reference to *Qur.* 32:13, "If We had so willed, We could have given every soul its guidance," al-Biqāʿī comments: "If there were in every country a prophet who informed people of the real truth about things and put an end to disputes and removed difficulties, it would be more wonderful than abandoning them to their ignorance, recalcitrance, and error."[9]

Again, after citing the *ḥadīth* that on Judgment Day there will be three groups of people, those walking, those riding, and those on their faces, he notes that someone questioned the Prophet, "How will they walk on their faces?" and that Muḥammad replied, "He who made them walk on their feet is able to make them walk on their faces!"[10] al-Biqāʿī comments: "The query was about the 'how.' Had it been about the reality, he would have explained the 'how' to him by saying, 'as the snake walks,' for example, or 'they will run on their hands,' or 'God will create something like feet on their heads.' "[11] God can do whatever He will; and this is a truth that we must accept "without asking how" (*bi-lā kayf*).

[8] *Tahdīm*, fol. 48a.

[9] *Tahdīm*, fol. 46b. This had been a standard argument against the Muʿtazilite doctrine of the optimum (*al-aṣlaḥ*); cf. al-Ijī, *Mawāqif*, VIII, 196.

[10] *Tahdīm*, fol. 53a; for the *ḥadīth*, see Aḥmad ibn Ḥanbal, *Musnad*, II, 354. For al-Ghazālī's own cmt. on this tradition, see his *al-Durrah al-fākhirah* (ed./tr. L. Gautier; Geneva, 1878), p. 51 [Arabic text]; pp. 44-45 [trans.].

[11] *Tahdīm*, fol. 53b. al-Suyūṭī (*Tashyīd*, fol. 3a) replies that God could have placed man's head on his back, or his mouth on his stomach, etc., but the actual arrangement is most marvelous; he cites *Qur.* 95:4 as decisive proof. This argument al-Suyūṭī takes directly from al-Ghazālī, though without acknowledgment; cf. *al-Maqṣad al-asnā*, p. 106, lines 11-15.

More practically, if God truly wished to improve our lot, He could command the Day of Judgment to come forthwith; or He could furnish us with a remedy for death; or He could create for us, here and now, an earthly paradise.[12] Still better, if He wished, He could make all the mountains of the earth of solid gold.[13]

One such example adduced by al-Biqāʿī is of particular interest, and could hardly have endeared him to his Damascene contemporaries. The city of Damascus is dominated on its western side by the bare and dusty flanks of Mt. Qāsiyūn, a mountain deemed sacrosanct by Damascenes as the burial place of patriarchs and prophets.[14] al-Biqāʿī suggests that God could have set Mt. Qāsiyūn, which now "blocks the good air from Damascus," in some other location, or He could at least have arrayed it in pleasant vegetation and populated it with exotic birds; and that, too, would have been more wonderful![15]

al-Suyūṭī's response to this is instructive. God could remove the mountain from Damascus (and indeed on Judgment Day He will remove it), but now it is most wonderful where it stands. God knows that the blockage of sweet air is "most salutary" (*aṣlaḥ*) for Damascus. Fresh air is not always beneficial for certain temperaments; indeed, in times of pestilence, vile places (*al-amkinah al-radīyah*) can even be most beneficial, according to physicians.[16]

Furthermore, God created mountains solely to anchor the earth (*Qur*. 79:32); in His wisdom, He set each mountain in a fixed place, expressly for this purpose. If Mt. Qāsiyūn were to be removed, it would "violate the wisdom of its anchoring" (*akhalla bi-ḥikmat al-irsāʾ*). Therefore, its actual location is the most wonderful. This may lead, to be sure, to certain lesser evils,

[12] *Tahdīm*, fol. 48b (Judgment Day); fol. 49a (remedy for death); fols. 48b-49a (earthly paradise).

[13] Cited in *Tashyīd*, fols. 3a-3b.

[14] See the description of Mt. Qāsiyūn by the Damascene historian and savant Ibn Ṭūlūn al-Ṣāliḥī, himself a native of the Ṣāliḥīyah quarter on the slopes of Mt. Qāsiyūn, *al-Qalāʾid al-jawharīyah*, p. 1ff.

[15] *Tahdīm*, fols. 48b-49a. The earlier historian Ibn Shaddād (d. 684/1285) praises Damascus expressly for its excellent location and its air, which he calls "most evenly balanced," *al-Aʿlāq al-khaṭīrah*, I, 13.

[16] *Tashyīd*, fol. 3b.

such as stagnant air, but these evils should be discounted in view of the greater good its present position affords mankind.[17]

We are familiar with this line of reasoning: there is a divine wisdom manifest in creation; what exists, exists not because God could not do otherwise, but because in His consummate wisdom He determined that this arrangement, and no other, is optimal.

al-Suyūṭī's arguments here are characteristic of the optimist stance so often assumed by al-Ghazālī's defenders. If the arguments seem weak, it is because the optimist is most vulnerable in respect to particular cases. The optimist wisely prefers to invoke general principles; and his opponent, in reply, always reverts to specifics. When al-Biqāʿī proffers the possibility of mountains of gold—a possibility few would find unappealing—al-Suyūṭī must labor noticeably to make mere ordinary mountains appear "more wonderful." If mountains were of gold, he argues, people would begin killing each other down to the last man, or they would abandon agriculture and other sources of livelihood, and we should all starve, etc.[18]

al-Samhūdī will offer a better response to such skepticism as al-Biqāʿī's, as we shall see; for a more convincing counter–argument must take into consideration the very nature of the possible.

## *B. THE PROBLEM OF CHANGE*

God has performed acts in the past which produced an undeniably superior state-of-affairs, and He could perform these once again. He could, for example, send down to us the quails and manna with which He once fed the Israelites, and this would be more wonderful since envy, rivalry, and hardship would cease.[19] Or He could send down as well as the Table (*al-māʾidah*) morning and night, as He once did for Jesus and his disciples

[17] *Ibid.* On the mythic significance of mountains, see A. J. Wensinck, "The Ideas of the Western Semites concerning the Navel of the Earth," *Verhandelingen der Koninklijke Akademie van Wetenschapen te Amsterdam,* N.S., 17:1 (1916), esp. pp. 1-10.

[18] *Tashyīd,* fols. 3a-3b.

[19] *Tahdīm,* fol. 47b; cf. *Qur.* 2:57, *Exodus* 16:4ff.

(*Qur*. 5:112-115); and this, too, would be more wonderful since henceforth "no one would be envied for his possessions."[20] Or He could send against every army of oppressors the "swarms of flying things," mentioned in the Qur'ān (105:3).[21]

Indeed, the revelation of the Qur'ān itself to a particular people at a particular time shows that God acts to produce the more wonderful:

> "We have revealed to you a scripture wherein is your reminder" (*Qur*. 21:10), i.e., your glory and dignity. We have no doubt that (the condition) to which the Arabs (before Islam) were brought through this Book . . . is better than the condition of poverty and want, abasement and destitution, rumormongering and neglect of the holy, in which they found themselves, and that it is more wonderful . . . By this it is clear that there is in the realm of possibility more wonderful than what is.[22]

Other changes for the better have occurred. Heaven and hell once stood empty and were only gradually peopled.[23] Individuals change; an unbeliever may turn to belief. If nothing is more wonderful than what already is, the conversion of infidels is folly; and yet, "every age shows that God guides unbelievers. Was the Prophet ignorant in wanting to call unbelievers to Islam?"[24]

## *C. THE RESPONSES OF AL-SUYŪṬĪ AND AL-SAMHŪDĪ*

al-Biqāʿī's error here is explained by al-Suyūṭī, as follows:

> (al-Biqāʿī) thinks that when an existing thing is pronounced "most wonderful," that assertion continues in force until Judgment

[20] *Tahdīm*, fol. 47b. In the Qur'ānic passage, Jesus prays: "O God, our Lord, send down upon us a Table out of heaven, that shall be for us a festival, the first and last of us, and a sign from Thee" (tr. Arberry, p. 146).

[21] *Tahdīm*, fol. 49a.

[22] *Tahdīm*, fols. 48a-48b.

[23] *Tahdīm*, fols. 51b-52a; see Abū Dā'ūd, *K. al-sunnah*, *bāb* 66 (#4744).

[24] *Tahdīm*, fol. 50a.

> Day, and that the creation of an opposite better than it, at a later time, is precluded.
>
> This is incorrect. All that God creates in its moment is more wonderful in that moment than anything else; but He may create something else at a later time, and that other will be more wonderful at that time than the first. . . .
>
> He may create in a single day many opposites in succession: an opposite in each hour; and each one more wonderful in that hour than another.[25]

This is in accord with al-Suyūṭī's dictum that "everything which exists is more wonderful for its moment than that from which it differs" (i.e., either that which is opposite to it, or that which it has replaced in time).[26] The "most wonderfulness" of a thing is relative; it may be most wonderful at one moment, but then at a later moment its opposite may be so. God creates for every moment one of two opposites as the most wonderful for that moment.[27]

al-Samhūdī, who further develops this notion, explains: "Divine wisdom requires that a thing be most wonderful and most perfect in relation to its time, even if its opposite be most wonderful and most perfect in relation to another time."[28] For example, night follows day and day, night; each is most wonderful and most perfect in its time but "were one of them to remain always, order would be impaired."[29]

The truth of this is shown, not only by nature, but by the divine law (*sharīʿah*) itself. Thus, the abrogation (*naskh*) of a particular legal judgment is possible; for such judgments stand in a nexus with their opposites. Both the judgment and the counter-judgment depend, not on some intrinsic positive good within them, but on an underlying reason (*ʿillah*), or *ratio legis*. Legality may adhere at one time to a ruling and at a later time to its very opposite "because of the conformity of each in its

[25] *Tashyīd*, fol. 4a, lines 5-12.
[26] *Ibid.*: *kull mawjūd abdaʿ fī waqtihi min khilāfihi.*
[27] *Tashyīd*, fol. 2b: *al-abdaʿ fī hādha al-waqt ījād aḥad al-ḍiddayn.*
[28] *Iḍāḥ*, p. 113, line 12.
[29] *Ibid.*

time to a *ratio legis*."[30] Just as abrogation is possible "if wisdom and beneficence require it," so, too, is the creation of another most perfect and most wonderful in the order of things; each successive perfection abrogates and supersedes its predecessor.

This has other practical consequences. There may be, for example, low prices (*rakhāʾ*) at one moment and high prices (*ghalāʾ*) at another;[31] there may be plenty in one country and drought in another; and the same is true of "life and death, ease and hardship, security and fear, sickness and health."[32] Just as a legal prescription is most perfect and most wonderful in its time, but may be superseded, so, too, are all of these circumstances of life most wonderful in their respective moments, though they change unceasingly.

For this reason, according to al-Suyūṭī, people would be well advised to remain in the situations in which they find themselves. Whenever they try to change their circumstances, they fall into a worse situation. In fact, it is itself a manifestation of "most-wonderfulness" (*abdaʿīyah*) that people are divided into various groups and classes: "Some are ascetics, others are greedy; some renounce worldly hope while others lust after it. If all were ascetics, however, commercial life with all its advantages would cease and no one could make a living. Hence, what God has made is the most marvelous."[33]

Furthermore, the perfections of things are not static and unchanging. If this were the case, it would imply that such perfections were somehow intrinsic to their possessors; but this is not so, nor is it what al-Ghazālī means.

"Most perfect," "most wonderful," etc., are merely relative (*iʿtibārī*) terms "which the intellect uses in considering, but which have no existence *in concreto* (*fiʾl-khārij*)."[34] When we say that a given condition is most wonderful, we mean that it is so, rel-

[30] *Iḍāḥ*, p. 114, line 6.

[31] The question of prices (*asʿār*) was a standard topic in Muʿtazilite and Shīʿite theological works; see, e.g., *Sharḥ al-uṣūl al-khamsah*, pp. 788-789, and Ibn al-Muṭahhar al-Ḥillī, *Kashf al-murād*, p. 214. For a discussion, see Daniel Gimaret, "Les théologiens musulmans devant la hausse des prix," *JESHO* 22 (1979), pp. 330-338.

[32] *Tashyīd*, fol. 2b; cf. *Iḍāḥ*, p. 114.

[33] *Tashyīd*, fol. 3b.

[34] *Iḍāḥ*, p. 115.

ative to a certain individual at a particular time and in relation to other individuals, but not that "the most wonderful" is some fixed and permanent quality existing *in concreto* within that individual. Rather, God has created and assigned that condition at that time to a particular individual, and He does so out of consummate wisdom (*ḥikmah bālighah*), but this does not mean that at a later time He will not assign another equally perfect condition to that individual.

The notion of relative perfection leads to some bizarre conclusions. It must be understood that when we say that a certain condition is most wonderful, we do not mean "most wonderful" according to some immutable and autonomous scale of values, as though perfection could be assayed and measured. We mean rather that it is most wonderful and most perfect at a given moment for a given individual. Thus, such conditions as lameness or blindness—indeed, all that we habitually term imperfections—are themselves manifestations of the "most wonderfulness" of things as they are. The poverty or the deformity of Zayd is most perfect, most wonderful, as is his affluence or bodily wholeness at some other time, simply because the divine wisdom has created and assigned those circumstances to him at that particular time. We ought not look at the world and judge one state or one thing superior to another, for this implies that things have within themselves some self-subsistent value.

This does not mean, however, that the imperfect is not imperfect, that lameness, for example, is not really lameness, but that the imperfect in all its forms is also a manifestation of the most wonderful. The creation of the imperfect is itself a sign of the divine wisdom and power: "Everything which exists is the most wonderful because the divine wisdom requires it, be it perfect or imperfect."[35]

## *D. THE BASIS OF AL-BIQĀʿĪ'S ATTACK*

In striving to uphold divine omnipotence, al-Biqāʿī goes so far as to reject the well-established tenet that God's power is unconnected with performance of the impossible. He associates

[35] *Ibid.*

this tenet with the detestable teachings of the philosophers, and so abjures it.[36] It must be noted, however, that in his many examples al-Biqāʿī offers none which represents an impossibility in the strict sense.

We may understand this in the light of al-Biqāʿī's polemical strategy, at least in part: to link al-Ghazālī with the teachings of suspect groups is to discredit him. al-Biqāʿī claims, for example, that the disputed statement lends support to the philosophers' teaching that the world is eternal, a teaching rejected decisively by al-Ghazālī in several works. This rejection notwithstanding, argues al-Biqāʿī, the statement implies that this is the only possible world. This is what the philosophers maintain, on the grounds that this world "is the utmost to which the divine power can attain."[37] For al-Biqāʿī, this seems to lead to the conclusion that God created out of some necessity of His nature; and, if so, then the world must always have existed (since there could have been no time at which a divine power acting by a necessity of its nature was inoperative).

We must keep in mind that it is al-Biqāʿī's intention to deflate the fatuous presumption of those who discover "divine wisdom" in the most unseemly circumstances. God's wisdom and power are beyond mortal ken; it is folly to pronounce upon them. In this sense, al-Biqāʿī's attack is reminiscent of the attack launched centuries earlier by Ibn Karrām (d. 255/869), the eponymous founder of the Karrāmīyah sect, against the optimism of the Muʿtazilites.

Thus, in his lost *Kitāb al-sirr*, Ibn Karrām asked: "Whose profit is it when (God) creates snakes, scorpions, and mice and then orders them to be killed?"[38] And again, "Human beings commit sins, whereas those creatures whose meat they eat: camels, cows, sheep, and the birds to which they give chase, do not bear any guilt. What kind of wisdom allows Him to let those

[36] *Tahdīm*, fol. 37b.

[37] *Tahdīm*, fol. 50b, citing al-Ijī, *Mawāqif*, VII, 244, line 6.

[38] The extracts occur in the 13th-century Persian writer Ibn al-Dāʿī al-Rāzī's *Tabṣirat al-ʿawāmm* and have been brought to light by J. van Ess (whose translation I here quote) in his "Ibn ar-Rēwandī, or the Making of an Image," *al-Abḥāth* 27 (1978/79), p. 7; see also the same scholar's *Ungenützte Texte zur Karrāmīya* (Heidelberg, 1980).

who sin and go astray loose on those who obey?"[39] The object here, as in al-Biqāʿī's case, is not to arraign the divine wisdom, but to castigate the impertinence of those who pontificate so blithely upon it.

al-Biqāʿī's attack is no unconsidered jeremiad, but proceeds from two fundamental convictions. The first is that the divine power is unlimited and, indeed, ineffable. The second is that the possible is whatever is conceivable. This notion of possibility was well characterized by Maimonides, and with examples which we should not be surprised to find in al-Biqāʿī's own treatise:

> They (sc. Muslim theologians) are of the opinion that everything that may be imagined is an admissible notion for the intellect. . . . For, as they say, according to intellectual admissibility (*tajwīz*), one place is not more appropriate for one particular body than another place. They also say with regard to all things that are existent and perceptible that supposing anything among them should be bigger than it is or smaller or different from what it is in shape or place—should a human individual, for instance, have the size of a big mountain having many summits overtopping the air, or should there exist an elephant having the size of a flea, or a flea having the size of an elephant—all such differences would be admissible from the point of view of the intellect.
>
> The whole world is involved in this method of admissibility as they practice it. For whatever thing of this kind they assume, they are able to say: it is admissible that it should be so, and it is possible that it should be otherwise; and it is not more appropriate that one particular thing should be so than that it should be otherwise.[40]

When al-Biqāʿī claims that God could create mountains wholly of gold or that He could have located man's mouth on his stomach, he does so on the basis of this notion of admissibility. And al-Ghazālī's defenders, such as al-Suyūṭī and al-Samhūdī, would

[39] J. van Ess, "Ibn ar-Rēwandī," p. 7.

[40] Maimonides, *Dalālat al-ḥā'irīn.* (Jerusalem, 1972), I, 113a; tr. Pines, p. 206. See also Alfred L. Ivry, "Maimonides on Possibility" in J. Reinharz and D. Swetschinski (eds.), *Mystics, Philosophers and Politicians* (Durham, NC, 1982), pp. 67-84.

agree: God could indeed perform all these actions; and yet, they would add, He does not because in His profound wisdom He chooses not to perform such actions.

It would seem, then, that the dispute in some measure centers on opposing views of the world itself.

For al-Ghazālī—and in this, he stands squarely in one tradition of Ashʿarite *kalām*—the world is an "act of skillfully accomplished design" (*fiʿl muḥkam*).[41] It is "expertly constructed" (*muḥkam fī ṣanʿatihi*) and "set in order" (*murattab*).[42] Such a world betokens a creator endowed with power: "Whoever sees a beautifully woven and joined cloth of silk brocade (*dībāj*) . . . and imagines that its weave is the product of a lifeless person lacking any capacity, or of a man without ability, has taken leave of his native wits and has plunged down the path of the foolish and the ignorant."[43] The world displays orderly disposition (*tarattub*), arrangement (*intiẓām*), and symmetry (*tanāsub*), as do the limbs and organs of the human body.[44]

This is, of course, the familiar cosmological proof. Its main purpose is to point to a creator characterized by power and skill, but it also indicates that the world itself possesses a certain coherence, however provisional. The world has order, structure, and measure. The things within it have their own just and proper place; and there are discoverable reasons for their placement. This is not, to be sure, because of any law of nature, or any exigency arising from things in themselves, but because God in His wisdom has so willed it.

For al-Biqāʿī, by contrast, the present world is only one of innumerable worlds which God could create.[45] Moreover, God

[41] *al-Iqtiṣād fi'l-iʿtiqād*, p. 80. The word *muḥkam*, used by al-Ashʿarī in an identical context (*K. al-lumaʿ*, p. 10), is difficult to translate: it denotes something solidly established, like a well-built house; or something finely meshed, like a coat of mail with closely woven links; it may also signify something imbued with wisdom (*ḥikmah*). See Lane, pp. 616-617.

[42] *Iḥyā'*, I, 96

[43] *Ibid.* For the comparison with the silk brocade, see al-Ashʿarī, *K. al-lumaʿ*, p. 10; there is a similar argument in al-Juwaynī, *Irshād*, p. 36.

[44] *al-Iqtiṣād*, p. 80.

[45] Cf. al-Baghdādī, *Uṣūl al-dīn*, p. 34: "Some [Qur'ān commentators] think God has 18,000 worlds, each of which is like the perceptible world, or larger; and some hold that there are 90,000 worlds; and others, 1,000 worlds." See also

could at any time, and in an instant, alter this world in countless ways. There is no obvious, or even discernible, rationale in the actual placement of things. God could just as easily have moved Mt. Qāsiyūn, or cloaked it in refreshing vegetation, as placed it, bare and dry as it is, in its present location. There is no reason which the intellect can discover as to why Mt. Qāsiyūn should be where it is and as it is; at best, we may say that God wanted it so, even though He knew it might be better otherwise.

These divergent views of the world issue ultimately from the self-same premise: God is omnipotent. As the Qur'ān repeatedly proclaims, "He is powerful over everything" (*huwa ʿalā kull shay' qadīr*; 2:20 and *passim*). The verse is cited both by al-Biqāʿī against al-Ghazālī[46] and by al-Ghazālī himself in a discussion of omnipotence.[47]

The premise that "God is powerful over everything" leads al-Biqāʿī ineluctably to the conclusion that this actual world is but one of an infinity of possible worlds which God can create. There is no point at which we may say with certainty: this is the best, this is the utmost, which God can create. For divine power there is no utmost which it cannot surpass.

For al-Ghazālī, the world is not merely the effect of brute power, but of power acting in concert with wisdom. To act with power entails acting with skill; and the actual world must bear the impress of that skill and that power. Omnipotence will be reflected in its effects.

It is clear, then, that we must examine not only the nature of omnipotence in itself, but its relation with its objects. When we say that divergent views of the world underlie the dispute, we are perforce speaking of the nature of the possible itself. We must ask how the term "possibility" is to be understood in our disputed statement. Does it mean everything conceivable, as al-

---

al-Ṭabarī, *Jāmiʿ al-bayān*, I, 23, for a discussion of the different meanings of "world." On the question of a plurality of worlds in ancient thought, see W.K.C. Guthrie, *A History of Greek Philosophy*, I, 106-115 [Anaximander], and II, 313-315 [Anaxagoras]; on the question in early Christian thought, see Jean Pépin, *Théologie cosmique et théologie chrẹtienne* (Paris, 1964), pp. 72-78.

[46] *Tahdīm*, fol. 46a.

[47] *Iḥyā'*, I, 96.

Biqāʿī seems to hold? And, if so, in what relation does it stand with the divine power?

## II
## THE PROBLEM OF OMNIPOTENCE

Both critics and defenders of the disputed statement agree that God is powerful, but they disagree over the scope and nature of that power. Indeed, the whole problem of divine power was part of a larger disagreement among various groups of Muslim thinkers from the earliest period.

In the view of al-Taftāzānī (d. 792/1390), none of the differing sects denied[48] that God is one or eternal (*ṣifāt al-dhāt*: attributes of essence); or that He is not a body occupying space (*ṣifāt salbīyah*: negative attributes); or that He may be described as "high" or "first" or "last" (*ṣifāt iḍāfīyah*: relative attributes); or that He possesses "attributes of action" (*ṣifāt al-afʿāl*), i.e., He creates, He punishes, etc. They did disagree, however, over the seven attributes designated variously as "existential attributes" (*ṣifāt wujūdīyah*), or "real existential attributes" (*sifāt thubūtīyah haqīqīyah*),[49] or "attributes based on determinants" (*ṣifāt al-maʿānī*).[50] These seven are: power, knowledge, will, life, hearing, sight, and speech.

A host of problems surrounds these seven attributes.[51] They are especially problematic because each may have for its objects things that are temporal and evanescent, and indeed the whole

[48] al-Taftāzānī, *Sharḥ al-Maqāṣid*, II, 53-54. For the dissenting view of the philosophers, see Fakhr al-dīn al-Rāzī, *al-Muḥaṣṣal*, p. 116; Ibn Ḥazm, *Fiṣal*, II, 155-169; Ibn al-Dāʿī al-Rāzī, *Tabṣirat al-ʿawāmm*, pp. 4-5. The Muʿtazilites, of course, denied the existence of separate, eternal attributes as such, but not that God is one and eternal, etc.; see Wensinck, *Muslim Creed*, p. 74ff.

[49] al-Taftāzānī, *Sharḥ al-Maqāṣid*, II, 53-54; al-Āmidī, *Ghāyat al-marām*, p. 38ff.; Aḥmad ibn Zarrūq, *Sharḥ ʿaqīdat al-Ghazālī*, pp. 19-20. In al-Bāqillānī's *K. al-tamhīd* (p. 262), these are, however, termed attributes of essence (*ṣifāt al-dhāt*) as well.

[50] See R. M. Frank, "*Al-Maʿnā*: some Reflections on the Technical Meanings of the Term," *JAOS* 87 (1967), p. 250.

[51] For the various opinions on the attributes, see O. Pretzl, *Die frühislamische Attributenlehre* (Munich, 1940); H. A. Wolfson, *The Philosophy of the Kalam* (Cambridge, 1976), pp. 112-235; and M. Allard, *Le problème des attributs divins* (Beirut, 1965).

realm of contingent, created being. If it be asserted, for example, that God's knowledge is eternal, it then becomes crucial to explain how or what God knew before the objects of knowledge (*maʿlūmāt*) existed. Can there be knowledge without an object of knowledge? If God be described as knowing only after the creation of cognoscible things, then He was previously unknowing; and His subsequent knowledge is somehow dependent on contingent and created things. This is clearly inadmissible. (The solution of the Karrāmīyah sect, that God has an individual act of knowledge for each knowable—that His knowledge comes to be created coincident with the thing to be known—proved unpalatable to the "orthodox.")[52]

Furthermore, there is considerable difficulty in determining what relation, if any, may obtain between an eternal and immutable attribute and objects that come to be and pass away in time. If we say, as do the philosophers, that there is no relation between divine knowledge or power and particular things,[53] we render God in some sense ignorant. But if we declare that there is such a relation, and that God knows particulars, we seem to surrender God's knowledge to the mercy of contingencies.

It is neither possible nor desirable to consider the doctrine of the divine attributes in any great detail here. The subject is notoriously complex, the literature extensive, and much of the discussions not germane to our purpose. We shall try merely to present the essential features of the Ashʿarite position, as they relate to our topic, and in their later, more codified form, as indeed they would have been known to the disputants themselves.

### *A. THE ATTRIBUTE OF POWER*

The Muʿtazilites had generally adhered to the doctrine that God is powerful essentially (*li-dhāt*), in order to avoid positing an eternal attribute outside the divine nature, and which

[52] al-Taftāzānī, *Sharḥ al-ʿAqā'id*, p. 79.

[53] al-Ghazālī, *Tahāfut al-falāsifah*, p. 223ff.; this is denied by Ibn Rushd, *Faṣl al-maqāl*, p. 18. See the excellent treatment in Michael E. Marmura, "Some Aspects of Avicenna's Theory of God's Knowledge of Particulars," *JAOS*, 82 (1962), pp. 299-312, and especially p. 300.

might seem to rival the divine or to contaminate His perfect oneness.[54]

Against this, the Ashʿarites proclaimed that God is powerful "by virtue of a power" (*qādir bi-qudrah*).[55] Power proceeds from God, not essentially but by virtue of something "superadded to Him" (*li-zāʾid ʿalayhi*), or, more precisely, by virtue of a "determinant superadded to His essence" (*li-maʿnā zāʾid ʿalā dhātihi*).[56] God is powerful "by virtue of a power," i.e., not powerful in His very nature, powerful without having something which can be called "power," as the Muʿtazilites aver; but rather, powerful because of something distinct called power, just as a human being is termed powerful or knowing by virtue of the power or knowledge which he possesses. The Muʿtazilite doctrine, that God is powerful without having something called power, is, in al-Taftāzānī's view, like saying "black without any blackness" (*aswad lā sawād lahu*), and is an obvious absurdity.[57]

Here the Ashʿarites employ the traditional argument, taken over from the Muʿtazilites, which is known as "analogy from the visible to the transcendental world" (*qiyās al-ghāʾib ʿalā al-shāhid*), e.g., "The reason (*ʿillah*) that something is knowing in this world (*fiʾl-shāhid*) is knowledge; so, too, in the transcendent world (*fiʾl-ghāʾib*). The definition of one who knows here is he in whom knowledge subsists (*man qāma bihi al-ʿilm*); so, too, its definition there."[58]

Thus, power subsists in God (*qāʾimah bi-dhāt al-rabb*)[59] and is a distinct and definable attribute. If what the Muʿtazilites maintained were true, and power, knowledge, and the rest proceeded from God essentially, all these attributes would be indistinguishable; there would be no difference between knowl-

[54] See Ibn Mattawayh, *al-Majmūʿ* (ed. Houben, as the work of ʿAbd al-Jabbār), I, 107; al-Taftāzānī, *Sharḥ al-ʿAqāʾid*, p. 77: "The Muʿtazilites follow this course to avoid invalidating divine unity, since there would result eternally existing things different from His essence, and the eternity of other than God."

[55] al-Āmidī, *Ghāyat al-marām*, p. 85.

[56] al-Ghazālī, *al-Iqtiṣād*, p. 81.

[57] al-Taftāzānī, *Sharḥ al-ʿAqāʾid*, p. 76.

[58] al-Ījī, *Mawāqif*, VIII, 45, line 8; according to al-Ījī (*ibid.*); this form of argument was rejected by al-Āmidī on the grounds that power in this world does not permit creation (*ījād*), whereas in the transcendent world it does.

[59] al-Āmidī, *Ghāyat al-marām*, p. 85.

edge or power or life or speech. And yet, "the predication of these attributes conveys a sound meaning (*fā'idah ṣaḥīḥah*), in contradistinction to our saying 'His essence is His essence' (*dhātuhu dhātuhu*)."[60] To declare God essentially powerful is, thus, a tautology comparable to saying "God is God."

The attributes are to be understood in the Ashʿarite view as something superadded to the divine essence; and yet, not in such a way as to be either autonomous, rival entities, or indistinguishable components of the divine nature. In the paradoxical formulation, they are "not God and nothing other than God" (*hīya lā huwa wa-lā ghayruhu*).[61] Moreover, these attributes are not necessarily existent, as God Himself is; in themselves they are merely possible, and yet the fact that they are in themselves possible does not prevent their being co-eternal with God, for they subsist in Him.[62]

Power is thus an attribute that is cognitively distinct and one, that is eternal and without any temporal inception (*azalī*), and that subsists in the divine nature. How, then, are we to understand the relation of such power to its manifold possible objects?

In order to avoid the consequence that power be in some way dependent on its objects, the *kalām* devised the expedient notion of a nexus (*taʿalluq*) between power and its objects. In reply to the question as to how divine power could remain perfect and immutable when the objects of that power undergo incessant change, it could thus be said that while God's power remains unchanged, the nexus that exists between His power and its objects changes, as those objects change. The interposition of this relation, or nexus, would lead to other thorny problems,[63] but it had the advantage of preserving the perfection of the di-

[60] al-Ījī, *Mawāqif*, VIII, 46, line 5.

[61] al-Taftāzānī, *Sharḥ al-ʿAqā'id*, p. 77.

[62] In his gloss to al-Taftāzānī's *Sharḥ al-ʿAqā'id* (see note 7 above), al-Biqāʿī objects to the notion that the attributes may be termed possible in themselves: "This is a harsh and difficult statement that ought not be applied to God's attributes. . . . It would be better to say that God's essence requires the existence of attributes as they are," *al-Nukat wa'l-fawā'id*, fol. 25b.

[63] Certain of these problems are discussed in great detail in al-Āmidī's *summa* entitled *Abkār al-afkār* (Princeton ms., New Series #1927), fol. 35aff. The complexity of al-Āmidī's discussion seems to me to render any summary here inadvisable, but I hope to deal with his treatment separately at another time.

vine attributes intact, without in any way diminishing their scope. Divine power remains unchanged; it is the nexus which changes.

Accordingly, the seven troublesome attributes are sometimes termed "attributes standing in a nexus" (*ṣifāt mutaʿallaqah*).[64] Knowledge stands in a nexus with knowable things (*maʿlūmāt*), power with objects of power (*maqdūrāt*), etc. In the case of power, it is further affirmed that it "stands in a nexus with all the objects of power,"[65] i.e., there is a relation between power and whatever can be done. For the term "objects of power" denotes *possibilia* themselves, as al-Ghazālī states: "It is a cardinal principle of omnipotence that it stands in a nexus with all objects of power. By 'objects of power' I mean all possible things" (*aʿnī biʾl-maqdūrāt al-mumkināt kullahā*).[66]

## *B. OMNIPOTENCE AND IMPOSSIBILITY*

The definition of omnipotence as the power to do not all things without exception, but all possible things, is familiar enough.[67] Nevertheless, the distinction continues to prove vexing. A contemporary writer has suggested, for example, that we distinguish between the doctrine of God as "almighty," i.e., as having power over all things, and the doctrine of God as "omnipotent," i.e., as having the "ability to do everything."[68] This second doctrine, that of "absolute omnipotence," maintains that "God can do everything absolutely; everything that can be expressed in a string of words that makes sense; even if that sense can be shown to be self-contradictory, God is not bound in action, as we are in thought, by the laws of logic."[69]

Certain of al-Ghazālī's opponents appear to advocate this extreme position. For simple piety, of course, as al-Sijilmāsī al-

[64] al-Ghazālī, *al-Iqtiṣād*, p. 93.

[65] *al-Iqtiṣād*, p. 82; cf. al-Āmidī, *Ghāyat al-marām*, p. 85.

[66] *al-Iqtiṣād*, p. 82.

[67] See, e.g., the Thomistic manual by J. Gredt, *Elementa philosophiae aristotelico-thomisticae*, II, 269: ". . . nomine omnipotentiae [intelligimus] potentiam, quae ad omnia efficienda extenditur, quae entis rationem habent seu in se contradictoria non sunt."

[68] P. Geach, *Providence and Evil* (Cambridge, 1977), p. 3.

[69] Geach, pp. 6-7.

Lamaṭī illustrates, "God's power is wholly efficacious and there is nothing of which it is incapable."[70] Does not the Qur'ān state that "He has power over everything"? And to the question as to whether God can create a world more excellent than this one, the Qur'ān also gives a definitive reply: "If He wish, He can remove you and bring a new creation."[71]

Needless to say, this doctrine, supported in Islamic theology by such texts as Qur. 2:20 (and within Christianity by such texts as Mark 10:27: "With God all things are possible"), skirts obvious difficulties. There are clearly acts which cannot be reconciled with omnipotence without violating logic.

These fall into two broad groups.[72] First, there are actions which are somehow contrary to the divine nature itself, even though they are not in themselves impossible, or even difficult. These include vicious acts, such as lying or committing injustice, as well as such bodily actions as running and walking. Here the problem is that all such acts are within the power of creatures; shall we say that their creator cannot perform them? And, of course, to assert that God can lie raises obvious questions about His goodness.

Second, there are actions in themselves impossible and which involve an intrinsic contradiction. Clearly, these are impossible for creatures, but are they also impossible for God? Such *per se* impossibilities include, for example, effecting the simultaneous truth of contraries (*al-jamʿ bayn al-ḍiddayn*), or rendering what once happened as though it had not been, or, further, for God

[70] *Dhahab*, p. 471. The doctrine of *potentia absoluta* was supported in Western Scholasticism by St. Peter Damian (1007-1072), who affirmed, for example, that God had power to make a past event as though it had not occurred: not only could He destroy Rome, He could make it never to have existed; furthermore, He could make a woman virgin again after defloration. See his *De divina omnipotentia* (ed. Cantin), pp. 402-406. This position is also ascribed by St. Bonaventura to the controversial chancellor of Chartres, the theologian Gilbert de la Porrée (ca. 1076-1154); see Bonaventura, *Commentaria in IV libros Sententiarum*, in *Opera theologica selecta*, I, 596. For a discussion of the question, see E. Coreth, *Metaphysik* (Innsbruck, 1980), pp. 411-413.

[71] *Dhahab*, p. 471, citing *Qur*. 14:19.

[72] See the discussions in Aquinas, *Summa theologiae*, Ia.25, 1-4, and *Summa contra Gentiles*, II, 25; also F. Suarez, *Tractatus de divina substantia ejusque attributis*, Lib. 3, cap. 9, 21, in *Opera omnia*, I, 229.

to create another God equal to Himself, etc. Such *per se* impossibilities were often expressed in the form of trick questions: Can God fit the world into a walnut or into an egg?[73] Can God create a stone too heavy for Himself to lift?[74]

To return to the first group, actions contrary to the divine nature, we find this a subject of discussion among Muslim theologians from an early period. Opinions were often sharply divided, as we might expect, and there is at times a certain vacillation which betrays the uneasiness which the subject provoked. For example, the Muʿtazilite Abū al-Hudhayl al-ʿAllāf (d.c. 227/840) held, in one report, that injustice (*ẓulm*) is impossible (*muḥāl*) for God; but in another he is said to have declared that "God is able to commit injustice . . . but He does not because of His wisdom and mercy."[75] The Basra Muʿtazilite Muḥammad ibn Shabīb reportedly affirmed that "God is able to oppress, wrong, and lie," but he qualified this with the proviso that "wrong and falsehood occur only through the agency of one from whom harm befalls, and you know that this does not come from God."[76] The view that God can commit wrong, but does not, a view widespread among the early Muʿtazilites, aroused derision among certain of their opponents, such as al-Māturīdī.[77]

Other Muʿtazilites, such as al-Naẓẓām (d. 231/845) and his student al-Jāḥiẓ (d. 255/868), held that God "cannot be described as having power to commit wrong and falsehood, nor to forgo performing what is optimal (*aṣlaḥ*)."[78] This position was found unacceptable, however, by more orthodox theologians, for it seems to deny power to God in a fundamental way; and so al-

[73] al-Muṭahhar b. Ṭāhir al-Maqdisī (d. 356/966), *K. al-badʾ waʾl-taʾrīkh* (ed. Huart), I, 106.

[74] See J. van Ess, "Göttliche Allmacht im Zerrbild menschlicher Sprache," *Mélanges de l'Université St.-Joseph*, 49 (1975-76), p. 651. For Ibn Ḥazm (d. 456/1064), these are "the questions of madmen," *Fiṣal*, II, 160, and in the same passage, he argues that God made the law of contradiction, for example, and could change it,or violate it, if He wished. This was also the opinion of Descartes; see Harry G. Frankfurt, "The Logic of Omnipotence," *Philosophical Review*, 73 (1964), pp. 262-263.

[75] al-Ashʿarī, *Maqālāt*, II, 556; the second opinion, II, 555.

[76] *Maqālāt*, II, 556.

[77] See his *K. al-tawḥīd*, p. 132.

[78] al-Ashʿarī, *Maqālāt*, II, 555; see also al-Shahrastānī, *K. al-milal*, p. 77.

Naẓẓām is called a "Zoroastrian" (*majūs*), i.e., a dualist, by later commentators, such as al-Taftāzānī.[79]

There were also those who believed that even to raise such a question smacked of impropriety: "It is not good to apply it to a pious Muslim and so, too, it may not be applied to God. . . . One should not say, 'If Abū Bakr had committed adultery and if ʿAlī had become an infidel, what would be the opinion concerning them?' So, too, we deem it wrong to say, 'If God had committed injustice. . . .' "[80]

This first group of difficulties leads to rather special complications within Islamic theology. At issue is not only the authorship of evil, but the authorship of acts in general. The Ashʿarites preferred to ascribe sole agency for all acts to God, in the sense that God is the creator of all acts while man merely "acquires" (*iktasaba*) them; the Muʿtazilites, by contrast, generally held that man could create his own actions.[81]

In order to escape the consequence of their view, namely, that God is ultimately responsible for evil, the Ashʿarites declare that there is no such thing as good or evil beyond what the divine law reveals as such. We cannot assess God's actions, pronouncing some good and others evil, for these categories have no objective validity. Whatever God wills is good; and since whatever happens cannot happen except as a result of His will, whatever happens is *ipso facto* good.

We are far here from one solution available to Western scholasticism: God cannot lie because the power to lie is at bottom no power at all, and so its absence cannot impugn omnipotence.[82] In the Ashʿarite view, God can declare tomorrow that

[79] al-Taftāzānī, *Sharḥ al-Maqāṣid*, II, 62.

[80] al-Ashʿarī, *Maqālāt*, II, 555. The question was, in any case, widely discussed; as documents preserved in the Cairo Genizah attest, the problem and its possible solutions were debated among Jewish (Karaite) Muʿtazilites. See G. Vajda, "Fragments muʿtazilites en judéo-arabe," *JA* 264 (1976), esp. p. 4. For the main Muʿtazilite arguments, see G. Hourani, *Islamic Rationalism* (Oxford, 1971), p. 97ff.

[81] On the subject of man's "acquisition" (*kasb/iktisāb*) of acts, see, among others, A. S. Tritton, *Muslim Theology*, pp. 67-68.

[82] See, e.g., Petrus Lombardus, *Libri IV sententiarum*, I, 260, and St. Thomas Aquinas, *De potentia Dei*, Q. 1, art. 6; tr. Shapcote, *On the Power of God*, I, 36. A good example may be found as well in Hugh of St. Victor's (1096-1141)

lying is good and veracity bad, and they will become good and bad forthwith. Now, if this solution seems to evade the central issue, the problem of the authorship of evil, nevertheless, other equally troubling difficulties arise. If God is the only true agent, what shall we say of such actions proper to creatures as walking, running, or the like? Is God the sole agent of every act of human and animal locomotion? Can a possible action have two agents (the problem of *al-maqdūr bayn al-qādirayn*)?[83]

Again, experience seems to show that certain causes generate predictable effects. If I move my hand, the ring on my finger moves as well. Is God the agent not only of my hand's motion, but of the ring's as well, and so on within the whole apparent chain of causes and effects? Is God sole agent of these generated effects (*al-mutawalladāt*) within nature?[84]

These subsidiary questions need not detain us further. It seems clear that creation of a more wonderful world is in no way incompatible with the divine nature; hence, it is not an impossibility in the first sense. The question is, therefore, whether production of a better world is in itself impossible. This appears to have been the interpretation of the disputed statement by certain of al-Ghazālī's opponents, such as al-Biqāʿī. If it is intrinsically impossible for God to create a more wonderful world, does this entail a lack in the divine omnipotence?

Certain of the so-called *impossibilia* and their relation to divine omnipotence are discussed in a brief text by an 11th–century Zaydī author named al-Ḥusayn ibn al-Qāsim. The text, entitled *Kitāb al-tawḥīd wa'l-tanāhī wa'l-taḥdīd*, has recently been

---

*De sacramentis*: God cannot kill Himself, but this does not limit His omnipotence, for the power to do this is not power at all (*Dico ergo quod Deus omnia potest; et tamen se ipsum destruere non potest. Hoc enim posse posse non esset, sed non posse. Itaque omnia potest Deus, quae posse potentia est*); *De sacr.* I.ii.22, in Migne, *Patrologia Latina*, vol. 176, p. 214. For further examples of this popular medieval topic, see the titles listed in P. Glorieux, *La littérature quodlibétique de 1260 à 1320* (Paris, 1925-35), e.g., vol. I, pp. 102-104, 113 [no. 9: Whether God can make Christ's humanity better], 116, 123, 125, 129, 130, 142 and 144 [no. 2: Giles of Rome on whether God can will two contraries simultaneously], among others.

[83] al-Ghazālī, *al-Iqtiṣād*, p. 86ff.

[84] *al-Iqtiṣād*, p. 95ff.

published, with a translation and commentary, by J. van Ess.[85] In this work, it is asked, for example, whether God can create His like (no, because if He created His like, it would be a created thing, whereas God is a creator);[86] or, whether God could kill Himself, if He wished (no, for death can befall only corporeal beings, but God is incorporeal);[87] or, whether God can create something infinite (no, for a body cannot be without limits), etc.[88] That God can perform none of these acts in no way limits His omnipotence, for such acts involve an internal contradiction (*tanāquḍ*); they are in themselves absurd (*muḥāl*), and so are not truly objects of power (*maqdūrāt*).[89]

Such acts are *per se* impossibilities (they are *muḥāl* or *mustaḥīl* or *mumtani' li-dhātihi*), in contradistinction to acts which are impossible "because of something else," impossibilities *propter aliud* (*li-ghayrihi*).

Now the creation of a better world would not seem to involve any intrinsic impossibility. It is not absurd, nor does it entail anything impossible for thought. It is a criterion of the *per se* impossible that it be inconceivable. As a modern Muslim theologian, resuming the earlier tradition, puts it: "The intellect cannot conceive for it [sc. the impossible] any existing quiddity. . . . It does not exist even in the mind."[90]

I can, of course, imagine a succession of outlandish permutations in the actual structure of things. I can picture pigs with wings, or fabulous mountains of gold, and while these may be impossible in the sense that I know they will never exist, they are not true impossibilities. The truly impossible has unimaginability as its very nature.

To posit the simultaneous truth of opposites, for example, is to posit an unimaginable state-of-affairs. It is false to assume that

[85] "Göttliche Allmacht im Zerrbild menschlicher Sprache," pp. 651-688 [see note 74 above].

[86] *Ibid.*, p. 657.

[87] *Ibid.*, p. 656. See note 82 above for a Scholastic answer to this question.

[88] *Ibid.*, p. 658.

[89] Cf. Aquinas, *De potentia Dei* (tr. Shapcote, I, 18-19): God "cannot make yes and no to be true at the same time," not "through lack of power, but through lack of possibility, such things being intrinsically impossible."

[90] Muḥammad 'Abduh, *R. al-tawḥid* (Beirut, 1977), p. 36.

such an intrinsic contradiction could somehow partake of being. It is in this sense that the truly impossible cannot be an "object of power." And to claim that God can effect the simultaneous truth of opposites is, far from extolling His omnipotence, rather to predicate an absurdity of Him; it is to predicate of Him a meaningless, nonsensical act which stands in no relation to the power to act.[91]

The examples which al-Biqāʿī puts forth, in an effort to demonstrate that God can perform the impossible, are really examples of logical possibilities which al-Ghazālī himself, we may safely assume, would concede to be within the scope of divine omnipotence. Omnipotence, however, does not function in isolation. It acts in concert with other divine attributes, such as knowledge and will. Furthermore, it acts according to the "dictates of wisdom." Thus, when al-Ghazālī's defenders reject al-Biqāʿī's examples as impossible, they do so, not because these are in themselves impossible (in themselves they are possible), but because they are impossible "for some other reason." And this "something else" which renders an inherent possibility impossible is, in this instance, the divine wisdom itself.

According to the disputed statement, "there is not in possibility more wonderful than what is," i.e., it is impossible that there exist anything more wonderful than what is. But if the creation of a more wonderful world is not possible, and yet is not in itself impossible, how are we to avoid impugning either the divine goodness or the divine power? Clearly, it is one thing to say that God's power remains unconnected with the *per se* impossible—that He cannot, for example, fit the universe into a walnut without either reducing the universe or fashioning a co-

[91] Ibn Ḥazm denies this (see note 74 above). He distinguishes four types of impossibility: relative impossibility (*muḥāl bi' l-iḍāfah*); the impossible-to-exist (*muḥāl fi'l-wujūd*); that which is impossible due to the structure of the human mind (*muḥāl fi-mā baynanā fī binyat al-ʿaql*), e.g., violation of the law of contradiction; and the absolutely impossible (*muḥāl muṭlaq*), which alone is impossible for God. See *al-Fiṣal*, II, 159, and Wolfson, *The Philosophy of the Kalam*, p. 584ff. Interestingly enough, the *amīr* ʿAbd al-Qādir tries to show that God can indeed perform the impossible; for example, God can make two contraries to be true at the same time and in the same place. He seeks to justify this view by examples drawn from the opposing motions of the spheres and by such Qur'ānic verses as 3:169. See his *K. al-mawāqif*, I, 213.

lossal walnut—and quite another to claim that the creation of a superior world is not in itself impossible, and yet that it cannot be.

al-Ghazālī's critics treat the statement as though it posited a *per se* impossibility in the creation of a better world; and they resort to scripture, as well as to common sense, in order to disprove it. His defenders reply, however, that creation of a better world is impossible, not in itself, but because of "something else."

Both sides seem to agree, in any case, that the divine power stands in a nexus with all possible objects of power, which are themselves infinite (*lā nihāyata lil-mumkināt*), such that "the creation of temporal being after being reaches to no limit, beyond which the emergence of a further temporal being is impossible to the intellect (to conceive)."[92] This connection of power with all possible objects is termed the "universality of power" (*ʿumūm al-qudrah*).[93] Furthermore, power is one and indivisible; it is only the relationship, or nexus, of power that changes in accord with its changing objects.

The element common to both power and to its objects is possibility; it is indeed the sole common factor (*wa-lā yushtarak fī amr siwā al-imkān*).[94] Possibility is itself the complement of power.

The question of whether God can perform impossibilities is answered by the formulation: the divine power stands in no nexus with the impossible. Omnipotence denotes the power to perform whatever is possible; and so, the central question of the dispute is seen to be, not whether God can perform the impossible in the strict sense, but whether His power is somehow limited by performance of the most wonderful. Possibilities are said to be limitless; to state that God has created, in this world, the most wonderful in possibility seems to involve a curtailment of His power. Can He not be supposed capable of creating world after world, each more wonderful than its predecessor, *ad infinitum*?

al-Biqāʿī purports to defend the thesis that God can perform

[92] al-Ghazālī, *al-Iqtiṣād*, p. 82; al-Ijī, *Mawāqif*, VIII, 60ff.
[93] al-Ijī, *Mawāqif*, VIII, 60.
[94] al-Ghazālī, *al-Iqtiṣād*, p. 82.

the impossible; this, we suggest, is a false, or at least a misleading, issue. It arises from a mistaken notion of the impossible. As Ibn al-Munayyir noted in a similar context, the impossible is treated as though it existed, or could exist in some sense, when in fact it stands in no relation whatever to existence.[95] It is the absence of any such relation that is expressed in the axiom: divine power stands in no nexus with the impossible. Power does not fall short or betray deficiency when faced with the impossible, for the impossible is that which by its very nature can neither be imagined nor performed.

## III
## THE ATTACK OF IBN AL-MUNAYYIR

Two of Ibn al-Munayyir's objections addressed the problem of divine power. These objections must be reconstructed from the response of al-Samhūdī, since Ibn al-Munayyir's work has apparently not survived. For this reason, it is often difficult to follow the course of Ibn al-Munayyir's arguments; what follows is, therefore, a tentative account.

### *A. THE QUESTION OF INCAPACITY (ʿAJZ)*

In his fourth precept, Ibn al-Munayyir takes umbrage at al-Ghazālī's formulation of the dilemma, and especially the sentence: "If God were not able (to produce a better world), it would be incapacity (*ʿajz*), contrary to divinity." Ibn al-Munayyir takes *ʿajz* here to denote "privation of power" (*ʿadam al-qudrah*). This, he notes, is "conventional usage," but it is an error: "A stone has no power, but it is not incapable; the eternal power stands in no nexus with the impossible, but it is not incapable."[96] Rather, incapacity is to be understood, as al-Ashʿarī held, as a "positive factor" (*maʿnā wujūdī*),[97] since mere absence of power, as in the case of the stone, does not render the stone

[95] In his gloss to al-Zamakhsharī's *Kashshāf* (Beirut, 1947), I, 88, note 1.

[96] Cited in *Iḍāḥ*, pp. 125-126.

[97] The term *maʿnā* is notoriously difficult to translate; it may mean "thing" or "cause" (synonymous with *ʿillah*), or even "accident."

impotent or incapable. Incapacity is the contrary of power, and not simply its lack.

Moreover, incapacity, like capacity (*istiṭāʿah* or *qudrah*), is something that really exists and is distinct from its agent; this, too, we know on the authority of al-Ashʿarī himself.[98] Incapacity "stands in a nexus with contingent being, just as power stands in a nexus with it, but in an opposite way" (*ʿalā al-muḍāddah*).[99] Furthermore, incapacity is applicable only to created being. A man can be capable or incapable, knowing or unknowing, etc., at various moments, but this cannot properly be said of God.

Ibn al-Munayyir's argument seems to be as follows: if *ʿajz* in the offending sentence denotes privation of power (*ʿadam al-qudrah*), then the statement is meaningless; for we cannot speak of privation of power as incapacity. There is no nexus between power and the impossible, but such lack of relation does not signify incapacity.

On the other hand, *ʿajz* cannot simply mean incapacity in the ordinary sense, as weakness or inability, since that is applicable only to created being, but not to God. "Incapacity," he explains, "is a determinant (*maʿnā*) that stands in relation to what cannot be done (*al-maʿjūz ʿanhu*) at the time it exists, just as temporally created power stands in relation to what can be done at the time it exists."[100] The unperformable (*al-maʿjūz ʿanhu*) at a given moment is something with which the incapable person stands in relation. Privation of power, on the other hand, enters into no such relationship; indeed, it is not susceptible of existence in relationship in any way.

al-Ghazālī is in error, according to Ibn al-Munayyir, because he makes the absence of a nexus of power incapacity, and yet there follows no "object of incapacity" (*al-maʿjūz ʿanhu*), no unperformable act, with which God's alleged incapacity could stand in nexus. If God did not make a superior world due to a privation of power on His part, this would not be because He was "incapable," but because no nexus of possibility obtained through which such a world could be produced.

98 al-Ashʿarī, *K. al-lumaʿ*, p. 54.
99 Cited in *Iḍāḥ*, pp. 125-126.
100 *Iḍāḥ*, p. 126, lines 2-3.

In other words, if al-Ghazālī's remark implies a privation of power, then this is not truly incapacity; and if it implies incapacity in our human sense, then there should be some "object of incapacity," with which His incapacity stands in nexus. As it is, however, there is not over against the divine power something to which it stands in a relation of incapacity.

### *B. AL-SAMHŪDĪ'S REBUTTAL*

This, contends al-Samhūdī, is distortion (*taḥrīf*) of al-Ghazālī's meaning. al-Ghazālī bases his position on the fact that God links (*anāṭa*) His creation of the most perfect with the requirements of wisdom. "But if we assumed in the description of possible things a perfection superadded to that (perfection) by which the world is characterized, and the creator were not capable of producing that perfection which wisdom required, then that denial of power (*intifā' al-qudrah*) over that possible would be incapacity, incompatible with divinity."[101] al-Ghazālī means by *ʿajz* a lack of divine power over certain possibilities. That al-Ashʿarī "does not call this defect '*ʿajz*' does not impair" al-Ghazālī's case.[102]

Furthermore, it is simply calumny (*tashnīʿ*) when Ibn al-Munayyir claims that al-Ghazālī makes the absence of a nexus of power "incapacity." This is certainly not what is meant.

When we say, "If God were not able to produce a better world, He would be incapable," we mean by that a denial of power (*intifā' al-qudrah*), and not "the privation of power" (*ʿadam al-qudrah*).[103] The implication of al-Ghazālī's statement is not that if God could not create a more wonderful world, He is to be deemed without power, as a stone, for example, is without power; but rather, that if this were the case, God could be described as incapable, i.e., as unable to realize a certain possibility.

Power or ability can be denied only of one in whom these

[101] *Ibid.*
[102] *Ibid.*
[103] al-Samhūdī here cites al-Maḥallī's cmt. on al-Suyūṭī's *Jamʿ al-jawāmiʿ*: *al-jahl intifā' al-ʿilm.*

attributes can exist, and this is certainly true of God. If God were unable to create some possible perfection, He could legitimately be described as incapable. This is what al-Ghazālī's statement means. (Of course, the force of the statement lies in the fact that the divine power is considered unimpeachable; since God's power is in no way deficient, what He has realized must be seen as perfect and as commensurate with His power.)

Finally, Ibn al-Munayyir is mistaken in any case in claiming tha *ʿajz* means the privation of power in common usage.[104]

## C. INFINITE POSSIBILITIES AND PERFECTION

In his eighth precept, Ibn al-Munayyir again considers a problem related to divine omnipotence. Briefly stated, the problem is that possibilities are said to be infinite, and yet the very idea of anything "most wonderful" or "most perfect" seems to limit those possibilities. al-Ghazālī's statement makes finite what is infinite, and so it is contradictory.

Ibn al-Munayyir states: "If the eternal power is capable of one number, it is capable of a number greater than that, since it cannot be enumerated or limited. Thus is faith in the efficacy of divine power, and the grandeur of its might, perfected."[105]

al-Ghazālī's statement excludes the addition of anything to creation beyond a fixed limit or furthest point termed perfection. But, asks Ibn al-Munayyir, "How can he deem possible belief in the limitation of divine power to a number that cannot be exceeded and a limit that cannot be surpassed?"[106]

For Ibn al-Munayyir, the notion that there is a "most perfect" with which divine power is connected is a limitation of omnip-

[104] Cf. Lane, p. 1961; *Lisān al-ʿarab*, VII, 236: *alʿajz naqīḍ al-ḥazm*; *al-ʿajz al-ḍuʿf*. But cf. Ibn Ḥazm, *al-Fiṣal*, II, 160, line 1: *ʿadam al-qudrah alladhī huwa al-ʿajz*; and the discussion in al-Fārābī's *"Jawāb masāʾil,"* in *Philosophische Abhandlungen* (ed. Dieterici), p. 90. See also Mullā Ṣadrā, *al-Ḥikmah al-mutaʿālīyah*, I/3, 3: "[*qudrah*] means an animal's being such that an action issues from it when it wishes it, and an action does not issue from it when it does not wish it; and the opposite of this notion is *ʿajz*." For treatment of a similar question, see R. M. Frank, "The Structure of Created Causality according to al-Ashʿarī," *SI* 25 (1966), p. 62ff.

[105] *Iḍāḥ*, p. 112, line 11.

[106] *Iḍāḥ*, p. 124, line 10.

otence (*quṣūr al-qudrah*). There can be no number to which another number cannot be added, and this is analogous to the infinitude of possibilities. How can we set a boundary to omnipotence? Does not al-Ghazālī himself state that "the creation of contingent beings reaches no limit beyond which the emergence of further contingent beings is impossible to the intellect?"[107]

In its simplest form, Ibn al-Munayyir's argument here seems to be this: if possibilities are indeed infinite, and if God's power stands in a nexus with them all, how may we speak of any "most perfect in possibility"? Will there not always be some further perfection possible for God?

It seems probable, however, judging from al-Samhūdī's reply, that the argument in Ibn al-Munayyir's eighth precept took the rather more complex form of a dilemma. This may be reconstructed as follows: If possibilities are conceded to be infinite, then it cannot be said that God's power stands in a nexus with any supreme perfection, for there will always be a further perfection conceivable; but if it be said that God's power does stand in a nexus with the utmost perfection, then possibilities are somehow limited, and yet we know that numbers, for example, are infinite.

Elsewhere, Ibn al-Munayyir states: "It is obvious that the perfections occurring in existing things are limited and reach a limit in God's knowledge which only He knows, in contradistinction to those perfections which may be expected from existents that do not occur, for their perfections are unlimited and reach to no end."[108]

He then adduces the Qur'ānic "We have created man in the most excellent stature" (95:4), and glosses it as meaning "the most excellent stature of (any) existing thing" (*al-mawjūd*). That is, such perfections as there are, occur only among actually existing things, but in the realm of possibility there are no limits to perfections, for "possibilities remain without limit" (*fa-tabqā al-mumkināt ʿalā ʿadam al-nihāyah*).[109]

[107] al-Ghazālī, *al-Iqtiṣād*, p. 82.
[108] *Iḍāḥ*, p. 120.
[109] *Ibid.*

Ibn al-Munayyir here inserts an assumed counter-objection: How may we overcome the uncertainty over whether divine power stands in a nexus with the most perfect, or not? He replies that the notion of "the most perfect, than which nothing is more perfect" is contradictory (*yunāqiḍ*). It is assumed that no limits may be assigned to possibilities; and yet, perfections are themselves possibilities. To suppose a "most perfect," above which there is nothing more perfect, is to render finite what is infinite, and this is impossible. Since God's power stands in no nexus with the impossible, He cannot be said to have limited possibilities.

If, however, we say with al-Ghazālī that this world is the most perfect in possibility, do we not in fact make finite the infinite possibilities with which God's power stands in nexus? This is clearly an impossibility; as such, it stands in no nexus with omnipotence. Therefore, this world cannot be the most wonderful in possibility.

## *D. AL-SAMHŪDĪ'S REBUTTAL*

In reply, al-Samhūdī affirms that God's power is indeed infinite, as al-Ghazālī himself maintains; and he cites al-Ijī as further support: divine power is infinite, both in itself and in its nexus. By infinite is meant "non-finite" (*al-lātanāhī*); what is infinite cannot be said "to stop at any limit beyond which a nexus with something else is impossible."[110]

It must be understood, however, that the divine power is infinite only in potency (*bi'l-qūwah*), while the nexus of that power with its objects remains finite in act (*bi'l-fi'l*).[111] This is because the objects of that power are finite by nature. Thus, when we say that possibilities are infinite, we are describing the infinite capability of the divine nature to realize possibility upon possibility, *ad infinitum*; but this capability, while infinite in it-

[110] al-Ijī, *Mawāqif*, VIII, 58, quoted in *Iḍāḥ*, p. 112.

[111] al-Ijī, *Mawāqif*, VIII, 58. The problem of whether an infinite power can produce infinite effects is discussed by St. Bonaventura, among others, in his *Commentaria in IV libros Sententiarum*, I.43.1; see also E. Gilson, *The Philosophy of St. Bonaventure* (NY, 1938), p. 170ff.

self, remains finite in act since its objects are created and contingent things, finite by nature.

How then, asks al-Samhūdī, can Ibn al-Munayyir claim that al-Ghazālī curtails omnipotence? For al-Ghazālī affirms that divine power is efficacious for "that which cannot be enumerated and limited."[112] This, however, is not the point. God could realize innumerable possibilities, but instead "He selects out of all of them the most perfect and the most complete which wisdom demands."[113]

Furthermore, the "impossibility of any addition" (*ʿadam imkān al-zāʾid*) to this present creation, a notion to which Ibn al-Munayyir takes exception, is not to be understood as a *per se* impossibility (*istiḥālah li-dhātihi*); it is God's profound "wisdom that renders impossible the creation (of anything additional)."[114] Hence, it is an impossibility "because of something else" (*li-ghayrihi*), i.e., God's wisdom, will, and power which have, respectively, selected, determined, and realized the best out of all possibilities.

We have already encountered the distinction between the impossible *per se* and the impossible *propter aliud*. al-Samhūdī explains it as follows:

> Whatever is not impossible *per se* can be characterized as possible, whether it be impossible for some extrinsic reason—e.g., that the non-occurrence of which stands in nexus to eternal knowledge—or not (impossible), like other existing things. Whatever can be characterized by the possibility of existence is among the totality of things within God's power. And so, the impossible *propter aliud* is among the totality of things within God's power.
>
> This is because of the efficacy of divine power (*li-ṣalāḥat al-qudrah*) to stand in a nexus with its production in terms of its (sc. the possible's) very nature. God, for example, is capable of making all unbelievers believers, as the Qur'ān indicates . . .

[112] *Iḍāḥ*, p. 112 (probably referring to *al-Iqtiṣād*, p. 82).
[113] *Ibid.*
[114] *Ibid.*

> But the absence of a prior act of divine volition that all believe, and (that volition's) specifying some for belief, but not others, prevent all from believing together. Nevertheless, this is possible as far as God Himself is concerned.[115]

A more wonderful world than this is possible, in that it may be conceived, but it is impossible, in that an extrinsic factor, the divine will, has determined that this present world is the most wonderful. Nor does this mean that the divine power falls short of some further, higher perfection, and so remains unconnected with the utmost perfection. As al-Samhūdī comments: "The mere possibility that there be a more perfect than this perfect does not imply the impossibility of a nexus between the divine power and the most perfect; for the possible is that, the existence and the non-existence of which are (both equally) possible."[116] And he elaborates:

> If we assume that God does not will the existence of that possible which is more perfect than that with which His power stands in nexus, then that with which His power stands in nexus *is* the most perfect in existence, even if the assumption of something more perfect than it be allowed vis-à-vis possibility.
>
> There is, then, neither contradiction nor impossibility in the nexus of the divine power with one degree of perfection beyond which the creator does not will anything more perfect in actual existence (*wuqūʿ*), even if that (further perfection) is allowed as a possibility (*wa-in jāza dhālika imkānan*).[117]

As we know, Ibn al-Munayyir conceded that there are limited perfections in existing things, but the fact that there remain limitless perfections within possibility invalidates al-Ghazālī's statement, in his view; for we can deem nothing ultimately most perfect. Not so, replies al-Samhūdī. It is true that further per-

[115] *Iḍāḥ*, p. 93. Cf. al-Ghazālī, *al-Iqtiṣād*, p. 85: "We may say that if it is present in God's knowledge that He will cause Zayd to die on Saturday morning, one may ask whether the creation of life for Zayd on Saturday morning is possible or impossible. The truth is, that it is both: possible in itself, but impossible in respect to the divine knowledge."

[116] *Iḍāḥ*, p. 123.

[117] *Ibid.*

fections may be assumed as possible, but since God has not willed their existence, they are inevitably inferior to what actually exists; it is the fact that God has willed what is that renders it most perfect.

Furthermore, we may speak off a "most perfect" in actual existence. When Ibn al-Munayyir twists the tenet, "the impossible stands in no nexus with divine power," to mean "the most perfect stands in no nexus with divine power," he is simply wrong. The consensus of the Muslim community disproves him. Does not that very community designate Muḥammad "the most excellent" (*afḍal*) of "those who have been and will be?"[118] This shows that there is, in fact, a most perfect than which nothing more perfect exists.

Degrees of perfection exist as well. They exist, for example, among the prophets, of whom God expresses a preference for some over others. Muḥammad is the most perfect and most marvelous of prophets, and there are degrees of perfection among the others. So, too, among nations: the community of Muḥammad is the best of nations, and within this community the best individual is Abū Bakr. Even in the "genus of non-prophetic perfection" (*jins kamāl ghayr al-anbiyā'*), we see, therefore, that there is a perfection beyond which nothing more perfect exists. Even so, this fact does not prevent the objects of God's power from being infinite in terms of possibility.[119]

Finally, against the charge that al-Ghazālī's statement makes finite what is infinite, al-Samhūdī replies that this involves no difficulty (*maḥdhūr*): it is divine volition itself which prevents the realization of the infinite. Indeed, there would be "contradiction and impossibility" only if "perfection stopped at no limit in existence, such that no perfect could exist but that a more perfect than it would have to occur," for then, divine power would remain unconnected with any most perfect.[120]

al-Samhūdī here turns Ibn al-Munayyir's own argument against him. al-Ghazālī's statement, he maintains, does not lead to a restriction of divine power to a finite number and a fixed term,

[118] *Ibid.*
[119] *Ibid.*
[120] *Ibid.*

but, even if it did, such a limit is required by the divine wisdom. Moreover, God's power is such that He can limit what it limitless in possibility.[121]

The divine power stands revealed in its creation of the limited, the fixed, and the finite, just as it is revealed in its creation of the imperfect, together with the perfect. That God can limit an infinitude of possibilities, far from implying incapacity on His part, is rather a sign of His very omnipotence.

In concluding this section, let us note that both al-Samhūdī and Ibn al-Munayyir accept the axiom that possibilities, the "objects of God's power," are endless, although they place quite different interpretations on this. Ibn al-Munayyir appears to hold that possibilities are literally infinite, and their infinitude is, as it were, a guaranty of God's infinite power. For al-Samhūdī, possibilities are infinite, but only in potency; in fact, they are limited, and yet God's power remains, in itself, infinite.

We have spoken throughout of possibility and possibilities as though the terms were self-evident, but now we must consider them more closely. For it is not immediately apparent what is meant by "possibility" in the disputed statement, nor is it clear that the disputants all understood the term in the same way.

# IV
# THE NATURE OF POSSIBILITY

In the transmissions of the disputed statement, the word *imkān* appears consistently, with the single exception of the version transmitted by Abū Bakr ibn al-ʿArabi. Now *imkān* and the related participial form *mumkin* (corresponding to Greek δύναμις and τὸ δυνατόν, of which indeed they are the translations) are most commonly used in Arabic to express "possibility" and "possible," respectively. To be sure, these are not the only terms used. The possible, in the sense of the "intellectually admissible," is expressed by the word *jā'iz* (*jā'iz ʿaqlī*); this was, in fact, the term originally favored by the *kalām*.[122] Frequently,

[121] *Iḍāḥ*, p. 124: *maʿa annahu taʿālā qādir ʿalā tanāhī mā lā yatanāhā imkānan.*

[122] See R. M. Frank, "*Al-Maʿnā*: Some Reflections on the Technical Meanings of the Term . . . ," *JAOS* 87 (1967), p. 250, note 13.

too, we find possibility rendered by the word *ṣiḥḥah*.[123] And the possible meaning the "contingent" is, in the early texts, such as the Arabic translation of Aristotle's *De interpretatione*, expressed by *al-muḥtamal* (corresponding to Greek τὸ ἐνδεχόμενον).[124]

At times it may seem that these terms are used somewhat loosely in the literature; often they appear interchangeable. Nevertheless, *imkān* and its related forms have quite precise meanings and a correspondingly exact nomenclature which was refined and elaborated over the course of time. A late writer such as Ismāʿīl b. Muṣṭafā al-Kalanbawī (d. 1205/1791), for example, lists no fewer than eight main types of possibility, and several subtypes, in his treatise on the modalities.[125] That possibility is employed in a variety of senses needs no emphasis, in any case.[126]

The possible falls between the extremes of the necessary, which must be, and the impossible, which cannot be. According to Murtaḍā al-Zabīdī, the possible is "what is neither necessary nor . . . impossible by its very nature."[127] At times, the possible is seen as tending toward one of these two extremes, waxing as it approaches the necessary and waning as it approaches the impossible. As Ibn Yaʿīsh al-Raqqī, in the account recorded by Abū Ḥayyān al-Tawḥīdī, puts it, the possible is at certain times

[123] So, for example, in al-Ṭūsī's cmt. on al-Rāzī's *Muḥaṣṣal*, p. 116. See also, ʿAbd al-Jabbār, *Mughnī*, VII, 12, and the *Sharḥ al-uṣūl al-khamsah*, p. 395; both cited in J. Peters, *God's Created Speech* (Leiden, 1976), pp. 80-81 and 199, respectively.

[124] See al-Fārābī, *Sharḥ li-kitāb Arisṭūṭālīs fi'l-ʿibārah* (ed. Kutsch and Marrow; Beirut, 1971), pp. 173-174. See now the superb translation and commentary on this work by F. W. Zimmermann, *al-Farabi's Commentary and Short Treatise on Aristotle's De Interpretatione* (London, 1981), p. 167ff.

[125] His *R. al-imkān* (Istanbul, 1309); the work is more correctly entitled *Miftāḥ bāb al-muwajjahāt*, for which see the description of the Yahuda mss., Mach 3306.

[126] See the Appendix below for a discussion of these senses. In general, see Aristotle, *De int.* 23a8-13 (Loeb ed., pp. 168-169) and al-Fārābī, *Sharḥ*, p. 181ff. (tr. Zimmermann, *al-Farabi's Commentary*, p. 174ff.); *An. Pr.* 32a18-20 [contingent] and 25a38-40 [possible]; *Met.* 1019a15-1020a17 (Loeb ed., p. 248ff). See also G. Ryle, *The Concept of Mind* (London, 1949), pp. 126-127; and, for a history of the subject, A. Faust, *Der Möglichkeitsgedanke* (Heidelberg, 1931).

[127] *Itḥāf*, IX, 430, line -10.

the "shadow" of the necessary, and at others the shadow of the impossible, according to the measure in which it approaches or withdraws from existence.[128] Again, he compares the possible to a kind of dream-state (*ru'yā*), lacking "body" or "nature"; it is one "of the shadows of the waking state" (*ẓill min ẓilāl al-yaqẓah*), i.e., a shadow of the necessary; but, as it diminishes, "it resembles the impossible," and it may of course remain in equilibrium between these two extremes.[129]

Existence is itself divisible into the necessary and the possible, but the necessary may be applied properly only to God, the necessarily existent being (*wājib al-wujūd*), whereas the shadowy mid-kingdom of the possible comprises "everything that is not God."[130] Everything that exists, or may exist, is possible, in that it may exist and it may not exist; the possible is in itself utterly neutral as to existence and non-existence.

This point deserves emphasis. There is an ingrained tendency to consider the possible weighted, as it were, in favor of either existence or non-existence. The possible, however, denotes "the negation of necessity for existence and non-existence simultaneously."[131]

The polymath Ibn Kamāl Pasha (d. 940/1533) discusses this point in a brief treatise addressed to the question of whether "one of the two extremities (i.e., existence or non-existence) is more fitting *per se* for the possible."[132] One group asserts that "non-existence is more fitting for *possibilia*" (*al-ʿadam awlā bi'l-mumkināt*), and by *possibilia* they mean such things as time and motion, described as "flowing possibilities" (*mumkināt sayyālah*), or "possibilities that are non-stationary" (*ghayr al-qārrah*).[133] But this, argues Ibn Kamāl Pasha, cannot be so, any

[128] al-Tawḥīdī, *al-Imtāʿ wa'l-mu'ānasah*, I, 216; see also his *al-Muqābasāt* (ed. Ḥusayn), p. 183.

[129] *Ibid.* Cf. also, Abū al-Baqā', *Kullīyāt* (Damascus, 1974), I, 308. For the *amīr* ʿAbd al-Qādir, possibility is the limbo (*barzakh*) between existence and non-existence; see his *K. al-mawāqif*, I, 99.

[130] al-Rāzī, *Mafātīḥ al-ghayb*, I, 178.

[131] al-Ghazālī, *Miʿyār al-ʿilm*, p. 249; al-Rāzī, *al-Mabāḥith al-mashriqīyah*, I, 114.

[132] *R. fī taḥqīq al-mumkin* (Atsız, no. 98), Yahuda ms. 298 (Mach 3133), fol. 47b, line 7.

[133] *R. fī taḥqīq al-mumkin*, fol. 48b, line 9.

more than that existence is *per se* more fitting for the possible. The possible is that in which the relation to existence as well as to non-existence is equal (*mutasāwī*). Were this not so, we should have to admit something in the very nature of the possible itself that impels it either to exist or not to exist, and this cannot be.

Possibility is, thus, "the absence of intrinsic necessity to exist or not to exist."[134] In itself, it is indifferent to both extremities. Possibility in this sense, as that which can exist and not exist equally, and in which there is no element of necessity, is designated "special possibility" (*al-imkān al-khāṣṣ*) in the technical terminology.

According to Ibn Sīnā—and al-Ghazālī follows him in this—most people mean by the possible merely "something that is not impossible *qua* not-impossible without considering whether it is necessary or not."[135] But to say that the possible is simply what is not impossible is to subsume the necessary, which is also not impossible, under the possible; and indeed, this is "possibility in the popular sense" (*al-imkān al-ʿāmmī*).[136] This results, however, in a division into only the impossible (*mumtaniʿ*) and the not-impossible (*mā laysa bi-mumtaniʿ*), under which both the necessary and the possible are ranged.[137]

What Ibn Sina here discusses is commonly designated in the literature as "general possibility" (*al-imkān al-ʿāmm*), in contradistinction to the aforementioned "special possibility" (*al-imkān al-khāṣṣ*). (The suggestion, implicit in his treatment, that the formulation derives from *ʿāmmah*, "ordinary people"—as opposed to the learned, *al-khawāṣṣ*,—is probably a somewhat playful etymology; it is rejected by later writers, one of whom declares that it is correctly derived from *ʿumūm*, "generality," rather than from *ʿāmmah*.)[138]

[134] al-Jurjānī, *Taʿrīfāt*, p. 30.

[135] Ibn Sīnā, *al-Shifā'*, I/3, 116-117.

[136] *ibid.*; cf. al-Ghazālī, *Miʿyār al-ʿilm*, p. 249.

[137] al-Ghazālī, *Miʿyār*, p. 249, and *Maqāṣid al-falāsifah*, p. 61.

[138] Ibn Malkā, *K. al-muʿtabar*, I, 80. I am indebted for this reference, and for several that follow, to Prof. R. Mach, who generously made available to me his extensive files of Arabic technical terminology. I shall identify citations drawn from his files, in this chapter and in the appendix, with the initials RM immediately thereafter.

Now "the learned" (i.e., the philosophers and, particularly, the logicians), dissatisfied with this bipartite division, introduced the necessary into their distinctions, together with the possible and the impossible, in order to define what they termed "special possibility." What is not possible is not, in this special sense, merely impossible, but rather "necessary either in its existence or in its non-existence" (*ḍarūrī immā fi'l-wujūd wa-immā fi'l-ʿadam*), i.e., what is not possible is either necessary *per se* or impossible *per se.*[139] The necessary is henceforth no longer merely "not impossible," like the possible itself; the necessary is what must exist, the impossible what must not exist. The possible, however, is itself utterly devoid of any intrinsic necessity; it is not necessary that it be, nor is it necessary that it not be.[140]

We shall return to this notion of "special possibility" in what follows, for it appears to be what is meant by *imkan* in the disputed statement.

## *A. IMKĀN VS. QUDRAH*

As we know, Abū Bakr ibn al-ʿArabī replaced the word *imkān* in the disputed statement with the word *qudrah*, so that the statement becomes: There is not in the divine power more wonderful than what is. This reading was corrected by Zakarīyā' al-Anṣārī, and by others. According to al-Santawī, for example, "*imkān* must not be explained as *qudrah*"; and he adds that this is the error of al-Ghazālī's opponents.[141]

Was this merely a careless misreading of the statement, or was it even a mischievous reworking of it? Although we cannot know with certainty, either explanation appears unlikely. *Imkān* and *qudrah* were considered synonymous in certain contexts. al-Fārābī, for example, states: "Possibility (*imkān*), potentiality (*qūwah*), power (*qudrah*), and capability (*istiṭāʿah*) are terms that must now be grasped as synonymous (*mutarādifah*), despite

[139] Ibn Sīnā, *al-Shifā'*, I/3, 117, lines 14-16.
[140] *Ibid.* Cf. also al-Ghazālī, *Miʿyār*, p. 249, and *Maqāṣid al-falāsifah*, p. 61.
[141] *al-Sayf al-ḥusām*, fol. 14a, line -6. [For al-Santawī, see Chapter Two, #22.]

the fact that many disciplines employ these words in divers senses."[142]

Of course, al-Fārābī is here trying to show that there is a common basis for all of these terms. In any case, it seems improbable that Abū Bakr ibn al-ʿArabī, with his repudiation of Aristotelian logic, would rely on such a source.

The problem is that for al-Ghazālī's opponents possibility is understood as "the power to act," i.e., as something in the agent, rather than in the object, of action. Now, Maimonides ascribes this very view to an unnamed "intelligent man from among the later *mutakallimūn*" who formulated it in order to establish God's creation of the world *ex nihilo*. For if possibility resides in the object of action, rather than in the agent, how could the world be created before such a substrate existed?[143] And so, "possibility resides in the agent, and not in the thing that is the object of action."[144]

Now, as it happens, this "intelligent man," to whom Maimonides refers, is probably none other than al-Ghazālī himself, as indeed Wolfson has pointed out.[145] In his *Tahāfut al-falāsifah*, al-Ghazālī states: "The meaning of possibility with reference to something created is that its creation is possible for an agent who has the power to create it, so that possibility is an attribution to the agent."[146]

It seems likely that this is the source of the confusion. An argument which al-Ghazālī devised for a quite specific and limited purpose, as part of his attempt to refute the doctrine of the world's eternity, seems to have been taken in a much wider sense, as though possibility were to be understood as residing exclusively in the agent.

If this is, indeed,the basis of Abū Bakr ibn al-ʿArabī's version it is easy to understand the dismay which the statement occasioned. It is axiomatic that God's power is infinite. If possibility

[142] al-Fārābī, *Sharḥ li-kitāb Arisṭūṭālis*, p. 182, lines 16-17; cf. Zimmerman, *al-Farabi's Commentary*, p. 176, for a slightly different translation.

[143] Maimonides, *Dalālat al-ḥā'irīn*, II, 30b, line -7; tr. Pines, p. 287. (RM)

[144] *Ibid.*

[145] Wolfson, *Philosophy of the Kalam*, p. 595.

[146] *Tahāfut al-falāsifah*, p. 77, line 3ff., as cited and translated in Wolfson, *Philosophy of the Kalam*, p. 595.

and power are synonymous, if indeed possibility resides solely in the agent, then in the case of God, it must be infinite, and to claim that nothing more wonderful remains in possibility is absurd as well as blasphemous.

It must be said, however, that this cannot have been what al-Ghazālī meant and that his defenders are right in vigorously repudiating it. Clearly, much of the confusion in the debate arises not merely from simple misunderstanding but from divergent views of possibility. We must now try to determine how possibility is to be understood in the disputed statement.

## *B. THE MEANING OF IMKĀN IN THE DISPUTED STATEMENT*

It seems clear that the term "possibility" in the disputed sentence is used in the sense of "special possibility." None of the other types of possibility is apposite here. al-Ghazālī does not mean, for instance, "there is not in potentiality" (*qūwah* or *imkān istiʿdādī*), or "there is not in future possibility" (*imkān istiqbālī*), "anything more wonderful than what is." Nor does he mean, as we might suppose from al-Biqāʿī's arguments, "inherent" or "conceptual possibility" (understood as intellectual admissibility: *tajwīz ʿaqlī*), according to which whatever is conceivable is possible.[147] As al-Samhūdī pointed out, there are further possibilities, and God is capable of producing them, but as long as they remain unactualized, they are inferior to what already exists.

al-Santawī puts the point forcibly: "The meaning of al-Ghazālī's statement . . . is that there is not (anything more wonderful than what is) in that, the existence and emergence (*ibrāz*) of which are possible in objective reality (*fi'l-khārij*). Nothing more wonderful than this existing world yet exists; rather, this existence is in fact more wonderful and more excellent than any possible one whose existence may be surmised (*yuqaddar wujūduhu*)."[148]

[147] For a list of other types of possibility, see the Appendix.

[148] al-Santawī, *al-Sayf al-ḥusām* fol. 13a, line 3.

Under general possibility (*al-imkān al-ʿāmm*), as we know, no further distinction is made than between the possible and the impossible, i.e., the impossible and the not-impossible, with the result that the possible and the necessary are subsumed under the not-impossible.[149] Accordingly, general possibility involves "the negation of necessity from one of the two alternatives," and specifically, the second part of the disjunction.[150] An example often used is "Every fire is hot." If we say, "Necessarily every fire is hot, or it is not," we negate necessity in the second part, i.e., "or it is not the case that necessarily every fire is hot." Again, if we say, "Every man is animal," we affirm necessity of the first part, but deny it of the second: "Necessarily every man is animal, or it is not the case that necessarily every man is animal."[151]

General possibility may thus be described as the alternative of the two subcontraries, appearing as the second parts of disjunctions.

Special possibility, on the other hand, is described as "the negation of necessity from both alternatives" (*salb al-ḍarūrah ʿan al-ṭarafayn*).[152] It is that "from which the necessary is excluded" (*kharaja al-wājib ʿanhu*).[153] As an example of this, al-Jurjānī offers: "Every man is one who writes."[154] Both writing and not writing are equally possible, and neither is necessary.[155] Or again, we may say, "Every man exists by special possibility," and we mean that "his existence is not necessary, nor is his non-existence."[156]

[149] al-Ghazālī, *Miʿyār*, p. 249.
[150] al-Jurjānī, *Taʿrīfāt*, p. 30.
[151] al-Isnawī, *Nihāyat al-sūl*, I, 165. (RM)
[152] al-Jurjānī, *Taʿrīfāt*, p. 30; Aḥmadnagarī, *Dustūr*, I, 172. See also al-Dasūqī, *Ḥāshiyah ʿalā al-Tahdhīb*, p. 274. (RM)
[153] al-Ghazālī, *Miʿyār*, p. 249.
[154] al-Jurjānī, *Taʿrīfāt*, p. 30; cf. also Maimonides, *Maqālah fī ṣināʿat al-manṭiq* (ed./tr. Efros), *Proceedings of the American Academy for Jewish Research*, 8 (1937/38), p. 10f. [Judaeo-Arabic text]; p. 39 [English tr.], who terms this *al-mumkin bi'l-ḥaqīqah*.
[155] al-Jurjānī, *Taʿrīfāt*, p. 30. al-Kalanbawī, *R. al-imkān*, p. 63, quibbles over this example, since "not writing is necessary to man during infancy," and he prefers: "Man is one who moves voluntarily."
[156] Aḥmadnagarī, *Dustūr*, I, 172. (RM)

Special possibility may therefore be expressed in the form of a conjunction, in contradistinction to general possibility, which takes the form of a disjunction. Under special possibility, both alternatives may be simultaneously true.

These may be represented on a Square of Opposition, thus:[157]

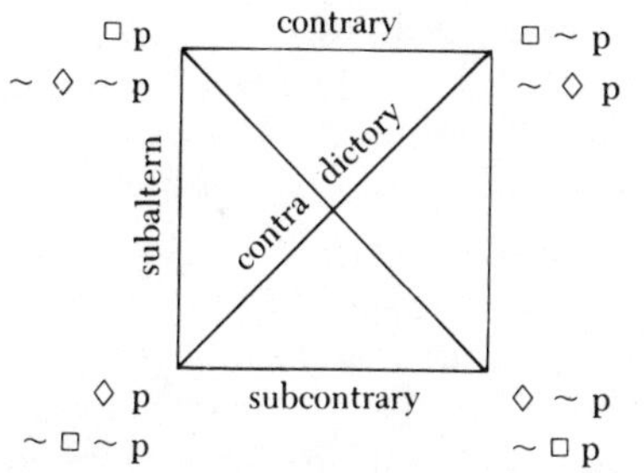


Special possibility then may be expressed as: "it is possible that *p* and it is possible that not-*p*" (◇ *p* • ◇ ~ *p*), whereas general possibility will be expressed as: "it is not necessary that not-*p*, or it is not necessary that *p*" (~ □ ~ *p* v ~ □ *p*). In accordance with the definitions discussed above, special possibility will involve a negation of necessity from both alternatives; general possibility, however, will require the negation of necessity from only one of the two alternatives.

It seems clear now that what is meant in the disputed statement is indeed "special possibility" (*al-imkān al-khāṣṣ*), or, at any rate, that this is how al-Ghazālī's defenders understood the matter. For Zakarīyā' al-Anṣārī, *imkān* is to be interpreted here as "opposite to impossibility and to necessity";[158] and Murtaḍā al-Zabīdī, we recall, noted that the term means "what is neither necessary nor impossible."[159] General possibility, however, carries with it an affirmation of necessity in one of its alternatives.

[157] I am indebted to Prof. R. Mach for this explanation. For the Square of Opposition, see, among others, R. McCall, *Basic Logic* (2d ed.; New York, 1970), p. 85. On the Square of Opposition in Islamic logic, see Naṣīr al-dīn al-Ṭūsī, *Asās al-iqtibās*, p. 100; and for a table of types of possibility, *ibid.*, p. 150. The notation here is as follows: p = proposition; □ = necessary; ◇ = possible; • = and; v = or; ~ = not.

[158] Cited in *Ḥikmat*, p. 31.

[159] *Itḥāf*, IX, 430, line -10.

As we know, it is, by contrast, the signal characteristic of special possibility to be devoid of necessity.[160] It is, as al-Ghazālī phrases it, "one" in regard to either of the extremities of existence or non-existence.[161] And, according to another commentator, "Everything that is not possible in terms of special possibility is either necessary or impossible, and both of these (latter) are possible in terms of general possibility."[162]

Now if this is so, and possibility in the disputed sentence is in fact special possibility, how does this affect our interpretation of it? What, indeed, does "special possibility" mean?

Although it is not always clear from the texts, it would seem that special possibility corresponds to contingency. Ibn Sīnā describes the contingent (*al-muḥtamal*) as that which relates to a future time, whereas the possible (*mumkin*) is "what has no continuance (*dawām*) in either its existence or its non-existence."[163] The contingent is that which is now non-existent but which may come to exist; the possible is that which now exists, but which may cease to exist at any time.[164] And yet, Ibn Sīnā notes, when people say "the possible" (*al-mumkin*), they mean the general sense, whereas in speaking of the contingent, they intend the special sense (*al-khāṣṣ*).[165]

Keeping in mind our definition of special possibility as that which equally can exist and not exist, we find that this corresponds exactly to the traditional notion of contingency: "*contingens est, quod potest esse et non esse.*"[166]

If the contingent is that in which there is no necessity either to exist or not to exist, it is also that which "requires something

[160] It should be noted that a "most special possibility" (*al-imkān al-akhaṣṣ*), denoting the denial of necessity absolutely, is also discussed in the literature; see al-Kalanbawī, *Miftāḥ bāb al-muwajjahāt*, fol. 39a. Cf. also, al-Taḥtānī, *Lawāmiʿ*, p. 106. (RM)

[161] *Miʿyār*, p. 249.

[162] al-Taḥtānī, *Lawāmiʿ*, p. 38, line 19. (RM)

[163] Ibn Sīnā, *al-Shifā'*, I/3, 114, line 14.

[164] Ibn al-Muqaffaʿ, *Manṭiq* (ms. Tehran/Majlis), fol. 62b, line -5. (RM)

[165] *al-Shifā'*, I/3, 114.

[166] St. Thomas Aquinas, *Summa theologiae*, I.86,3, cited in Eisler, *Wörterbuch der philosophischen Begriffe*, I, 849 [s.v. "Kontingenz"]; see also, N. Abbagnano, *Dizionario di filosofia* (Turin, 1961), p. 162. Cf., too, Aristotle, *De gen. animal.*, 731b.25, and al-Ghazālī, *Maqāṣid al-falāsifah*, p. 232.

other than it for its existence and its non-existence."[167] This is, of course, preeminently true of the world itself; indeed, it is the basis for the proof *a contingentia mundi* for the existence of God. This has as a consequence that the contingent can always be otherwise; contingency signifies "das Andersseinkönnen," to borrow Eisler's definition.[168] As such, it corresponds to actuality, or to the factual. The contingent judgment "All the kings who ruled in France in the eighteenth century were named Louis" is, as its author points out, "a statement of fact, but clearly is not the expression of any law. The proposition relates to a limited number of individuals who happened to have the same name given to them; but we recognize that their names might have been different, and that their being kings of France was not dependent on their possessing the name in question. This then we may call a judgment of actuality."[169]

We are now in a position to interpret the disputed statement. We understand "*laysa fi'l-imkān* . . ." to mean: there is not in the realm of contingency, i.e., the realm of things that equally can be and not be, and that require for their existence or non-existence something outside themselves, anything more wonderful than what is. This, it would seem, is what al-Samhūdī means when he paraphrases the statement: ". . . there is not in the possibility by which every possible is to be described. . . ."

The point here is that the contingent, or the actual, is in itself indifferent to existence or non-existence; it requires something outside itself to effect its coming-to-be and its passing away. This "something" which confers existence as well as non-existence on the things of this world, and the world itself, also confers their condition of "most-excellentness." That which confers existence and its concomitant of insuperable excellence is the divine power, acting in concert with wisdom and will. It is not anything inhering in the world itself.

[167] al-Rāzī, *al-Mabāḥith al-mashriqīyah*, I, 114.

[168] Eisler, *Wörterbuch*, I, 849. Cf. Duns Scotus: the contingent is "something whose opposite could have occurred at the time that this actually did," in *Philosophical Writings* (tr. A. Wolter), p. 59.

[169] J.N. Keynes, *Studies and Exercises in Formal Logic* (4th rev. ed.; London, 1906), p. 88. Cf. also, R. Carnap, *Meaning and Necessity* (Chicago, 1960), p. 175. (RM)

The divine power, says Aḥmad Zarrūq, is "the attribute that necessitates the emergence of a possible whose existence rather than non-existence is willed; and the proof (of power) is this emergence."[170]

When we say, "There is not in the realm of contingency anything more wonderful than what is," we mean on the one hand that the things in this realm retain their character of radical contingency, that they do not themselves cause either their existence or its perfection; and, on the other, that they are as they are, only because God has made them so. They can of course be annulled and superseded by subsequent, more wonderful and equally contingent things.

Furthermore, these contingent things never lose their character of radical contingency. At the same time, however, they may become either necessary or impossible "because of something else" (*propter aliud*). The world itself is radically contingent, and remains so in its very nature. Nevertheless, as soon as it exists, it becomes necessary. It is, and remains, contingent *per se*, but it becomes necessary *propter aliud* (i.e., it is *mumkin li-dhātihi*, but *wājib li-ghayrihi*).[171]

Conversely, what does not exist is also possible *per se*, but impossible *propter aliud*. Another order of things is in itself possible. One may conceive it, and do so without any internal contradiction. And yet, while it remains perfectly possible in itself, it is impossible "because of something else."

This, we would suggest, is the real root of the disagreement, on this point, between al-Biqāʿī and such defenders of al-Ghazālī as al-Suyūṭī and al-Samhūdī. al-Biqāʿī is right, in that whatever is conceivable is possible; however, he fails to allow for the necessitating action of the divine will and wisdom in the designation of certain *possibilia* for existence, and others for non-existence.

For al-Ghazālī's defenders, and for al-Samhūdī especially, the fact that certain possibilities remain unrealized is itself a sign of

[170] Aḥmad Zarrūq, *Sharḥ ʿAqīdat al-Ghazālī*, p. 59.

[171] al-Ghazālī, *Miʿyār*, p. 250. Cf. Ibn Sīnā, *al-Najāh*, p. 226f. For a useful summary of the concept and its development, see Abbagnano, *Dizionario*, p. 162.

the divine wisdom. Their very absence argues forcefully for the unsurpassable excellence of what is. The fact that they do not exist, at a given moment, indicates that God's wisdom has decreed, and His power realized, their non-existence at that moment. Consequently, what does exist, by the very fact of its existence, must be most excellent. If it were not, it would not exist.

This is the significance of the definition of possibility, in the disputed sentence, as "special possibility," or contingency. The contingent is in itself neutral in regard to both existence and non-existence; it is, as it were, inert, vis-à-vis both extremities. Only the divine power, and nothing else, is capable of effecting its existence and its non-existence.

There is a tendency, which al-Biqāʿī betrays in his arguments, to suppose the possible endowed with a specious status bordering on existence, but this is incorrect. If a possible thing, such as an alternative location for Mt. Qāsiyūn, does not exist, it is because the divine wisdom has decreed its non-existence; in itself it remains possible, but in fact it is impossible. *Possibilia* are not simply incipiently existing things, verging on realization; they are things whose non-existence the divine wisdom intends, and so they cannot, at this moment, exist.

It is in this sense, in the view of al-Ghazālī's defenders, that "there is not in possibility more wonderful than what is."

FOUR

# *Creation as "Natural Necessity"*

## I
## THE SECOND MAJOR CHARGE

For al-Ghazālī, the world is not only "the most wonderful in possibility," it is "according to the necessarily right order, in accord with what must be and as it must be and in the measure in which it must be."[1] This affirmation of a "necessarily right order" (*al-tartīb al-wājib al-ḥaqq*) led his critics to associate the statement with certain doctrines of the philosophers, and especially the doctrine which its opponents term *ījāb dhātī*, creation by "natural necessity."[2]

Thus, in mentioning the vexed question, the 15th–century author Kamāl al-dīn ibn Abī Sharīf claims that it arises from al-Ghazālī's "confusion (*dhuhūl*) in basing himself on the methods of the philosophers."[3] This charge is countered by Ḥāmid al-Shāfiʿī, among others, who argues that it is not "necessity," but the divine decree (*qaḍā' Allāh*) which produces things, and that this is what al-Ghazālī meant.[4] Interestingly enough, Kamāl al-dīn b. Abī Sharīf's younger brother Burhān al-dīn b. Abī Sharīf takes up the cudgels in al-Ghazālī's defense against his brother: "In the Proof of Islam's statement there is no compulsion (*ījāb*) of any sort and no curtailment of divine power, or any denial of power (to create) other than this world; rather, He is able to produce infinite worlds. . . ."[5]

It is tempting to dismiss al-Ghazālī's detractors as obscuran-

[1] *Iḥyā'*, IV, 223.

[2] The notion enters Western Scholasticism as the question of whether God creates *per necessitatem naturae*; see, for example, St. Thomas Aquinas, *Summa contra gentiles*, II, 23. For an extended discussion, see B. Zedler, "Saint Thomas and Avicenna in the '*De Potentia Dei*,' " *Traditio* 6 (1948), pp. 105-159.

[3] *al-Musāmarah fī sharḥ al-Musāyarah*, p. 61; cited also in *Dhahab*, p. 474.

[4] *al-Dalīl wa'l-burhān*, fol. 134a, *paen.*

[5] Cited in *Dhahab*, p. 479, line -7ff.

tists and to relegate their charges against him to mere quibbles over words; to do this is, however, to misunderstand what is truly at issue. At first sight, it might seem that to speak of a "necessarily right order" is simply another way of expressing the traditional and quite orthodox belief that whatever exists, is the result of the divine predetermination; that, as the *ḥadīth* has it, "what strikes you was not there to miss you," etc. Or we may accept al-Ghazālī's own explanation, that the *ḥadīth* embodies what the ordinary reader is capable of understanding, whereas the initiated perceive, beyond this, that what is "must be" (*wājib al-ḥuṣūl*).[6] Both of these explanations of the disputed statement and its immediate context are, indeed, employed by al-Ghazālī's defenders.

As we have seen, to certain of al-Ghazālī's earliest critics such as al-Ṭurṭūshī, al-Māzarī, and Ibn Rushd, he is at best a clumsy epigone of the philosophers, and particularly Ibn Sīnā, and at worst, a corruptor of the unwary. He parrots the philosophers without understanding them. This view persisted, even if it was voiced more circumspectly. Ibn al-Munayyir, al-Biqāʿī, Kamāl al-dīn b. Abī Sharīf, and al-Sijilmāsī al-Lamaṭī level the same or similar accusations. These are minority opinions, but they arise from an authentic perplexity, nor are they without foundation.

It is probably impossible for us to recapture the sense of alarm which certain of al-Ghazālī's later "Ṣūfī" works (or passages thereof) provoked in more traditionally minded readers. The passage in which our vexed question occurs is a good case in point. Here we find alongside the traditional components of pious discourse—the Qur'ānic allusion, the quotation from *ḥadīth*—phrases and terms that emerge laden with alien associations: "necessarily right order," "comes to be necessarily," "there is not in possibility," etc. It is not a question of usage alone (although the terminology may well have carried a barbarous ring in this context). It is that notions adopted from suspect disciplines appear, without disclaimer or qualification, side by side with the language of time-honored piety. Moreover, these phrases are introduced as though intended to provide a rationalistic basis for the

[6] *K. al-arbaʿīn*, p. 245.

more traditional precepts, precepts, it need hardly be stressed, which the common reader is expected to accept unquestioningly.

The alarming and discordant note which these phrases and terms strike may account for the persistence of the interpolation theory. To many readers they may have sounded strange and unfamiliar, as though an alien voice intruded upon a well-known (or at least reasonably predictable) discourse.[7]

However well founded the accusation that al-Ghazālī submitted unduly to the influence of the philosophers, it would carry serious weight only if it could be shown that he had in some way subscribed to an outright heresy on their part. To object to his use of philosophical terminology or his reliance on Aristotelian logic was a long-lost cause, even by the time of Ibn al-Munayyir in the 13th century, although, of course, objections to these persisted. Indeed, as has often been noted,[8] it was al-Ghazālī's introduction of the methods and vocabulary of philosophy which made possible the further development of the *kalām* in the works of Fakhr al-dīn al-Rāzī, al-Ijī, al-Taftāzānī, and others. In order to invalidate the statement by linking it with the philosophers, it was, therefore, necessary to show that it led to some untenable and long-repudiated conclusion. It is for this reason, we suspect, that al-Biqāʿī sought, albeit tortuously, to connect it with the doctrine of the world's eternity.[9]

This lies ultimately behind the charge of undue philosophic influence on al-Ghazālī. If his opponents do not press it vigorously, it is probably because the underlying issues no longer appeared charged with the urgency they once had; the doctrine of the eternity of the world was simply no longer a vital question for theologians of the later periods. And if the matter appeared settled, it was very largely due to al-Ghazālī's own refutation of this doctrine in his *Tahāfut al-falāsifah*. Needless to say, it was

[7] The interpolation theory persists in modern scholarship; see, for example, Hava Lazarus-Yafeh, "Philosophical terms as a Criterion of Authenticity in the Writings of al-Ghazzālī," *SI* 25 (1966), pp. 111-121. I find her argument unconvincing.

[8] See, e.g., J. van Ess, *Die Erkenntnislehre des ʿAḍudaddīn al-Icī*, p. 29.

[9] See Chapter Three above, section I. D.

well-nigh impossible to claim convincingly that the chief demolisher of this doctrine had in some way secretly supported it.

Nevertheless, the charge had its uses. al-Ghazālī's immersion in the methods and doctrines of the philosophers was common knowledge, and the influence of this immersion demonstrable. Concerning any debatable point in his writings, those who contested it could easily claim the malign intrusions of the philosophers into otherwise irreproachable teaching. And although none of his opponents based his attack solely on the obvious affinity of the statement with the doctrines of Ibn Sīnā, for example, the inclusion of this charge added gravity to the attack. Sometimes we may suspect that "the philosophers" are invoked principally as a convenient form of dismissal of an irksome question; but this is not often the case.

The charge is serious enough, but it is made too late. The elements to which exception was taken had long since been successfully incorporated into dogmatic theology. Certainly, this is true for the discussions in the 15th-16th centuries, when interest in the issue was at its height. Only if it could be shown that al-Ghazālī somehow included within such passages as that in the *Iḥyā'* doctrines that were clearly beyond the pale, could he be tellingly attacked on this score. This would be equivalent to showing that the disputed statement meant not what its supporters thought but something quite different, something repellent to orthodox sensibilities. The doctrine of "creation by natural necessity" offered just such a possibility.

## II
## THE DOCTRINE OF NATURAL NECESSITY

In his fifth point, and in the conclusion of his treatise as well, Ibn al-Munayyir maintained that the controversial statement was in agreement with the philosophical doctrine that God creates "by natural necessity" (*bi-ījāb dhātī*).[10] This means, first, that God creates not as an act of free choice (*ikhtiyār*), but as a very condition of His nature (*dhāt*); and, second, that whatever

[10] Cited in *Iḍāḥ*, p. 97. Cf. the discussion in al-Bāqillānī, *K. al-tamhīd*, p. 34ff., over whether God is not simply a "nature" (*ṭabī'ah*), from whose existence the world must come to be (*wajaba ḥudūth al-'ālam 'an wujūdihi*).

He creates is perforce "most excellent," since "from the perfect only the perfect may issue."[11]

What is meant by this doctrine is explained further by al-Ghazālī himself in his exposition of the philosophers' views. An agent may act by "sheer nature" (*ṭabʿ maḥḍ*), i.e., "without knowledge of either what is done or the doing (itself)."[12] Or he may act with will (*irādah*). Will presupposes knowledge; and indeed, it is in this sense that God, or "the One," acts, for "His will is His knowledge":

> Everything emanates from the divine nature while He knows that it is emanating from Him. Its emanation is not incompatible with His nature, such that it would be averse (*kārih*) to it; there is in Him no aversion to it. He, therefore, consents to its emanating from Him, and this may be termed will.[13]

Divine knowledge is the source of this emanation (*fayaḍān*). This is not knowledge as we experience it, for human knowledge is in fact either belief (*iʿtiqād*), or opinion (*ẓann*), or fancy (*takhayyul*). Our knowledge is only exact and disinterested and productive of "true intellectual knowledge" (*ʿilm ʿaqlī ḥaqīqī*) in certain pursuits, such as geometry.[14] God's knowledge, however, is not only consummate and disinterested; it is itself the cause for the existence of things: "His very act of mental apprehension suffices for the thing apprehended actually to exist" (*nafs taṣawwurihi kāfin li-ḥuṣūl al-mutaṣawwar*).[15] The divine knowledge comprehends the good in itself that is "universal order" (*al-niẓām al-kullī*).[16] His knowledge of this order produces it, and it flows from Him in series of emanations. His nature (*dhāt*), says al-Ghazālī, is one "from which every existent emanates necessarily in the most complete and perfect way according to its possible arrangement within (universal order), unto the farthest limits of order."[17]

[11] *Ḥikmat*, p. 15.
[12] *Maqāṣid al-falāsifah*, p. 235.
[13] *Ibid.*
[14] *Ibid.*
[15] *Ibid.*, p. 237.
[16] *Ibid.*
[17] *Ibid.* This is based on Ibn Sīnā, *al-Shifā'*, *Ilāhīyāt*, II, 414ff.; cf. also, Ibn Sīnā, *al-Najāh*, p. 284ff. The doctrine receives extensive development in the

The necessary order of things emanating from the divine in accord with His perfect knowledge is described as providence (*ʿināyah*), corresponding to the Greek πρόνοια, from which source much of the doctrine derives. This is not, of course, providence as used in ordinary religious parlance; it is a disinterested providence which acts on behalf of universal order and not, as Ibn Sīnā emphasizes "for our sakes."[18]

It is undeniable that al-Ghazālī's insistence on the perfect rightness of the actual owes much to this doctrine. One of the cardinal theses of philosophic providence, in its various ancient as well as in its Islamic forms, is that the cosmos manifests a rational and, indeed, necessary order and that, as a result of this order, the cosmos is surpassingly beautiful as well. This notion is of great antiquity. Pohlenz, for one, traces it back as far as the pre-Socratic Diogenes of Apollonia (fl. 440-430 BC). Diogenes held that the underlying substance of the universe possessed intelligence for otherwise, "it would not be possible . . . so to be divided up that it has measures of all things—of winter and summer and night and day and rains and winds and fair weather. The other things, too, if one wishes to consider them, one would find disposed in the best possible way" (διακείμενα ὡς ἀνυστὸν κάλλιστα).[19]

This is a key tenet as well of the Stoic doctrine of providence, with the added notion that the order and beauty of the cosmos are purposeful. They are intended to benefit its inhabitants, and most especially man himself. The universe, according to Chrysippus, is "a whole composed of gods and men and those things which have come to be for their sakes."[20] This universe is often compared to a great and magnificent house in which nothing necessary is lacking; and "when we see a well-built house we ask not only by whom but for whom it is built."[21] The teleological view serves a double purpose: it indicates man's proper sta-

---

work of Ṣadr al-Dīn al-Shīrāzī (Mullā Ṣadrā); see his *al-Ḥikmah al-mutaʿālīyah*, VII, 55ff. For another, earlier treatment, see Ibn Rushd, *Talkhīṣ mā baʿd al-ṭabīʿah* (ed. Amīn; Cairo, 1958), p. 160ff.

[18] *al-Shifāʾ*, *Ilāhīyāt*, II, 414.

[19] M. Pohlenz, *Die Stoa*, II, 56; the translation is from Kirk and Raven, *The Presocratic Philosophers*, p. 433.

[20] Pohlenz, I, 99 [citing *SVF*, II, 527-528].

[21] *Ibid.*

tus; and it indicates that the world owes its just and ordered existence to a providential agent. "If you see some great and beautiful building, would you infer, because the architect is not immediately visible, that it must have been built by mice and weasels?"[22]

We find a similar emphasis in the earlier Islamic philosophers. al-Kindī (d. 252/866), for example, states:

> In the order of this world and its arrangement (*tartīb*) . . . and in the perfection of its form for what is best in the existence of each thing that comes to be and in the passing away of each thing that passes away, in the permanence of every permanent (*thābit*) thing, and the transience of every transitory thing, there is a mighty proof for supremely perfect design (*atqan tadbīr*)[23] (and every design presupposes a designer) and for wisest wisdom (*aḥkam ḥikmah*) (and for all wisdom there is one who is wise), because this is all connected.[24]

And, in a discussion of providence, al-Fārābī (d. 339/950) declares that it "pervades particular things and all the parts of the world, and its conditions are set in the best-appointed and most perfect places . . . and all the things by which it is sustained are delegated (*mawkūl*) from the one who sustains them necessarily in the utmost perfection and wisdom."[25]

The emphasis on order and design in creation serves to indicate that things do not happen accidentally or at random: "the whole cannot come to be by chance (*bakht*) and coincidence (*ittifāq*); and so, too, with the world as a whole"—and the proof of this is "the wonderful order" (*al-niẓām al-badīʿ*) which exists in all parts of the world, one with the other."[26]

[22] Cicero, recapitulating the Stoic viewpoint, in *De natura deorum*, II:17; tr. McGregor, *The Nature of the Gods*, p. 130.

[23] The word *tadbīr*, like *ʿināyah*, serves to render Greek πρόνοια; thus, the treatise on providence by Alexander of Aphrodisias, extant only in Arabic, is entitled alternatively *Fī'l-ʿināyah* or *K. al-tadbīr*. See A. Neuwirth, *ʿAbd al-Laṭīf al-Baġdādī's Bearbeitung von Buch Lambda der aristotelischen Metaphysik* (Wiesbaden, 1976), p. 190. The Arabic text of Alexander's treatise has been published by Hans-Jochen Ruland in *Die arabischen Fassungen von zwei Schriften des Alexander von Aphrodisias* (Diss., Saarbrücken, 1976).

[24] al-Kindī, *Rasāʾil*, I, 215.

[25] al-Fārābī, *K. al-jamʿ* (ed. Dieterici), p. 26, line 2ff.

[26] *Ibid.*, p. 23.

These examples, together with those adduced in Chapter One, make it clear that there are unmistakable affinities between the providence of the philosophers and the Ghazālian optimism. These are no doubt due in part to such common sources as Galen's *De usu partium*. Indeed, al-Fārābī cites it explicitly as one of his authorities for the doctrine.[27]

Nevertheless, there are equally unmistakable differences between the two applications of this ancient doctrine, and chiefly in al-Ghazālī's conception of the divine will. al-Ghazālī borrows various concepts and terms from the philosophic doctrine of providence, but he bends them to serve his own purposes. The borrowings are obvious: we note the recurrence, in al-Ghazālī's text, as well as in those of al-Fārābī and al-Kindī, of such terms as *tartīb* and *tadbīr*; there is, further, the striking emphasis on wisdom in creation, and on its necessary order; and, finally, there is the rather unexpected word *badīʿ*, which al-Fārābī uses to describe the universal order and of which the elative form *abdaʿ* appears in al-Ghazālī's statement, ostensibly for the same purpose.

And yet, the fundamental divergence between the philosophers and al-Ghazālī resides in the latter's adherence to the principle of divine free choice (*ikhtiyār*).

There is no need for choice in, say, the Avicennian system. Perfect knowledge expressed in will, which is itself merely "consent" (the term used is *rāḍin*), determines the series of necessary emanations that flow from the One down to the furthest reaches of the sublunary world. And perfect knowledge precludes choice. Choice implies some motive or preference, either of which sway the will to action. In the Avicennian system, however, God is wholly disinterested and acts for no "purpose"; certainly, "the supreme causes do not do what they do for our sakes."[28] Rather, these causes and the divine itself act impartially and necessarily in conformity with universal order.

[27] *Ibid.*, p. 26. It is worth noting that J. Schacht considered Galen's *De usu partium* to have influenced the Muʿtazilite doctrine of the optimum as well; see his "New Sources for the History of Muhammadan Theology," *SI*,1 (1953), pp. 23-42.

[28] Ibn Sīnā, *Ishārāt*, III, 154; see also note 18 above.

Such supreme aloofness preserves unimpaired the transcendent perfection of the divine. Freedom to choose is not seen here as an attribute of the highest perfection. The One who knows perfectly knows necessarily. For such knowledge there are no alternatives; there is only the right and the good, known and effectuated forthwith. It is for a similar reason that in Eastern Christianity, for example, St. Maximus the Confessor (c. A.D. 580-662) would assert that human free will is actually a token of human imperfection. A perfect nature does not need choice: "it knows naturally what is good."[29]

All of these elements, which make up what al-Ghazālī's critics mean by *ījāb dhātī*, appear clearly in a text by the physician and philosopher ʿAbd al-Laṭīf al-Baghdādī (557-629/1162-1231):

> We maintain neither that God's activity primarily has as its end the order and well-being of the world, nor that these things come to be without His knowledge and will and consent. We do not maintain further that the existence of these things has something other than Him as cause. Rather, we maintain that their existence and order follow on His existence, for He is perfectly good. . . .
>
> He does the good as does the fire that warms everything in its vicinity without its existence and warmth existing for the sake of that which it warms; but rather, in order to preserve continually its own proper nature.
>
> Thus it is with God as well. For to all existing things He gives as much of good and rank as they can and will accept. Could we further assume that the fire knows and wills its own intrinsic nature and the warmth and light that issue from it, the simile would be fully apposite.[30]

Knowledge and will alone preserve God from acting by "sheer nature," as fire or any other such natural object acts.[31] Never-

[29] Cited in Vladimir Lossky, *The Mystical Theology of the Eastern Church* (London, 1973), p. 125.

[30] Cited in F. Rosenthal, *Das Fortleben der Antike im Islam* (Zürich, 1965), p. 215. This portion of the Arabic text remains unpublished and was unavailable to me.

[31] For unqualified "natural necessity," see the passage in the *Muṇḍaka Upaniṣad*: "As a spider emits and draws in (its thread), as herbs arise on the earth, as the hairs of the head and body from a living person, so from the Imperishable

theless, will (in the sense of consent or allowance) is only a function of knowledge; and the divine knowledge is ultimately indistinguishable from the divine nature itself.

What is of moment here, in connection with the charge of "natural necessity" brought against al-Ghazālī in his controversial statement, is that God, in the view of the philosophers, cannot not know; hence, He cannot not will. It would be imprecise to claim, as adversaries of the doctrine do, that God is in effect governed by necessity, as though necessity were some higher principle to which He were subordinate. Rather, he is the source of necessity. And yet, the fact remains that He cannot, for example, choose not to act simply because choice is inappropriate for His nature.

It follows from this that there cannot have been a time in which the divine nature was not fully active. Otherwise, it would be necessary to assume that at one moment He was inactive and then chose to act; and yet, this would entail some change in the divine nature. A necessary consequence of the doctrine of *ījāb dhātī* is, then, the eternity of the world. If the world had been created *ex nihilo*, as scripture claims, then there was some time at which the divine knowledge was not fully realized.

Against this, it would be argued, for example, that any action whatsoever implies the initiation of a process occurring in time. If we accept the philosophers' arguments, how may we speak of action in any sense of God's part?[32]

It is not possible here to enter into the complex of arguments for and against the world's eternity; these have, in any case, been rather thoroughly explored.[33] At issue is the fact that the

---

arises everything here," in S. Radhakrishnan (ed.), *A Sourcebook in Indian Philosophy*, p. 51; see also C. A. Scharbau, *Die Idee der Schöpfung in der vedischen Literatur* (Stuttgart, 1932), p. 98ff.

[32] So al-Ghazālī, *al-Iqtiṣād*, p. 104.

[33] See, for example, al-Ghazālī, *Tahāfut al-falāsifah*, pp. 21-78, and the response of Ibn Rushd, *Tahāfut al-tahāfut* (ed. Bouyges), pp. 4-117; Maimonides, *Guide* (tr. Pines), pp. 281-327. See also Wolfson, *Philosophy of the Kalam*, pp. 355-466, and E. Behler, *Die Ewigkeit der Welt*, Teil 1 (Paderborn, 1965), especially p. 149ff. For a useful discussion, see George F. Hourani, "The Dialogue between al-Ghazālī and the Philosophers on the Origin of the World," *The Muslim World*, 48 (1958), pp. 183-191; 308-314. On the issue from a Scholastic viewpoint, see Bernardino M. Bonansea, "The Question of an Eternal World in the Teaching of St. Bonaventure," *Franciscan Studies*, 34 (1974), pp. 7-33.

doctrine of *ījāb dhātī* not only deprives God of free choice, but leads inevitably to belief in the eternity of the world.

## III
## THE DIVINE WILL (*IRĀDAH*)

Divine will, like divine power, is also one of the seven problematic "attributes of essence" or "existential attributes." It, too, is "something superadded to the divine nature." God does not will essentially, but "by virtue of a will." Furthermore, this will stands in a nexus with its objects, all of which are possible objects of will (*murādāt*). And again, as in the case of power, it is said that will does not stand in any nexus with the impossible. God's will is, in the paradoxical formulation, "not God and nothing other than God." It is not (as the philosophers hold) indistinguishable from the divine nature itself.

The character of the divine will is described in the sentence: "What He wills, is and what He does not will, is not."[34] This extends to the least, seemingly insignificant, occurrence: ". . . not even the casual glance of a spectator nor the stray thought in the mind come to be outside the sphere of His will."[35] Will is also expressed by the term *mashī'ah*, "volition," and so it is that the word *shay'*, "thing," deriving from this same root, is sometimes glossed as "what has been willed [sc. by God] to exist."[36]

The divine will serves a precise and unique function. Possibilities, as explained earlier, are in themselves equal with regard to existence and non-existence; they have within themselves no predisposition either to be or not to be. There must be something extrinsic to them that determines their status. This cannot be the divine nature itself, for it, too, is "one," as al-Ghazālī puts it, "in relation to opposing alternatives."[37] Nor can it be the divine power, for it is undifferentiated and does not determine at what moment a thing may be or not be; power merely effectuates its existence or non-existence. There is thus a need to

[34] al-Ghazālī, *al-Iqtiṣād*, p. 108.
[35] al-Ghazālī, *K. al-arbaʿīn*, p. 6.
[36] See al-Jawharī, *al-Ṣiḥāḥ*, I, 58-59; Ibn Manẓūr, *Lisān al-ʿarab*, I, 97-98.
[37] al-Ghazālī, *al-Iqtiṣād*, p. 101.

posit for some attribute the function of determining when and how things shall be. This attribute is will. Its unique function is termed the "specifying [or: determining] action of the will" (*takhṣīṣ al-irādah*).[38]

In defending al-Ghazālī's position, his supporters draw on the exposition he furnishes in his doctrinal *kalām* work *al-Iqtiṣād fi'l-iʿtiqād*; and so, in what follows, we shall briefly restate this.

According to al-Ghazālī, there are four basic doctrinal positions on the divine will. Of these, only the first, that of the philosophers, and the fourth, that of the *ahl al-ḥaqq* or "party of truth" (i.e., the Ashʿarites), need concern us here.[39]

The philosophers assert that the world exists through God's very nature (*bi-dhāt Allāh*). They deny that there is any attribute such as will superadded to His nature. Since God's nature is eternal, the world is also eternal; it is related to the divine as effect to cause: it is like light cast by the sun or the shadow which a person projects.[40]

Against this, the Ashʿarites affirm that "the world comes to be at that time when the eternal will stands in nexus with its coming-to-be."[41] And yet, the will of God is eternal and suffers no alteration *qua* eternal attribute when it determines the creation of the world in time. This involves a difficult problem, to be sure; and this problem lies at the heart of all the varying opinions on divine will. al-Ghazālī poses this underlying problem thus: "Why does the divine will stand in nexus with temporal creation at a specific time (*fī waqt makhṣūṣ*), neither earlier nor later, despite the fact that the relations of (various) times to the will are equal?"[42] That is, why did God will the world's

[38] *Ibid.*; cf. also, al-Āmidī, *Ghāyat al-marām*, p. 53. See the discussion of *takhṣīṣ* in Ibn Sīnā, *al-Shifā'*, *Ilāhīyāt*, I, 38-39, which lies at the basis of al-Ghazālī's view.

[39] al-Ghazālī, *al-Iqtiṣād*, p. 101. The second position is that of the Muʿtazilites who hold that God acts by a temporal will "not in a substrate" (*lā fī maḥall*), but this is like saying, "He wills by a will subsisting in something other than Himself," and is an absurdity "beyond discussion;" cf. *al-Iqtiṣād*, p. 106. The third position is that of the Karrāmīyah.

[40] *al-Iqtiṣād*, p. 103.

[41] *Ibid.*, p. 104.

[42] *Ibid.*

creation at one moment rather than another? What induced His will to act at that moment, and not earlier or later?

The philosophers avoid this difficulty with their doctrine of the world's eternity. Nevertheless, they cannot escape the evidence for the "specifying effects of the divine attributes" (*khuṣūṣ al-ṣifāt*), for these are manifest in the world itself: "the world is specified in a specific measure and a specific position" (*al-ʿalam makhṣūṣ bi-miqdār makhṣūṣ wa-waḍʿ makhṣūṣ*), even though "its contraries remain possible in the intellect."[43] Nevertheless, the eternal nature cannot be said to conform better to some possibilities than to others.[44] That is, the world as we experience it is in fact "specified." Certain things exist, but not others (although these others could exist). The fact that certain things do exist, and in a certain specified way, demonstrates that the world has indeed itself been specified. Hence, there must be something which specified the existence of things as they are, as well as the non-existence of that which remains a mere possibility in the mind. It is this specifier that we call will. Through will, things created in time come to be when they do. The will distinguishes these things from "opposites belonging to the same genus."[45]

The world thus bears witness to the determining and discriminating action of will. Even so, a further perplexity arises. Why does this will choose one thing but not another? Are not both opposites equal in respect to possibility? In replying to this doubt, al-Ghazālī also provides the answer to his first and fundamental question: why does the will act at one time rather than another?

The question, he claims, is itself erroneous. It is like asking, why does knowledge entail disclosure of the knowable (*inkishāf al-maʿlūm*)? That, in turn, is like asking, why is knowledge knowledge?[46] The acts of distinguishing and of specifying are the will's acts *par excellence*. To ask why it distinguishes or specifies one time or one thing rather than another is to ask, why is it a

[43] *Ibid.*

[44] *Ibid.*: *al-dhāt al-qadīmah lā tunāsib baʿḍ al-mumkināt dūna baʿḍ.*

[45] *Ibid.*; p. 106: *fa-mayyazathā ʿan aḍdādihā al-mumāthilah lahā.* Cf. al-Ijī, *Mawāqif*, IV, 48.

[46] *al-Iqtiṣād*, p. 107; cf. also, *Tahāfut al-falāsifah*, p. 37.

will, or why is will will? It is these very actions that constitute will: "the true nature (of the will) is to distinguish a thing from what is like it."[47]

Whatever exists has been created by God's power; but, in order to exist at all, a thing stands in need of the divine will "in order to direct power to its object and specify (the object) for (power)."[48] Every object of power is at the same time an object of will: *kull maqdūr murād.*[49] Things that exist in time are objects of power. Therefore, things created in time are also objects of will: *kull ḥādith murād.*[50]

This syllogism has predictable consequences: "Evil (*al-sharr*), disbelief (*al-kufr*), and sin (*al-maʿṣīyah*) are created in time," and so they, too, are necessarily objects of will, for "what God wills, is and what He does not will, is not."[51]

In the following chapter we shall discuss some of the solutions which al-Ghazālī offers to the problem of evil. The point here is that evil in all its forms is willed. It does not occur simply as a secondary consequence of some greater good, or as a necessary concomitant of the good. Or, rather it may come to be for these reasons, but it is nevertheless fully intended; it is a contingent thing specified by the divine will.

Although al-Ghazālī composed *al-Iqtiṣād fī'l-iʿtiqād* as a manual of dogmatic theology and did not himself regard the methods of the *kalām* as the only, or even the best, approach to higher truth, there is no reason to conclude that his exposition here conflicts with his later, more complex views.[52] Indeed, at the end of the controversial *Iḥyā'* passage itself he declares that "good and evil are foreordained. What is foreordained comes necessarily to be after a prior act of divine volition" (*baʿd sabq al-mashī'ah*).[53] It is, of course, this very point which his defenders single out in denying that al-Ghazālī subscribes to the doctrine of "natural necessity" (*ījāb dhātī*); and they would appear to be in the right. Everything that occurs, does occur necessarily, but

[47] *al-Iqtiṣād*, p. 107: *ḥaqīqatuhā tamyīz al-shay' ʿan mithlihi.*
[48] *Ibid.*
[49] *Ibid.*
[50] *Ibid.*
[51] *Ibid.*, p. 108.
[52] On this, see his *al-Munqidh min al-ḍalāl* (ed. Jabre), pp. 16-17.
[53] *Iḥyā'*, IV, 223.

not because in and of itself it must. It occurs necessarily because of God's prior decree and volition.

In his treatise on the divine names, al-Ghazālī states: "All the events that occur in the world, the evil and the good, the helpful and the harmful, are not outside the divine volition, but rather are willed by God."[54] Even more explicitly, and again relying on the philosophical terminology that so provoked his critics, he states: "Everything that enters into existence enters only by necessity (*bi'l-wujūb*). It is necessary that it exist, even if it is not necessary *per se* (*wājib li-dhātihi*), but rather necessary by the eternal decree (*wājib bi'l-qaḍā' al-azalī*), against which no one can rebel."[55]

Thus, the necessity in the natural order results from the divine decree and does not proceed inevitably from the divine nature itself. If God wished, He could obliterate this universe and bring forth a new and different order; if God had wished, He could have foregone creating this universe at all.[56] God's will is characterized by choice, as is His power. As Nāṣir al-dīn al-Ṭūsī (d.672/1274) notes: "He is powerful from whom an act may issue or not issue. This possibility is power."[57]

God's action therefore proceeds from will. Will, however, is based on "what wisdom demands" (*mā taqtaḍīhi al-ḥikmah*). This gives rise to another objection which we must briefly consider.

## IV
## THE FUNCTION OF WISDOM

al-Biqā'ī took exception to the notion that God acts "according to the dictates of wisdom." God is not bound by reason or by wisdom; He does what He will.[58] The objection seems to

[54] *al-Maqṣad al-asnā*, p. 102, lines 9-11.

[55] *al-Maqṣad al-asnā*, p. 103, lines 4-5.

[56] *al-Iqtiṣād*, p. 174; *Iḥyā'*, I, 111.

[57] In his commentary on Fakhr al-dīn al-Rāzī's *al-Muḥaṣṣal*, p. 116; cf. al-Jurjānī, *Ta'rīfāt*, p. 149.

[58] See Chapter Three, section 1, above. Cf. Ibn Ḥazm's remark that God does what He wishes without regard for reason, cited in G. E. von Grunebaum, "Concept and Function of Reason in Islamic Ethics," *Oriens* 15 (1962), p. 6, note 1 [citing *al-Iḥkām li-uṣūl al-aḥkām* (Cairo, 1345), VIII, 120]. For the phrase "what wisdom demands," see al-Rāghib al-Iṣfahānī, himself an influence on al-Ghazālī, in his *Tafṣīl al-nash'atayn*, pp. 17 and 39.

be that al-Ghazālī's insistence on wisdom masks an imputation to God of subservience to some ruling principle.

al-Ghazālī uses "wisdom" in rather a precise way. Someone is wise who knows "the most excellent of things (*afḍal al-ashyā'*) by the most excellent of sciences," i.e., whoever knows God (insofar as He can be known), who is Himself the "most excellent of things," is wise.[59] Moreover, God is "the truly wise" (*al-ḥakīm al-ḥaqq*) since He knows "the most exalted of things (*ajall al-ashyā'*) by the most exalted knowledge."[60]

In God's case, to be wise means "to arrange causes and direct them to their effects," for He is "the cause of all causes" (*musabbib kull al-asbāb*).[61] Exploiting the fact that the divine name *al-ḥakam*, "the arbiter," derives from the same root as *ḥikmah*, "wisdom," al-Ghazālī remarks that God's providential design (*tadbīr*) is the foundation for the establishment of causes. God's decree and foreordainment proceed from this faculty of wise arbitration, both in general and in particular. Predestination, allied with wisdom, determines the enduring and unchanging course of heavens and earth, the stars and the spheres, as well as those purely temporal effects (*al-musabbabāt al-ḥādithah*), the motions of which are "limited, measured, and perceptible," and it does this "instant by instant."[62]

We have already discussed the effects of this divine wisdom and will in the natural order. We must now look, however, at a particular instance of this wisdom in relation to a point of marked dispute.

## V

## THE CREATION OF THE IMPERFECT

As we have seen, al-Ghazālī and his supporters hold that God purposely creates the imperfect together with the perfect, and that the imperfect is itself most wonderful. We may be tempted to think that the strange insistence on this point arises from a wish to dissociate al-Ghazālī's position even more sharply

[59] *al-Maqṣad al-asnā*, p. 130.
[60] *Ibid.*
[61] *al-Maqṣad al-asnā*, p. 98.
[62] *Ibid.*

from that of the philosophers who maintain that "from the perfect only the perfect may issue."

This may be true in part; ultimately, however, the position develops from the premise that whatever occurs is the result of divine will directed by wisdom. It may seem grotesque to insist that it is a measure of God's power and wisdom that He can create the imperfect and defective as well as the perfect, as though creation of the perfect alone implied some shortcoming in the divine nature! And yet, this is the position which al-Ghazālī's supporters maintain.

Furthermore, whether or not al-Ghazālī's defenders stress this doctrine more than they might in order to distance him from the philosophers, there is a more important reason for their insistence. To say that God deliberately and primordially wills the creation of the imperfect helps to explain the very disparity among the things of this world. Poverty and wealth, sickness and health, misery and bliss, etc., are "most wonderful" just because God has willed them for a particular individual at a particular moment; and, indeed, has willed them from all eternity.

In part, this is a result as well of what has been termed "the principle of plenitude."[63] This means that all possible niches in the order of things must be occupied. The absence of any item in the inventory of being would constitute an impairment of divine generosity and wisdom. That the perfect order of the whole be realized, all sorts of things and circumstances along the whole "chain of being" must come into existence—the deleterious and the nugatory as well as the beneficial and the grand. We have already noted examples of this from the texts of the dispute.

The cosmos is not only the arena in which the *coincidentia oppositorum* is enacted; it is a "filled cosmos." This is why it is said that "nothing can be added" to the actual order of things. In the words of al-Jazā'irī:

[63] The phrase was coined by A. Lovejoy in his *The Great Chain of Being*; see especially p. 52. For a detailed critique of Lovejoy's application of his principle, see now Simo Knuuttila (ed.), *Reforging the Great Chain of Being: Studies of the History of Modal Theories* (Dordrecht, 1981).

> The "state of being most wonderful" is a way of saying (*kināyah*) "reaching the brink of the impossible": the production of this world is by virtue of free choice and divine will in a way that unites wisdom and all possible benefits, such that increase to them is not possible, like a filled vessel (*inā' mumtali'*) to which one cannot add.[64]

And he comments further:

> The existing world allows full measure to everything that can be in accord with instances of wisdom (*ḥikam*) and excellence, so that increase and decrease and transformation into some other form are not possible, even by so much as a gnat's wing. The Prophet's statement attests to this: "If you knew about the invisible world, you would choose things as they are" (*al-wāqiʿ*).[65]

What does not exist, or what does not yet exist, cannot exist. It is, however, only extrinsically impossible; God's prior decree has ordained that it shall not be. The Ṣūfī ʿAyn al-Quḍāt al-Hamadānī, himself an early subject of al-Ghazālī's influence, states this clearly: "Anything which is possible must exist from eternity. Thus does God's *sunnah* proceed in this world and the next. You will never find any alteration in God's *sunnah*. Everything which does not yet exist is considered impossible (*muḥāl*), i.e., by something other than it, not *per se* (*lā bi-dhātihi*). . . . The reason for this is that it is God who is the cause for the existence of what exists."[66]

Does this not return full circle to the original question, that the order of things is somehow necessary? The answer is, of course, yes; everything that is, comes necessarily to be, but its necessity is governed by the divine decree. It is necessary only because God wills it, and not otherwise. In His eternal foreordainment, God decrees certain things, His will specifies them, and His power executes them; and the very priority of these things, the fact that their existence was preceded by divine volition, guarantees their necessity and their necessary excellence.

How may we know this in everyday life? First, it is through

[64] *Ḥikmat*, p. 43.
[65] *Ḥikmat*, p. 44.
[66] *Zubdat al-ḥaqā'iq*, in *Muṣannafāt* (ed. ʿUṣayrān; Tehran, 1341), p. 18.

imperfection that we come to recognize perfection. To this Ibn al-Munayyir may object, "What need is there to know the perfect?" on the grounds that "the best for man would be not to be aware of the perfect."[67]

To this al-Samhūdī replies that man is one upon whom a religious obligation has been enjoined—he is *mukallaf*—and he has the obligation to know in order to fulfill the requirements of gratitude (*shukr*).[68] Unawareness of the perfect (*ʿadam al-istishʿār biʾl-kamāl*) leads to heedlessness, and so ignorance cannot be best. Since it is through opposites that we know at all, contemplation of them arouses us to bless: "seeing one opposite reveals the great perfection of its opposite, and its excellence."[69] Therefore, when we see a sinner or an afflicted person, we offer a prayer of thanksgiving.[70]

Ibn al-Munayyir has a further objection: even if we do need to know the perfect, we do not need to know it through the imperfect. Simple apprehension (*taṣawwur*) of the perfect is possible, just as we know straightaway that God is perfect and that an imperfect god is impossible.[71] And, he adds, could not God, in any case, have created us from the outset with knowledge of the perfect?

The reply to this is that God could create in us a direct and immediate knowledge of the perfect; however, wisdom demands that we acquire knowledge in this indirect way. Thus do we come to realize that it is God who links "causes with effects," and so we are moved to gratitude. The blessed come to knowledge of their superior state through seeing the pain of unbelievers in hell and, through their knowledge, they are prompted to offer continual thanks.

Even conceding that through the imperfect we recognize the perfect, Ibn al-Munayyir further objects: could not God have been content to let the world's very contingent and created character alone suffice to illustrate His supreme perfection? The

[67] Cited in *Iḍāḥ*, p. 135, line 1.
[68] *Ibid.*
[69] *Ibid.*: *shuhūd al-ḍidd yuẓhir akmaliyat ḍiddihi wa-ḥusnahu.*
[70] *Iḍāḥ*, p. 133; cf. *Luke* 18:10-14.
[71] *Iḍāḥ*, p. 133.

contingent is by nature imperfect, and so "what need would there be to create man blind or deaf" as well?[72] Furthermore, would not one imperfect individual suffice: "how is it that the imperfection of created things is more abundant than (their) perfection?"[73]

al-Samhūdī replies, first, that this merely substantiates his claim that what al-Ghazālī meant is that "the matter redounds to (God's) volition and free choice, and not to necessity or compulsion" (*iḍṭirār*).[74] In a creation governed by necessity, a preponderance of imperfection would not occur; since it does in fact occur, we must assume that it is so willed and intended by God.

He reverts here to an argument introduced earlier by al-Suyūṭī:

> You try to deny the divine wisdom in the creation of the imperfect and the fact that God does what He will. You describe the God of profound wisdom by that from which one must declare Him remote. It is known that gold and silver are more perfect than rock and that God is capable of creating mountains wholly of gold and silver. The more marvelous, however, is what He does make. If all were of gold and silver, people would forgo earning by professions.[75]

God likes people to pursue even the "base professions" (*al-ḥiraf al-khasīsah*), "so that the world's business may be carried out in an orderly way."[76] al-Samhūdī cites approvingly the dictum of Ibn ʿAṭāʾ Allāh: "The existence of the needy is a boon from God for the affluent since they discover (in them) someone to bear their provisions from them into the afterworld."[77] Thus,

[72] *Ibid.*

[73] *Ibid.* Cf. Ibn Sīnā's treatment of this question in *Shifāʾ*, *Ilāh.*, II, 634, *al-Najāh*, p. 476, and *Ishārāt*, III, 207-208: the extremes of either great good fortune or abject misery are rare, in actuality it is the median state that predominates. Cf. also Leibniz, *Essais de theodicée*, p. 109ff.

[74] *Iḍāḥ*, p. 133.

[75] *Ibid.*

[76] *Ibid.* For the "base professions" (tanner, weaver, barber, etc.), see R. Brunschvig, "Métiers vils en Islam," *SI*, 16 (1962), pp. 41-60.

[77] *Iḍāḥ*, p. 134. For the 10th-century Ismāʿīlī writer Abū al-Fawāris A. Ibn Yaʿqūb, the disparity among people is a sign of wisdom (*al-tafāwut fī'l-ʿālam ḥikmah*), for otherwise, order would be incomplete (*lam yatimmi niẓām*); this, too, explains why Zayd is selected for the imamate, but not ʿAmr. See his *al-*

nothing is without its reason in the world designed by wisdom. Even discrepancies serve, for they occasion gratitude.[78] All promotes, all contributes to, the admirable order of the world.

As to why God did not remain satisfied to create only one afflicted or imperfect individual, al-Samhūdī remarks:

> Divine wisdom requires the universalization (*taʿmīm*) of all creation. . . . A multiplicity reminds people of God's blessing, and they thank Him for it over and over again. A paucity would not suffice for this causal connection whereas a multiplicity does; for a multiplicity proceeds in accordance with wisdom. God made the qualities of perfection and imperfection dissimilar in His creation so that there would not appear in the majority one afflicted with a defect . . . without there appearing also someone else more severely afflicted with tribulation than he. . . . Thus, there opens for the (less afflicted) the path to gratitude to God for His blessing to him in saving him from the worse affliction.[79]

This bracing observation is supported by *ḥadīth*: "Abū Hurayrah said, 'Consider those beneath you, do not consider those who are above you!' "[80] Presumably, consideration of those more fortunate might prompt feelings other than gratitude.[81] And al-Samhūdī cites as well the *ḥadīth* in which Adam, having observed the discrepancies between rich and poor, handsome and

---

*Risālah fi'l-imāmah* in S. N. Makarem, *The Political Doctrine of the Ismāʿīlīs* (Delmar, NY, 1977), p. 18 [Arabic]; pp. 33-34 [English translation].

[78] According to al-Suyūṭī, *Tashyīd*, fol. 2a, lines 16-25, God "made the types of affliction various with the intention of prompting gratitude," e.g., a poor, starving man sees a wealthy man who is desperately ill and each thanks God for not having afflicted him as severely as the other; a ruler thanks God that he is not among the ruled while the latter observe the ruler's fears and dangers, and so thank God for not making them rulers.

[79] *Iḍāḥ*, p. 136.

[80] *Ibid.*; see Aḥmad ibn Ḥanbal, *Musnad*, II, 254.

[81] See, e.g., the anecdote cited in R. Mottahedeh, *Loyalty and Leadership in an Early Islamic Society* (Princeton, 1980), p. 77, in which a poor man exclaims, "As a pauper I do not pray to God; to Him pray the powerful and the wealthy." Traditionally, of course, in Islamic belief, the poor are said to enjoy a precedence over the rich in paradise, which they enter, according to different reports, "40 autumns," or even 500 years, before the affluent; see Ibn Qayyim al-Jawzīyah, *Ḥādī al-arwāḥ*, pp. 101-103.

ugly, exlaims, "O Lord! If only You had made Your servants equal!" And to which God replies: "I love to be thanked!"[82]

And, continues al-Samhūdī, does not al-Ghazālī himself point out that of the various things for which any reasonable man must be grateful to God in whatever poverty, illness, or terror befalls him, the first and foremost is that his plight is not worse than it is; for it can always be worse, since "the objects of God's power are endless."[83]

God can, of course, augment His favor to a particular individual as well. For example, he may increase the mystic knowledge of one person while limiting that of another. In both cases, His action is "most wonderful." In the one case, He knows that the individual is capable of absorbing further knowledge without detriment, whereas in the other, He knows that not to increase his knowledge is preferable. Certain individuals are incapable of accepting such knowledge, and so God prevents it "lest his absorption distract him from what is beneficial . . . for one who is absorbed in love does not feel even the pain of a swordblow."[84]

In summary we may say that the imperfect serves in the providential scheme of things not only to lead us to knowledge and to stand, in al-Ghazālī's words, as a "ransom" for the perfect, but that it also serves to signify that the world is willed as it is. The world as it is, is the product of God's free choice. Hence, the term "necessity" in the *Iḥyā'* passage denotes not "intrinsic necessity" (*wujūb dhātī*), but rather, in al-Samhūdī's phrase, "necessity by free choice" (*wujūb bi'l-ikhtiyār*). This he explains as follows:

> The most excellent and the most perfect occur necessarily by reason of the priority of divine predestination, and the volition which executes it and the wisdom which demands it.
>
> Hence, necessity in this sense is necessity by free choice because it has its source in priority of knowledge . . . and in vo-

[82] *Iḍāḥ*, p. 134; see Aḥmad ibn Ḥanbal, *Musnad*, V, 135.

[83] *Iḍāḥ*, p. 136, citing *Iḥyā'*, IV, 111. For al-Ghazālī's concept of gratitude and its possible sources, see S. van den Bergh, "Ghazālī on 'Gratitude towards God' and its Greek Sources," *SI*, 7 (1957), pp. 77-98.

[84] *Iḍāḥ*, p. 119; the example of the sword-blow is probably taken from *K. al-arba'īn*, p. 267.

lition. . . . Thus, absence (of necessity) is impossible due to the perfect efficacy of the will, the power consequent to it, and the extensive wisdom which requires placing things in their proper places (*fī maḥallihā*).[85]

## VI
## THE OBJECTIONS OF AL-SIJILMĀSĪ AL-LAMAṬĪ

al-Samhūdī glosses the final lines of the *Iḥyā'* passage as meaning that this world demonstrates "a specified order which must occur . . . because the priority of a divine volition necessitates its occurrence."[86]

This, replies al-Sijilmāsī al-Lamaṭī, is conceded (*musallam*), but it proves nothing; it is certainly no proof that the world is most wonderful and most perfect. We have here, he argues, only two alternatives: al-Ghazālī's statement (and al-Samhūdī's defense of it) either conforms to the Muʿtazilite doctrine of "the optimum" (*al-aṣlaḥ*), or it is a mere *petitio principii* (*muṣādarah ʿan al-maṭlūb*), "for he furnishes no proof that what must be, due to the nexus of knowledge and will, is the most wonderful and the most perfect, (and that) other than it does not remain in possibility."[87]

To say that the divine will and the divine knowledge precede the creation of their objects does not prove that these objects are necessarily the best, unless one adheres to the belief that God is somehow obliged to provide the best (i.e., that there is some necessity to which He is subject). On the other hand, if the statement is seen as not deriving from the Muʿtazilite position, al-Samhūdī's argument simply begs the question; in his argument, al-Samhūdī tacitly assumes that if divine will precedes the creation of something, that thing will perforce be best. This, however, is the very point requiring proof.

[85] *Iḍāḥ*, p. 73; cited also in *Dhahab*, p. 483, and *Ḥikmat*, p. 34. See al-Ghazālī's statement in *al-Maqṣad al-asnā*, p. 103: "Everything that enters into existence enters only by necessity, for it is necessary that it exist; if it is not necessary intrinsically (*li-dhātihi*), nevertheless, it is necessary by the eternal decree."

[86] *Iḍāḥ*, p. 73: *al-tartīb al-mutaʿayyan lā budda min ḥuṣūlihi.*

[87] *Dhahab*, p. 483.

Unless some necessity dictates God's production of the most wonderful, there is no reason to suppose that He must produce it, or that nothing better remains in possibility (or, indeed, that He must bring forth anything at all). God is not capricious, but He is unpredictable to human reason. There is no intellectual basis (as the Muʿtazilites wrongly suppose), nor is there any principle in the nature of things (as the philosophers teach), which entitles us to assume that God will act in a given way.

al-Lamaṭī next turns to the oft-invoked "divine wisdom" which requires "the assignment of things to their proper places," and he asks, "What do you mean by wisdom?"[88]

Wisdom denotes either knowledge, which is the apprehension of things in their true quiddity (*taṣawwur al-ashyāʾ bi-taḥaqquq al-māhīyah*), or action that is "ordered and masterful, comprising everything needed in respect to beauty (*zīnah*) and perfection."[89]

On the one hand, if wisdom be taken to mean knowledge, it will not require "the necessity of the most wonderful" (*wujūb al-abdaʿ*), to the exclusion, that is, of less than the most wonderful, "since by necessity (*ḍarūratan*) divine knowledge stands in nexus with everything."[90] On the other hand, if wisdom be understood as action, it too does not convey the desired result (*lā yufīdukum*): ". . . to express the efficacious nexus of power (*taʿalluq al-qudrah al-tanjīzī*) as a cause for effecting only the most wonderful and most perfect, on the ground that (wisdom denotes) masterful and skillful action, does not demand restricting it to the most wonderful and denying it of other individuals in the sphere of possibility."[91]

In short, to invoke "wisdom" is either to resort to a belief in causality (*taʿlīl*) and a denial of free choice (*nafy al-ikhtiyār*), as do the philosophers, or it is to flee to the position of the Muʿtazilites, who uphold God's wisdom as action, solely in order to avoid imputing to Him either stinginess or injustice.[92]

[88] *Dhahab*, p. 484.
[89] *Ibid.*, citing *Maqāṣid al-falāsifah*, p. 240.
[90] *Dhahab*, p. 484.
[91] *Ibid.*
[92] *Ibid.*

In combatting al-Samhūdī, al-Lamaṭī has recourse to the earlier arguments of Aḥmad ibn al-Munayyir: to say that God produces the most wonderful limits His omnipotence and His omniscience. Indeed, al-Lamaṭī contends that al-Samhūdī has not accurately grasped Ibn al-Munayyir's arguments. In recapitulating Ibn al-Munayyir's attack, al-Lamaṭī attempts to reduce al-Samhūdī's arguments to their alleged philosophical (or Muʿtazilite) presuppositions or to show that they are based on simple fallacies. When he cites the *Maqāṣid al-falāsifah* against al-Samhūdī, he does so as though this ostensibly neutral exposition of the philosophers' views represented al-Ghazālī's own position, as if to say: the very words of your own master disprove you. al-Lamaṭī proceeds thus with impunity, for he is convinced that the disputed statement has been interpolated into al-Ghazālī's works. He is even willing to entertain the possibility that al-Ghazālī's own defense of the statement in the *Imlāʾ* is itself a wholesale interpolation.[93]

At this point, it would be well to keep in mind that the vehemence of the debate is fired not only by the desire to prove al-Ghazālī right or wrong in his statement, but also to claim him and his spiritual authority as a prize. Whether one represented a stricter, more traditionalist Ashʿarism (as al-Biqāʿī does), or a more rationalistic, *kalām*-based position (as al-Samhūdī does), or even a mystical and esoteric tendency (as we find in Ibn ʿArabī, al-Shaʿrānī and al-Jazāʾirī), one's particular doctrinal emphasis could be immensely enhanced by claiming al-Ghazālī as a sponsor. In this sense, al-Lamaṭī seeks not to discredit al-Ghazālī, but to reclaim him; he seeks the "original," narrowly orthodox al-Ghazālī behind the obfuscations of his defenders.

Unfortunately, al-Lamaṭī's arguments remain virtually unanswered; or, rather, they are considered only to be dismissed as unworthy of reply.

al-Jazāʾirī, for instance, transmits al-Lamaṭī's attack on al-Samhūdī's gloss of the phrase "necessary order" but notes only that it "eloquently proclaims (al-Lamaṭī's) lack of understanding."[94] To the criticism that al-Samhūdī commits the fallacy of *petitio*

[93] *Dhahab*, p. 496.
[94] *Ḥikmat*, p. 34.

*principii*, al-Jazā'irī replies drily: "this is something that may be disregarded."[95]

Murtaḍā al-Zabīdī responds at greater length, but relies on an *ad hominem* approach. al-Lamaṭī's own lack of insight is responsible for his attack. Murtaḍā al-Zabīdī exclaims indignantly: "This is an astonishing matter! If a peephole (*kūwah*) into the transcendent world had been opened for (al-Lamaṭī), he would have beheld what the godly (*al-ṣāliḥūn*) behold, and some of the secrets disclosed to initiates would have been revealed to him."[96] Thus, to a man who prayed, "O Lord! Show us the world as You see it!" the Prophet replied in rebuke, "Do not speak thus! God does not see the world as you see it. Say rather, 'O Lord! Show me the world as the godly man sees it!' "[97] It would behoove al-Lamaṭī, Murtaḍā al-Zabīdī continues, to strive for a perception of the truth like al-Ghazālī's, rather than to carp at that which he misunderstands.

For Murtaḍā al-Zabīdī, al-Ghazālī is "one of the great masters of esoteric truth " (*min akābir ahl al-bāṭin*); comprehension of his teaching is recondite for those who pursue mere exoteric knowledge. It becomes these latter to bow to him in such matters, for "the *ahl al-ẓāhir* are no proof against the *ahl al-bāṭin* in any way."[98]

## VII
## AL-GHAZĀLĪ AND THE PHILOSOPHERS

It is clear from al-Ghazālī's own writings, and in particular the *Tahāfut al-falāsifah*, that he rejects the notion of necessary creation. In the *Tahāfut*, for example, he asserts the primacy of the divine will in opposition to the philosophical doctrine of the world's eternity.[99] And again, in rejecting belief in causality, he affirms that the divine will acts by free choice (*ikhtiyār*).[100]

Nevertheless, it is also clear that he is heavily indebted to the

[95] *Ḥikmat*, p. 37.
[96] *Itḥāf*, IX, 459, line -7.
[97] *Ibid.*
[98] *Itḥāf*, IX, 460, line 1ff.
[99] *Tahāfut al-falāsifah*, pp. 21-78, and especially p. 37.
[100] *Ibid.*, pp. 277-296, especially p. 283, lines 4-5.

philosophers. This he himself admits. His method is eclectic, and unashamedly so. For he subscribes to the principle attributed to ʿAlī ibn Abī Ṭālib: "Do not know the truth by the men, but rather, know the truth, and then you will know who follow it."[101] To be sure, this does not prevent him from recommending that the ignorant and the ill-informed be kept from exposure to works of philosophy:

> Just as it is obligatory to keep one who is not a skilled swimmer from slippery places along the shore, so is it obligatory to preserve people from studying these books; just as it is obligatory to keep young boys from handling snakes, so is it obligatory to keep the ears from becoming too familiar with such utterances.[102]

Philosophy presents a double danger to the "weak-minded," in that they are inclined either to accept it or to reject it *in toto*; and yet, either course is hazardous.

Those who reject philosophy outright run the risk of ignoring useful and, indeed, self-evident truths, such as are provided by mathematics and astronomy. Moreover, such people bring religion itself into disrepute. When such a well-intentioned but ignorant person rejects, for example, the philosophers' account of lunar and solar eclipses, "someone may hear who knows these things through conclusive demonstration (*bi'l-burhān al-qāṭiʿ*) and he does not doubt demonstration, but comes to view Islam as founded upon ignorance and the rejection of proof. Thus, his love for philosophy increases, as does his hatred for Islam."[103]

al-Ghazālī enunciates the rule to be observed: if the philosophical doctrine is "reasonable in itself and corroborated by proof, and is not in conflict with the Book and the *sunnah*, then why should one flee and renounce it?"[104]

To be sure, the philosophers are all in varying degrees tainted by disbelief and apostasy. As al-Ghazālī notes further, they have

[101] *al-Munqidh min al-ḍalāl*, p. 25. On the issue in general, see Michael E. Marmura, "Ghazālī's Attitude to the Secular Sciences and Logic," in G. Hourani (ed.), *Essays in Islamic Philosophy and Science* (Albany, 1975), pp. 100-111.

[102] *al-Munqidh*, p. 27.

[103] *al-Munqidh*, pp. 21-22.

[104] *al-Munqidh*, p. 26.

as well the lamentable habit of sprinkling throughout their writings citations from the Qur'ān and *ḥadīth*. An unwary reader may be led thereby to believe that their works are acceptable in all points:

> When someone considers their books, such as the [*Rasā'il* of the] Ikhwān al-ṣafā' and the like, and sees how they mix into their doctrines the wise sayings of the prophets and the words of Ṣūfis, he may at times deem [these books] right and accept them and form a high opinion of them. Thus, he hastens to accept the falsehoods that are mixed therein because of the good opinion he formed of what he saw and approved. This is a kind of gradual progression into error.[105]

Ironically, al-Ghazālī's opponents discover the same sort of danger in his works, and claim to detect the deleterious influence upon him of such works as the *Rasā'il* of the Ikhwān al-ṣafā'. The charge was made within his own lifetime, and he responded to it in his "autobiography," in a way that suggests that our disputed statement may have been one of the points at issue:

> A group of people, whose minds have not firmly grasped the religious sciences and whose perceptions have not penetrated the farthest objectives of doctrinal teachings, has taken issue with certain statements published in our writings on the mysteries of the religious sciences. They claim that these statements come from the Ancients (*al-awā'il*), despite the fact that some of these are the off-spring of (my own) reflections (*muwalladāt al-khawāṭir*),—for it is not impossible that one hoof strike where another has already struck!—and still others occur in the scriptures, while the import of most of them may be found in Ṣūfi works.[106]

This disavowal notwithstanding, al-Ghazālī proceeds to defend the use of philosophy: "Suppose that (these statements) exist nowhere but in their writings. . . . Were we to open the gate and proceed to relinquish every truth to which the mind of an infidel had preceded us, we would be forced to forego much

[105] *al-Munqidh*, p. 27.
[106] *al-Munqidh*, p. 26.

of the truth."[107] And he gives a concrete example: the reasonable man "does not loathe honey even if he finds it in the cupping-glass, for he knows that the cupping-glass does not change the intrinsic nature of the honey."[108]

Most people, he continues, cannot grasp this:

> For when you trace and ascribe a statement to a person of whom they think highly, they accept it, even if it be false; but if you ascribe it to one of whom they hold a low opinion, they reject it, even if it be true. And so, they everlastingly recognize the truth by means of men, rather than recognizing men by means of the truth; and this is the ultimate error![109]

Acting on this principle, al-Ghazālī wishes to establish what is useful, and what baneful, in the works of the philosophers. Certain subdivisions of philosophy, such as arithmetic and geometry, he points out, are indifferent with regard to revealed truth and may be deemed harmless. Logic, too, is in itself neutral, although it offers a potential danger. For example, those whom its clarity impresses may come to believe that certain heretical doctrines which it supports are also true.[110] In any case, logic is not the private province of the philosophers. In former ages, theologians employed it too, although with different terminology. Furthermore, the name logic (*manṭiq*) is itself used by philosophers solely in order to intimidate (*tahwīlan*).[111]

While mathematics, astronomy, and even logic may be considered neutral, the metaphysical doctrines of the philosophers pose a distinct danger, and it is these doctrines which al-Ghazālī seeks to expose and demolish in the *Tahāfut al-falāsifah*. In-

[107] *Ibid.*

[108] *Ibid.* al-Ghazālī's argument here may be compared with the similar line of reasoning used by the great Orthodox theologian St. Gregory Palamas (1296-1359) who declares that there is benefit in the works of pagan philosophers, just as there is therapeutic efficacity in the flesh of serpents; such works are a mixture of "honey and hemlock." See his *Triads*, ed./tr. J. Meyendorff, *Défense des saintes hésychastes* (Louvain, 1959), I, 56-57.

[109] *al-Munqidh*, pp. 26-27. Appropriately enough, al-Lamaṭī will invoke this principle to justify his attack on the disputed statement; see *Dhahab*, p. 497.

[110] *al-Munqidh*, p. 23.

[111] *Tahāfut al-falāsifah*, p. 16.

deed, in that work he analyzes and refutes no fewer than twenty "heretical" doctrines held by the philosophers.[112]

Even so, while philosophers from earliest times, up to and including al-Fārābī and Ibn Sīnā, are to be considered heretics, their works are not utterly devoid of truth.[113] Truth and falsehood lie side-by-side within their works, and this is the essence of the problem. To extract from such a farrago the useful truths it undoubtedly contains is no task for the ignorant. For the ignorant, again in al-Ghazālī's words, fail to see that

> . . . the propinquity of the counterfeit (*zayf*) to the good coin does not render the good coin counterfeit, just as it does not make the counterfeit good. So, too, the propinquity between truth and falsehood does not make the true false, nor the false true.[114]

In short, al-Ghazālī takes the truth where he finds it. And in the case at hand, he has clearly borrowed from his predecessors among the philosophers. It is perhaps disingenuous when he claims that his statements come solely from his own independent thoughts or from the Qur'ān and *sunnah* or from the pronouncements of Ṣūfī masters. al-Ghazālī owes a distinct and undeniable debt to al-Fārābī and to Ibn Sīnā, as well as to various works of Greek philosophy in Arabic translation, such as Galen's *De usu partium* or the same author's *Compendium* of Plato's *Timaeus*. In particular, al-Ghazālī has borrowed from these authors a notion of providence which he seeks to reconcile with traditional Islamic belief.[115]

The obvious impediment to use of such doctrines as philo-

[112] *Tahāfut*, pp. 18-20. The three erring doctrines with which the philosophers are consistently charged are belief in the world's eternity, the denial of divine free choice, and causality; see Ibn al-Dāʿī al-Rāzī, *Tabṣirat al-ʿawāmm*, p. 4.

[113] *al-Munqidh*, p. 20.

[114] *al-Munqidh*, p. 27.

[115] See, for example, his characteristic gloss of the traditional pious term *rushd* ("right guidance") by *ʿināyah*: "By right guidance, we mean the divine providence which assists a person by directing him to his goals and enabling him (to obtain) that in which there is benefit . . ." *Iḥyā'*, IV, 94, line 14. The term *ʿināyah* is, of course, not originally—or exclusively—a philosophical term; disputes such as the present one no doubt gained in intensity and in acerbity because of the wide and shifting range of connotations which such terms possessed.

sophic providence is that the doctrine presupposes a strict necessitarianism. Such necessitarianism is unacceptable from the orthodox standpoint, not simply because it entails restricting God's freedom and will,[116] but also because of its two corollaries: causality and the eternity of the world.

The problem here is not merely to deny necessity. Rather, it must be denied, but not sacrificed entirely. If we affirm necessity of God, we seem to render Him subject to some superior agency. We imply that there is some sense in which He must act. However, if we deny necessity of Him utterly, we are left with a universe in which everything occurs purely by chance and there is no observable continuity. This is not only contrary to our experience, which suggests that indeed there is a certain regularity and predictability in the scheme of things, but also it leads to a diminishment of the sovereign efficacy of the divine will. In a happenstance universe there is no room for such a will.

Between these two extreme positions, representing the necessitarianism of Aristotle, on the one hand, and the Epicurean view of the universe as the product of chance, on the other, the *kalām*, as Wolfson has shown,[117] occupies a curious middle ground. Whereas Muslim theologians virtually unanimously deny that there is any necessary connection between cause and effect—"the connection between what is deemed a cause in the habitual course of events (*fi'l-ʿādah*) and what is deemed an effect is not necessary (*ḍarūrī*) in our opinion," states al-Ghazālī[118]—they do not thereby accept a universe surrendered to blind chance. Rather, the universe is the direct effect of the divine will. Whatever exists, is created directly by God without any intermediary

[116] In passing, we may note that Leibniz formulated his theodicy very much in reaction to the necessitarianism of Spinoza which he saw as constraining God: "Spinoza . . . seems explicitly to have professed a blind necessity, having denied understanding and will of the author of things. . . . To the extent one can understand him, he recognizes no goodness in God, strictly speaking, and he teaches that all things exist through the necessity of the divine nature, without God's making any choice." *Essais de theodicée*, p. 217.

[117] *The Philosophy of the Kalam*, p. 520. For a summary of the necessitarian view, see Maimonides, *Dalālat al-ḥā'irīn*, II, 40a; tr. Pines, pp. 302-303. See also Ibn al-Dāʿī al-Rāzī, *Tabṣirat al-ʿawāmm*, p. 5.

[118] *Tahāfut al-falāsifah*, p. 277.

agency, and it is created instant by instant. What to us appears to be continuity and continuance in the course of things is in actuality the result of God's continuous creation, atom by atom and instant by instant, of all existing things.

If (to use a famous example) we observe that cotton burns when placed in fire, this is not because the fire is itself the agency of burning, but because God directly wills that in this instance the fire shall burn and the cotton be burnt. God could just as readily will, however, that the cotton not be burnt when placed in the fire. al-Ghazālī explains:

> Our adversary maintains that the agent of burning (*fā'il al-iḥtirāq*) is the fire alone and that it is an agent by its very nature, not by choice. Hence, it cannot avoid (doing) what is its own nature after it encounters a substrate receptive to it.
>
> But we deny this. Rather, we hold that the agent of burning—in the creation of (charred) blackness in the cotton, in separating its components, in making it flame or ashes—is God Himself, either by means of angels or by other means. As for the fire, it is inanimate (*jamād*) and possesses no agency (*fa-lā fi'l lahā*).[119]

Fire kindles and cotton burns when they are placed together. This is to be explained, not as the result of cause and effect, but as "custom" (*'ādah*). That we observe a certain regularity and predictability in the course of events—water quenches thirst, bread satisfies hunger, light appears at sunrise, decapitation and death are simultaneous, etc.—[120]is due merely to custom. None of these apparent agents, the water, the bread, the sun, or the headsman's sword, is truly an agent; nor is there any necessary connection between them and their apparent objects:

> Their simultaneous occurrence is due to the prior decree of God who created them so as to be interrelated (*'alā al-tasāwuq*), and is not because this [occurrence] is necessary in itself (*ḍarūrī fī nafsihi*), and not subject to rupture (*ghayr qābil lil-farq*). On the contrary, the creation of satiety without eating may be an object of divine power or even the prolongation of

[119] *Tahāfut*, pp. 278-279.
[120] For these examples, see *Tahāfut*, p. 277.

> life despite decapitation, and so on with all the things whose simultaneous occurrence is associated (*al-muqtaranāt*).[121]

While he accepts the doctrine of "custom" and rejects causality, al-Ghazālī is at pains to emphasize the necessary connection between God's will and its objects. This is, of course, to avoid any diminution of the divine will, but it also serves his hortatory purpose in the *Iḥyā'* passage.

Doubtless it is easier to accept whatever happens to one if one is convinced that it is the result, the direct and necessary result, of the divine will, and not either a product of chance or the effect of an unbreakable chain of impersonal causality. If it is believed, for example, that one's affluence or poverty, or health or illness, are created directly and intentionally by God, and at every instant of their continuance, these varying circumstances come to seem charged with significance—a significance no less powerful for being incomprehensible. Furthermore, granting the premise that whatever happens is the direct result of God's will and so happens necessarily, it must seem "right and just," however abject and miserable the afflicted individual may appear to himself.

In conclusion, we may conjecture that the inculcation of *tawakkul*, in al-Ghazālī's teaching, called for a sharp emphasis on the necessity established by the divine will in nexus with its objects. This was not, as opponents would claim, for the purpose of smuggling into orthodox theology various repudiated doctrines, but rather to borrow, indeed to usurp, from these doctrines those elements which because of their coherence and rational appeal might serve to enhance and strengthen his particular brand of Ashʿarite Ṣūfism.

Whether or not these elements were introduced in order to solicit a certain class of readers—those who, like al-Ghazālī himself, had delved into philosophy and who would respond more readily to the blandishments of reason than to the summons of

[121] *Tahāfut*, p. 278. Departures from the habitual course of events, as in these final examples, are termed a "breach of custom" (*kharq al-ʿādah*); this notion serves to account for miracles.

scriptural authority—we cannot say with certainty, but it does not appear unlikely. As noted earlier, it is al-Ghazālī's practice to interject into discourse fashioned out of more or less traditional elements, phrases and concepts drawn from another more strictly rationalizing tradition. This has the effect of proferring, almost in passing, as it were, to those more skeptical and sophisticated of his readers a rationalistic account of what was finally an ineffable mystery: the secret of predestination, God's "secret" *par excellence*.

When, therefore, al-Ghazālī is accused of "revealing God's secret," what is meant is that he attempts to explain this secret in rationalistic terms, instead of confining himself to an assertion of its ultimate inscrutability. In doing this, he relies in part on philosophical terminology; to his critics, this reliance, however equivocal, betrays a secret and inexcusable sympathy for heretical doctrines.

It cannot be denied that al-Ghazālī shows a penchant for philosophical terminology and method, but he also avails himself of certain key concepts even in their metaphysics, which he generally repudiates. The notion of providence, as elaborated earlier by al-Fārābī and Ibn Sīnā, is one such instance. However, the role of necessity in that doctrine has been replaced in the Ghazālian adaptation by the divine will itself. The necessity that obtains, results from the efficacy of that will in acting upon its objects.[122]

Whatever sympathy he may have with certain aspects of philosophy, and however much he appropriates its language and methodology, al-Ghazālī's attitude toward it remains inimical. In this he finds himself allied with various other sectarians, their differences notwithstanding:

[122] It is the emphasis on the divine free will that explains the apparent discrepancy between al-Ghazālī's position in the *Iḥyā'* passage and the passage in *Tahāfut al-falāsifah*, p. 41ff., where he criticizes the philosophers for holding that "the universal order of the world cannot be in any way other than that in which it exists." For the philosophers, the perfect order of the world is the necessary effect of the divine will which cannot will less than what is perfect; for al-Ghazālī, what exists is "most wonderful" because God has willed it so, but it could always be different.

> I do not rise to defend any specific theological school. On the contrary, I consider all the sects united as one against them [the philosophers]. For other sects may sometimes differ with us in some particular (*fi'l-tafṣīl*), but these [philosophers] oppose the very foundations of religion. So let us join together against them, for in the face of calamities (personal) rancors vanish.[123]

However petty or private the rancors and contentions among rival sects might appear in view of the greater threat posed by philosophy, they were hardly insubstantial. It is to certain of these divisive issues, linked with the third and final charge brought against al-Ghazālī, that we now turn our attention.

[123] *Tahāfut al-falāsifah*, pp. 13-14.

FIVE

# The Problem of the Optimum

## I

## THE CHARGE OF MU'TAZILISM

If the offending statement reminded critics of certain heretical teachings of the philosophers, it was even more strongly reminiscent of Muʿtazilite formulations and, in particular, the notorious and distinctive Muʿtazilite doctrine that God is somehow obliged to provide "the best" (*al-aṣlaḥ*) for His creation.[1]

Aḥmad ibn al-Munayyir, in the 13th century, first brought the charge that Muʿtazilite influences had shaped al-Ghazālī's position in the controversial passage.[2] The charge became standard thereafter. For al-Biqāʿī, for example, the statement is "like the doctrine of those who hold that a concern for providing the optimum (*riʿāyat al-aṣlaḥ*) is incumbent upon God."[3] The orthodox, he continues, rallied to refute this doctrine, but the fact that al-Ghazālī had accepted it and incorporated it into his writings undermined their refutation and misled people. al-Ghazālī may be irreproachable, but he is not infallible; this is clearly a lapse (*zallah*) on his part.[4]

Badr al-dīn al-Ḥanbalī, one of the few who cites al-Biqāʿī with approval, also interpreted al-Ghazālī's phrase "necessary order"

[1] In this chapter, as in the Introduction, I discuss the doctrine largely as it bears on the disputed issue; the history and development of the doctrine of the optimum are complex and fascinating and merit a study that is beyond the scope of the present work. For other discussions, see also *EI*², I, 713; Wensinck, *The Muslim Creed*, p. 79ff.; Meyerhof and Schacht, *The Theologus Autodidactus of Ibn al-Nafīs*, pp, 78-79; R. Brunschvig, "Muʿtazilisme et optimum (*al-aṣlaḥ*)," *SI*, 39 (1974), pp. 5-23; W. M. Watt, *The Formative Period of Islamic Thought*, p. 239f., and G. Vajda, "Le problème de l'assistance bienveillante de Dieu, du 'mieux' et de la nécessité de la loi révélée selon Yūsuf al-Baṣīr," *Revue des études juives*, 134 (1975), pp. 31-74.

[2] Ibn al-Munayyir's seventh precept; *Iḍāḥ*, p. 85.

[3] *Tahdīm*, fol. 37b; see also, *Itḥāf*, IX, 443.

[4] *Tahdīm*, fol. 37b.

(*al-tartīb al-wājib*) in the light of Muʿtazilite precedents, as though the phrase meant "the order obligatory for God."[5] On the contrary, he declares, nothing is obligatory for God: "Had God created twice what He has created, or only believers and no unbelievers, or only unbelievers and no believers, it would be admissible. Had He created only inorganic matter, it would be admissible. Everything that He makes is wisdom and right, justice and generosity."[6]

al-Sijilmāsī al-Lamaṭī, in the 18th century, declared that if the statement was not to be understood in accord with the philosophers' teachings, then it might only be understood in Muʿtazilite terms.[7] What he meant was that the statement subjected God to necessity in some form—if not the "natural necessity" of the philosophers, than the moral necessity, the obligation, of the Muʿtazilites. For Ashʿarites, the imposition of necessity in either form was objectionable. (The dual interpretation of the statement is possible since deontic as well as ontological necessity may be rendered in Arabic by the same term: *wujūb*.)

This charge seems to have been especially galling to certain of al-Ghazālī's defenders. Aḥmad ibn al-Munayyir had couched it in strong terms: "In this tenet of the obligation upon God to perform the optimal, al-Ghazālī removes the veil with his frank utterance. He follows the teachings of the Muʿtazilah here to an extreme degree, and without either explanation or reasoned argument (*bi-lā ta'wīl wa-lā taʿlīl*)."[8]

The suggestion that al-Ghazālī stood exposed, and in his own words, as an adherent of the Muʿtazilites drew a sharp reply from al-Samhūdī. This, he exclaims, is "your ruin, O hurler of inanities from the shadows of a fanaticism that produces the blindness of a sick understanding!"[9] To the contrary, declares al-Samhūdī, there is no mutual implication (*lā yulāzim*) between the justice of God's acts, which wisdom demands, and the obli-

[5] "*Jawāb su'āl,*" fol. 39a.

[6] *Ibid.*, fol. 40a. The Qadarīyah had claimed that God could not restrict Himself to creation of inanimate matter (*jamādāt*); see al-Baghdādī, *Uṣūl*, p. 152.

[7] *Dhahab*, p. 483.

[8] Cited in *Iḍāḥ*, p. 85.

[9] *Ibid.*

gation to do what is optimal. Indeed, wisdom may at times demand what is incompatible with "the optimal."[10]

Furthermore, no single school, such as Ashʿarism, has a monopoly on truth. al-Samhūdī calls attention to the fact that al-Ghazālī himself denounced the intolerance of certain Ashʿarites who went so far as to term the great al-Bāqillānī "erring" (*ḍalāl*) because of some minor divergence in doctrine.[11] Whoever fancies that Ashʿarism is the sole arbiter of correct doctrine equates himself and his co-sectarians with the Prophet, who was sinless.

In any case, al-Samhūdī notes further, al-Ghazālī decisively rejected the doctrine of the optimum in several of his works.[12] He rejected it, moreover, in incontrovertible terms. This proves that he cannot have subscribed, in some surreptitious way, to the doctrine.

These are the charges and the responses that surround the third major difficulty with the disputed statement. While it is true that al-Ghazālī formally rejected the doctrine of the optimum, he also drew upon it to a certain extent in devising his own theodicy. This is not surprising in so avowedly eclectic a thinker. Ashʿarite theology was, in any case, permeated with Muʿtazilite themes, concepts, and terms. It would have been strange indeed if in discussions of this question, and in attempts to formulate rival responses, later Ashʿarite theologians had not availed themselves of notions, and even particular expressions, forged by the Muʿtazilites in earlier discussions.

# II

## MUʿTAZILITE AFFINITIES AND PARALLELS

The Muʿtazilite tenet that God must provide the best for man struck critics as outrageous and untenable. In the first place, it was repellent to speak of obligation in regard to God. And, in the second place, it was manifestly false to state that God had

[10] *Iḍāḥ*, p. 88.

[11] *Iḍāḥ*, p. 89, alluding to al-Ghazālī's *Fayṣal al-tafriqah bayn al-Islām wa'l-zandaqah* [Bouyges, no. 43]; the passage occurs on p. 131ff. of the Cairo, 1961, edition.

[12] See, for example, *Iḥyā'*, I, 99f., *al-Iqtiṣād fi'l-iʿtiqād*, p. 184ff., and *al-Qusṭās al-mustaqīm* (Beirut, 1959), p. 94ff.; for a translation of the last passage, see now R. J. McCarthy, *Freedom and Fulfillment*, pp. 326-327.

provided the best: anyone can see that the world teems with the most egregious and horrifying diseases, afflictions, miseries, and misfortunes. As the formidable Ẓāhirī theologian and jurisprudent Ibn Ḥazm (d. 457/1064) remarked, "It is as though believers in the 'optimum' were absent from the world; or, when they are present, it is as if their intellects had been stripped from them and their senses numbed."[13]

Sometimes Ashʿarite theologians display an almost unseemly eagerness in pointing out the miseries of existence as proof of God's freedom from obligation. Thus, al-Taftāzānī can declare that "if the best for man had been obligatory upon God, He would not have created the infidel, the pauper, and the person tormented in this world and the next, and especially (not) those beset with illnesses, pains, trials, and disasters."[14]

To understand al-Ghazālī's position, it is useful to see it as a middle course between these two extremes: on the one hand, the Muʿtazilite insistence, often to the point of absurdity, on the requisite rightness and justice of things as they are; and, on the other, the Ashʿarite insistence, often to the point of heartlessness, on sheer voluntarism, and the sovereign and ungovernable will of God. In the present instance, it seems likely that al-Ghazālī wished to salvage certain elements of the Muʿtazilite theodicy in order to render the Ashʿarite position more palatable.

Unfortunately, it is difficult to assess this final charge against al-Ghazālī. On this point, his critics are consistently vague. They tend to lump together both philosophers and Muʿtazilites. They cite neither specific passages nor examples of Muʿtazilite influence.

The charge is not frivolous, nor is it entirely an attempt to discredit by association. There are good grounds for suspicion, but none of the critics will follow these to their possible sources. Even by Aḥmad ibn-al-Munayyir's time, Muʿtazilism had long been extinct as a force to be reckoned with; nevertheless, the

[13] *al-Fiṣal fi'l-milal*, III, 121.

[14] *Sharḥ al-Maqāṣid*, II, 123. The characteristic Ashʿarite position on this point struck outside observers; see, for example, Maimonides, *Dalālat al-ḥā'irīn*, III, 33b; tr. Pines, p. 467.

charge raised disquieting questions and uneasy echoes of old disputes long considered settled.

Certainly there are Muʿtazilite precedents for key tenets in al-Ghazālī's version of theodicy. Let us consider three of these before turning to the doctrine of the optimum itself.

## *A. THE PERFECT RIGHTNESS OF THE ACTUAL*

As we have seen, this is the cardinal principle underlying al-Ghazālī's belief that "there is not in possibility more wonderful than what is." The earlier Muʿtazilite theologian al-Naẓẓām (d. between 220/835 and 230/845) had advocated a similar position, though in more extreme form.

al-Naẓẓām held that God can neither add to, nor subtract from, things as they are:

> God cannot (*lā yaqdir*) do for mankind other than what has within it benefit (*ṣalāḥ*) for them. He cannot reduce the felicity of the blessed by one atom because their felicity is a benefit for them; to decrease that in which there is benefit is injustice (*ẓulm*).
>
> He is not able to increase the torments of the damned by one atom, nor to decrease them in any way.[15]

In this view, it is God's own justice that constrains Him. God acts, as Aquinas put it, "*de necessitate justitiae.*"[16] Furthermore, this constraint operates not only in the afterlife, but extends to God's governance of this world as well:

> [al-Naẓẓām] said further that God could not blind a sighted person nor make ill a well person nor impoverish a rich person, for He knows that sight, health and riches are most salutary (*aṣlaḥ*) for them. So, too, God cannot enrich a pauper or restore a sick

[15] al-Baghdādī, *al-Farq bayn al-firaq*, pp. 115-116; see also the same author's *Uṣūl al-dīn*, p. 239, and al-Shahrastānī, *K. al-milal*, p. 78. For a Persian account, see Ibn al-Dāʿī, *Tabṣirat al-ʿawāmm*, p. 48.

[16] *In 4 libros Sententiarum* (dist. 43, q. 2, art. 2): ". . . ex justitia sua determinetur ad aliquod unum faciendum, ita quod aliud facere non possit: et sic falsum est," in *Opera omnia* (Parma ed.), VI, 351.

man to health, for He knows that sickness and poverty are most salutary for them.[17]

In al-Naẓẓām's view, the constraint of divine justice extended as well to the creation of particular creatures: "God could not create a snake or a scorpion or any body (*jism*) of which He knew that something other might be more beneficial in His creation."[18]

What al-Ghazālī's critics considered a necessary implication of his statement—that God cannot but do the "most wonderful," that He is, in effect, constrained by His own justice—is here, in al-Naẓẓām's view, openly stated. If what exists were not "the most salutary," it would not exist at all. In His justice, God does nothing that is not of ultimate benefit for His creatures. In fact, He has already performed the optimal for them in all respects. God holds nothing better in abeyance. If He did, we should be justified in calling Him "miserly" (*bakhīl*).[19]

Furthermore, al-Naẓẓām's position, like al-Ghazālī's later, was seen by critics as deriving directly from alien and unacceptable sources. Thus, according to the heresiographer al-Shahrastānī (d. 548/1153), al-Naẓẓām

> . . . took this doctrine from the ancient philosophers inasmuch as they assert that the Generous One (*al-jawād*) cannot hoard anything which He does not do. Whatever He brings forth and produces is an object of power. If there were in His knowledge and power something more excellent (*aḥsan*) and more perfect (*akmal*) than what He has created, in respect to order (*niẓām*) and design (*tartīb*), and advantage (*ṣalāḥ*), He would create it.[20]

When al-Ghazālī's adversaries denounced his statement, they did so with exceptional vehemence because the underlying issues were dangerously familiar. If they accused him of circumscribing God's omnipotence, it was partly because earlier, suspect thinkers, like al-Naẓẓām, had done so blatantly, and in

[17] al-Baghdādī, *al-Farq*, pp. 115-116.

[18] *Ibid.*

[19] This was also the view of ʿAbbād ibn Sulaymān; see Ibn Ḥazm, *Fiṣal*, III, 92.

[20] *K. al-milal*, p. 78. The doctrine was generally considered to have come from the philosophers; see *Itḥāf*, II, 179.

alarmingly similar terms. Thus, in the present debate, there is often the disquieting awareness that the disputed passage is being read and considered in the light of other such unmentioned—and indeed, perhaps, half-forgotten—texts and passages.

### *B. THE CORRELATION OF PERFECT AND IMPERFECT*

For al-Ghazālī, the surpassing excellence of the world depends upon the simultaneous presence within it of perfect and imperfect; in his view, perfect and imperfect are correlated.

Certain Muʿtazilites had espoused this notion as well and had given it forceful expression. For example, al-Naẓẓām employed it to show that the just order of the world depends upon a mixture of opposing components; apparently, he introduced the notion in response to dualist teachings.[21]

al-Jāḥiẓ (d. 255/868), a student of al-Naẓẓām, elaborated the view in a striking passage of his *Kitāb al-ḥayawān*. There he stated that benefit (*maṣlaḥah*) involves a mixture (*imtizāj*) of good and evil: the harmful is intermixed with the helpful, the repugnant with the pleasurable, the many with the few.[22] If evil were total, creation would perish, but if good were total, the requisite testing (*miḥnah*), the trial-and-error conducive to thought, would also cease.[23]

It is the opposition of things within creation that provokes thought. Without thought, there could be neither discrimination (*tamyīz*) nor choice (*takhyīr*). Knowledge itself would no longer be possible. As we know, this was a cardinal point in the Ghazālian theodicy, and espoused by such disputants as al-Suyūṭī

[21] For his attack on the dualists, see al-Baghdādī, *al-Farq*, p. 117, line 5ff. The idea of the "mixture" may owe something to Iranian dualism itself; see J. van Ess, "Theology and Science: the Case of Abū Isḥāq an-Naẓẓām," *The Second Annual United Arab Emirates Lecture in Islamic Studies* (Ann Arbor, 1978), p. 15.

[22] *K. al-ḥayawān*, I, 204; for another discussion of this passage, see I. Geries, *Un genre littéraire arabe: al-Maḥâsin wa-l-Masâwî* (Paris, 1977), p. 44ff.

[23] The notion of *miḥnah* as "trial and error" is expounded also by al-Māturīdī, *K. al-tawḥīd*, p. 179.

and al-Samhūdī: it is through the opposition of good and evil, perfect and imperfect, that we acquire knowledge.

Without this thought-provoking mixture of good and evil, al-Jāḥiẓ stated, men and angels "would revert to the condition of beasts and to a state of stupidity and rusticity"; rational beings would become automatons and "like the stars in their forced labor (*sukhrah*) which are even more lacking in freedom to roam than the beasts."[24] Who, he asked, "would be pleased to become sun and moon, fire and frost, or one of the stations of the zodiac, a bit of cloud or a galaxy, a mere measure of water or of air?"[25]

Furthermore, this mixture of things is necessary in order to instill trust in God (*tawakkul*). Otherwise, "the fruit of trust in God would be vain," and we should have no certainty that God is "the preserver, the defender, the averter from harm."[26]

The world, a mixture of seemingly disparate things, forms a unified whole. It is a coincidence of opposites. In this grand unity, what appears injurious results ultimately in benefit. Indeed, God ensures consummate benefit by unifying opposing elements into a single whole: "through the combination (of disparate things) divine beneficence is perfected."[27] For this reason, no part of the cosmos may be eliminated without detriment to the whole: "In the negation of a single one is the negation of all."[28] The cosmos is like a living body; to remove or alter one part is to damage all.

In this totality, each thing is of equal value. To try to remove one part, or even to consider it contemptible, is to impugn the wisdom that designed the order of things. No part is more worthy than another. Each thing bespeaks God; each is a sign of Him: "Do you not see that the mountain is not more indicative (*adall*) of God than the pebble and that the praiseworthy peacock is not more indicative of Him than the disapproved pig?"[29]

[24] *K. al-ḥayawān*, I, 204.
[25] *K. al-ḥayawān*, I, 205.
[26] *Ibid.*
[27] *K. al-ḥayawān*, I, 206: *bi'jtimāʿihā tatimm al-niʿmah.*
[28] *Ibid.*
[29] *Ibid.*

In this passage from al-Jāḥiẓ, various themes appear that played an important role in the debate around al-Ghazālī's statement: the correlation of good and evil, the requisite play of opposites that prompts knowledge, the crucial role of trust in God, and the emphasis on the final significance of each thing in the grand order of the world. As we know, al-Ghazālī and his defenders availed themselves of these points. There are obvious affinities, but there is also a sharp distinction.

In his justification for things as they are, al-Jāḥiẓ possesses an underlying assurance that everything, however lowly, repulsive, or useless it may seem—the humble pebble or the unclean pig—yet has some ultimate *raison d'être*. Moreover, each thing is ultimately beneficial, and beneficial specifically for human beings. Even though we often fail to recognize it, each thing on earth is, in his view, fundamentally good.

The Ghazālian position offers no such assurance. The good is good, the imperfect is imperfect, to be sure, and there may be reasons for this, but the reasons are, finally, provisional. Good and evil, perfect and imperfect, depend upon God's will. We have no assurance that they will remain as they are at this moment, or that they will be ultimately explicable to human reason. Then, too, for al-Ghazālī and his followers, the imperfect and the less perfect have no intrinsic worth, but are significant only in serving as a "ransom" for the more perfect.

There are other differences as well. And, of course, many of the points which al-Jāḥiẓ makes are not uniquely his, or even uniquely Muʿtazilite, but derive from ancient sources.[30] al-Ghazālī would have had access to such ideas from various earlier authors, and not only Muʿtazilites. But the fact that such notions played a part in early Muʿtazilite speculation, and that so illustrious an author as al-Jāḥiẓ gave them prominence, may have strengthened his critics' suspicions.

[30] The idea of the world as "mixture" is one such example, and may go back to the pre-Socratic Empedocles; see, e.g., W.K.C. Guthrie, *A History of Greek Philosophy* (Cambridge, 1965), II, 147ff. Muslin thinkers may have learned of this through Aristotle, *Metaphysics*, 985a.6-7 and 1075a.20. See also note 21 above.

## *C. THE WORDING OF THE DISPUTED STATEMENT*

### *1. The Emphasis on Justice*

The repeated stress on justice and right in the *Iḥyā'* passage alarmed opponents. The Muʿtazilites had accorded the highest importance to the principle of divine justice. al-Ghazālī's insistence on the point, and in such a context, must have seemed suspicious.

Apparently, Aḥmad ibn al-Munayyir did raise this point, but his main objection here is somewhat different. In the doctrinal work entitled *Qawāʿid al-ʿaqā'id* (incorporated within the first book of the *Iḥyā'*), al-Ghazālī stated in defense of God's justice that since injustice consists in "the use of property belonging to another" (*al-taṣarruf fī milk ghayrihi*), God can in no sense be capable of injustice.[31] Ibn al-Munayyir sought to turn this definition against al-Ghazālī, explicating the disputed statement as though it meant that if God had foregone creating a better world, it would somehow be a misuse of another's property. In other words, Ibn al-Munayyir sought to reduce the disputed statement to absurdity, and to do so by quoting al-Ghazālī against himself.[32]

As al-Samhūdī is quick to note, such a reading is perverse and has no bearing on the disputed question. The issue is not whether God misuses what belongs to another, but whether He may be termed unjust if He fails to create a superior world.[33]

Furthermore, since everything ultimately belongs to God, it is meaningless to speak of His misuse or misappropriation of another's property. Of course, Ibn al-Munayyir knows this—his attempted *reductio ad absurdum* rests upon it—but al-Samhūdī is eager to emphasize the point. God has no need of possessions:

> His misuse of a possession cannot conceivably occur, nor His claim upon something which is other than He, (a claim) to the detriment of man. This is an intrinsic impossibility for God.[34]

[31] *Iḥyā'*, I, 100.
[32] *Iḍāḥ*, p. 82, line 7.
[33] *Ibid.*
[34] *Ibid.*

Moreover, in regard to the real point at issue, al-Samhūdī counters,

> . . . the production of other than the most wonderful is doubtless possible in relation to God, for His power is efficacious to produce it, but His production (of other than the most wonderful) is not injustice in this rejected sense.[35]

For al-Samhūdī, injustice was to be understood, in the disputed passage, in a different sense. It was not injustice in the narrow juridical sense, as Ibn al-Munayyir had attempted mischievously to maintain; nor was it, by any means, injustice as the Muʿtazilites had understood the term. Rather, al-Samhūdī follows a well-established, earlier tradition. *Ẓulm*, the word used by al-Ghazālī, does mean injustice, but it must be understood here in the sense of "displacement," in contradistinction to *ʿadl*, or the "proper placement" of things by God. Thus, for al-Samhūdī, the force of the Ghazālian dilemma was that if we term God "unjust" (*ẓālim*), we mean that He has "positioned a thing in other than its proper place."[36] But this leads to an obvious absurdity since God, and only He, determines what place is proper for a thing.

This interpretation could be justified by reference to al-Ghazālī's own works. For example, in discussing justice, al-Ghazālī stated:

> God created the parts of existing things, the corporeal as well as the spiritual, the perfect as well as the imperfect, . . . and

[35] *Ibid.*

[36] *Ibid.* Of course, *ẓulm* may denote wrongdoing in general, but it is used particularly of tyrannous wrong; among the Shīʿites, the first three caliphs were denigrated as "the three malefactors" (*al-ẓalamah al-thalāthah*), implying thereby a violent abrogation of the legitimate rights of others. See I. Goldziher, "Spottnamen der ersten Chalifen bei den Schi'iten," in *Gesammelte Schriften*, IV, 296. See also the discussion in al-Tawḥīdī, *al-Hawāmil wa'l-shawāmil* (Cairo, 1951), p. 84ff. For *ẓulm* in the special sense as "displacement," see further Roy Mottahedeh, *Loyalty and Leadership in an Early Islamic Society* (Princeton, 1980), p. 179. The notion is well illustrated by the verses of Jalāl al-Dīn Rūmī: "What is justice? Placing (something) in its place. / What is injustice? Placing in other than its place. / What is justice? Watering the trees. / What is injustice? Giving water to the thorns." Cited in Murtaḍā Muṭahharī, *ʿAdl-i ilāhī* (Tehran, 1352/1973), p. 62.

> in this He is generous (*jawād*). He ordered them in places suitable for them; in this He is just.[37]

The act of creation betokens God's generosity, the subsequent arrangement and ordering of created things His justice:

> He positioned the earth as the lowest and He set the water above it, and the air above the water, and the heavens above the air. Were this arrangement to be reversed, order would be impaired.[38]

The usual objection to this notion was to claim that injustice would then result from any displacement of things. In some instances, this was considered literally true. Thus, the 10/16th-century polymath Ibn Kamāl Pasha could write:

> When the knowing Creator takes a twisted plank, a broken stone, and a defective brick and then places it in a spot suitable and fit for it, that is justice and right on His part, for which He deserves praise. . . . Whoever places vile things (*khabā'ith*) in their proper places and positions (has done) wisdom and justice and right. It is folly (*safah*) and injustice (*ẓulm*) only if he sets them in other than their fitting places.[39]

The principle extends to the most banal and ordinary objects:

> He who places a turban on the head and a shoe on the foot, kohl upon the eye, and sweepings in the refuse heap has placed a thing in its place and has not wronged (*lam yaẓlim*) the shoe and the sweepings, since these are their places.[40]

al-Suyūṭī had invoked this principle to justify the actual location of Mt. Qāsiyūn. It is important, for it marks a fundamental divergence between Ashʿarites and Muʿtazilites. For the Ashʿarites, justice is determined by God and is disclosed in the actual order of things. It is not an abstract, objective notion to which the human intellect, by its own power, has access; rather, it is revealed to us in the placement and arrangement of things as they are. By contrast, injustice represents a displacement, or

[37] *al-Maqṣad al-asnā*, p. 105.
[38] *al-Maqṣad al-asnā*, pp. 105-106.
[39] *Rasā'il Ibn Kamāl* (Istanbul, 1316), I, 126.
[40] *Ibid.*

disarray, of things, the violation of an order determined not by reason, but by divine command.

Obviously, then, from the Ashʿarite perspective, God cannot be conceived as unjust. Commandment alone establishes what is just or good or right, and who could command God? Justice is not some value which God observes and respects; rather, it is He who creates justice.

The conviction found forceful expression in the well-known *ḥadīth*, cited by al-Biqāʿī against the Muʿtazilite view:

> Were God to punish the inhabitants of heaven and earth, He would punish them without being unjust (*ẓālim*) to them. And were He to have compassion on them, His compassion would be better for them than their own actions.[41]

Centuries later, Murtaḍā al-Zabīdī confirms this quite traditional position from the other side of the debate. Thus, with reference to al-Ghazālī's own endorsement of it, he states:

> If God made all of them enter heaven without prior virtue on their part, it would be His right; and if He sent them all down into hell without any fault on their part, it would be His right. No one can lay claim against Him for a deserved reward, for it is through His magnanimity that He rewards.[42]

On this point at least, al-Ghazālī's defenders seem right in rejecting the charge of Muʿtazilite taint. al-Ghazālī's position accords well with a perfectly "orthodox" definition of justice. Indeed, his belief in the perfect rightness of the actual may easily be construed as deriving from an understanding of divine justice as "the proper placement of things."

[41] Ibn Mājah, *Sunan*, I, 29; Aḥmad ibn Ḥanbal, *Musnad*, V, 182, 185, 189. The *ḥadīth* is cited in *Tahdīm*, fol. 52a, and may perhaps be best understood as an emphatic reaction against Muʿtazilite and Qadarite formulations.

[42] *Itḥāf*, II, 186 [commenting on *Iḥyā'*, I, 99-100]. Cf. al-Ashʿarī, *K. al-lumaʿ*, p. 71 [tr., p. 99]: "Whatever God does, He is just (*ʿādil*), though He punish the faithful in hell and reward the faithless in heaven; even so, He is just." For an earlier Ṣūfī reaction to such a position, see Farīd al-dīn ʿAṭṭār, *K. tadhkirat al-awliyā'* (ed. Nicholson), I, 153-154: Abū Yazīd al-Bisṭāmī (d. ca. 261/874) said, "He is my disciple who stands on the brink of hell (*dūzakh*) and takes by the hand everyone being conveyed to hell and dispatches him to heaven and then enters hell in his place"; tr. A. J. Arberry, *Muslim Saints and Mystics*, p. 120.

## 2. *The Terms "aṣlaḥ" and "abdaʿ"*

The repeated use of the elatives (*aḥsan, akmal, atamm*) in the *Iḥyāʾ* passage had a suspicious ring for opponents.[43] After all, the heretical Muʿtazilite doctrine had been called *al-aṣlaḥ*, and sometimes the words *aḥsan* or *afḍal* were used as well. It is important not to read too much into this; they are common words. But common words often carry the impress of doctrinal affiliations and cannot be used without evoking those affiliations. In this context, al-Ghazālī's choice of words could not help but remind hostile readers of comparable Muʿtazilite formulations. It was perhaps just because his words seemed to echo typical Muʿtazilite formulations that al-Biqāʿī, for one, reversed the disputed statement with such righteous defiance, as we have seen.

The root *ṣ-l-ḥ* and its derivatives are familiar enough from the Qurʾān. The injunction "to perform good works" (*ʿamala al-ṣāliḥāt*) occurs repeatedly (2:62, 5:69, 18:110, etc.). We read often of those "who believe and do right" (6:48) and especially of those "who repent and do right" (2:160, 4:146, 5:39, etc.). Right action forms the outward complement of the requisite inner state of belief and repentance. Believers are enjoined to perform good works (*iṣlāḥ*): to aid widows and orphans (2:220) and to give alms (4:114).

The same root also conveys meanings of order, rightness, harmony, and well-being. In its fourth form, the verb may thus mean "to set in order, to set right, to promote or establish harmony." Of the earth, it is said that it has been "set right"; hence the command, "Do not spread corruption in the earth after it has been set in order (*baʿd iṣlāḥihā*; 7:56, 7:85).[44]

[43] *Iḍāḥ*, p. 98.

[44] The contrary of *aṣlaḥa* is *afsada*, and the latter term has a comparable, if opposite, range of meanings: to wreak wickedness and corruption and, also, to do what is wrong or incorrect. The Qurʾān speaks harshly of "those who spread corruption (*yufsidūn*) in the earth and do not do good" (*lā yuṣliḥūn*); see Qur. 26:152 and 27:48. Paret's translation of 26:152 conveys this contrast well: ". . . und die Unheil auf der Erde anrichten and nicht für Frieden und Ordnung sorgen," *Der Koran*, p. 260.

With reference to Qur. 2:205, "God does not love wrongdoing" (*fasād*), al-Suyūṭī—here following the gloss of al-Ṭībī to al-Zamakhsharī's *Kashshāf*—comments: "*Ifsād* means the removal of something from a laudable condition without

The noun form *ṣalāḥ* combines the senses of right action and benevolence; it is more than our "piety." It suggests action which contributes positively to well-being and harmony. Its attainment signals a high degree of virtue. Of al-Ḥasan al-Baṣrī, that early exemplar of righteousness, we read that as a young man "he advanced in *ṣalāḥ* and knowledge to a preeminent degree."[45]

When we translate *al-aṣlaḥ* as "the best" or "the optimal" or "the most salutary," we lose an essential nuance of the word. These translations are correct, but they are too bland. A truly virtuous believer possesses *ṣalāḥ*; he is enjoined to perform good works; there is goodness and right in the very earth upon which he walks. In Muʿtazilite parlance, when it is said that God performs, or must perform, what is *aṣlaḥ*, there is the sense that He possesses and exercises, in transcendent fashion, the very virtues which He enjoins upon mankind. Accordingly, the standard phrase "the obligation to provide the best" (*wujūb riʿāyat al-aṣlaḥ*) might be better rendered as "the obligation to provide what is most righteous." From the Muʿtazilite standpoint, the obligation to provide the most righteous means that God is bound by, or at least observes, a moral norm. He must not merely provide what is "most perfect." A world that is technically "most perfect" is not inevitably a "most righteous" world. Rather, God must provide a world in which justice and goodness are exemplified, and He must do so for the sake of the creatures dwelling therein.

The words al-Ghazālī originally chose in his *Iḥyā'* passage—*aḥsan, akmal, atamm*—probably reflected a certain reliance on Muʿtazilite precedents. However, when he later came to defend his sentence in the *Imlā'*, he substituted the more neutral term *abdaʿ*, and he qualified it further by adding "than the form

---

any valid purpose," and he notes further: "For this reason, it is said, 'O You Whose wrongdoing is beneficence!' " (*yā man ifsāduh ṣalāḥ*). In good optimist fashion, al-Suyūṭī explains further: "What we consider *ifsād* [on God's part] is in relation to ourselves and our limited vision, but in the divine vision, all is goodness" (*ṣalāḥ*). See *Tashyīd*, fol. 8b-9a; also cited in *Itḥāf*, IX, 437, line 6ff.

[45] Ibn al-Jawzī, *al-Ḥasan al-Baṣrī* (Cairo, 1931), p. 14. *Ṣalāḥ* is used as well in more homely fashion, e.g., Ibn al-Muqaffaʿ, *al-Adab al-kabīr* (Beirut, n.d.), p. 11: "The basic principle in the proper regimen of the body (*ṣalāḥ al-jasad*) is that you not overburden it with eating, drinking and sexual intercourse."

of this world." The effect was to distance the revised sentence from possible Muʿtazilite parallels. The word *abdaʿ* places greater emphasis on the world itself as a divine artifact. The world *aḥsan* (which he had first used) could also mean "best" in the moral sense, as well as "most excellent" and "most beautiful." Thus, it may have seemed too suggestive of Muʿtazilite usages. By contrast, the word *abdaʿ* directed attention to what is amazing, unexpected, and ingenious in the structure of the world; it implied nothing about the creator's moral nature.

It is reasonable to assume that such affinities and parallels as the preceding played a certain part in the debate, if only indirectly. They illustrate to what extent Muʿtazilite notions and even turns of phrase had permeated theological discourse. Thus, a certain confusion enters the debate. The disputants are quick to suspect dubious concepts and phrases that smack of Muʿtazilite origins, but they are neither familiar enough with the earlier sources nor, in the end, serious enough about the final charge to pursue it tenaciously. At the same time, however, the whole issue of Muʿtazilism has the strange and unexpected power of kindling tempers and arousing theological passions.

The single consistent point made by al-Ghazālī's critics is that he seems to adhere to the very principle that underlies the doctrine of the optimum, and it is to this that we now turn our attention.

## III
## RATIONAL GOOD AND EVIL

The doctrine of the optimum was not the creation of a blind and fatuous piety bent on denying the evidence of the senses, but proceeded from a sound basis: the conviction that moral values possess an objective validity.

The charge against al-Ghazālī rests finally on the suspicion that he shared this conviction. Thus, says al-Samhūdī, ". . . al-Ghazālī's critics wrongly assume that he bases his argument on the Muʿtazilite belief in a principle of good and evil discoverable by the intellect" (*al-ḥusn wa'l-qubḥ al-ʿaqliyān*).[46]

[46] *Iḍāḥ*, p. 77.

Belief in such a "rational good and evil" lay at the heart of the optimum. To be sure, extreme forms of the doctrine, such as those propounded by al-Naẓẓām or ʿAbbād ibn Sulaymān or al-Kaʿbī, would be repudiated, especially by the later Basra Muʿtazilah.[47] Abū ʿAli al-Jubbāʾī (d. 303/915) even composed a treatise against al-Kaʿbī on this very point, and his son Abū Hāshim (d. 321/933) also wrote against the radical position of the Baghdad school.[48] Then, too, the *qāḍī* ʿAbd al-Jabbār (d. 415/1025), the last great Muʿtazilite theologian, argued forcefully against those whom he called "partisans of the optimal" (*aṣḥāb al-aṣlaḥ*), and by this term he designated those who held, for example, that certain acts are obligatory because of a benefit that accrues to the obligatee.[49] On the contrary, he was prepared to argue, nothing obliges God: He acts neither for His own advantage nor under the compulsion of any necessitating agency. Like us, God recognizes the obligatory and fulfills it.[50] For God as for us, obligation flows from the very nature of the obligatory.

Nevertheless, despite these later cautious nuances, the fundamental Muʿtazilite principle remained unchanged: good and evil are objective, and the human intellect is inherently capable of recognizing them. In fact, we grasp the good or evil of actions as we grasp "directly perceived phenomena" (*al-mudrakāt*).[51] We know at once (to use the standard examples) that injustice, lying, and ingratitude are evil, just as we know straightaway that justice, truthfulness, and gratitude are good.[52]

The idea that the intellect can discern the good or the evil of actions by its own power characterized the Muʿtazilah from an early date. Bishr ibn al-Muʿtamir (d. 210/825), the founder of

[47] On ʿAbbād ibn Sulaymān (d. ca. 250/864), see Ibn Ḥazm, *Fiṣal*, III, 92, and, in general, *EI*², I, 4-5. On Abū al-Qāsim al-Kaʿbī (d. 319/931), see Brunschvig, "Muʿtazilisme et optimum," p. 11, and, in general, *EI*², I, 1002, and *GAS*, I, 622-623.

[48] See D. Gimaret, "Matériaux pour une bibliographie des Ǧubbāʾī," *JA*, 264 (1976), p. 281 (Abū ʿAlī) and 307 (Abū Hāshim).

[49] *Mughnī*, XIV, 28.

[50] *Mughnī*, XIV, 14.

[51] *Mughnī*, VI/1, 18.

[52] *Mughnī*, VI/1, 58 and 61. The moral qualities of these acts are self-evident and recognized as such by men of all faiths, including even dualists and "believers in metempsychosis" (*aṣḥāb al-tanāsukh*); see *Mughnī*, XIII, 301-302.

the Baghdad school, eulogized this function of the human intellect in the following verses:

> How excellent a scout is the intellect,
> And a companion in both hardship and ease!
> How excellent a judge (*ḥākim*), drawing inference
> From the judgment of the visible to the invisible!
> It is a thing among whose actions it is
> To distinguish the good from the evil![53]

As we know, the Ashʿarites repudiated this notion. Speaking of the intellect's capacity to judge good and evil, al-Ijī states flatly, "We declare its judgement invalid" (*abṭalnā ḥukmahu*), for "God is the judge (*ḥākim*) and 'He decrees whatever He will' (Qur. 5:1)."[54] al-Ijī defines the Ashʿarite position with utmost concision: "The Law establishes and clarifies" (i.e., good and evil); and, in commenting on this, al-Jurjānī explains, "There is no good and no evil proper to acts prior to the law's emergence."[55]

The position leads to obvious difficulties. The Shīʿite theologian Ibn al-Muṭahhar al-Ḥillī (d. 726/1326) summarized the Ashʿarite view as follows:

> [the Ashʿarites] hold that good and evil are made known only by the divine law: whatever the law commands is good and whatever it forbids is evil. If not for the law, there would be no good and no evil. If God had commanded what He has forbidden, the evil would be turned into the good.[56]

But such a position leads inevitably, in al-Ḥillī's view, to "the conceivability of wrongdoing by God and the violation of what is obligatory."[57]

[53] al-Jāḥiẓ, *K. al-ḥayawān*, VI, 292, cited in ʿAbd al-Ḥalīm Balbaʿ, *Adab al-Muʿtazilah* (Cairo, 1959), p. 370. For the great Ismāʿīlī theologian Ḥamīd al-Dīn Kirmānī (d. after 411/1020), the intellect is that which "considers, selects, and prefers the most excellent (*afḍal*) thing, with the greatest preponderance of good in its final consequences." See his *al-Aqwāl al-dhahabīyah* (Tehran, 1397/1977), p. 67, *paen*.

[54] *Mawāqif*, VIII, 195-196.

[55] *Mawāqif*, VIII, 182: *al-sharʿ huwa al-muthbit lahā wa'l-mubayyin*. Cf. also, al-Āmidī, *al-Iḥkām fī uṣūl al-aḥkām*, I, 69-70.

[56] *Kashf al-murād*, p. 185.

[57] *Ibid.*

To avoid such an implication, the Muʿtazilah had affirmed God's perfect justice. But to declare God just presupposes that we know, and can state, what justice truly is. Justice or goodness, injustice or evil, cannot be arbitrarily established, if we wish convincingly to uphold God's justice. On the contrary, these must be qualities inherent in acts.

For Muʿtazilites as well as Ashʿarites, evil denotes that which is repugnant (*qabīḥ*), good that which is attractive (*ḥasan*).[58] For the Muʿtazilites, however, evil is further defined as "that which by its very nature merits blame when committed."[59] Good and evil are not determined merely by divine command.[60] The good or the evil of an act is a "superadded qualification" (*ḥukm zā'id*);[61] each such act possesses an "intelligible aspect" (*wajh maʿqūl*) by which it is known for what it is;[62] and acts are good or evil because of "something by which they are specifically characterized."[63]

What, then, specifically characterizes an evil act? In the definition of ʿAbd al-Jabbār (whose account we here follow), such an act is one that effects "injury in which there is no benefit or the avoidance of a greater injury." Furthermore, the injury in-

[58] The terms are comparable to Greek αἰσχρός and καλός in combining the senses of moral and physical repulsiveness and attractiveness; see further, G. Hourani, *Islamic Rationalism* (Oxford, 1971), p. 49f. The *qāḍī* ʿAbd al-Jabbār is at pains to emphasize that the moral, and not the aesthetic, sense is primary in these terms; see *Mughnī*, VI/1, 20-25. In *Iḥyā'*, I, 100, al-Ghazālī seeks to show that "evil" is relative: "The evil (*qabīḥ*) is what is incompatible with purpose, so that something may be evil in one individual's opinion, good in another's; for it conforms to the object of one, but not the other."

[59] *Mughnī*, VI/1, 9: *al-qabīḥ min ḥaqqihi an yastaḥiqq bi-fiʿlihi al-dhamm.* By contrast, the good is that for performance of which "its agent does not merit reproof in any way." See *Mughnī*, VI/1, 31, and also, the student of ʿAbd al-Jabbār, Muḥammad Ibn al-Ṭayyib al-Baṣrī (d. 436/1044), *K. al-muʿtamad* (Damascus, 1964-65), I, 364.

[60] So *Mughnī*, VI/1, 59: "It cannot be that that because of which the evil on our part is evil, is the divine prohibition. . . and it cannot be that that because of which the good is good, is the divine command." Cf. also, *Mughnī*, VI/1, 115ff. Elsewhere, ʿAbd al-Jabbār states that the law and the principles discoverable by reason coincide and are complementary: "The law is to be deemed that which discloses matters established in the intellect, and is not something at variance with [the intellect]." *Mughnī*, XIV, 23.

[61] *Mughnī*, VI/1, 7.

[62] *Mughnī*, VI/1, 57.

[63] *Ibid.*

flicted is undeserved; and, finally, it is an act committed by a capable and freely acting agent whose commission of the act merits blame.[64]

The definition is precise and juridical, as befits a *qāḍī*, but it is precise for significant theological reasons as well: the definition is meant to have universal application, and to apply to God as well as to man. In accord with the Muʿtazilite principle—so loathsome to many Ashʿarites!—"the essential natures of things do not differ in this world and in the transcendent world," a good act is good regardless of agent, and an evil act is evil regardless of agent.[65] If God failed to bestow a deserved reward, "He would merit reproof, just as one of us would merit reproof if he did not do what is fair."[66] The definition of the evil act must be such as to allow for its hypothetical commission by God while excluding its actual occurrence. As al-Ḥillī put it, God's commission of evil remains a "fundamental possibility" (*imkān aṣlī*), in that His power is equal to it, but it is also a "concomitant impossibility" (*imtināʿ lāḥiq*), in that it would be contrary to His wisdom.[67]

It is this hypothetical possibility, implicit in any doctrine of objective good and evil, that appalled Ashʿarite opponents of Muʿtazilism; and al-Ghazālī's critics find it voiced in the disputed passage. Such a dilemma as al-Ghazālī poses has force and meaning only within the context of a belief in "rational good and evil." Certainly, in traditional Ashʿarite terms, it has no meaning, for whatever God does, is right and just.

To his critics, furthermore, al-Ghazālī seems to stand back, as it were, and regard the cosmos with a critical and appraising eye; to them, he seems to assess creation—and the creator—according to some objective standard of good and evil such as the Muʿtazilah had propounded. If God has not created the most wonderful in possibility, He has somehow done less than He might have. Moreover, He has failed to meet His obligation

[64] *Mughnī*, VI/1, 18. The definition is offered with reference to lying, on which see also *Sharḥ al-uṣūl al-khamsah*, p. 303, and al-Ḥillī, *Kashf al-murād*, p. 187.

[65] *Mughnī*, XIV, 13.

[66] *Mughnī*, XIV, 15.

[67] *Kashf al-murād*, p. 188.

to provide what is best. For its opponents, such a tacit imputation seems to lurk in the *Iḥyā'* passage. It was outrageous enough to imply that God might be obliged, but it was intolerable to suggest that He might fail to discharge even such inconceivable obligations.

## IV
## AL-GHAZĀLĪ AND THE OPTIMUM

The third charge against al-Ghazālī is peculiar. It is easy to show that he rejected the doctrine of the optimum, and did so in no uncertain terms. His attacks on the doctrine strike the same sharp and peremptory note we observe in other Ashʿarite discussions; and, ironically, it is the same note we have found in al-Biqāʿī's attack on al-Ghazālī. Clearly, discussions of optimism could be as irritating and even maddening to medieval Muslim theologians as they are to modern skeptics.[68]

In the third section of his doctrinal work *Qawāʿid al-ʿaqā'id*, al-Ghazālī devotes eight of his ten points to refutation of the Muʿtazilites, and specifically on this point.[69] Thus, he affirms that God can enjoin upon man what is beyond his strength; God can inflict pain on man—indeed, He can torment man—without hope of reward and for no reason; in short, God can do with man what He will.[70] And yet, in all this, God remains wise, just, merciful, and good. Of the Muʿtazilites al-Ghazālī can say, using a contemptuous and unexpected rhyme to stress the gulf between their pretensions and divine transcendence: "Things divine are too exalted in their majesty (*jalāl*) to be weighed on the scales of the Muʿtazilites" (*ahl al-iʿtizāl*).[71]

In defending al-Ghazālī against this charge, al-Samhūdī draws

[68] For an extreme example, see the violent and obscene outburst of the Ṣāḥib Ibn ʿAbbād when approached by a Sunnī theologian eager to discuss the optimum, as reported by al-Tawḥīdī, *Akhlāq al-wazīrayn*, pp. 121-122; in another version (*ibid.*, pp. 123-124), Ibn ʿAbbād exclaims, "He wanted to dispute with me about *al-maṣlaḥah*, so—by God!—I considered crucifying him on the Bāb al-Maslaḥah!" Of course, al-Tawḥīdī's anecdotes should be taken with a grain of salt!

[69] See *Iḥyā'*, I, 99ff. For the *Qawāʿid al-ʿaqā'id*, incorporated in the first part of the *Iḥyā'*, see Bouyges, no. 27.

[70] *Iḥyā'*, I, 99.

[71] *Iḥyā'*, I, 100.

attention to three points on which al-Ghazālī differed most markedly from the Muʿtazilites. Peculiar as the charge may seem at first sight, it was taken quite seriously by the disputants. There are good reasons for this, as we shall see.

First, while al-Ghazālī unequivocally rejected the Muʿtazilite conception of objective good and evil, he did admit that the human intellect is capable, by itself, of perceiving good and evil in aesthetic terms; e.g., man can perceive degrees of perfection. In al-Samhūdī's view, this is both the source of the critics' confusion and the basis of the disputed passage. If God had produced other than the most wonderful, He could be deemed deficient, and our intellects could perceive this.[72] It should be remembered, too, that "most wonderful" and "optimal" are not equivalent: God may create, and does create, the less than perfect, but this is itself most wonderful. al-Samhūdī's first point is well taken. al-Ghazālī and other Ashʿarites did hold that the human intellect possessed an autonomy of judgment in the aesthetic realm.[73] But it is difficult to see how this defense would ultimately strengthen al-Ghazālī's case. While it would clearly be preferable to imply that if God had not created a most wonderful world, He could be deemed guilty of shoddy workmanship, rather than to imply that He was either miserly or unjust; even so, such an imputation could hardly escape the critics' censure.

What al-Samhūdī means, of course, is that man's very faculty of perception should enable him to see that this world is, indeed, most wonderful. Unfortunately, no later disputant addresses this point, or any of al-Samhūdī's other points in defense of al-Ghazālī on this charge.

In al-Samhūdī's opinion, the error of the Muʿtazilites was to assume that there must be mutual implication (*mulāzamah*) between "perfect generosity and wisdom" and "the optimal," but

[72] *Iḍāḥ*, p. 98.

[73] See, e.g., *Iḥyā'*, IV, 256ff. See also Fakhr al-Dīn al-Rāzī, *K. al-arbaʿīn fī uṣūl al-dīn* (Hyderabad, 1353), pp. 246-249, where it is argued that while the intellect is perfectly capable of ascertaining what is pleasing or unpleasing to our nature, as well as what is perfect (such as knowledge) or imperfect (such as ignorance), only the law can establish the qualities of acts.

this is not so; there is, in fact, an incompatibility (*khilāf*) between them.[74] For we know that God is just, generous, and wise, but at the same time, we know that He does not do what is "optimal." Here al-Samhūdī falls back on the stock Ashʿarite response: "If the best were obligatory on God, He would perform it. But it is obvious that He does not. This shows that it is not obligatory upon Him."[75] Another stock response, which al-Ghazālī himself employs, was to state that if God were obliged to do the best for man, He would have created him, and let him remain, in paradise; since this is manifestly not the case, the Muʿtazilite doctrine is disproved.[76]

Following al-Ghazālī further, al-Samhūdī claims that the Muʿtazilites fell into error through their reliance on analogy (*muqāyasah*) between the creator and the created, for "they make His wisdom comparable to human wisdom."[77] al-Ghazālī had made this charge forcefully; for him, the whole doctrine of the optimum was nothing better than an example of "personal opinion" (*ra'y*), unsupported by either scripture or reason.[78]

It was a misuse of analogy, in the Ashʿarite view, that led the Muʿtazilites to impose obligation upon God. For the Muʿtazilites, the obligatory (*al-wājib*) was a category of the good and defined as that which merits blame when not performed; it was thus the direct opposite of the evil act.[79] Certain acts, such as gratitude to a benefactor, are obligatory by nature, and our knowledge of this is necessary (*ḍarūrī*).[80]

Given the Muʿtazilite insistence on objective, "rational" good and evil and their unswerving belief in God's justice, it would have been inconceivable to absolve God from performance of the obligatory. It would have been illogical as well, for if the obligatory follows from the very nature of an action, then such

[74] *Iḍāḥ*, p. 99.
[75] *Iḍāḥ*, p. 100.
[76] *Iḥya'*, I, 99; *al-Qusṭās al mustaqīm*, p. 94.
[77] *Iḍāḥ*, p. 100, citing *al-Qusṭās al-mustaqīm*, p. 94.
[78] This is the argument in *al-Qusṭās*, pp. 94-95.
[79] *Mughnī*, XIV, 7. The obligatory act stands in opposition to the evil act which merits censure when performed (the obligatory is: *fī ḥukm al-ḍidd lil-qabīḥ*).
[80] *Mughnī*, VI/1, 43.

actions must be obligatory for God as well. But how to conceive of God's obligations?

Clearly, the notion caused the Muʿtazilites themselves some discomfort. The *qāḍī* ʿAbd al-Jabbār's elaboration of the problem is especially careful. As he explains, the obligatory, too, possesses its "intelligible aspect" (*wajh maʿqūl*), but this is not to be confused with any "cause" (*ʿillah*). An act is not obligatory either because of a command (*amr*), or because of some necessitating agent who compels by means of utterance or gesture (*dalālah*). Speech and gesture disclose the obligatory nature of an obligation, but are not its causes.[81] "A sign (*dalīl*) reveals the state of the thing signified (*ḥāl al-madlūl*), but it is not what it is because of this."[82] The aspect of an obligatory act is not what makes it obligatory, but that by which we recognize its obligatory nature.[83]

The point was important for two reasons. First, the obligatory is so by its very nature; it is not arbitrarily established. And, second, since the obligatory is not the result of the compelling agency of an "obligator" (*mūjib*), it is proper to speak of obligation with respect to God. It might be said in certain contexts that "God obligates Himself" (*awjaba ʿalā nafsihi*),[84] but for ʿAbd al-Jabbār and his followers, what is obligatory for God arises, as it does for us, from the very nature of obligatory acts.[85]

However obligation might be qualified, it was plainly unacceptable for al-Ghazālī when applied to God. In his view, nothing was obligatory for God; indeed, "obligation is unthinkable

[81] *Mughnī*, XIV, 22.

[82] *Ibid.*

[83] *Ibid.*: "The aspect of obligation must be such that, when it is known, the obligatoriness of the act is also known."

[84] According to al-Bazdawī, the Muʿtazilah cited Qur. 11:6, "No creature is there crawling on the earth but its provision rests on God" (*ʿalā Allāh rizquhā*), with the explanation, "He obligates Himself (to provide) nourishment, for the word '*ʿalā*' places obligation upon Him." al-Bazdawī counters that the preposition here betokens, not obligation, but "elevation" (*ʿulūw*); see his *K. uṣūl al-dīn*, p. 126.

[85] *Mughnī*, XIV, 14: "If it is possible for us to know the binding force of an obligation without definition, nothing prevents its being necessary for God as well, and without the coercion of any obligator."

with regard to Him."[86] In any case, a concern to provide the best is proper to the world of human affairs and to human calculations of gain and loss, but is absurd in God's case; for "whence might the provision of the best be enjoined?"[87]

In his second point, al-Samhūdī argues that the Muʿtazilites assumed that God must do what is best for every individual, but al-Ghazālī did not claim this. In fact, for al-Ghazālī, what God decrees for a particular individual may be disastrous for him personally, even if it is "most wonderful" in the general scheme of things. Indeed, "dazzling wisdom" may demand denying to an individual what is "optimal" for him.[88]

A good illustration of this point is provided by the subject of divine grace, although al-Samhūdī does not mention it. Muʿtazilites and Ashʿarites held sharply opposing views on the subject; and certain of the early discussions prefigure points in our later debate.

Thus, the problem of grace (*luṭf*) was closely linked with definitions of divine power. In the words of Abū ʿAlī al-Jubbāʾī, ". . . there is with God no grace that may be described as the power (*qudrah*) to make one whom He knows will not believe, believe upon receiving it."[89] Grace was sometimes said to be something "in God's possession" (*ʿind Allāh*). The force of this was to suggest that God had on hand—in storage, as it were—some largesse of grace, but this could lead to the objection that God has withheld some good from His creatures. To deny that God has at His disposal any further grace was, therefore, to acquit Him of the imputation of miserliness.[90]

The formulation of the problem goes back to Abū al-Hudhayl

[86] *Iḥyāʾ*, I, 99: *lā yuʿqal fī ḥaqqihi al-wujūb*.

[87] *Iḥyāʾ*, I, 100.

[88] *Iḍāḥ*, p. 99.

[89] al-Ashʿari, *Maqālāt*, II, 575. Little has been written on this important subject. For a discussion of Muʿtazilite and Shīʿite conceptions of grace, see Abdulaziz A. Sachedina, *Islamic Messianism* (Albany, 1981), pp. 120-134; see also Martin J. McDermott, *The Theology of al-Shaikh al-Mufīd (d. 413/1022)*, (Beirut, 1978), pp. 76-82. For ʿAbd al-Jabbār, grace was defined as "that which induces an act of obedience in such a way that it occurs as freely chosen," *Mughnī*, XIII, 9; cf. also, *Sharḥ al-uṣūl al-khamsah*, p. 779.

[90] This was, in fact, the majority view of the Muʿtazilah, according to Ashʿarī, *Maqālāt*, I, 247.

al-ʿAllāf (d.ca. 226/840), the teacher, and later the rival, of al-Naẓẓām. Abū al-Hudhayl taught that the things knowable and possible to God constitute a discrete totality (*kull wa-jamīʿ*) and so, reach to a limit (*ghāyah*).[91] If this were not so, he argued, God could be considered miserly (*bakhīl*); hence, "He cannot put aside the optimal and do what is less than optimal."[92]

al-Ashʿarī, who transmits this view, objects. In his opinion,

> God can do less than what He does do and the like (of what He does), because He is not incapable (*ghayr ʿājiz*). If He were not to be described as able to do (less than the optimal), He could be characterized by impotence (*ʿajz*).[93]

Even in this brief exchange, we may note early formulations of themes with which we have already become familiar in our later debate. On the one hand, there is the claim that God must act to the utmost of His power, or else be considered miserly; and, on the other, there is the striking—and characteristic—Ashʿarite view that the vastness of divine power and capability is paradoxically displayed only most fully in God's freedom to perform less than, or other than, what is "optimal." The singular notion that the imperfect itself stands as a token of God's sovereign will and freedom is clearly prefigured here.

The problem is whether God's power as manifested in grace is finite and circumscribed, or infinite. If God could bestow enabling grace on unbelievers and yet does not, He is parsimonious; however, if He possesses no further grace—if, in His generosity and justice He has expended all in His possession—then, He is somehow impotent against the persistence of disbelief and the obduracy of evildoers. Furthermore, if God has provided all the grace at His disposal, then everything should be "for the best," and yet, how explain the continued existence of evildoers and the fate of sinners in hell?

These questions are intricate and deserve consideration in their own right. For our purposes, it is enough to note that they form

[91] *Maqālāt*, II, 576-577.
[92] *Maqālāt*, II, 577, line 4.
[93] *Ibid.* For a discussion of Abū al-Hudhayl's position, see R. M. Frank, *The Metaphysics of Created Being*, pp. 25-26.

a persistent, if shadowy, parallel with our own debate. Some of the vehemence of that later debate may have resulted from the fact that al-Ghazālī's statement raised, yet again, issues that for Ashʿarites had long seemed firmly settled, and it raised these issues in somewhat broader terms. The Ghazālian dilemma carried echoes, as it were, of earlier, equally perplexing dilemmas that had divided theological opinion and impaired consensus.

For al-Ghazālī, as for Ashʿarites generally, God possesses a grace which He uses when and as He will, and this grace is unlimited.[94] Moreover, God is free not merely to withhold grace, but even to misguide. Citing *Qur.* 16:93, "He leads astray whom He will and guides whom He will," al-Bazdawī comments:

> He misguides men, and this is a cause of harm to them. . . . This verse demonstrates that God does to men that which is not beneficial for them. . . . God wills disbelief from men, as well as harm.[95]

In the Ashʿarite view, which al-Ghazālī accepts and defends, God acts for no motive and no end, and certainly not for the good of a particular individual (though God is free to do so, if He will).[96] On this point, Ashʿarism and the Avicennian system are closer to each other—though for different reasons!—than either is to Muʿtazilism.[97] al-Ghazālī's "most wonderful" is to be understood in cosmic terms and not, as the Muʿtazilites would have it, in specific individual terms.

In his third and final argument, al-Samhūdī points out that al-Ghazālī's view of the imperfect as a ransom for the perfect differs radically from Muʿtazilite tenets.[98] According to the Muʿtazilites, each thing was created with its own specific benefit in view, even if that benefit might be deferred. But this is hardly compatible with al-Ghazālī's declaration that some beings serve merely to ransom other, higher beings—as, for example, sacrificial animals serve to ransom human souls.

[94] See, for example, al-Juwaynī, *Irshād*, p. 174 [trans. p. 265].
[95] *K. uṣūl al-dīn*, p. 127.
[96] *Iḥyā'*, I, 100.
[97] See Ibn Sīnā, *Ishārāt*, III, 154-155.
[98] *Iḍāḥ*, pp. 103-105.

Indeed, there is a profound difference between the Muʿtazilites and al-Ghazālī and his fellow Ashʿarites on this score. In the Muʿtazilite view, God does nothing without purpose, and in all that He does, He intends only benefit. How might this tenet be reconciled with the sufferings of the innocent, and specifically the sufferings of infants and animals?

The Muʿtazilites could not comfortably claim that children underwent pain as a means of "grace," i.e., as something prompting to freely chosen faith or virtue. Nor could they claim that children's suffering was the requisite tribulation through which reward might be won. Children possessed no juridical status of responsibility: they were not *mukallaf* under Islamic law. For God to inflict suffering upon them, in this world or in the next, would be supremely unjust.

Various solutions were offered to this ultimately insoluble problem. One solution regarded such sufferings as admonitions, or moral precepts, for adults. In the anthropocentrist theodicy of the Muʿtazilah, nothing could be purposeless, nothing could be in vain; even ostensibly meaningless suffering had to serve and be of use, specifically for man. Sometimes this led to peculiar notions, such as that God could create nothing imperceptible to man, for the imperceptible cannot serve as a sign or precept: "God can never create anything but that through which man may be given signs and benefit. He cannot create something no one sees or perceives."[99] So, too, the sufferings of children served as sign and admonition; their sufferings were a warning for the perspicacious, and they also provided a convenient means for putting mothers and fathers to the test.[100]

The most popular solution was to claim that in the next world God made up for the sufferings which innocents underwent in this world. God indemnified unmerited suffering by providing a recompense (*ʿiwaḍ*).[101] In the majority view, God inflicted pain on infants as an admonition to adults, but He then recompensed

[99] al-Ashʿarī, *Maqālāt*, I, 251. The view had been advocated earlier by the Qadarīyah, according to al-Baghdādī, *Uṣūl*, p. 152.

[100] al-Nāshi' al-Akbar (d. 293/905), *K. al-awsaṭ*, in: J. van Ess, *Frühe muʿtazilitische Häresiographie*, p. 99.

[101] See also Goldziher, *Vorlesungen*, p. 100; tr., p. 91.

those infants in the hereafter.[102] Some Muʿtazilites denied that God caused any undeserved pain. Others, including al-Naẓẓām, held that infant suffering is, indeed, God's doing, but that it occurs through "the necessary course of nature."[103]

If the problem of infant suffering seemed intractable, the problem of animal suffering was, in its way, even more so. It was hard to maintain that animals suffered as an admonition for man, nor could it be shown that the pain animals endure was somehow beneficial for them.

Such considerations led the Muʿtazilites to posit a recompense for animals, too, in the hereafter. Opinions varied as to the nature of this recompense. Some held that animals would be lavishly treated in paradise and clothed in "the most beautiful forms": others believed that God might recompense them in this world, as well as in the hereafter; still others contented themselves with the belief that God does recompense animals, but in ways we cannot understand.[104]

In their scrupulous concern for the precise workings of divine justice, the Muʿtazilites often found themselves entangled in unexpected intricacies which aroused derision among their opponents. It was asked, for example, what God would do in the case of a believer whose hand had been cut off and who then apostasized; and, conversely, in the case of an infidel whose hand had been cut off and who then came to believe. The simplest response was to claim that another hand would be substituted, but solutions could become complicated: by some it was held that the hand of the apostasizing believer would be attached to the repentant infidel, while the infidel's hand (which had been amputated while he still disbelieved) would be affixed to the apostate. Still others rejected this, on the ground that belief and disbelief are not "the hand and the foot."[105]

The Ashʿarites were inclined to pour scorn on such solutions; they found especially distasteful the whole notion of recompense for animal suffering. On this point, al-Ghazālī himself remarks

[102] al-Ashʿarī, *Maqālāt*, I, 253.
[103] al-Nāshi', in van Ess, *Frühe muʿtaz. Häresiographie*, p. 100; cf. also p. 98.
[104] al-Ashʿarī, *Maqālāt*, I, 254-255.
[105] *Maqālāt*, I, 252.

caustically that Muʿtazilites believe that "whenever any bedbug or flea is hurt by being rubbed or struck, God is obliged to gather and reward it with a recompense."[106] Indeed, animal suffering seems to have presented no serious problem for the Ashʿarites. According to al-Bazdawī,

> Dogs and horses have no reward, nor do insects, beasts of prey and vermin. . . . Reward in the hereafter is nothing but paradise, and they have no paradise. Rather, they are crammed together and then reduced to dust and do not enter paradise. Piety does not exist among horses, insects and beasts of prey. . . .[107]

The three points which al-Samhūdī marshals, when taken together with al-Ghazālī's own explicit rejection of the doctrine of *al-aṣlaḥ*, suffice to dispel the crude charge that he was somehow covertly Muʿtazilite in the controversial *Iḥyā'* passage. But, of course, the matter is not so simple. However repellent the bases of the doctrine of the optimum might be, it had, nevertheless, a certain appeal. The emphasis on God's generosity and justice, even the possibility of His provision of the optimal, was attractive; it was the Muʿtazilite insistence that God was duty-bound to act or be in a certain way that angered the Ashʿarites. Certainly, this is true in al-Ghazālī's case. Even after denouncing and ridiculing the Muʿtazilite formulation of the doctrine, he is unwilling to exclude it utterly. He leaves open the possibility that God provides "the optimal," but he connects it, characteristically, with the "secret of predestination." As he puts it, "Indeed, there is a mystery in doing what is best (*li-fiʿl al-aṣlaḥ sirr*) that derives from the knowledge of God's secret in predestination."[108]

According to strict Ashʿarite doctrine, God afflicts individuals, not for their own good or for the sake of future reward or in the hope of later recompense, but simply because He wills so to afflict them; nor are these afflictions to be regarded necessar-

106 *al-Iqtiṣād*, p. 182.
107 *K. uṣūl al-dīn*, pp. 128-129.
108 *al-Qusṭās al-mustaqīm*, p. 95.

ily as goods in disguise. God creates evils and He inflicts them.[109] We cannot know ultimately why.

The candid acceptance of evil from God permitted the Ashʿarites a certain "realism" in viewing the world; it relieved them of any need to search out far-fetched and implausible rationalizations for human misery. Whatever its advantages, however, such an attitude could only raise renewed questions about God's justice and mercy. The Ashʿarite position was not merely too harsh, it was simply inadequate: by denying that there was any question, it flew in the face of common sense as well. The difficulty was, however, that a variety of answers to such questions lay ready to hand, as it were, in Muʿtazilite teaching. The explanations were embedded within "heretical" doctrine; they were dangerous and to be treated gingerly. It was necessary to extract what was useful and appealing from such doctrine, but to cast aside what was harmful.

al-Ghazālī is often praised as a great synthesizer. Whether his syntheses were finally successful is still a subject of debate. That he was shrewdly eclectic, however, is everywhere apparent throughout his later work. One passage from his *Qawāʿid al-ʿaqāʾid* illustrates this tendency with special aptness. The passage reaffirms several key points in the more famous and controversial text that sparked our long debate. It does so, moreover, with conscious reference to, and reliance upon, Muʿtazilite concepts.

Nothing exists, al-Ghazālī declares,

> . . . except what is created by God's action and emanates from His justice in an existence that is most excellent (*aḥsan*), most perfect (*akmal*), most complete (*atamm*), and most just (*aʿdal*), for God is wise in His acts, just in His judgments. God's justice is not to be compared with man's (*lā yuqās ʿadluhu bi-ʿadl al-ʿibād*).[110]

[109] God creates evils, but a certain pious etiquette is to be observed in regard to them. According to the lexicographer Ibn Manẓūr, "In praising God, excellent things are connected with Him, and not evil things. The object is not to deny anything of His power and creative action. Thus, in prayer it is recommended that one say, 'O Lord of heavens and earth!' and not, 'O Lord of dogs and swine!' even though He is their lord." *Lisān al-ʿarab*, VI, 67.

[110] *Iḥyāʾ*, I, 80, line -11ff. As though to complete the connection, al-Zabīdī

al-Ghazālī makes quite deliberate use of Muʿtazilite notions and turns of phrase, but he does so for the purpose of refuting a cardinal Muʿtazilite principle: the analogy between this world and the transcendent, between man and God.

And a few lines later, he resorts to the same procedure, with even more explict reference to the doctrine of the optimum:

> God is generous (*mutafaḍḍil*) in creating, in inventing and in imposing obligation,—not out of any necessity (*wujūb*)—and He is lavish in providing favors and "the optimal" (*al-aṣlaḥ*)—not out of any obligation (*luzūm*).[111]

This has a double force: it rebukes the Muʿtazilites and, at the same time, it usurps a key point in their doctrine. It plucks the notion of necessity from the heart of the doctrine while preserving what is acceptable in it: the divine generosity and justice that freely and unconditionally bestow what is best.

## V
## THE SOLUTION OF AL-SUYŪṬĪ

al-Suyūṭī offers a compromise solution that is novel in the context of the debate.

For him, two points in the *Iḥyā'* passage were especially problematical. The first was the disputed sentence itself. This al-Suyūṭī transmitted not in its usual form, but as follows: "There is not in possibility more wonderful than what God has produced."[112]

The second troublesome point lay in the dilemma itself which al-Suyūṭī rephrased slightly thus:

> If there were (a more wonderful world), and God withheld it while having power (to produce it), it would be miserliness contrary to divine generosity, and injustice contrary to justice; or, if He did not have the power, it would be impotence contrary to the divine omnipotence.[113]

---

glosses the string of elatives in this passage by inserting the single word *abdaʿ*, "most wonderful." See *Itḥāf*, II, 32, line 17.

[111] *Iḥyā'*, I, 80, line -5, Cf. also, *Iḥyā'*, I, 99, line 7ff.

[112] *Tashyīd*, fol. 7b: *laysa fi'l-imkān abdaʿ mimmā awjada Allāh.*

[113] *Ibid.*

For some, al-Suyūṭī noted, these statements betrayed undue reliance on Muʿtazilite doctrines, whereas for others they were in conformity with the beliefs of the *ahl al-sunnah* and, specifically, the orthodox belief that God acts out of pure generosity (*faḍl*).[114]

In his own opinion, he strove for the middle ground:

> I say that al-Ghazālī only wanted to establish a proof according to the doctrine of both groups, so that his claim for the absence of possibility (of a more wonderful world) might be perfected according to both schools.
>
> It is as though he said: "It is impossible by consensus (*ijmāʿ*) of both parties. As for the *ahl al-sunnah*, because hoarding by God would be a denial of generosity. . . . And as for the Muʿtazilites, because hoarding by God would be injustice (*ẓulm*), which is a denial of justice (*ʿadl*).[115]

al-Ghazālī's purpose in this was not to confirm the teaching of one school over another; rather, al-Suyūṭī argues, he drew on both schools to strengthen and consolidate his arguments.[116]

al-Suyūṭī compares the various passages in which the disputed statement occurs and believes somewhat different tendencies can be detected in each. Thus, it was only in the *Iḥyā'*, he claims, that al-Ghazālī sought to achieve such a reconciliation. In the *Jawāhir al-Qur'ān* (*i.e.*, the *Kitāb al-arbaʿīn*), by contrast, al-Ghazālī omitted any mention of "justice," restricting himself instead to "generosity" (*faḍl, jūd*). Moreover, he did this either to satisfy the demands of "orthodox" doctrine or, quite simply, out of sheer disregard for such "innovating" (*mubtadiʿ*) sects as the Muʿtazilah. In this, too, he may have been motivated by a desire for approval or, still more simply, by a desire to eradicate all ambiguity from his controversial words.[117]

al-Suyūṭī's reasoning is as follows. In the *Iḥyā'*, al-Ghazālī consciously constructed the problematic passage so that it might

[114] See, for example al-Ashʿarī, *K. al-lumaʿ*, p. 20; tr., p. 27. Cf. also the *ḥadīth*: "God is generous and loves generosity" (*jawād yuḥibb al-jūd*), al-Tirmidhī, *Sunan*, VIII, 32.

[115] *Tashyīd*, fol. 7b.

[116] *Ibid.*

[117] *Tashyīd*, fol. 8a.

be unassailable from either an Ashʿarite or a Muʿtazilite standpoint. But later, when he paraphrased the passage in such works as the *Imlāʾ* and the *Kitāb al-arbaʿīn*, he recast, or left out, controversial phrases so as to bring his statements into conformity with accepted Ashʿarite teaching.

There is a further side to al-Suyūṭī's argument. He could not deny the manifest affinity of al-Ghazālī's words with certain Muʿtazilite teachings, but, unlike al-Ghazālī's other defenders, he chose to capitalize on this affinity.

Naturally, al-Suyūṭī was eager to demonstrate al-Ghazālī's unimpeachable "orthodoxy." Thus, he could explain al-Ghazālī's use of the word "miserliness" as mere hyperbole (*mubālaghah*); it is as though he said, "Doubtless the Creator is generous and not miserly, for He is remote from miserliness."[118] But such a demonstration of orthodoxy was *de rigueur*, in any case, in the volatile and contumacious atmosphere in which the debate, in al-Suyūṭī's time, took place.

Nevertheless, in his treatise, more clearly than in any other work of the dispute, we see the result of al-Ghazālī's ambiguous use of Muʿtazilite concepts and phrases. A curious and elusive mirror effect sets in. As we have seen, al-Biqāʿī often drew on traditional anti-Muʿtazilite arguments in attacking al-Ghazālī—who had himself appropriated Muʿtazilite arguments against the Muʿtazilites themselves—and al-Suyūṭī will avail himself of strangely transformed Muʿtazilite arguments to rebut al-Biqāʿī. For example, al-Suyūṭī will argue that God is not obliged to do the best, but in fact He does do the best in every case, and out of sheer magnanimity. For al-Suyūṭī, just as God "knows all types of speech, but selected for His book the most eloquent of all and then revealed it, so that anything more eloquent than it cannot be,"[119] so, too, with regard to creatures:

> God knows, for every being, all of the ways in which it is possible to produce it, but He chooses the most wonderful way and then produces it accordingly. Nevertheless, He retains the power efficacious to produce it in numerous other ways. How-

[118] *Ibid.*
[119] *Tashyīd*, fol. 2b.

ever, these are not the most wonderful. The most wonderful is the way in which God does produce.[120]

In short, God could produce things in other ways, but He does not. The effect of this line of reasoning is to preserve God's sovereign power and freedom in principle, while simultaneously proferring the assurance that, in practice, God will always act to produce "the most wonderful." God may not be obliged to provide the best, but in fact, He always has and He always will:

> Granted, it is not incumbent upon God to do the optimal, but He does do what is most wonderful in what He makes, as pure grace and favor—but not out of obligation. He causes His obedient ones to enter paradise,—out of generosity, not obligation. If He wished, He could make them enter hell, but He does not do that.[121]

Here al-Suyūṭī's argument strangely mirrors the early Muʿtazilite position that God can commit evil, but in fact never does.[122] God can forgo doing what is optimal, but He does not. Such a strategy as al-Suyūṭī here employs was a way of preserving principle while rendering it tolerable in practice. The assimilation of what was both useable and desirable in Muʿtazilite teaching, an assimilation initiated by al-Ghazālī, here finds its curious culmination in the work of his 16th-century defender. The critics were right to express alarm and dismay, but their attacks proved ineffectual. If the discredited doctrine of the optimum had been reinstated, it was under a different designation—*al-abdaʿ*, "the most wonderful"—but at the same time, its sting, the imposition of moral obligation upon God, had long been conclusively drawn.

## VI
## QUESTIONS OF MERCY

In his doctrinal works, al-Ghazālī hewed closely to Ashʿarite teaching; elsewhere, however, as in our disputed passage, he subtly modified or mitigated his position. He did this

[120] *Tashyīd*, fols. 2b-3a.
[121] *Tashyīd*, fol. 3b.
[122] See the discussion in Chapter Three above, section II.B.

by drawing on various sources, philosophic as well as Muʿtazilite. Against his stark assertion that whatever afflictions befall man are right and just, one must set the various more or less rationalistic explanations which he often offers for the problem of human suffering. Presumably, he engages in such explanation to afford helpmeets for those not fully and firmly established in "trust in God."

In any case, the harsh insistence on the sovereign inscrutability of the divine will might be proper and even useful in deflating the presumption of Muʿtazilite or philosophic optimists, but it would be cold comfort indeed when offered under ordinary circumstances to a suffering individual. Suffering craves reasons. Explanation often serves as an anodyne. It is always easier to suffer "for a reason."

The strict Ashʿarite position left little room for such explanations. As critics noted, the frank ascription to God of all agency raised disturbing questions about the divine mercy and justice. al-Ghazālī himself formulates such questionings as follows:

> Perhaps you will ask, "What is the meaning of God's being 'compassionate' (*raḥīm*) and 'the most compassionate of the compassionate' (*arḥam al-rāḥimīn*)? A compassionate person does not see someone afflicted, injured, tormented, and ill without rushing to remove that from him, if he is able to remove it. Now God is able to ward off every misfortune and to avert all poverty and grief and to remove every sickness and every injury. But the world overflows with sicknesses, tribulations, and calamities. He is able to remove all of them and yet, He leaves His servants in travail to disasters and misfortunes."[123]

al-Ghazālī answers this fundamental question in several ways, all of which draw on thinly disguised philosophic or Muʿtazilite precedents.

[123] *al-Maqṣad al-asnā*, p. 67. Compare the more vivid, earlier formulation by Ibn Ḥazm, *Fiṣal*, II, 157-8. al-Ghazālī's question may owe something to earlier, bolder expressions of doubt. For example, the theologian Jahm ibn Safwān (executed 128/745) used to stop with his companions before lepers and other unfortunates and exclaim, "Look! The 'Most Compassionate of the compassionate' does such things!" One of Jahm's followers supposedly remarked, too, that "nothing is more harmful (*aḍarr*) to creatures than their creator." See H. Ritter, "Risālat Ibn Sīnā fi'l-arzāq," *RAAD*, 25 (1950), p. 200; as also his *Das Meer der Seele* (Leiden, 1955), p. 159.

*A. The True Nature of Mercy*

Doubts often arise from a misapprehension of the true nature of divine mercy. After all, human compassion is interested. It is "not without a painful tenderness (*riqqah mu'limah*) which befalls the compassionate person and impels him to fulfill the need of the object of compassion."[124] By contrast, God's compassion is perfectly disinterested: it "consists in considering the object of compassion for his own sake, not for the sake of relief from (one's own) pain and solicitude."[125]

In the *basmalah*, God is invoked as "the compassionate" (*raḥmān*) and "the merciful" (*raḥīm*). The word *raḥīm* may be applied to other beings, but *raḥmān* applies only to God. His compassion is both perfect (*raḥmah tāmmah*) and universal (*raḥmah ʿāmmah*): it grants good to those in need and it does so for their sakes, out of concern (*ʿināyah*) for them. Then, too, it comprehends the undeserving as well as the deserving.[126]

The true nature of this impartial and consummate mercy is exemplified in other ways as well.

*B. Suffering Is Medicinal*

Suffering is like a prescribed cure which we must endure for our ultimate good. We mistake true compassion. We think that one who inflicts pain is uncompassionate, but this is not always so. The cupping (*ḥijāmah*) of an infant provides an instructive example:

> The mother feels tender concern for the little one and forbids cupping, but the father, who is intelligent, inflicts it forcibly on him. The ignoramus thinks that the mother, and not the father, is the compassionate one. But the reasonable person knows that the father's infliction of cupping on the child represents perfect compassion . . . and that the mother is (the child's) enemy in the guise of a friend.[127]

[124] *al-Maqṣad al-asnā*, p. 66.
[125] *Ibid.*
[126] *al-Maqṣad al-asnā*, p. 65.
[127] *al-Maqṣad al-asnā*, pp. 68-69. al-Baghdādī attributes this explanation to the Qadarīyah; see his *Uṣūl al-dīn*, p. 240. al-Shahrastānī, *K. al-milal*, p. 121, ascribes it to al-Jubbā'ī.

Thus, God is the intelligent father, and our sufferings are merely the distasteful medicine that heals us in the end. Those who side with the mother fail to see that out of a particular evil a general good may arise.[128]

### C. *Suffering Occasions Gratitude*

Misfortunes may be exemplary. They are direct and visible tokens of God's favor to those not so afflicted. They prompt man to gratitude (*shukr*). The afflicted individual may console himself with the thought that no matter how horrendous his state, there are countless others in a worse condition than he; hence, he, too, may be grateful. The misfortune of one illustrates and enhances the good fortune of another. As we have seen, this is the case with the blessed in paradise, whose bliss is augmented by contemplation of the agonies of the damned. As al-Ghazālī explains elsewhere:

> The pain of unbelievers in hell is also a blessing, but with regard to others, not with regard to themselves; for the afflictions of one group are benefits to another (*maṣā'ib qawm ʿinda qawm fawā'id*).[129]

Even the most severely afflicted may feel thankful when they reflect on the plight of unbelievers and those ignorant of God:

> Jesus passed a man who was blind and leprous, crippled, and afflicted with paralysis on both sides. His flesh was flaking away with leprosy. He said, "Praise God for saving me from that with which He has afflicted so many of His creatures!"
>
> Jesus exclaimed, "O you! What affliction can I see that has been spared you?" The man replied, "O spirit of God! I am better off than those in whose hearts God has not placed what He has placed in mine—I mean, knowledge of Him!"[130]

[128] The medicinal explanation is a common topos. See also, *Iḥyā'*, IV, 86; *K. al-arbaʿīn*, p. 268; and ʿAyn al-Quḍāh, *Nāmah-hā* (ed. Munzavī; Tehran, 1969), II, 222: "You would inflict the pain of cupping on a beloved child to cure it; so, too, does God act toward us." See also J. van Ess, *Die Gedankenwelt des Ḥāriṯ al-Muḥāsibī* (Bonn, 1961), p. 181. For its use by Leibniz, see his *Lettres et opuscules inédits* (ed. Foucher de Careil; Paris, 1854), pp. 173-174.

[129] *Iḥyā'*, IV, 111.

[130] *Iḥyā'*, IV, 298-299.

*D. Apparent Evil, Real Good*

Evils are often goods in disguise. In fact, there is no evil that does not contain some good hidden within it, such that "if the evil were removed, the good contained within it would become nothing."[131] A favorite example is that of a diseased hand, the amputation of which is an apparent evil, but ultimately, a genuine good.[132] There is divine wisdom even in our sufferings:

> God created nothing without there being wisdom in it, and He created nothing without there being blessing in it, either for all people or for some of them. Thus, in God's creation of suffering (*al-balā'*), there is blessing, too, either for the sufferer or for someone else.[133]

Events are not what they seem. Ostensible outrages may conceal great, though hidden, good—if not the goodness of God's mercy, then the goodness of His justice. The classic example is the famous Qur'ānic tale of Moses and the servant (18:61ff).[134] The belief that all events work toward the good

> . . . removes from one's mind the objection of "why?" and "how?" so that one is not surprised at whatever occurs in the world, including what the ignorant consider disorder, commotion, and deviation from the right course.[135]

al-Ghazālī illustrates this with a tale. A man who had achieved contentment with God's decree (*riḍā' bi'l-qaḍā'*) used to say in every circumstance, "There is something good in whatever God decrees!"

> He was in a desert with his people. He had only a donkey upon which his tent was packed, a dog who kept watch for them, and

[131] *al-Maqṣad al-asnā*, p. 68.

[132] *Ibid.* See also our translation of the *Iḥyā'* text, line 77ff.

[133] *Iḥyā'*, IV, 111, line -7ff. The Muʿtazilite insistence that God does nothing without intending benefit seems quite apparent in this passage. On the issue of "meaningless" suffering, see Emmanuel Levinas, "La souffrance inutile," *Giornale di Metafisica*, N.S., IV (1982), pp. 13-25 [The whole number of this journal is devoted to the question].

[134] See, too, the story of the Prophet at the Well in *K. al-arbaʿīn*, p. 269. For a discussion of this motif, see S. Thompson, *The Folktale* (Berkeley, 1977), p. 130.

[135] *K. al-arbaʿīn*, p. 268.

> a rooster who awoke them. A fox came and took the rooster. His people were sad, but he said, "It is a good thing!" A jackal came and killed the donkey. His people were sad, but he said, "A good thing!" Then the dog was stricken and died, but he said, "A good thing!" His people were astonished at this. But in the morning (they learned that) others had been taken captive in their vicinity and their children kidnapped. The location of some of them would have been revealed as well by the rooster's cry, that of others by the dog's barking, and that of still others by the donkey's braying. So he said, "(Now) do you believe that there is good in whatever God decrees? For if God had not destroyed the animals, you would have perished!"[136]

The reverse of this principle also may hold true: apparent goods are often really evils. Thus, property, status, and even family life are hindrances to true piety. Worldly happiness is perilous. al-Ghazālī cites approvingly the anonymous adage: "The believer endures against tribulation, but only the righteous endures against well-being."[137] The comforts and securities of this world are like honey filled with poison which the ignorant consume.[138] Hence, with regard to the attractions of family life, al-Ghazālī reminds his reader, "Your wives and children are enemies to you, so guard against them!"[139]

All suffering is of only two sorts: qualified or restricted (*muqayyad*) and absolute (*muṭlaq*).[140] All the afflictions of this world, including poverty, illness, and bodily pain, are qualified sufferings, and so may contain secret blessings. Only separation from God in the afterlife merits the designation of absolute suffering, and in this there may be no benefit for the sufferer himself.[141]

By contrast, the sufferings of this world are goods in disguise, and we should even be grateful for them, "just as a boy after

[136] *Ibid.* Compare the story of Akiba with the same theme in the Babylonian Talmud, *Berakhot* 60B (Jerusalem, 1966 ed.; Vol. I, p. 120, line -5), cited in H. Schwarzbaum, "The Jewish and Moslem Versions of some Theodicy Legends," *Fabula*, 3 (1960), p. 127.

[137] *Iḥyā'*, IV, 60.

[138] *Iḥyā'*, IV, 87.

[139] *Iḥyā'*, IV, 60.

[140] *Iḥyā'*, IV, 110.

[141] *Ibid.*

reaching the age of reason and maturity thanks his master and father for his blows and discipline."[142]

*E. Evil Occurs per accidens*

God never wills evil for its own sake (*li-dhātihi*), but only for the good that it contains. God decrees the good *per se*, the evil only *per accidens.*[143]

This principle, which al-Ghazālī derives from Ibn Sīnā,[144] he interprets in accord with the *ḥadīth qudsī*, "My mercy outstrips My wrath" (*sabaqat raḥmatī ghaḍabī*).[145] God wills evil as an expression of wrath, but His mercy manifests itself in the willing of good, and mercy takes precedence over wrath. The evil that God wills is always for the sake of some ultimate and overriding good, although it may reveal itself in the lineaments of wrath.[146]

Common to all these explanations is the tacit belief that evils are actually good or, at least, redound to the good. The calamities that befall individuals work in some unforeseeable way to their future advantage. Seemingly purposeless or even atrocious happenings possess a secret rationale.

Such explanations were basically homiletic. They pressed into service examples drawn from folklore as well as from common experience. They were intended to persuade, exhort, and reassure the reader in an immediate and credible way. On the question of suffering, doctrinal pronouncements alone could not suffice.

As his defenders noted, al-Ghazālī wrote in order to convince his readers to become *mutawakkilūn*, those who trust and abandon themselves to God. To this end, he employed exempla and anecdotes, Ṣūfī sayings, and more or less vulgarized philosoph-

[142] *Iḥyā'*, IV, 113.
[143] *al-Maqṣad al-asnā*, p. 68.
[144] See his *Ishārāt*, III, 206-207.
[145] See Muslim, *Ṣaḥīḥ*, IV, 2107ff.
[146] *al-Maqṣad al-asnā*, p. 68. Cf. the parable in ʿAṭṭār's *Muṣībat-nāmah*, in which Maḥmūd of Ghazna sends out soldiers to extort tribute so that his audience chamber, previously empty because of his justice, will fill with clamoring supplicants. The moral is, "Injustice and affliction are necessary so that the essential attribute of God as Lord become manifest." Cited in Ritter, *Das Meer der Seele*, pp. 62 and 253.

ical precepts—all in the attempt to strengthen his readers for eventual acceptance of a more difficult truth.

That these explanations owe something to philosophic or Muʿtazilite antecedents is hardly surprising. Most of the practical "solutions" available for such problems as suffering had been elaborated by Muʿtazilite theologians. These explanations could not be formally conceded, but elements could be extracted from them or they could be used, in a loose and informal fashion, for hortatory purposes.

In any case, all such explanations are merely provisional. For al-Ghazālī, in the end, we can only accept God's mercy on faith. The divine mercy is bound up with "God's secret," the mystery of predestination. It is this difficult truth that one must finally acknowledge:

> Do not doubt in any way that God is the most compassionate of the compassionate . . . for beneath this is a mystery, disclosure of which the law forbids. Be content then with prayer, do not hanker after disclosure! You have been informed by hints and signs if you are among His people. Reflect! . . . for I deem you one endowed with insight into God's secret of predestination.[147]

[147] *al-Maqṣad al-asnā*, pp. 69-70.

# Conclusion

al-Ghazālī borrowed from a variety of sources in shaping his thought, but his peculiar version of theodicy was ultimately a logical outgrowth of orthodox Ashʿarite doctrine. This was no systematic theodicy; it emerged under pressure of debate in the works of succeeding generations of disputants. In a sense, it may be called a collective exposition of theodicy, the lineaments of which became manifest only gradually over several centuries. Nevertheless, all the disputants drew with surprising fidelity on a single provocative passage; in the works of different thinkers, or in different periods, one tendency already implicit in the original text might be emphasized to the detriment of others. Then, again, the text might elicit questions, not previously considered, that in turn prompted later commentators to develop still other tendencies latent in the Ghazālian viewpoint. For all the longevity of the debate and the often fragmentary nature of the texts themselves, there is a coherence and consistency in the position of al-Ghazālī and his followers that invite synopsis. Let us try to summarize the characteristic features of this Islamic version of theodicy.

First, the actual world, at each instant of its continuance, is unsurpassably right and just; it has been determined by divine decree, specified by divine will, and effected by divine power. The world, at this precise instant, cannot be better. Nevertheless, it can change. The perfect rightness of the actual entails no unchanging and inviolate order of things. (That would imply that things possessed some intrinsic necessity, which they do not have.) Rather, God can, and does, change the "most wonderful" order of the world, and He does so incessantly. However, each change, each new configuration of things, is right and just; each new configuration is "most wonderful." The world is a succession of equally perfect and most wonderful states of affairs.

Second, the world is radically contingent: everything within it could be otherwise. No aspect of this world is intrinsically necessary. Nevertheless, while the world, in itself, is radically contingent, it is also strictly necessary. It is necessary "because of something else": the prior action of the divine will. Thus, according to this line of reasoning, one can say, without fear of contradiction, that "what strikes you was not there to miss you," and, at the same time, that "it could be otherwise." Each thing, each event, each individual, is contingent; each, by nature, can be and not be. However, if it be, it is necessary for as long as it may exist. What exists, exists necessarily; what does not exist, does not exist necessarily.[1] But neither the existence or the non-existence of a thing is intrinsic to it. Nothing in the world—nor the world itself— has within it any factor that determines, or necessitates, its existence or its non-existence. Existence and non-existence are assigned to each contingent thing by the divine wisdom; and assigned, moreover, at every instant of its continuance in being or non-being. It is the divine decree that imposes necessity, and existing things are necessary only because of this decree.

The crucial principle in the Ghazālian theodicy is the radical contingency of things. To say that a thing is "possible" does not mean that it already partakes, in some shadowy and unspecified way, of existence. True, a possibility may exist in the mind, though not in actuality. But such mental possibilities are themselves contingencies: they exist in the mind because the divine will has decreed that they shall so exist. "Not even the casual glance of a spectator, nor the stray thought in the mind, come to be outside the sphere of His will."[2] The hypothetical and alternative worlds which the mind conceives are indeed possible; however, since they do not exist in actuality, they are inevitably inferior to what does so exist. God could create these hypothetical, alternative worlds; the fact that He does not is itself a sign that they are not truly superior to the actual world.

Third, the very imperfections of the world—disease, defi-

[1] See the verses to this effect by Naṣīr al-Dīn Ṭūsī, as cited in M. Muṭahharī, *ʿAdl-i ilāhī*, p. 71.

[2] *K. al-arbaʿīn*, p. 6.

ciency, vice—contribute to the surpassing excellence of the world. In the grand scheme of things, they, too, are "most wonderful." Through imperfection, we are enabled to discern perfection and, ultimately, to have some sense of the consummate perfection that is God's. The imperfect, too, exists necessarily, for God has willed it; it is a sign of the specifying action of His will. To say that it could be otherwise and that it would be better otherwise, is (while true in theory!) to rebuke God's will and impugn His wisdom. The very fact that God can, and does, create the imperfect in all its forms, stands as an undeniable proof of His freedom, omnipotence, and will.

These are the salient features of the Ghazālian theodicy. Against its critics it may be said that these features are indeed compatible with traditional Ashʿarite theology; and, in fact, that they represent a natural outgrowth of this theology. The Islamic version of theodicy which al-Ghazālī and his followers elaborated may be seen as the extreme development of the pious maxim: "What He wills, is; what He does not will, is not." The perfect rightness of the actual is the inevitable expression of that will.

This point may be clearly seen in one final example. Sometime after 905/1500, five years before his death, the indefatigable al-Suyūṭī composed a little treatise on the subject of earthquake.[3] The work is interesting and important, not only because al-Suyūṭī tried to chronicle all the earthquakes known to him up to 1500, but also because he sought to account for the occurrence of such cataclysmic disasters. As we have repeatedly seen, al-Suyūṭī represents a strongly "optimistic" position in our own debate, and so his testimony is of particular interest.

In explaining earthquakes, al-Suyūṭī places primary emphasis on the divine will. Earthquakes occur solely through divine decree (*qaḍā'*). When God wishes to terrify man, He sends earthquakes.[4] al-Suyūṭī rejects explanations based on natural causes. The philosophers are wrong to state that earthquakes occur when too many vapors (*abkhirah*) accumulate below ground; rather,

[3] His *Kashf al-ṣalṣalah ʿan waṣf al-zalzalah*, ed. Saʿdānī (Fez, 1971). Works on earthquake are rare in Arabic; for two other treatises, both based on al-Suyūṭī, see Mach 4787-4788.

[4] *Kashf al-ṣalṣalah*, pp. 1, 3, 9, 11.

all the mountains of the earth are subterraneanly linked by "roots" (*ʿurūq*) to the legendary Mt. Qāf, the "mother of mountains,"[5] and

> . . . when God wishes to send earthquake upon a village, He commands that mountain and it then agitates the root upon which the village rests, and so it quakes and dashes the village. This is why one village is agitated, but not another.[6]

To be sure, God may intend such events for benefit; citing a tradition transmitted in the name of ʿĀʾishah, al-Suyūṭī will claim, for example, that earthquakes are "a mercy, a blessing, and an admonition to believers, but a warning, a sign of wrath, and a punishment to miscreants."[7] Ultimately, however, they occur because God has foreordained them, and we cannot know why. They are a divinely decreed evil (*sūʾ al-qaḍāʾ*), as in the following anonymous verses which al-Suyūṭī quotes regarding an earthquake that struck Ḥims in the year 552/1157:

> Earthquakes, occurring through an eternal decree
> Which the Lord of Heaven ordains, terrified us.
> They wrecked the stronghold of Shayzar and Ḥamāh;
> They destroyed the people through the evil of divine decree,
>
> And many towns, fortresses, and boundary defenses,
> Things established to endure forever.[8]

Earthquakes are "evil," and God ordains them. Such is the Ashʿarite view. This seems a far cry from theodicy or any semblance of "optimism." And yet, reading al-Suyūṭī's treatise in the light of the larger debate, we can reasonably assume that it was written to quell, if not to answer fully, the inevitable mur-

[5] *Kashf al-ṣalṣalah*, p. 3. For Mt. Qāf, see A. J. Wensinck, "The Ideas of the Western Semites concerning the Navel of the Earth," *Verhandelingen der Koninklijke Akademie van Wetenschappen te Amsterdam*, N.S., 17 (1916), pp. 5-6.

[6] *Kashf al-ṣalṣalah*, p. 1.

[7] *Kashf al-ṣalṣalah*, p. 4.

[8] *Kashf al-ṣalṣalah*, p. 41 [metre: *khafīf*]. For Shayzar (not Shīrāz, as some manuscripts have it!), see Yāqūt, *Muʿjam al-buldān*, III, 353. Of course, the belief that God directly causes earthquake is hardly unique to Islam; see, for example, the prayers in time of earthquake in the old Roman *Missal* ("*Omnipotens sempiterne Deus, qui respicis terram et facis eam tremere*," etc.).

murings of doubt which such disasters provoke. The treatise itself gives no hint of this, to be sure. al-Suyūṭī is concerned to present an imperturbable "orthodoxy" in the face of such events. His treatise appears to be little more than a compilation of traditions assembled for the edification of the pious. And the reader has the impression that these selected traditions embody immemorial beliefs that have suffered neither alteration nor skeptical inquiry. Such is the impression which al-Suyūṭī perhaps wishes to create in his reader. He represents an Ashʿarism that has been tested, strengthened, and modified by long and acrimonious debate. It possesses a fatalistic cast, but is not to be confused with fatalism, though it is tempting to think of it as an "optimistic fatalism." Each earthquake that al-Suyūṭī records, year by year, has been foreordained by the divine will. What would otherwise be a mere list of disasters acquires heightened significance when thus prefaced by a traditionalist insistence on divine will: each of these events, from the minor tremors to the great quakes, from the dawn of time to today, God has expressly and individually willed and predestined. From the Ashʿarite viewpoint, the ultimate justification of events, however appalling, lay in the inscrutable but unfailing efficacy of divine will; this, too, was an assurance that might justify theodicy.

Nevertheless, it must be conceded that al-Ghazālī's critics have a strong case. al-Ghazālī urges unquestioning acceptance of the divine will, but he does this on the basis of a prior rationalization and justification of the actions of that will. Unquestioning acceptance of God's will, "trust in God," occur as final stages on the mystic path; to approach these stages, the aspirant to *tawakkul* traverses numerous intermediary stages, at which reason and rational understanding must assist him.

Of course, reason as such is not the issue. More seriously, as his critics claim, there is a hidden necessity in the Ghazālian theodicy. It is placed at a remove, as it were, in the very will of God. To say that whatever occurs, occurs necessarily is, in one sense, merely to affirm that there is an irrefragable and direct connection between the divine will and its objects. But such an assertion seems to bind the will of God inescapably with its objects.

This is the hidden problem of theodicy: to affirm the necessary rightness of things without simultaneously subjecting God to necessity. Leibniz faced the difficulty in affirming, against the necessitarianism of Spinoza, that God acts *sub ratione boni*, and not *sub ratione perfecti*.[9] The problem is to assert the necessary rightness of things as they are, but to do so in a way that they are seen as proceeding from God's will, wisdom, and power, and not from a necessity of His nature.

To accomplish this, al-Ghazālī took from other formulations of theodicy which presupposed an outright necessitarianism: the providence of the philosophers, the "optimum" of the Muʿtazilites. At the same time, however, he attempted to mitigate, if not remove entirely, the dangerous and unacceptable premises upon which they were based. The successful assimilation of these other formulations depended upon a special understanding of possibility, for nothing in the world could be seen as existing necessarily in its own right; each thing was to be seen as necessary and inevitable, only because the divine will, acting in accord with wisdom, had determined it.

In this version of theodicy, divine wisdom is the ultimate justification for things as they are. Whatever happens for good and evil in the world results from the eternal decree of God, but this decree itself has been issued in accord with what "wisdom demands." In the Islamic theodicy, divine wisdom is the final refuge of necessity.

The debate whose long history we have considered did not end with the death of the last disputant in the 19th century, but it continued under other forms and in other terms. The underlying issues have a singular vitality, perhaps because they are not susceptible to plausible resolution. In the 20th century, for example, we observe familiar themes re-emerging in the writings of the Egyptian scholar Aḥmad Amīn, who can speak of the

[9] In his demonstration of his Proposition 33, Spinoza stated that "things have been produced by God in the highest degree of perfection, since they have necessarily followed from the existence of a most perfect nature," *Ethics*, tr. p. 69. In annotating the *Ethics*, Leibniz protested that God acts "by reason of the good, or according to will" (*sub ratione boni seu secundum voluntatem*); see G. Friedman, *Leibniz et Spinoza*, p. 136.

"benefit of suffering" (*niʿmat al-alam*) in neo-Muʿtazilite terms.[10] Muʿtazilite notions of good and evil are also very much an issue for much of contemporary Shīʿite thought, and the brilliant discussions of the late Iranian theologian Murtaḍā Muṭahharī deserve special note in this regard.[11]

The disputed sentence of al-Ghazālī continues to possess its own life and has become something of a catch-phrase. One may perhaps hear an echo of it as well in verses by the great Tunisian poet Abū al-Qāsim al-Shābbī (1909-1934), verses in which several themes of our own debate are echoed and restated in modern terms:

> Reflect! The order of life
> Is a subtle, marvelous, unique order,
> For nothing but death endears life,
> And only the fear of tombs adorns it;
> Were it not for the misery of painful life,
> People would not grasp the meaning of happiness.
> Whomever the scowling of the dark does not terrify,
> Does not feel the bliss of the new morning.[12]

[10] *Fayḍ al-khāṭir* (Cairo, 1948), I, 82-84.

[11] See his *ʿAdl-i ilāhī* which first appeared in 1973, and has now been translated into Arabic as *al-ʿAdl al-ilāhī* by M. ʿAbd al-Munʿim al-Khāqānī (Beirut: Dār al-Hādī, 1981). Muṭahharī was assassinated in 1979.

[12] *Dīwān* (Beirut, 1972), pp. 342-343. The first line reads: *taʾammul . . . fa-inna niẓām al-ḥayāh niẓām daqīq badīʿ farīd.*

# *Appendix: Types of Possibility*

What follows is a listing and brief description of the major types of possibility which are discussed in Arabic treatises of logic.

(1) *imkān istiʿdādī*: potentiality (*qūwah*).[1] This is used to denote the "readiness" (*tahayyuʾ*) or "propensity" (*istiʿdād*) of "one thing for another thing," e.g., the human spermatozoon which, "while it exists is man in potentiality, but not in actuality."[2]

(2) *imkān dhātī*: inherent possibility. This means that "the relation of affirmation and negation is such that the intrinsic nature of the object is not denied . . . even if something extrinsic denies it."[3] A thing that is inherently possible remains so, although it may be rendered necessary or impossible by "something else." The world, for example, could be described as possible in this sense only before its creation; afterwards, it became "necessarily existent," not because of anything in its nature, but because of the divine volition.[4]

Such necessity accrues to a possible only "on the condition that it exist" (*bi-sharṭ wujūd*).[5] The number 4, for example, is considered necessarily even, and yet, "it is not necessary to affirm evenness of it in all the circumstances that can be supposed."[6] As an inherently possible thing, it may not exist at all: "Its existence is not something necessitated by its intrinsic nature."[7]

[1] al-Kalanbawī, *R. al-imkān*, p. 48; also, al-Jurjānī, *Taʿrīfāt*, p. 30; al-Aḥmadnagarī, *Dustūr*, I, 190-191; Mullā Ṣadrā, *al-Ḥikmah al-mutaʿālīyah*, I/3, 2-3.

[2] al-Kalanbawī, *R. al-imkān*, p. 42.

[3] *Ibid*, p. 48; al-Jurjānī, *Taʿrīfāt*, p. 30.

[4] al-Ghazālī, *Miʿyār*, p. 250.

[5] al-Kalanbawī, *R. al-imkān*, p. 10.

[6] *Ibid.*, p. 6.

[7] *Ibid.*; also al-Aḥmadnagarī, *Dustūr*, I, 189 (RM).

*Imkān dhātī* is further described as synonymous with *tajwīz ʿaqlī*, intellectual admissibility, for "there does not follow anything impossible from supposing it to occur. This type of the possible may never actually occur at all . . . and is sometimes reckoned impossible (*muḥāl*)."[8]

Inherent possibility is, then, a "relative thing" (*amr iʿtibārī*) which the mind brings to bear on a thing when considering "the relation of its quiddity to existence" and, as its name shows, "it is inseparable from the quiddity of the possible (*lāzim li-māhiyat al-mumkin*); it subsists in it and cannot possibly be divorced from it."[9]

(3) *imkān dhihnī*: conceptual possibility. This is apparently a variant of *tajwīz ʿaqlī*; it is used in contrast with *imkān khārijī*, actual, or objective, possibility. This means the possibility that arises when "the mind forms a simple apprehension of things and surmises about them (*yataṣawwar ashyāʾ wa-yuqaddiruhā*), regardless of its knowledge of their impossibility and possibility *in concreto*, and its lack of knowledge" thereof.[10] This occurs when "a thing is presented to the mind, but, not knowing its impossibility, one says, 'This is possible,'—not because the mind knows it to be possible, but because it does not know that it is impossible."[11]

Objective possibility (*imkān khārijī*), on the other hand, denotes the knowledge that something is possible in reality, either through knowing that it actually exists or through the knowledge that something comparable to it exists.[12]

(4) *imkān wuqūʿī*: actual possibility. al-Jurjānī identifies this with *imkān istiʿdādī* (#1 above).[13] It is also sometimes called *al-imkān bi-ḥasab nafs al-amr*, "possibility in accord with objective reality."[14] This is that in which "the contrary alternative is necessary neither *per se* nor *propter aliud*; and no absurdity

[8] Abū al-Baqāʾ, *Kullīyāt*, I, 309 (RM)

[9] *Ibid.*

[10] Ibn Taymīyah, *K. al-radd ʿalā al-manṭiqīyīn*, p. 318 (RM). See also al-Tahānawī, *Kashshāf*, II, 1353, line 16.

[11] Ibn Taymīyah, *K. al-radd*, p. 318.

[12] *Ibid.*

[13] al-Jurjānī, *Taʿrīfāt*, p. 30.

[14] al-Kalanbawī, *R. al-imkān*, pp. 61-62.

follows in any way if we assume the actual occurrence of the first part of the disjunction (*al-ṭaraf al-muwāfiq*)."[15] When we say, for example, in relation to a past or present time, "Zayd's writing yesterday or at this time is possible in this sense," this assertion is true only if Zayd actually wrote then, or writes now; but possibility, in this sense, extends to the future as well, so that "when we say 'his writing tomorrow is possible,' this assertion is true even if this writing tomorrow does not occur."[16]

This is so because possibility, in this sense, depends on an agent acting with choice (*al-fāʿil al-mukhtār*), choice being defined as "the possibility to act or not to act" (*ṣiḥḥat al-fiʿl waʾl-tark*).[17] Choice "destroys the principle of necessity" (*hādim li-qāʿidat al-ījāb waʾl-ḍarūrah*): Zayd's standing "is possible at the time he is not standing, and his not standing is possible at the time he is standing."[18]

(5) *imkān manṭiqī*: logical possibility.[19] This means that "the relation of affirmation or denial is such that the second part of the disjunction is without intrinsic necessity, i.e., necessity at all times the subject exists, even if there exist a 'descriptive or temporal necessity' (*ḍarūrah waṣfīyah aw waqtīyah*) in the second part of the disjunction."[20] For example, when we say "the moon is not in eclipse," it is necessary at that time to describe the moon as "not in eclipse," but this entails no intrinsic necessity, since "eclipse and its absence are not necessary at all times of the moon's existence, but only at certain times."[21] The descriptive and temporal necessity in the second part of the disjunction does not negate the possibility in the first part.

More specific types of possibility, related to the preceding, are as follows, in ascending order of specificity:

(6a) *imkān ḥīnī*: occasional possibility. This denotes "the denial of necessity from the second part of the disjunction at

[15] al-Jurjānī, *Taʿrīfāt*, p. 30.
[16] al-Kalanbawī, *Miftāḥ bāb al-muwajjahāt*, fol. 39b.
[17] *Ibid.*
[18] *Ibid.*, and *R. al-imkān*, p. 62.
[19] This type is found only in al-Kalanbawī under this designation; see *R. al-imkān*, p. 59.
[20] *Ibid.*
[21] *Ibid.*; for this example, cf. al-Ghazālī, *Miʿyār*, p. 249.

some times of the description of the subject" (*fī baʿḍ awqāt waṣf al-mawḍūʿ*).[22] It is contradictory to descriptive necessity (*al-munāqiḍ lil-ḍarūrah al-waṣfīyah*).[23]

(6b) *imkān waqtī*: temporal possibility. Contradictory to temporal necessity.[24] It is "to deny necessity from the second part of the disjunction at a specific time (*waqt muʿayyan*) for the subject."[25]

(6c) *imkān dawāmī*: continual possibility. This means "the denial of necessity from the second part of the disjunction at any time." (*fī waqt mā*).[26] This is also called *imkān intishārī*, "diffused (?) possibility."[27] For example, when we say, "Every moon is eclipsable (*dhū maḥw*) by virtue of diffused possibility," what is meant is that "the denial of 'eclipsable' from 'moon' is not necessary at any time."[28]

(7) *imkān istiqbālī*: future possibility. This can only be a kind of "special possibility" (see above, p. 175ff.), since it denotes the denial of necessity from both extremities.[29] It is "true possibility" (*imkān ḥaqīqī*), for "neither its non-existence nor its existence is necessary."[30] It denotes the denial of necessity absolutely (*salb muṭlaq al-ḍarūrah*) and under any form whatever (intrinsic, descriptive, temporal, etc.)[31] Future possibility is "the possibility of a thing in relation to future time," and so is devoid of necessity, for "what determines one of the two extremities (i.e., existence or non-existence) is dependent on the arrival of that time."[32]

[22] al-Kalanbawī, *R. al-imkān*, p. 65. Cf. also al-Samarqandī, *Sharḥ al-Qusṭās fi'l-manṭiq* (ms. Yale, Nemoy 1410) fol. 37a, line 3 (RM).

[23] al-Kalanbawī, *Miftāḥ*, fol. 37b, *paen.*

[24] al-Kalanbawī, *Miftāḥ*, fol. 38b, line 1.

[25] al-Kalanbawī, *R. al-imkān*, p. 65.

[26] *Ibid.*

[27] al-Samarqandī, *Sharḥ*, fol. 37a, line 6 (RM).

[28] *Ibid.*

[29] al-Kalanbawī, *R. al-imkān*, p. 65.

[30] *Ibid.*

[31] *Ibid.*

[32] *Ibid.* Also al-Samarqandī, *Sharḥ*, fol. 36b, line 19 (RM). For an excellent study of types of possibility, see the Persian work of Ismāʿīl Vāʿiẓ Javādī entitled *Ḥudūth va qidam* (Tehran, 1347/1968), especially p. 215ff. (I am indebted to Dr. Hossein Modarressi Tabātabā'i for this reference.)

# *Bibliography*


Abbagnano, Nicola. *Dizionario di filosofia*. Turin, 1961.

ʿAbd al-Bāqī, M. Fuʾād. *al-Muʿjam al-mufahras li-alfāẓ al-Qurʾān al-karīm*. Cairo, 1378.

ʿAbd al-Ḥamīd, M. Muḥyī al-Dīn. *R. al-ādāb fī ʿilm ādāb al-baḥth waʾl-munāẓarah*. 3d ed. Cairo, 1361/1942.

ʿAbd al-Jabbār al-Asadābādī. *al-Mughnī fī abwāb al-tawḥīd waʾl-ʿadl*:

vol. 6/1: *al-Taʿdīl waʾl-tajwīr*. Ed. A. al-Ahwānī and I. Madkūr. Cairo, 1962.

vol. 13: *al-Luṭf*. Ed. A. al-ʿAfīfī. Cairo, 1962.

vol. 14; *al-Aṣlaḥ. Istiḥqāq al-dhamm. al-Tawbah*. Ed. M. al-Saqā. Cairo, 1965.

———. *Sharḥ al-uṣūl al-khamsah*. Ed. ʿAbd al-Karīm ʿUthmān. Cairo, 1965. [On the authorship of this work see Introduction, note 55.]

ʿAbd al-Qādir b. Muḥyī al-Dīn al-Jazāʾirī. *Dhikrā al-ʿāqil wa-tanbīh al-ghāfil*. Beirut, 1966.

———. *Le livre d'Abd-el-Kader intitulé Rappel à l'intelligent, avis à l'indifférent*. Tr. Gustave Dugat. Paris, 1858.

———. *K. al-mawāqif fīʾl-taṣawwuf waʾl-waʿẓ waʾl-irshād*. 3 vols. Damascus, 1966-67.

ʿAbduh, Muḥammad. *R. al-tawḥīd*. Beirut, 1977.

Abelard, Peter. *Opera*. Ed. Victor Cousin *et al.* 2 vols. Paris, 1849-1859.

Abū al-Baqāʾ al-Ḥusaynī al-Kaffawī. *Kullīyāt*. 4 vols. Damascus, 1974.

Abū Dāwūd. *Sunan*. 4 vols. Cairo, 1935.

Abū Nuʿaym al-Iṣfahānī. *Ḥilyat al-awliyāʾ wa-ṭabaqāt al-aṣfiyāʾ*. 10 vols. Beirut, 1967-68.

Ahlwardt, Wilhelm. *Verzeichnis der arabischen Handschriften*. (*Die Handscriften-Verzeichnisse der Königlichen Bibliothek zu Berlin*: vols. 7-9, 16-22). 10 vols. Berlin, 1887-1899.

Aḥmad ibn Ḥanbal. *Musnad*. 6 vols. Cairo, 1313/1895.

al-Aḥmadnagarī, ʿAbd al-Nabī. *Jāmiʿ al-ʿulūm fī iṣṭilāḥāt al-funūn al-mulaqqab bi-Dustūr al-ʿulamāʾ*. 4 vols. Beirut, 1975.

St. Albertus Magnus. *Opera omnia*. 38 vols. Paris, 1890-99.

———. *Opera omnia*. Ed. B. Geyer *et al.* Aschendorff, 1951-.

Alexander of Hales. *Summa theologica*. Ed. B. Klumper. 4 vols. Quaracchi, 1924-48.

Allard, Michel. *Le problème des attributs divins dans la doctrine d'al-Aš'arī et de ses premiers grands disciples*. Beirut: Imprimerie Catholique, 1965.

Altunsu, Abdülkadir. *Osmanlı Şeyhülislâmları*. Ankara, 1972.

al-Āmidī, Sayf al-Dīn. *Abkār al-afkār*. Arabic ms., Princeton University Library, New Series, vol. no. 1927.

———. *Ghāyat al-marām fī 'ilm al-kalām*. Cairo, 1391/1971.

———. *al-Iḥkām fī uṣūl al-aḥkām*. 2 vols. s.1, 1401/1981.

Amīn, Aḥmad. *Fayḍ al-khāṭir wa-huwa majmū' maqālāt adabīyah wa-ijtimā'īyah*. 6 vols. Cairo, 1948.

Anonymous. *Relaçaõ do grande terremoto, que houve na Praça de Mazagam em o primeiro de Novembro de 1755. Referem se os seos effeitos, e ruinas que causou, e brevemente se mostra de que procedem os tremores de terra*. Lisbon, 1756.

Anonymous. *Tathbīt qawā'id al-arkān bi-an Laysa fi'l-imkān abda' mimmā kān*. Arabic ms., Yahuda Collection, vol. 3233 (Mach 3026).

Antes, Peter. "The First Aš'arites' Conception of Evil and the Devil," in: *Mélanges offerts à Henry Corbin*, ed. S. H. Nasr. Tehran, 1977.

Arberry, A. J. *Sufism*. London, 1950.

Aristotle. *The Categories. On Interpretation. Prior Analytics*. Tr. H. P. Cooke and H. Tredennick. Cambridge, Mass. and London, 1973 [The Loeb Classical Library]

———. *Generation of Animals*. Tr. A. L. Peck. Cambridge, Mass. and London, 1953. [The Loeb Classical Library]

———. *The Metaphysics*. Tr. H. Tredennick. 2 vols. Cambridge, Mass. and London, 1968. [The Loeb Classical Library]

———. *On the Soul*. Tr. W. S. Hett. Cambridge, Mass. and London, 1964. [The Loeb Classical Library]

Arnim, J. von. *Stoicorum veterum fragmenta*. 4 vols. Leipzig, 1903-1924; rpt. Stuttgart, 1964.

Āṣafīyah. *Fihrist-i kutub-i 'arabī va fārsī va ūrdū makhzūnah-i Kutub-khānah-i Āṣafīyah*. 4 vols. Hyderabad, 1333-55/1914-37.

al-Ash'arī, Abū al-Ḥasan. *al-Ibānah 'an uṣūl al-diyānah*. Ed. F. H. Maḥmūd. Cairo, 1977.

———. *Maqālāt al-islāmīyīn wa-ikhtilāf al-muṣallīn*. Ed. H. Ritter. 2 vols. and index vol. Istanbul, 1929-33. [Bibliotheca Islamica, 1]

———. *The Theology of al-Ash'arī. The Arabic Texts of Ash'arī's K.*

*al-Luma*ʿ *and Risālat Istiḥsān al-Khawḍ fī ʿIlm al-Kalām*. Ed. and tr. Richard J. McCarthy. Beirut, 1953.
Āshtīyānī, Jalāl al-Dīn. *Muntakhabātī az āthār-i ḥukamā-yi ilāhī-yi Īrān/ Anthologie des philosophes iraniens*. Vol. 4. Mashhad, 1358/1978.
Asín Palacios, Miguel. *La Espiritualidad de Algazel y su Sentido Cristiano*. Vol. 4: *Crestomatía algazeliana*. Madrid, 1941.
Atsız. "Kemalpaşa-oglu'nun eserleri," *Şarkiyat mecmuası*, 6 (1966), pp. 71-112; 7 (1972), pp. 83-135.
ʿAṭṭār, Farīd al-Dīn. *K. tadhkirat al-awliyā'*. Ed. R. A. Nicholson. 2 vols. London and Leiden, 1905-1907. [Persian Historical Texts, 3]
———. *Muslim Saints and Mystics. Episodes from the Tadhkirat al-Auliyā'*. Tr. A. J. Arberry. London, 1966.
St. Augustine. *Concerning the City of God against the Pagans*. Tr. H. Bettenson. New York: Penguin, 1972.
———. *Confessions*. Tr. W. Watts. 2 vols. Cambridge, Mass., and London, 1950. [The Loeb Classical Library]
———. *La Genèse au sens littéral en douze livres/De Genesi ad litteram libri duodecim*. Ed. and tr. P. Agaësse and A. Solignac. 2 vols. Paris, 1972.
Aulus Gellius. *The Attic Nights*. Tr. J. C. Rolfe. 3 vols. Cambridge, Mass. and London, 1946-52. [The Loeb Classical Library]
ʿAyn al-Quḍāh al-Hamadhānī. *Muṣannafāt*. Ed. A. ʿUṣayrān. Tehran, 1341/1962.
———. *Nāmah-hā*. Ed. A. ʿUṣayrān. 2 vols. Tehran, 1969.
Badawī, ʿAbd al-Raḥmān. *Mu'allafāt al-Ghazzālī*. Cairo, 1961.
Baghdad. *Fihris al-makhṭūṭāt al-ʿarabīyah fī Maktabat al-Awqāf al-ʿĀmmah fī Baghdād*. Cpl. ʿAl. Jubūrī. 4 vols. Baghdad, 1973-74.
al-Baghdādī, ʿAbd al-Qāhir. *al-Farq bayn al-firaq*. Ed. M. Badr. Cairo, 1328/1910.
———. *Uṣūl al-dīn*. Istanbul, 1346/1924.
Balbaʿ, ʿAbd al-Ḥalīm. *Adab al-Muʿtazilah*. Cairo, 1959.
Bālī-zādeh, Muṣṭafā b. Sulaymān. *K. sharḥ Fuṣūṣ al-ḥikam*. Kirmān (?), 1309/1891 or 2.
Bankipore. *Catalogue of the Arabic and Persian Manuscripts in the Oriental Public Library at (Bankipore) Patna*.26 vols. Patna, 1908-.
al-Bāqillānī, Abū Bakr M. *K. al-tamhīd*. Ed. Richard J. McCarthy. Beirut, 1957.
St. Basil the Great. *Homélies sur l'Hexaéméron*. Ed. and tr. S. Giet. 2d rev. ed. Paris, 1968. [Sources chrétiennes, 26]

al-Baṣrī, M.b.ʿA.b. al-Ṭayyib. *K. al-muʿtamad fī uṣūl al-fiqh*. Ed. M. Ḥamīd Allāh. 2 vols. Damascus, 1384/1964-65.

al-Bayḍāwī, ʿAl. b. ʿUmar. *Anwār al-tanzīl wa-asrār al-ta'wīl*. Ed. H. O. Fleischer. 2 vols. Leipzig, 1846.

al-Bazdawī [al-Pazdawī], M.b.M. *K. uṣūl al-dīn*. Ed. Hans Linss. Cairo, 1383/1963.

Behler, Ernst. *Die Ewigkeit der Welt. Problemgeschichtliche Untersuchungen zu den Kontroversen um Weltanfang und Weltendlichkeit im Mittelalter*. Teil 1: *Die Problemstellung in der arabischen und jüdischen Philosophie des Mittelalters*. Munich, 1965.

Bell, Joseph Norment. *Love Theory in Later Ḥanbalite Islam*. Albany: SUNY Press, 1979. [Studies in Islamic Philosophy and Science]

Bergsträsser, G. "Hunain ibn Ishaq über die syrischen und arabischen Galen-Übersetzungen." *Abhandlungen für die Kunde des Morgenlandes*, 17:2 (1925).

Billicsich, Friedrich. *Das Problem des Übels in der Philosophie des Abendlandes*. 3 vols. Vienna: A. Sexl, 1952-59.

al-Biqāʿī, Burhān al-Dīn Ibrāhīm b. ʿUmar. *Maṣraʿ al-taṣawwuf*. Ed. ʿAbd al-Raḥmān al-Wakīl. Cairo, 1372/1953.

———. *al-Nukat wa'l-fawā'id ʿalā Sharḥ al-ʿAqā'id*. Arabic ms., Yahuda Collection, vol. 2306 (Mach 2245).

———. *Tahdīm al-arkān min Laysa fi'l-imkān abdaʿ mimmā kān*. Arabic ms., Garrett Collection, vol. 464H (Hitti 798)

Bonansea, Bernardino M. "The Question of an Eternal World in the Teaching of St. Bonaventure," *Franciscan Studies*, 34 (1974), pp. 7-33.

St. Bonaventura. *Itinerarium mentis in Deum*. Ed. and tr. Philotheus Boehner. St. Bonaventure, N.Y., 1956.

———. *Opera theologica selecta*. 5 vols. Quaracchi, 1934-1964.

Bonitz, H. *Index Aristotelicus*. 2d ed. Berlin, 1870; rpt. Graz, 1955.

Bousquet, G. H. *Ih'ya ou Vivification des sciences de la foi; analyse et index*. Paris, 1955.

Bouyges, Maurice. *Essai de chronologie des oeuvres de al-Ghazali*. Ed. M. Allard. Beirut, 1959.

Bowker, John. *Problems of Suffering in Religions of the World*. Cambridge, 1970.

Brentano, Franz. *Religion und Philosophie*. Ed. F. Mayer-Hillebrand. Bern, 1954.

———. *Vom Dasein Gottes*. Ed. A. Kastil. Leipzig, 1929.

Brockelmann, Carl. *Geschichte der arabischen Litteratur*. 2d ed. 2 vols.

Leiden, 1943-49; and *Supplement* (to 1st ed.), 3 vols., Leiden, 1937-42.

Brunschvig, Robert. "Métiers vils en Islam," *Studia Islamica*, 16 (1962), pp. 41-60.

———. "Muʿtazilisme et optimum (*al-aṣlaḥ*)," *Studia Islamica*, 39 (1974), pp. 5-25.

al-Bukhārī, M. b. Ismāʿīl. *Ṣaḥīḥ*. Ed. L. Krehl. 4 vols. Leiden, 1862-1908.

*The Cambridge History of Later Medieval Philosophy, from the Rediscovery of Aristotle to the Disintegration of Scholasticism 1100-1600*. Ed. Norman Kretzmann, Anthony Kenny and Jan Pinborg. Cambridge, 1982.

Capelle, Wilhelm. "Zur antiken Theodicee," *Archiv für Geschichte der Philosophie*, 20 (1907), pp. 173-196.

Carnap, Rudolf. *Meaning and Necessity*. Chicago, 1960.

Cicero. *De natura deorum*. Tr. H. Rackham. London, 1933. [The Loeb Classical Library]

———. *The Nature of the Gods*. Tr. H.C.P. McGregor. Baltimore: Penguin, 1972.

Copleston, Frederick. *A History of Philosophy*. Vol. 2: *Mediaeval Philosophy*. 2 vols. Garden City, N.Y.: Image Books, 1962.

Corbin, Henry. *Creative Imagination in the Ṣūfism of Ibn ʿArabī*. Tr. Ralph Mannheim. Princeton, 1969.

———. *Histoire de la philosophie islamique*. Vol. 1: *Des origines jusqu' à la mort d'Averroes (1198)*. Paris, 1964.

———. "The Ismāʿīlī Response to the Polemic of Ghazālī," in: S. H. Nasr (ed.), *Ismāʿīlī Contributions to Islamic Culture* (Tehran, 1398/1977), pp. 69-98.

———. *Trilogie ismaélienne*. Tehran and Paris, 1961.

Coreth, Emmerich. *Metaphysik. Eine methodisch-systematische Grundlegung*. 3d ed. Innsbruck: Tyrolia Verlag, 1980.

Cornford, F. M. *Plato's Cosmology*. Indianapolis: Bobbs-Merrill, n.d.

Damascus. *Fihris makhṭūṭāt Dār al-kutub al-Ẓāhirīyah. al-Taṣawwuf*, 1. Damascus, 1398/1978.

al-Damīrī, Kamāl al-Dīn. *Ḥayāt al-ḥayawān al-kubrā*. 2 vols. Cairo, 1305.

Danziger, Raphael. *Abd al-Qadir and the Algerians: Resistance to the French and Internal Consolidation*. New York: Holmes and Meier, 1977.

Dār al-Kutub al-Miṣrīyah. *Fihrist al-makhṭūṭāt*. 2 vols. Cairo, 1961-63.

al-Dawwānī, Jalāl al-Dīn M. *R. (fī) īmān Fir'awn.* Arabic ms., Garrett Collection, vol. 464H (Hitti 2197). See also, Mach 2180.

De Vogel, C. J. *Greek Philosophy.* Vol. 3: *The Hellenistic-Roman Period.* 2d ed. Leiden, 1964.

Diels, Hermann. *Die Fragmente der Vorsokratiker.* Ed. Walther Kranz. 6th rev. ed. 3 vols. Berlin, 1951.

Dols, Michael W. *The Black Death in the Middle East.* Princeton: Princeton University Press, 1977.

Dozy, R. *Supplément aux dictionnaires arabes.* 2 vols. Leiden, 1881; rpt. Beirut, 1968.

Duns Scotus, Joannes. *Opera omnia.* 26 vols. Paris: Vivès, 1891-95.

———. *Philosophical Writings: a Selection.* Tr. Allan Wolter. Indianapolis: Bobbs-Merrill, 1962.

al-Dusūqī [al-Dasūqī], M.b.A. *Ḥāshiyat 'alā al-Tahdhīb* in: 'Ubayd Allāh al-Khabīsī, *Sharḥ 'alā Tahdhīb al-manṭiq wa'l-kalām.* Cairo, 1355/1936.

Eisler, Rudolf. *Wörterbuch der philosophischen Begriffe.* 4th rev. ed. 3 vols. Berlin, 1929.

*The Encyclopaedia of Islam.* 4 vols. and Supplement. Leiden, 1913-34.

*The Encyclopaedia of Islam.* 2d ed. 4 vols. to date. Leiden, 1960-.

*The Encyclopedia of Philosophy.* Ed Paul Edwards. 8 vols. New York, 1972.

van Ess, Josef. "Disputationspraxis in der islamischen Theologie. Eine vorläufige Skizze," *Revue des études islamiques,* 44 (1976), pp. 23-60.

———. *Die Erkenntnislehre des 'Aḍudaddīn al-Īcī.* Wiesbaden: Franz Steiner, 1966.

———. *Frühe mu'tazilitische Häresiographie. Zwei werke des Nāši' al-Akbar (gest. 293H)* Wiesbaden, 1971. [Beiruter Texte und Studien, 11]

———. *Die Gedankenwelt des Ḥāriṯ al-Muḥāsibī.* Bonn, 1961. [Bonner Orientalistische Studien, N.S., 12]

———. "Göttliche Allmacht im Zerrbild menschlicher Sprache," *Mélanges de l'Université Saint-Joseph,* 49 (1975-76), pp. 651-688.

———. "Ibn ar-Rēwandī, or the Making of an Image," *al-Abḥāth,* 27 (1978/79), pp. 5-26.

———. "Neuere Literatur zu Ġazzālī," *Oriens,* 20 (1967), pp. 299-308.

———. "Skepticism in Islamic Religious Thought," *al-Abḥāth,* 21 (1968), pp. 1-18.

———. "Theology and Science: the Case of Abū Isḥāq an-Naẓẓām,"

*The Second Annual United Arab Emirates Lecture in Islamic Studies*. Ann Arbor, 1978.

———. *Ungenützte Texte zur Karrāmīya*. Heidelberg, 1980. [Sitzungsberichte der Heidelberger Akademie der Wissenschaften, Philosophisch-historische Klasse, 1980:6]

———. *Zwischen Ḥadīṯ und Theologie. Studien zum Entstehen prädestinatianischer Überlieferung*. Berlin, 1975. [Studien zur Sprache, Geschichte und Kultur des islamischen Orients, 7]

al-Fārābī, Abū Naṣr. *Alfarabi's philosophische Abhandlungen*. Ed. Friedrich Dieterici. Leiden, 1890.

———. *Sharḥ al-Fārābī li-kitāb Arisṭūṭālīs fi'l-ʿibārah*. Ed. W. Kutsch and S. Marrow. 2d rev. ed. Beirut, 1971.

———. *al-Farabi's Commentary and Short Treatise on Aristotle's De Interpretatione*. Tr. F. W. Zimmermann. London: published for The British Academy by the Oxford University Press, 1981. [Classical and Medieval Logic Texts, 3]

Faust, August. *Der Möglichkeitsgedanke. Systemgeschichtliche Untersuchungen*. 2 vols. Heidelberg, 1931.

Festugière, A. J. *Etudes de philosophie grecque*. Paris, 1971.

Feuerbach, Ludwig. *Werke*. 6 vols. Frankfurt: Suhrkamp, 1975.

*Fihris al-kutub al-mawjūdah bi'l-maktabah al-Azharīyah*. 6 vols. Cairo, 1946-52.

*Fihrist al-kutub al-ʿarabīyah al-maḥfūẓah bi'l-Kitābkhānah al-Khidīwīyah al-Miṣrīyah*. Cairo, 1308.

Frank, Richard M. "*Al-maʿná*: Some Reflections on the Technical Meanings of the Term in the Kalām and its Use in the Physics of Muʿammar," *Journal of the American Oriental Society*, 87 (1967), pp. 248-259.

———. *The Metaphysics of Created Being according to Abū l-Hudhayl al-ʿAllāf. A Philosophical Study of the Earliest Kalām*. Istanbul: Nederlands Historisch-Archaeologisch Instituut in Het Nabije Oosten, 1966.

———. "The Structure of Created Causality according to al-Ašʿarī," *Studia Islamica*, 25 (1966), pp. 13-75.

Frankfurt, Harry G. "The Logic of Omnipotence," *The Philosophical Review*, 73 (1964), pp. 262-263.

Friedmann, Georges. *Leibniz et Spinoza*. Rev. ed. Paris, 1962.

Friedrich, Otto. *The End of the World: a History*. New York: Coward, McCann and Geoghegan, 1982.

Frierson, William Manton. *The Problem of Evil: A Metaphysical and Theological Inquiry*. Ph.D. dissertation, Emory University, 1977.

Galen. *Galeni compendium Timaei Platonis, aliorumque dialogorum synopsis quae extant fragmenta.* Ed. Paul Kraus and Richard Walzer. London, 1951. [*Plato Arabus*, vol. 1; *Corpus Platonicum Medii Aevi*, ed. R. Klibansky]

———. *De usu partium.* Ed. George Helmreich. 2 vols. Lepzig: Teubner, 1907.

———. *On the Usefulness of the Parts of the Body.* Περὶ χρείας μορίων. *De usu partium.* Tr. Margaret T. May. 2 vols. Ithaca: Cornell, 1968.

———. *Pseudo-Galeni in Hippocratis de Septimanis commentarium.* Ed. G. Bergsträsser. Leipzig, 1914. [Corpus medicorum graecorum, X, 2, 1]

Gannūn, ʿAl. *Aḥmad Zarrūq.* Tetuán, 1954.

Geach, Peter. *Providence and Evil.* Cambridge, 1977. [The Stanton Lectures, 1971-72]

Geries, Ibrahim. *Un genre littéraire arabe: al-Maḥâsin wa-l-Masâwî.* Paris, 1977.

al-Ghazālī, Abū Ḥāmid. *al-Durrah al-fākhirah fī kashf ʿulūm al-ākhirah.* Ed. and tr. Lucien Gautier. Geneva, 1878.

———. *al-Fayṣal al-tafriqah bayn al-Islām waʾl-zandaqah.* Cairo, 1961.

———. *Iḥyāʾ ʿulūm al-dīn.* 4 vols. Cairo, 1334/1916.

———. *al-Imlāʾ fī mushkilāt al-Iḥyāʾ.* Arabic ms., Berlin, Pm. 545 (Ahlwardt 1714).

———. *al-Iqtiṣād fīʾl-iʿtiqād.* Ed. İbrahim A. Çubukçu and Hüseyin Atay. Ankara, 1962. [Ankara Üniversitesi Ilâhıyat Fakültesi Yayınları, 34]

———. *Jawāhir al-Qurʾān.* Beirut, 1977.

———. *K. al-arbaʿīn fī uṣūl al-dīn.* Cairo, 1344.

———. *Makātīb-i fārsī-yi Ghazzālī bi-nām-i Faḍāʾil al-anām min rasāʾil Ḥujjat al-Islām.* Ed. ʿAbbās Iqbāl. Tehran, 1333/1954.

———. *Maqāṣid al-falāsifah.* Ed. Sulaymān Dunyā. Cairo, 1961.

———. *al-Maqṣad al-asnā fī sharḥ maʿānī asmāʾ Allāh al-ḥusnā.* Ed. Fadlou A. Shehadi. Beirut, 1971.

———. *Miʿyār al-ʿilm fī fann al-manṭiq.* Beirut, 1978.

———. *al-Munqidh min al-ḍalāl.* Ed. and tr. Farid Jabre. Beirut, 1959.

———. *al-Mustaṣfā min ʿilm al-uṣūl.* 2 vols. Cairo, 1356/1937.

———. *Naṣīḥat al-mulūk.* Ed. Jalāl Humāʾī. Tehran, 1315-17/1936-38.

———. *Ghazālīʾs Book of Counsel for Kings.* Tr. F.R.C. Bagley. London: Oxford University Press, 1964.

———. *al-Qusṭās al-mustaqīm.* Beirut, 1959.

———. *Tahāfut al-falāsifah*. Ed. Maurice Bouyges. Beirut, 1927. [Bibliotheca Arabica Scholasticorum, Série arabe, 2]

[pseudo-Ghazālī]. *al-Ḥikmah fī makhlūqāt Allāh*. Aleppo and Cairo, 1352/1934.

Gilson, Etienne. *History of Christian Philosophy in the Middle Ages*. New York, 1955.

———. *The Philosophy of St. Bonaventure*. New York, 1938.

Gimaret, Daniel. "Matériaux pour une bibliographie des Ǧubbā'ī," *Journal asiatique*, 264 (1976), pp. 277-332.

———. "Les théologiens musulmans devant la hausse des prix," *Journal of the Economic and Social History of the Orient*, 22 (1979), pp. 330-338.

———. "Les *Uṣūl al-ḫamsa* du Qāḍī ʿAbd al-Ǧabbār et leurs commentaires," *Annales islamologiques*, 15 (1979), pp. 47-96.

Glorieux, P. *La littérature quodlibétique de 1260 à 1320*. 2 vols. Paris, 1925-35. [Bibliothèque thomiste, 5 and 21]

Götze, Albrecht. "Persische Weisheit in griechischem Gewande. Ein Beitrag zur Geschichte der Mikrokosmos-Idee," *Zeitschrift für Indologie und Iranistik*, 2 (1923), pp. 60-98.

Goitein, Hirsch. *Das Problem der Theodicee in der älteren jüdischen Religionsphilosophie (Teil 1)*. Berlin, 1890. [Inaugural-Dissertation, Albertus-Universität zu Königsberg]

Goldziher, Ignaz. *Gesammelte Schriften*. Ed. J. DeSomogyi. 6 vols. Hildesheim, 1967-73.

———. *Le livre de Mohammed Ibn Toumert*. Algiers, 1903.

———. *Muslim Studies (Muhammedanische Studien)*. Ed. S.M. Stern; tr. C. R. Barber and S. M. Stern, 2 vols. Chicago, 1968-71.

———. *Vorlesungen über den Islam*. 2d ed. Heidelberg, 1925.

———. *Introduction to Islamic Theology and Law*. Tr. Andras and Ruth Hamori. Princeton: Princeton University Press, 1981.

Gredt, Joseph. *Elementa philosophiae aristotelico-thomisticae*. 13th ed. 2 vols. Barcelona, 1961.

Grosseteste, Robert. *Die philosophischen Werke des Robert Grosseteste, Bischofs von Lincoln*. Ed. Ludwig Bauer. Münster, 1912 [Beiträge zur Geschichte der Philosophie des Mittelalters; Texte und Untersuchungen, 9]

Guthrie, W.K.C. *A History of Greek Philosophy*. Vols. 1 & 2. Cambridge, 1965; rpt. 1978.

Ḥā'irī, ʿAbd al-Ḥusayn. *Fihrist-i Kitābkhānah-i Majlis-i Shūrā-yi Millī . . . kutub-i khaṭṭī (fārsī va ʿarabī)*. Vol. 9; pt. 1. Tehran, 1346/1968.

Ḥājjī Khalīfah [Kātib Chelebī]. *Kashf al-ẓunūn ʿan asāmī al-kutub wa'l-funūn*. 2 vols. Tehran, 1967.

———. *Mīzān al-ḥaqq fī ikhtiyār al-aḥaqq*. Istanbul, 1286/1869.

———. *The Balance of Truth*. Tr. G. L. Lewis. London, 1957.

al-Ḥanbalī, Badr al-Dīn. "*Jawāb su'āl*." Arabic ms., Yahuda Collection, vol. 3166 (Mach 3029).

Hartmann, Eduard von. *Philosophie des Unbewussten*. 10th ed. 3 vols. Leipzig, 1889.

Hebel, Johann Peter. *Schatzkästlein des rheinischen Hausfreundes*. Ed. W. Weber. Zürich: Manesse, n.d.

Herman, Arthur L. *The Problem of Evil and Indian Thought*. Delhi: Motilal Banarsidass, 1976.

Hick, John. *Evil and the God of Love*. London, 1966.

Hidding, K.A.H. "Der Hochgott und der mikrokosmische Mensch," *Numen*, 18 (1971), pp. 94-102.

Hirschberger, Johannes. *Geschichte der Philosophie*. Vol. 1: *Altertum und Mittelalter*. 12th rev. ed. Freiburg, 1976.

———. "Omne ens est bonum," *Philosophisches Jahrbuch der Görres-Gesellschaft*, 53 (1940), pp. 292-305.

Hitti, Philip K. *et al*. *Descriptive Catalog of the Garrett Collection of Arabic Manuscripts in the Princeton University Library*. Princeton: Princeton University Press, 1938.

Hourani, George F. "The Chronology of Ghazālī's Writings," *Journal of the American Oriental Society*, 79 (1959), pp. 225-233.

———. "The Dialogue between al-Ghazālī and the Philosophers on the Origin of the World," *The Muslim World*, 48 (1958), pp. 183-191, 308-314.

———. "Ibn Sīnā's 'Essay on the Secret of Destiny,' " *Bulletin of the School of Oriental and African Studies*, 29 (1966), pp. 25-48.

———. *Islamic Rationalism. The Ethics of ʿAbd al-Jabbār*. Oxford: Clarendon, 1971.

Hugh of St. Victor. *De sacramentis*, in: J.-P. Migne, *Patrologia latina*, vol. 176 (Paris, 1880).

Humā'ī, Jalāl. *Ghazzālī-nāmah. Sharḥ-i ḥāl va āṡār va ʿaqā'id*. Tehran, 1342/1963.

Hume, David. *Dialogues concerning Natural Religion*. Ed. Nelson Pike. Indianapolis: Bobbs-Merrill, 1970.

Ibn ʿAbd al-Karīm, M. *Hamdān ibn ʿUthmān Khūjah al-Jazā'irī wa-mudhakkirātuhu*. Algiers, 1972.

Ibn Abī Sharīf, M.b.M. *al-Musāmarah fī sharḥ al-Musāyarah lil-Kamāl ibn al-Humām*. Ed. M. Muḥyī al-Dīn ʿAbd al-Ḥamīd. Cairo, 1940.

Ibn al-ʿArabī, Muḥyī al-Dīn. *Fuṣūṣ al-ḥikam.* Ed. A. ʿAfifi. Cairo, 1309.
———. *The Bezels of Wisdom.* Tr. R.W.J. Austin. Ramsey, N.J.: Paulist Press, 1980.
———. *al-Futūḥāt al-makkīyah.* 4 vols. Būlāq, 1293/1876.
———. *Kleinere Schriften des Ibn al-ʿArabī.* Ed. H. S. Nyberg. Leiden, 1919.
Ibn al-Dāʿī al-Rāzī. *Tabṣirat al-ʿawwām fī maʿrifat maqālāt al-anām.* Ed. ʿAbbās Iqbāl. Tehran, 1313/1944-45.
Ibn al-ʿImād, ʿAbd al-Ḥayy. *Shadharāt al-dhahab fī akhbār man dhahab.* 8 vols. Cairo, 1350-51/1931-32.
Ibn al-Jawzī, Abū al-Faraj. *al-Ḥasan al-Baṣrī.* Cairo, 1931.
Ibn al-Khaṭīb, Lisān al-Dīn. *al-Iḥāṭah fī akhbār Gharnāṭah.* Ed. M. ʿAl. ʿInān. 3 vols. Cairo, 1395/1975.
Ibn al-Marzubān, Bahmanyār. *al-Taḥṣīl.* Ed. Murtaḍā Muṭahharī. Tehran, 1349/1970.
Ibn al-Muqaffaʿ. *al-Adab al-kabīr wa'l-adab al-ṣaghīr.* Beirut, n.d.
Ibn al-Murtaḍā. *K. ṭabaqāt al-Muʿtazilah.* Ed. S. Diwald-Wilzer. Beirut, 1961. [Bibliotheca Islamica, 21]
Ibn al-Muṭahhar al-Ḥillī. *Kashf al-murād fī sharḥ Tajrīd al-iʿtiqād.* Ṣaydā, 1353.
Ibn al-Ṣalāḥ al-Shahrazūrī. *Fatāwā.* Cairo, 1348.
Ibn Ḥajar al-ʿAsqalānī. *al-Durar al-kāminah fī aʿyān al-mi'ah al-thāminah.* Hyderabad, 1348-50.
Ibn Ḥajar al-Haythamī, A. *al-Fatāwā al-ḥadīthīyah.* Cairo, 1356/1937.
Ibn Ḥāmid al-Shāfiʿī, M. *al-Dalīl wa'l-burhān ʿalā annahu laysa fi'l-imkān abdaʿ mimmā kān.* Arabic ms., Yahuda Collection, vol. 598 (Mach 3027).
Ibn Ḥazm, Abū M. ʿA. *al-Fiṣal fi'l-milal wa'l-ahwā' wa'l-niḥal.* 5 vols. Cairo, 1964.
Ibn Kamāl Pasha. *Rasā'il Ibn Kamāl.* 2 vols. Istanbul, 1316/1898.
———. *R. fī taḥqīq ann al-mumkin lā yakun aḥad al-ṭarafayn.* Arabic ms., Yahuda Collection, vol. 298 (Mach 3133). [=*R. fī taḥqīq al-mumkin*]
Ibn Khaldūn. *The Muqaddimah. An Introduction to History.* Tr. Franz Rosenthal. 2d ed. 3 vols. Princeton: Princeton University Press, 1967.
Ibn Khallikān. *Wafayāt al-aʿyān wa-anbā' abnā' al-zamān.* Ed. M. Muḥyī al-Dīn ʿAbd al-Ḥamīd. 6 vols. Cairo, 1367.
Ibn Mājah, M. b. Yazīd. *Sunan.* 2 vols. Cairo, 1952
Ibn Malkā al-Baghdādī, Abū al-Barakāt. *al-Muʿtabar fi'l-ḥikmah.* 3 vols. Hyderabad, 1357.

Ibn Manẓūr. *Lisān al-ʿarab*. 20 vols. Būlāq, 1308; rpt. Cairo, n.d.
Ibn Maryam, M.b.M.b.A. *al-Bustān fī dhikr al-awliyāʾ waʾl-ʿulamāʾ bi-Tilimsān*. Algiers, 1326/1908.
[Ibn Mattawayh, Abū M.] *K. al-majmūʿ fiʾl-muḥīṭ biʾl-taklīf*. Ed. J. J. Houben (as the work of ʿAbd al-Jabbār). Vol. 1. Beirut, 1965.
Ibn Qayyim al-Jawzīyah. *Ḥādī al-arwāḥ ilā bilād al-afrāḥ*. Cairo, 1962.
Ibn Rushd, Abū al-Walīd *K. faṣl al-maqāl*. Ed. George F. Hourani. Leiden, 1959.
———. *Averroes on the Harmony of Religion and Philosophy*. Tr. George F. Hourani. London: Luzac, 1961. [E.J.W. Gibb Memorial Series, N.S., 21]
———. *Tahāfut al-tahāfut*. Ed Maurice Bouyges. Beirut, 1930. [Bibliotheca Arabica Scholasticorum, 3]
———. *Tahāfut al-tahāfut (The Incoherence of the Incoherence)*. Tr. Simon van den Bergh. 2 vols. London: Luzac, 1954. [E.J.W. Gibb Memorial Series, N.S., 19]
———. *Talkhīṣ mā baʿd al-ṭabīʿah*. Ed. ʿUthmān Amīn. Cairo, 1958.
Ibn Shaddād. *al-Aʿlaq a-khaṭīrah*. Vol. 1. Damascus, 1957.
Ibn Sīnā, Abū ʿA. *Dānishnāmah-i ʿalāʾī*. Ed. M. Moʿīn. Tehran, 1331.
———. *al-Ishārāt waʾl-tanbīhāt*. Ed. Sulaymān Dunyā. 3 vols. Cairo, 1366/1947.
———. *al-Najāh fiʾl-ḥikmah al-ilāhīyah*. s.l., 1357/1938.
———. *al-Shifāʾ: al-Ilāhīyāt*. Ed. Ibrāhīm Madkūr *et al*. 2 vols. Cairo, 1960.
———. *al-Shifāʾ: al-Manṭiq*, 3: *al-ʿibārah*. Ed. Ibrāhīm Madkūr and M. al-Khaḍīrī. Cairo, 1390/1970.
Ibn Taymīyah, Taqī al-Dīn. *Bayān muwāfaqat ṣarīḥ al-maʿqūl li-ṣarīḥ al-manqūl*, on margin of: *Minhāj al-sunnah al-nabawīyah fī naqḍ al-kalām, al-shīʿah waʾl-qadarīyah*. 2 vols. Būlāq, 1321.
———. *K. al-radd ʿalā al-manṭiqīyīn*. Bombay, 1949.
———. *Majmūʿat al-rasāʾil al-kubrā*. 2 vols. Cairo, 1323.
Ibn Ṭufayl, M.b. ʿAbd al-Malik. *Ḥayy ibn Yaqẓān*. Ed. and tr. Léon Gauthier, 2d rev. ed. Beirut, 1936.
Ibn Ṭūlūn al-Ṣāliḥī, Shams al-Dīn M. *al-Qalāʾid al-jawharīyah fī taʾrīkh al-Ṣāliḥīyah*. Damascus, 1949.
———. *Rasāʾil taʾrīkhīyah*. Damascus, 1348.
Ibn Zarrūq, A. *Sharḥ ʿaqīdat al-Imām al-Ghazālī*, on margin of: ʿAbd al-Qādir b.A. al-Fākihī, *al-Kifāyah fī sharḥ Bidāyat al-hidāyah*. Cairo, 1296/1879.
al-Ijī, ʿAḍud al-Dīn. *al-Mawāqif fī ʿilm al-kalām*. 8 vols. Cairo, 1325/1907.

Ikhwān al-ṣafā'. *Rasā'il.* 4 vols. Beirut, 1957.
Iqbāl, A. al-Sharqāwī. *Maktabat al-Jalāl al-Suyūṭī.* Rabat, 1397/1977.
Ismā'īl Pasha al-Baghdādī. *Hadīyat al-'ārifīn, asmā' al-mu'allifīn wa-āthār al-muṣannifīn.* Istanbul, 1951-55.
———. *Iḍāḥ al-maknūn fi'l-dhayl 'alā Kashf al-ẓunūn.* Tehran, 1967.
al-Isnawī, 'Abd al-Raḥīm. *Nihāyat al-sūl fī sharḥ Minhāj al-wuṣūl ilā 'ilm al-uṣūl lil-Qāḍī al-Bayḍāwī.* 2 vols. Cairo, n.d.
Ivry, Alfred L. "Maimonides on Possibility," in: J. Reinharz and D. Swetschinski (eds.) *Mystics, Philosophers and Politicians: Essays in Honor of Alexander Altman,* (Durham, N.C., 1982), pp. 67-84.
Izutsu, Toshihiko. "Creation and the Timeless Order of Things: a Study in the Mystical Philosophy of 'Ayn al-Quḍāt," *The Philosophical Forum,* 6 (1972), pp. 124-140.
al-Jāḥiẓ. *K. al-ḥayawān.* Ed. M. Hārūn. 8 vols. Cairo, 1938-43.
James, William. *Pragmatism: A New Name for Some Old Ways of Thinking.* Cambridge: Harvard University Press, 1978.
Jastrow, Marcus. *A Dictionary of the Targumim, the Talmud Babli and Yerushalmi, and the Midrashic Literature.* Rpt. New York, 1971.
al-Jawharī, Ismā'īl b. Ḥammād. *al-Ṣiḥāḥ.* 6 vols. Cairo, 1957; rpt. Beirut, 1979.
al-Jazā'irī, Hamdān b. 'Uthmān. *Ḥikmat al-'ārif bi-wajh yanfa' li-mas'alah "Laysa fi'l-imkān abda' mimmā kān."* Arabic ms., Yahuda Collection, vol. 3036 (Mach 3031).
———. *Itḥāf al-munsifīn wa'l-udabā' bi-mabāḥith al-iḥtirāz 'an al-wabā'.* Istanbul, 1254.
al-Jīlī, 'Abd al-Karīm. *al-Insān al-kāmil.* 2d ed. Cairo, 1908.
Job of Edessa. *The Book of Treasures.* Syriac text, ed, and tr. by A. Mingana. Cambridge, 1935.
al-Jurjānī, A. b. M. *al-Ta'rīfāt.* Cairo, 1938.
al-Juwaynī, Abū al-Ma'ālī. *al-Irshād ilā qawāṭi' al-adillah fī uṣūl al-i'tiqād.* Ed. and tr. J.D. Luciani. Paris, 1938.
Kaḥḥālah, 'Umar Riḍā. *Mu'jam al-mu'allifīn.* 15 vols. Damascus, 1957-61.
al-Kalabādhī, M.b. Ibrāhīm. *The Doctrine of the Sufis.* Tr. A. J. Arberry. Cambridge, 1935; rpt. 1977.
al-Kalanbawī, Ismā'īl. *R. al-imkān.* Istanbul, 1309.
———. *Miftāḥ bāb al-muwajjahāt.* Arabic ms., Yahuda Collection, vol. 2452 (Mach 3306).
Kant, Immanuel. *Werke* [Akademie-Textausgabe] 9 vols. Berlin: de Gruyter, 1968.

Kāshānī, Afẕal al-Dīn. *Muṣannafāt*. Ed. M. Mīnūvī & Y. Mahdavī. 2 vols. Tehran, 1331-37/1952-58.

al-Kattānī, ʿAbd al-Ḥayy. *Fihris al-fahāris waʾl-athbāt wa-muʿjam al-maʿājim*. 2 vols. Fez, 1346-47/1927-28.

al-Kattānī, M.b. Jaʿfar. *K. salwat al-anfās wa-muḥādathat al-akyās*. 3 vols. Fez, 1316/1898-99.

Keynes, J. N. *Studies and Exercises in Formal Logic*. 4th rev. ed. London, 1906.

Khalīqī, Ḥusayn. *Āfirīnish va naẕar-i faylasūfān-i islāmī dar bārah-i ān*. Tabriz, 1975.

al-Khayyāṭ, Abū al-Ḥusayn. *K. al-intiṣār*. Ed. and tr. A. Nader. Beirut, 1957.

Khushaim, Ali Fahmi. *Zarrūq the Sufi: A Guide in the Way and a Leader to the Truth*. Tripoli, Libya, 1976.

al-Kindī, Yaʿqūb b. Isḥāq. *Rasāʾil*. Ed. M. Abū Riḍā. 2 vols. Cairo, 1369/1950.

King, William. *An Essay on the Origin of Evil*. London. 1731.

Kirk, G. S., and Raven, J. E. *The Presocratic Philosophers: a Critical History with a Selection of Texts*. Cambridge: Cambridge University Press, 1963.

Kirmānī, Ḥamīd al-Dīn. *al-Aqwāl al-dhahabīyah*. Ed. Ṣalāḥ al-Sāwī. Tehran, 1397/1977.

———. *Rāḥat al-ʿaql*. Ed. M. Kāmil Ḥusayn and M. Muṣṭafā Ḥilmī. Cairo, 1953. [The Ismaili Society Series C, no. 1]

al-Kisāʾī, M.b.ʿAl. *The Tales of the Prophets of al-Kisāʾī*. Tr. Wheeler M. Thackston, Jr. Boston: Twayne, 1978. [Library of Classical Arabic Literature, 2]

Kister, M. J. " 'Rajab is the month of God . . .' A Study in the Persistence of an early Tradition," *Israel Oriental Studies*, 1 (1971), pp. 191-223.

Knuuttila, Simo, ed. *Reforging the Great Chain of Being: Studies of the History of Modal Theories*. Dordrecht: Reidel, 1981.

Kolakowski, Leszek. *Religion. If There Is No God . . . On God, the Devil, Sin and other Worries of the So-called Philosophy of Religion*. New York and Oxford: Oxford University Press, 1982.

Kopperschmidt, Josef. "Rhetorik und Theodizee. Studie zur hermeneutischen Funktionalität der Rhetorik bei Augustin," *Kerygma und Dogma*, 17 (1971), pp. 273-291.

al-Kutubī, M. b. Shākir. *Fawāt al-wafayāt*. Ed. I. ʿAbbās. 5 vols. Beirut, 1973-77.

Lactantius. *De ira Dei liber/Vom Zorne Gottes*. Ed. and tr. H. Kraft and A. Wlosok. Darmstadt, 1971. [Texte zur Forschung, 4]

———. *The Minor Works*. Tr. Mary F. McDonald. Washington, D.C., 1965. [The Fathers of the Church, 54]

Lane, Edward William. *An Arabic-English Lexicon*. 8 vols. London, 1863-1885; rpt. Lahore, 1978.

Lazarus-Yafeh, Hava. "Philosophical Terms as a Criterion of Authenticity in the Writings of al-Ghazzālī," *Studia Islamica*, 25 (1966), pp. 111-121.

Leibniz, Gottfried Wilhelm. *Discours de métaphysique*. Ed. Henri Lestienne. Paris: Vrin. 1975.

———. *Lettres et opuscules inédits*. Ed. Louis Alexandre Foucher de Careil. Paris, 1854; rpt. Hildesheim, 1975.

———. *Philosophical Papers and Letters*. Ed. and tr. Leroy E. Loemker. 2d ed. Dordrecht: Reidel, 1976.

———. *Die philosophischen Schriften von G.W. Leibniz*. Ed. C. J. Gerhardt. 7 vols. Berlin, 1885; rpt. Hildesheim, 1960-61. [Vol. 6, *Essais de theodicée*.]

———. *Theodicy. Essays on the Goodness of God, the Freedom of Man and the Origin of Evil*. Tr. E. M. Huggard. New Haven: Yale University Press, 1952.

Leopardi, Giacomo. *Tutte le opere*. Ed. Francesco Flora. 4 vols. Milan: Mondadori, [1945].

Levinas, Emmanuel. "La souffrance inutile," *Giornale di Metafisica*, N.S., 4 (1982), pp. 13-25.

Long, A. A. *Hellenistic Philosophy: Stoics, Epicureans, Sceptics*. London: Duckworth, 1974.

Lossky, Vladimir. *The Mystical Theology of the Eastern Church*. London, 1973.

Lovejoy, Arthur O. *The Great Chain of Being: a Study of the History of an Idea*. Cambridge, Mass.: Harvard University Press, 1976.

Luther, Martin. *The Bondage of the Will*. Tr. Henry Cole. Grand Rapids: Eerdmans, 1931.

Macdonald, Duncan B. "The Life of al-Ghazzālī, with Especial Reference to his Religious Experiences and Opinions," *Journal of the American Oriental Society*, 20 (1899), pp. 71-132.

Mach, Rudolf. *Catalogue of Arabic Manuscripts (Yahuda Section) in the Garrett Collection, Princeton University Library*. Princeton: Princeton University Press, 1977.

———. *Der Zaddik in Talmud und Midrasch*. Leiden, 1957.

Madelung, Wilferd. *Der Imam al-Qāsim ibn Ibrāhīm und die Glaubenslehre der Zaiditen*. Berlin, 1965.

Maimonides. *Dalālat al-ḥā'irīn/Moreh ha-nevukhim*. Ed. Joseph Kafah. 3 vols. Jerusalem, 1972.

———. *The Guide of the Perplexed*. Tr. Shlomo Pines. Chicago: University of Chicago Press, 1963.

———. "*Maqālah fī ṣināʿat al-manṭiq* = Maimonides' Treatise on Logic. The Original Arabic and Three Hebrew Translations," Ed. and tr. Israel Efros; *Proceedings of the American Academy for Jewish Research*, 8 (1937-38).

Makarem, Sami Nasib, ed. *The Political Doctrine of the Ismāʿīlīs (The Imamate): an Edition and Translation . . . of Abū l-Fawāris Aḥmad ibn Yaʿqūb's ar-Risāla fīl-Imāma*. Delmar, N.Y.; Caravan Books, 1977.

Makdisi, George. "Ashʿarī and the Ashʿarites in Islamic Religious History," *Studia Islamica*, 17 (1962), pp. 37-80; 18 (1963), pp. 19-39.

———. "Muslim Institutions of Learning in 11th Century Baghdad," *Bulletin of the School of Oriental and African Studies*, 24 (1961), pp. 1-56.

———. *The Rise of Colleges: Institutions of Learning in Islam and the West*. Edinburgh: Edinburgh University Press, 1981.

al-Makkī, Abū Ṭālib. *Qūt al-qulūb*. 4 vols. Cairo, 1351/1932.

al-Malaṭī, Abū al-Ḥusayn. *K. al-tanbīh wa'l-radd ʿalā ahl al-ahwā' wa'l-bidaʿ*. Ed. Sven Dedering. Istanbul, 1936. [Bibliotheca Islamica, 9]

Malebranche, Nicolas. *Entretiens sur la métaphysique et sur la religion*. Paris: Vrin, 1965. [= *Oeuvres complètes*, 12]

al-Maqdisī, Muṭahhar b. Ṭāhir. *Bad' al-khalq wa'l-ta'rīkh/Le livre de la création et de l'histoire*. Ed. Clément Huart. 6 vols. Paris, 1899-1919.

al-Maqqarī, A.b.M. *Nafḥ al-ṭīb min ghuṣn al-Andalus al-raṭīb*. Ed. I. ʿAbbās. 8 vols. Beirut, 1968.

Marmura, Michael E. "Ghazālī's Attitude to the Secular Sciences and Logic," in: G. F. Hourani (ed.), *Essays on Islamic Philosophy and Science* (Albany: SUNY Press, 1975), pp. 100-111.

———. "Some Aspects of Avicenna's Theory of God's Knowledge of Particulars," *Journal of the American Oriental Society*, 82 (1962), pp. 299-312.

Massignon, Louis. *La passion de Husayn Ibn Mansûr Hallâj. Martyr mystique de l'Islam exécuté à Bagdad le 26 mars 922*. 2d ed. 4 vols. Paris: Gallimard, 1975.

Mates, Benson. *Skeptical Essays.* Chicago: University of Chicago Press, 1981.

al-Māturīdī, Abū Manṣūr. *K. al-tawḥīd.* Ed. F. Kholeif. Beirut, 1970.

Maurer, Armand. "Ockham on the Possibility of a Better World," *Mediaeval Studies,* 38 (1976), pp. 291-312.

McCall, Raymond J. *Basic Logic.* 2d ed. New York: Barnes & Noble, 1970.

McCarthy, Richard Joseph. *Freedom and Fulfillment: an Annotated Translation of al-Ghazālī's al-Munqidh min al-Ḍalāl and Other Relevant Works of al-Ghazālī.* Boston: Twayne, 1980. [Library of Classical Arabic Literature, 4]

McDermott, Martin J. *The Theology of al-Shaikh al-Mufīd (d. 413/1022).* Beirut: Dar el-Machreq, 1978.

Merleau-Ponty, Maurice. *Signs.* Tr. Richard C. McCLeary. Evanston: Northwestern University Press, 1964.

Meyerhoff, Max and Joseph Schacht. *The Theologus Autodidactus of Ibn al-Nafīs.* Oxford, 1968.

Milton, John. *Christian Doctrine,* in: *Complete Prose Works, vol. 6 [ca. 1658-ca. 1660].* New Haven: Yale University Press, 1973.

———. *Paradise Lost and Selected Poetry and Prose.* Ed. Northrop Frye. New York: Holt, Rinehart, 1962.

Mīr Dāmād. *K. al-qabasāt.* Ed. M. Mohaghegh. Tehran, 1977.

Morabia, Alfred. "Surnaturel, prodiges prophétiques et incubation dans la ville de l'Envoyé d'Allah," *Studia Islamica,* 42 (1975), pp. 93-114.

Morsy, Magali. "Le tremblement de terre de 1755 d'après des témoignages d'époque," *Hespéris Tamuda,* 16 (1975), pp. 89-98.

Moses bar Kepha. *Der Hexaemeronkommentar des Moses bar Kepha.* Tr. Lorenz Schlimme. 2 vols. Wiesbaden: Harrassowitz, 1977. [Göttinger Orientforschungen; Syriaca, 14]

Mottahedeh, Roy P. *Loyalty and Leadership in an Early Islamic Society.* Princeton: Princeton University Press, 1980.

Mukhtār, Suhayr. *al-Tajsīm ʿind al-Muslimīn, madhhab al-Karrāmīyah.* Alexandria, 1971.

Mullā Ṣadrā, M. *al-Ḥikmah al-mutʿālīyah fi'l-asfār al-ʿaqlīyah al-arbaʿah.* 9 vols. Najaf, 1378/1958.

Muslim b. al-Ḥajjāj, al-Qushayrī. *Ṣaḥīḥ.* 5 vols. Cairo, 1955-56.

Muṭahharī, Murtaḍa. *ʿAdl-i ilāhī.* [Tehran], 1352/1973; rpt., n.d.

———. *al-ʿAdl al-ilāhī.* Tr. by M. ʿAbd al-Munʿim al-Khāqānī. Beirut: Dar al-Hadi, 1981.

al-Mutanabbī. *Sharḥ dīwān al-Mutanabbī.* Ed. I. Yāzijī. Beirut, 1887.

Nakamura, Kōjirō. "A Bibliography on Imām al-Ghazālī," *Orient* [Tokyo], 13 (1977), pp. 119-134.

Nasafī, ʿAzīz al-Dīn b. M. *K. al-insān al-kāmil*. Ed. M. Molé. Tehran, 1962. [Bibliothèque iranienne, 11]

al-Nashshār, ʿA. Sāmī. "Abū Ḥāmid al-Ghazzālī wa-muʿāriḍūhu min ahl al-sunnah," *Majallat Kullīyāt al-Ādāb* [Baghdad], 1 (1959), pp. 195-211.

Nāṣir-i Khosraw. *Zād al-musāfirīn*. Berlin: Kaviyani, 1341/1922.

Nasr, Seyyed Hossein. *An Introduction to Islamic Cosmological Doctrines: Conceptions of Nature and Methods Used for its Study by the Ikhwān al-Ṣafā, al-Bīrūnī, and Ibn Sīnā*. Rev. ed. London: Thames and Hudson, 1978.

Neuwirth, Angelika. *ʿAbd al-Laṭīf al-Baġdādī's Bearbeitung von Buch Lambda der aristotelischen Metaphysik*. Wiesbaden: Steiner, 1976.

Nicholson, Reynold A. "A Moslem Philosophy of Religion," *Le Muséon* [3d Series], 1 (1915), pp. 83-87.

———. *Studies in Islamic Mysticism*. Cambridge, 1921.

Norden, Eduard. "Beiträge zur Geschichte der griechischen Philosophie," *Fleckeisens Jahrbücher* (*Jahrbücher für classische Philologie*), 19th Supplementbd. (1893), pp. 431-439.

Nwyia, Paul. *Ibn ʿAṭā' Allāh (m. 709/1309) et la naissance de la confrérie šāḏilite*. Beirut, 1971.

O'Flaherty, Wendy Doniger. *The Origins of Evil in Hindu Mythology*. Berkeley: University of California Press, 1980.

Origen. *De principiis libri IV/Vier Bücher von den Prinzipien*. Ed. and tr. Herwig Görgemanns and Heinrich Karpp. Darmstadt, 1976. [Texte zur Forschung, 24]

Palamas, St. Gregory. *Défense des saints hésychastes*. Ed. and tr. J. Meyendorff. 2 vols. Louvain, 1959. [Spicilegium Sacrum Lovaniense; Etudes et documents, 30]

Pépin, Jean. *Théologie cosmique et théologie chrétienne (Ambroise, Exam. 11, 1-4)*. Paris, 1964.

Pietro Damiani. *Letttre sur la toute-puissance divine*. Ed. and tr. André Cantin. Paris, 1972. [Sources chrétiennes, 191]

Peters, J.R.T.M. *God's Created Speech: a Study in the Speculative Theology of the Muʿtazilī Qāḍī l-Quḍāt Abū l-Ḥasan ʿAbd al-Jabbār bn Aḥmad al-Hamadānī*. Leiden, 1976.

Petrus Lombardus. *Magistri Petri Lombardi Parisiensis episcopi Sententiae in IV libris distinctae*. 3d ed., 2 vols. [in 3]. Grottaferrata: Editiones Collegii S. Bonaventurae, 1971-81.

Pike, Nelson, ed. *God and Evil: Readings on the Theological Problem of Evil.* Englewood Cliffs, N.J.: Prentice-Hall, 1964.

Plato. *The Collected Dialogues.* Ed. Edith Hamilton and Huntington Cairns. Princeton: Princeton University Press, 1961.

———. *Platonis opera,* I. Ed. J.Burnet, Oxford, 1967.

Plotinus. *Enneads.* Tr. A.H. Armstrong. 3 vols. London, 1967-. [The Loeb Classical Library]

Pohlenx, Max. *Die Stoa: Geschichte einer geistigen Bewegung.* 4th ed. 2 vols. Göttingen, 1970.

Pope, Marvin H., tr. *Job.* New York: Doubleday, 1965. [The Anchor Bible]

Pretzl, O. *Die frühislamische Attributenlehre.* Munich, 1940.

Proclus Diadochus. *In Platonis Timaeum commentaria.* Ed. E. Diehl. 3 vols. Leipzig: Teubner, 1903-04.

———. *Commentaire sur le Timée.* Tr. A.J. Festugière. 5 vols. Paris: Vrin, 1966-68.

al-Qādirī, M. *Muḥammad al-Qādirī's Nashr al-mathānī: the Chronicles.* Ed. Norman Cigar. London: published for The British Academy by the Oxford University Press, 1981. [Fontes Historiae africanae; Series Arabica, 6]

*Qur'ān.* Cairo, 1371/1952.

———. *The Koran Interpreted.* Tr. A.J. Arberry. 2 vols. New York: Macmillan, 1967.

———. *Der Koran.* Tr. Rudi Paret. Stuttgart: Kohlhammer, 1979.

al-Qushayrī, Abū al-Qāsim. *al-Risālah al-Qushayrīyah.* 2 vols. Cairo, 1966.

Radhakrishnan, Sarvepalli and Charles A. Moore, eds. *A Sourcebook in Indian Philosophy.* Princeton: Princeton University Press, 1957.

al-Rāghib al-Iṣfahānī, Abū al-Qāsim. *K. tafṣīl al-nash'atayn wa-taḥṣīl al-sa'ādatayn.* Beirut, 1319.

Raza Library, Rampur. *Catalogue of the Arabic Manuscripts in Raza Library, Rampur. Vol.* 4: *Sufism, Holy Scriptures, Logic and Philosophy.* Compiled by Imtiyaẕ 'Alī 'Arshī. Rampur, 1971.

al-Rāzī, Abū Bakr M.b. Zakarīyā'. *Rasā'il falsafiyah.* Ed. Paul Kraus. Cairo, 1939; rpt.Tehran, n.d.

al-Rāzī, Fakhr al-Dīn. *K. al-arba'īn fī uṣūl ad-dīn.* Hyderabad, 1353.

———. *Mabāḥith al-mashriqīyah fī 'ilm al-ilāhīyāt wa'l-ṭabī'īyāt.* Hyderabad, 1343.

———. *Mafātīḥ al-ghayb al-mushtahar bi'l-Tafsīr al-kabīr.* 8 vols. Istanbul, 1307-8/1889-90.

al-Rāzī, Fakhr al-Dīn. *Muḥaṣṣal afkār al-mutaqaddimīn wa'l-muta'akh-khirīn* [with: Naṣīr al-Dīn al-Ṭūsī, *Talkhīṣ al-Muḥaṣṣal*] Cairo, 1323.

*Realencyklopädie für protestantische Theologie und Kirche*. Ed. Albert Hauck. 3d rev. ed. 22 vols. Leipzig, 1896-1909.

Reinert, Benedikt. *Die Lehre vom tawakkul in der klassischen Ṣūfik*. Berlin, 1968.

*Die Religion in Geschichte und Gegenwart*. Ed. Kurt Galling, 3d ed. 6 vols. Tübingen, 1962.

Ricoeur, Paul, *The Symbolism of Evil*. Tr. E. Buchanan. Boston, 1969.

Ritter, Hellmut. *Das Meer der Seele*. Leiden, 1955.

———. "Risālat Ibn Sīnā fi'l-Arzāq," *Revue de l'Académie arabe de Damas* [*Majallat al-Majma' al-'ilmī al-'arabī*], 25 (1950), pp. 199-209.

———. "Studien zur Geschichte der islamischen Frömmigkeit, I," *Der Islam*, 21 (1933), pp. 1-83.

Rosenthal, Franz. *Das Fortleben der Antike im Islam*. Zürich, 1965.

———. *A History of Muslim Historiography*. Leiden, 1968.

Ruland, Hans-Jochen. *Die arabischen Fassungen von zwei Schriften des Alexander von Aphrodisias*. Diss., Saarbrücken, 1976.

Russell, Jeffrey Burton. *The Devil: Perceptions of Evil from Antiquity to Primitive Christianity*. New York: New American Library, 1979.

Ryle, Gilbert. *The Concept of Mind*. London, 1949.

Sachedina, Abdulaziz Abdulhussein. *Islamic Messianism: The Idea of Mahdi in Twelver Shi'ism*. Albany: SUNY Press, 1981.

Sa'dī. *The Gulistān of Shaikh Muṣliḥu 'D Dīn Sa'dī of Shīrāz*. Ed. J. Platts. London, 1874.

al-Ṣafadī, Khalīl b. Aybak. *al-Wāfī bi'l-wafayāt*. Vol. 1, ed. H. Ritter. Leipzig, 1931-.

al-Sakhāwī, Shams al-Dīn. *al-Ḍaw' al-lāmi' li-ahl al-qarn al-tāsi'*. 12 vols. Cairo, 1353-55.

al-Samarqandī, Shams al-Dīn. *Sharḥ al-Qusṭās fi'l-manṭiq*. Arabic ms., Yale (Nemoy 1410).

al-Samhūdī, Nūr al-Dīn. *Iḍāḥ al-bayān li-man arāda al-ḥujjah min "Laysa fi'l-imkān abda' mimmā kān."* Arabic ms., Berlin, Pm. 226 (Ahlwardt 5102).

———. *Wafā' al-wafā' bi-akhbār dār al-Muṣṭafā*. 4 vols. Cairo, 1954-55.

al-Santawī, 'Abd al-Raḥmān. *al-Sayf al-ḥusām fi'l-dhabb 'an kalām Ḥujjat al-Islām*. Arabic ms., Yahuda Collection, vol. 2249. (Mach 3028).

Sartain, E. M. *Jalāl al-dīn al-Suyūṭī*. Vol. 1: *Biography and Back-*

*ground*; vol. 2: al-Suyūṭī, *K. al-taḥadduth bi-niʿmat Allāh*. Cambridge, 1975.

Schacht, Joseph. "New Sources for the History of Muhammadan Theology," *Studia Islamica*, 1 (1953), pp. 23-42.

Schaeder, Hans Heinrich. "Die islamische Lehre vom Vollkommenen Menschen, ihre Herkunft und ihre dichterische Gestaltung," *Zeitschrift der Deutschen Morgenländischen Gesellschaft*, 79 (1925), pp. 192-268.

Scharbau, Carl Anders. *Die Idee der Schöpfung in der vedischen Literatur. Eine religionsgeschichtliche Untersuchung über den frühindischen Theismus*. Stuttgart, 1932.

Schmitz, Hermann. *System der Philosophie*. 5 vols. [in 10]. Bonn: Bouvier, 1964-80.

Schopenhauer, Arthur. *Werke*. 10 vols. Zürich: Diogenes, 1977.

Schreiner, Martin. "Beiträge zur Geschichte der theologischen Bewegungen im Islam," *Zeitschrift der Deutschen Morgenländischen Gesellschaft*, 52 (1898), pp. 463-563.

Schwartz, Richard B. *Samuel Johnson and the Problem of Evil*. Madison: University of Wisconsin Press, 1975.

Schwarz, Michael. "The Letter of al-Ḥasan al-Baṣrī," *Oriens*, 20 (1967), pp. 15-30.

Schwarzbaum, Haim. "The Jewish and Moslem Versions of some Theodicy Legends," *Fabula*, 3 (1960), pp. 119-169.

Sezgin, Fuat. *Geschichte des arabischen Schrifttums*. 8 vols. Leiden, 1967-.

al-Shābbī, Abū al-Qāsim. *Dīwān*. Beirut, 1972.

Shabbūḥ, Ibrāhīm. *Fihris al-makhṭūṭāt al-muṣawwarah (Maʿhad al-makhṭūṭāt al-ʿarabīyah)*. Cairo, 1959.

al-Shahrastānī, M.b. ʿAbd al-Karīm. *K. al-milal waʾl-niḥal*. Ed. M. Badrān. Cairo, 1370/1951.

al-Shaʿrānī, ʿAbd al-Wahhāb. *Al-Ajwibah al-marḍīyah ʿan aʾimmat al-fuqahāʾ waʾl-ṣūfīyah*. Arabic ms., Yahuda Collection, vol. 584 (Mach 2821).

———. *al-Ṭabaqāt al-kubrā*. 2 vols. Cairo, 1373/1954.

———. *al-Yawāqīt waʾl-jawāhir*. 2 vols. Beirut, n.d.

Shestov, Lev. *In Job's Balances: on the Sources of the Eternal Truths*. Tr. C. Coventry. London, 1932.

al-Sijilmāsī al-Lamaṭī, A.b. Mubārak. *al-Dhahab al-ibrīz min kalām Sīdī ʿAbd al-ʿAzīz*. Cairo, 1961.

Spinoza, Benedict de. *Opera*. Vol. 2: *Tractatus de intellectus emendatione. Ethica*. Ed. Konrad Blumenstock, Darmstadt, 1980.

Spinoza, Benedict de. *Ethics*. Ed. James Gutmann. New York: Hafner, 1957.

Stegmüller, Friedrich. *Repertorium Commentariorum in Sententias Petri Lombardi*. 2 vols. Würzburg: F. Schöningh, 1947.

Steinschneider, Moritz. *Die arabischen Übersetzungen aus dem Griechischen*. Graz, 1960 (rpt.).

Stetkevych, Suzanne Pinckney. "Toward a Redefinition of *'Badīʿ* Poetry," *Journal of Arabic Literature*, 12 (1981), pp. 1-29.

Stieglecker, Hermann. "Die islamische Lehre vom Guten und Bösen," *Orientalia*, N.S., 4 (1935), pp. 239-245.

Suárez, Francisco. *Opera omnia*. 30 vols. Paris, 1856-78.

al-Subkī, ʿAbd al-Wahhāb. *Ṭabaqāt al-Shāfiʿīyah al-kubrā*. 10 vols. Cairo, 1964-76.

al-Suyūṭī, Jalāl al-Dīn. *Bughyat al-wuʿāh fī ṭabaqāt al-lughawīyīn wa'l-nuḥāh*. Cairo, 1326.

———. *Kashf al-ṣalṣalah ʿan waṣf al-zalzalah*. Ed. A. al-Saʿdānī. Fez, 1971.

———. *Naẓm al-ʿiqyān fī aʿyān al-aʿyān*. Ed. P. K. Hitti, New York, 1927.

———. *K. al-taḥadduth bi-niʿmat Allāh* = E. M. Sartain, *Jalāl al-dīn al-Suyūṭī*, vol. 2.

———. *Tashyīd al-arkān min "Laysa fi'l-imkān abdaʿ mimmā kān."* Arabic ms., Yahuda Collection, vol. 303 (Mach 3030).

al-Ṭabarī, Abū Jaʿfar. *Jāmiʿ al-bayān ʿan ta'wīl āy al-Qur'ān*. 30 vols. Cairo, 1373/1954

al-Taftāzānī, Saʿd al-Dīn. *Sharḥ al-Maqāṣid*. 2 vols. s.l., 1277.

———. *Sharḥ . . . al-Taftāzānī ʿalā matn al-ʿAqā'id*. Istanbul, 1326/1908; rpt. Baghdad, n.d.

al-Tahānawī, M. *Kashshāf iṣṭilāḥāt al-funūn*. Ed. A. Sprenger. 2 vols. Calcutta, 1862; rpt. Tehran, 1967.

al-Taḥtānī, Qutb al-Dīn al-Rāzī. *Lawāmiʿ al-asrār fī sharḥ Maṭāliʿ al-anwār*. 2 vols. Istanbul, 1277/1861.

Ṭālibī, ʿAmmār. *Ārā' Abī Bakr ibn al-ʿArabī al-kalāmīyah*. 2 vols. Algiers, 1974 [?]. Vol. 2= AB.b.al-ʿArabī, *al-ʿAwāṣim min al-qawāṣim*.

Ṭāshköprüzāde, Aḥmed. *Miftāḥ al-saʿādah wa-miṣbāḥ al-siyādah*. 3 vols. Hyderabad, 1328-56/1910-37.

al-Tawḥīdī, Abū Ḥayyān. *Akhlāq al-wazīrayn*. Ed. M. al-Ṭanjī. Damascus, 1965.

———. *al-Hawāmil wa'l-shawāmil*. Ed. A. Amīn. Cairo, 1370/1951.

———. *K. al-imtāʿ wa'l-mu'ānasah*. Ed. A. Amīn and A. al-Zayn. 3 vols. Beirut, 1953.

———. *al-Muqābasāt*. Ed. M. Ḥusayn. Baghdad, 1970.

Tazieff, Haroun. *When the Earth Trembles*. Tr. Patrick O'Brian. New York: Harcourt, Brace and World, 1964.

Teilhard de Chardin, Pierre. *The Phenomenon of Man*. New York: Harper, 1961.

al-Temini, Abdeljelil. *Recherches et documents d'histoire maghrébine*. Tunis, 1971.

St. Thomas Aquinas. *On the Power of God (Quaestiones disputatae de potentia Dei)*. Tr. Lawrence Shapcote. Westminster, Md.: The Newman Press, 1952.

———. *Opera omnia*. 25 vols. Parma, 1852-1873; rpt. New York, 1948.

———. *Summa contra Gentiles*. Tr. A. Pegis *et al*. 5 vols. Notre Dame: University of Notre Dame Press, 1975.

———. *Summa theologiae*. Latin text and English translation. Ed. T. Gilby. 60 vols. London, 1963-.

Thompson, Stith. *The Folktale*. Berkeley: University of California Press, 1977.

al-Tirmidhī, M.b. ʿĪsā. *Sunan*. 10 vols. Ḥimṣ, 1965-68.

Topitsch, Ernst. *Vom Ursprung und Ende der Metaphysik*. Munich: DTV, 1972.

Tritton, A. S. *Muslim Theology*. London: Luzac, 1947.

al-Ṭūsī, Naṣīr al-Dīn. *Asās al-iqtibās*. Tehran, 1326/1947.

Ullmann, Manfred. *Die Medizin im Islam*. Leiden and Köln, 1970. [Handbuch der Orientalistik: 1. Abt.; Ergänzungsbd. 6; 1er Abschnitt]

Vāʿiẓ Javādī, Ismāʿīl. *Ḥudūth va qidam*. Tehran, 1347/1968. [Intishārāt-i Dānishgāh-i-Tihrān, 1212]

Vajda, Georges. "De quelques fragments muʿtazilites en judéo-arabe. Notice provisoire," *Journal asiatique*, 264 (1976), pp. 1-7.

———. "La finalité de la création de l'homme selon un théologien juif du IX siècle," *Oriens*, 15 (1962), pp. 61-85.

———. "Le problème de l'assistance bienveillante de Dieu, du 'mieux' et de la nécessité de la loi révélée selon Yūsuf al-Baṣīr," *Revue des études juives*, 134 (1975), pp. 31-74.

———. *Un recueil de textes historiques judéo-marocains*. Paris, 1951.

van den Bergh, Simon, "Ghazālī on 'Gratitude towards God' and its Greek Sources," *Studia Islamica*, 7 (1957), pp. 77-98.

Viner, Jacob. *The Role of Providence in the Social Order: an Essay in Intellectual History*. Princeton: Princeton University Press, 1976.

Voltaire, François Marie Arouet de. *Correspondance, t. 4 (janvier 1754-*

*décembre 1757).* Ed. Theodore Besterman. Paris: Gallimard, 1978. [Bibliothèque de la Pléiade]

———. *Mélanges*. Paris: Gallimard, 1965. [Bibliothèque de la Pléiade]

Von Grunebaum, Gustave E. "Concept and Function of Reason in Islamic Ethics," *Oriens*, 15 (1962), pp. 1-17.

Watt, W. Montgomery. "The Authenticity of the Works Attributed to al-Ghazālī," *Journal of the Royal Asiatic Society* (1952), pp. 24-45.

———. *The Formative Period of Islamic Thought*. Edinburgh, 1973.

———. *Free Will and Predestination in Early Islam*. London, 1948.

———. "The Study of al-Ghazālī," *Oriens*, 13/14 (1961), pp. 121-132.

Wehr, Hans. *al-Ġazzālī's Buch vom Gottvertrauen (Das 35. Buch des Iḥyā' ʿulūm al-dīn)*. Halle/Saale, 1940.

Weinrich, Harald. *Literatur für Leser: Essays und Aufsätze zur Literaturwissenschaft*. Stuttgart: Kohlhammer, 1971.

Wensinck, A. J., *et al*. *Concordance et indices de la tradition musulmane*. 7 vols. Leiden, 1936-68.

———. "The Ideas of the Western Semites concerning the Navel of the Earth," *Verhandelingen der Koninklijke Akademie van Wetenschapen te Amsterdam*, N.S., 17:1 (1916).

———. *The Muslim Creed*. Cambridge, 1932.

———. *La pensée de Ghazzālī*. Paris, 1940.

William of Ockham. *Scriptum in librum primum Sententiarum*. Ed. G. Gál. 4 vols. St. Bonaventure, N.Y.: Franciscan Institute, 1967-79. [*Opera theologica*, 1-4]

Winter, Michael. "Shaʿrānī and Egyptian Society in the Sixteenth Century," *Asian and African Studies* [Jerusalem], 9 (1973), pp. 313-338.

Wolff, Christian. *Philosophia prima sive Ontologia*. Ed. Jean Ecole. 2d ed. Frankfurt and Leipzig, 1736; rpt. Hildesheim, 1962 [*Gesammelte Werke*, 2 Abt., Bd. 3]

Wolfson, Harry Austryn. *The Philosophy of the Kalam*. Cambridge, Mass.: Harvard University Press, 1976.

al-Yāfiʿī, a. M. ʿAl. *K. marham al-ʿilal al-muʿḍilah*. Ed. E. Denison Ross. Calcutta, 1910 [Bibliotheca Indica]

Yale. *Arabic Manuscripts in the Yale University Library*. Compiled by L. Nemoy. New Haven, 1956.

Yāqūt, Ibn ʿAl. *K. irshād al-arīb ilā maʿrifat al-adīb*. Ed. D. S. Margoliouth. 7 vols. Leiden, 1913. [E.J.W. Gibb Memorial Series, 6]

———. *K. muʿjam al-buldān*. Ed. F. Wüstenfield, 6 vols. Leipzig, 1870; rpt. Tehran, 1965.

Yver, G. "Si Hamdan ben Othman Khodja," *Revue africaine*, 57 (1913), pp. 96-138.

al-Zabīdī, M. Murtaḍā. *Itḥāf al-sādat al-muttaqīn bi-sharḥ asrār Iḥyā' 'ulūm al-dīn*. 10 vols. Cairo, 1311/1894.

al-Zamakhsharī, M.b.'Umar. *al-Kashshāf 'an ḥaqā'iq ghawāmiḍ al-tanzīl wa-'uyūn al-aqāwīl fī wujūh al-ta'wīl*. 4 vols. Beirut, 1947; rpt., n.d.

Zedler, Beatrice H. "Saint Thomas and Avicenna in the '*De Potentia Dei*,' " *Traditio*, 6 (1948), pp. 105-159.

al-Ziriklī, Khayr al-Dīn. *al-A'lām: Qāmūs tarājim*. New ed. 8 vols. Beirut, 1979.

# Index

Note: The Arabic article al- is not considered in filing when it occurs at the beginning of an entry; thus, al-Ghazālī will be found under G, al-Biqāʿī under B, etc.

*Library of Congress Cataloging in Publication Data*

Ormsby, Eric L. (Eric Linn), 1941-
Theodicy in Islamic thought.

Revision of thesis (Ph.D.)—Princeton University, 1981.
Bibliography: p.
Includes index.
1. God (Islam)—History of doctrines. 2. Ghazzālī, 1058-1111—
Metaphysics. I. Title.
BP166.2.076 1984 297'.211 84-3396
ISBN 0-691-07278-7 (alk. paper)